THE BARNETBY BOYS

A brief account of events in Barnetby and the fate of its Boys during the Great War 1914-1919

TO THE GLORY OF GOD
AND IN HONOURED MEMORY OF
THE BARNETBY BOYS
WHO GAVE THEIR LIVES
THAT WE MAY LIVE IN FREEDOM AND IN PEACE

THE BARNETBY BOYS

A brief account of events in Barnetby and the fate of its Boys during the Great War 1914-1919

compiled by
Roger O. Frankish

Reveille PRESS

Acknowledgements

I WOULD like to thank The Right Hon. The Earl of Yarborough, for use of the facilities at the Brocklesby Estate Office and for access to the book 'Charles Sackville Pelham, Lord Worsley' and permission to use images and material from that book. I would like to thank Mr Martin Middlebrook for the research notes that my father had sent to him. I am indebted to the staff of the Commonwealth War Graves Commission in searching their records and archives to identify the memorials of the 'Barnetby Boys' (before computerisation of records now available on the internet). I am grateful to the following Museums/Archives for their most valuable assistance: The Imperial War Museum, London, The National Archives (formerly Public Record Office) Kew, The National Archives of Canada, and The Ministry of Defence (Departmental Records – Archives). I am also grateful to the curators of the following Army Museums for their assistance: The Royal Artillery Institution, Woolwich; Royal Engineers, Chatham; The Prince of Wales's Own Regiment of Yorkshire, York; The King's Regiment, Liverpool; Durham Light Infantry, Durham (Durham County Council) and The King's Own Scottish Borderers, Berwick-upon-Tweed. My thanks go to the librarians and staff of the following libraries for their assistance: Grimsby Central Library & Hull Central Library (Humberside County Council, as then was), Retford Library (Nottinghamshire County Council), Long Eaton Library (Derbyshire County Council), Rotherham Metropolitan Borough Council Museum and Arts Services and Doncaster Library. I would like to thank Mr. M. Fish, Bigby (the then Archivist of the Great Central Railway), for loan of the Great Central Railway Journals. For the loan of photographs/material I am indebted to Mrs J. Manning, Barnetby, Mrs. J. Brumpton, Barnetby, Mr. J. Lowish, Barnetby, Mr. A. Tailby, Nettleton, Mr. Rimmington, Brigg, the late Mrs. E. Underwood, Brigg and the late Mrs Hastings, Brigg.

Reveille Press is an imprint of
Tommies Guides Military Booksellers & Publishers

Gemini House
136-140 Old Shoreham Road
Brighton
BN3 7BD

www.tommiesguides.co.uk

First published in Great Britain by
Reveille Press 2014

For more information please visit
www.reveillepress.com

© 2014, Roger Frankish

A catalogue record for this book is available from the
British Library.

All rights reserved. Apart from any use under UK
copyright law no part of this publication may be
reproduced, stored in a retrieval system, or transmitted,
in any form or by any means, without prior written
permission of the publisher, nor be otherwise circulated in
any form of binding or cover other than that in which it is
published and without a similar condition being imposed
on the subsequent publisher.

ISBN 978-1-908336-83-5

Printed and bound in the UK

Preface

IN December 1920, a Memorial Cross was erected in the St Barnabas Church grounds to the memory of the servicemen from, or associated with, Barnetby who fell during the First World War, 1914 - 1919. That Memorial was dedicated to 'The Barnetby Boys who gave their lives that we may live in freedom and in peace also as a thanksgiving for the safe return of the others who served in that war'.

This account of the 'Barnetby Boys' who died during the First World War started simply as a photographic record showing all their Memorials. It included only the barest information about each 'Boy' and the location of his Memorial, the idea being that this would eventually be placed in the Church as a permanent record. Since then I came across more information and things just snowballed from there. Having an interest in the First World War in the first place helped but having visited those battlefields and war cemeteries was an added incentive. People often think it strange when I tell them I spend part of my holiday visiting such places. But then possibly I have more reason than many to justify those visits having had two blood relatives and a 'Barnetby Boy' connected to my family by marriage killed in France and Flanders and my father wounded twice during his brief spell of active service in France. Everyone I have met on my visits has been awed by the experience, especially those who have witnessed the nightly Last Post ceremony at 8 p.m. at the Menin Gate Memorial to the Missing at Ypres.

Someone interested in what I had already done urged me to find additional information so as to make a broader written account. That is what I have done and this is the result.

This account is primarily about the 'Barnetby Boys' who fought and died during the Great War of 1914-1918 but I have also taken into account three men from Somerby. I have also included such snippets of information that I have found concerning any of the 'other' Barnetby men as the war affected them, plus events in, or connected with, the village that happened during the war and not necessarily directly related to it. Some of this may seem rather uninteresting, for in many cases it simply refers to men who were at home on leave, and it was not easy to write something about them apart from what had been reported in the newspapers. However many of the names will no doubt be familiar to a few of the elder inhabitants of the village and recall memories of those 'other' men who survived the war. Other items of information give some indication of what went on in the village during the war in an effort to support those servicemen. One item that many people today are totally unaware of included the participation in a national scheme that seems remarkable for its simplicity, yet was none the less vital.

I have also included one or two brief items that have no connection with Barnetby at all that relate to the grim realities of war and may be of interest to anyone visiting the area concerned.

The Memorials of the Second World War 'Boys' have been traced too but so far only two have been visited due to their locations being far wider spread – a list of those appears in the appendix. Also in the appendix I have included items about two men not connected with the village that I consider are of some local interest.

R. O. Frankish,

Barnetby-le-Wold

Contents

Acknowledgements . . . . *v*

Preface . . . . *vii*

Illustrations . . . . *x*

Maps . . . . *xiii*

Appendices . . . . *xiv*

Poetry . . . . *xiv*

    Introduction 1

1 An idea materializes 9

2 1914 15

3 1915 45

4 1916 73

5 1917 121

6 1918 195

7 1919 249

    Appendices 275

    Poetry 312

    Bibliography 318

Illustrations
Photographs
All photographs are by Roger Frankish unless otherwise stated.

Grimsby Chums in Training and some 'Barnetby Boys' *(various postcards)* 19
Barnetby level crossing *(postcard)* 23
King's Road, Barnetby; subway (underpass) at Barnetby *(postcards)* 25
Woburn Abbey Cemetery, Cuinchy; le Touret Cemetery & Memorial 31
HMS Good Hope, HMS Monmouth, HMS Glasgow and SMS Nürnberg*(I.W.M.)* 35
SMS Scharnhorst *(Arthur Renard)* 36
A. B. H. Bull *(Hull & Lincolnshire Times – hereinafter referred to as Hull Times)* 41
Portsmouth Naval Memorial 41
Railway service badge *(G.C.R. Journal)* 49
Panoramic views of the Loos battlefield 56
Ptes E. Denton, W. Denton & A. Denton *(Hull Times)* 57
Patriotic Barnetby family *(Hull Times)* 61
L/Sgt T. Hall *(Hull Times)* 62
L/Sgt A. Tweed; Pte C. F. Andrew *(Hull Times)* 64
Loos Memorial to the Missing 65
Sister Ellen Andrew headstone; Loos Memorial; G. C. R. Memorial 66
Menin Gate Memorial to the Missing 80
Lt Bott & Sgt Bowness Memorials 82
View of enemy held high ground the Bluff 83
L/Cpl G. H. Smith *(Hull Times)* 90
L/Cpl G. H. Smith headstone; Special memorials Gordon Dump Cemetery ... 91
Cpl G. W. Insley *(Hull Times)* 96
Pte J. W. Rapson *(Long Eaton Advertiser courtesy Derbyshire C. C.)* 98
Pte J. W. Rapson headstone 98
Cpl J. W. Lobley *(Hull Times)* 101
Cpl J. W. Lobley initial burial site, view from London Cemeter. 103
Lochnagar Crater & Thiepval Memorial 104
Pte C. R. Frankish & sister Amy *(postcard)* 111
Railway troops of 111th Coy R. E. in France and at Longmoor *(G.C.R. Journal)*. . 112
Pte C. Gostelow headstone 117
Two views of Ancre British Cemetery 117
Pte C. R. Frankish convalescing at home *(E. Waby, Photographer, Barnetby)* 119
Sgt H. Lowish *(courtesy Mr John Lowish)* 123

The Barnetby Boys

L/Cpl F. Thompson headstone	126
L/Cpl C. F. Wilson headstone	127
L/Cpl G. W. Smith *(courtesy Mrs Joyce Brumpton)*	130
L/Cpl G. W. Smith attestation paper *(National Archives of Canada)*	131
L/ Cpl G. W. Smith headstone; Pte W. Blair *(latter Hull Times)*	134
Sgt G. W. Thacker attestation paper *(National Archives of Canada)*	140
Sgt G. W. Thacker *(Hull Times)*	141
Initial burial site of G. W. Smith & G. W. Thacker; Canadian Cemetery	147
Sgt G. W. Thacker headstone; Pte R. W. Robinson *(courtesy Mrs June Manning)*	147
Pillbox on Hindenburg Line near Héninel	151
Pte R. W. Robinson headstone; Cpl C. P. Blanchard *(latter Hull Times)*	152
Cpl C. P. Blanchard headstone	153
Pte H. Dawson headstone; Chili Trench Cemetery	157
Initial burial site of Pte H. Dawson	158
Aerial photograph of battlefield near Ecoust St Mein *(I.W.M.)*	161
Arras Memorial, Faubourg d'Amiens Cemetery	164
Mur des Fusillées, Arras	165
Gunner E. Vessey	165
Vauxbuin French Military Cemetery; French Military Cemetery, Terny-Sorny *(latter postcard)*	167
Gunner E. Vessey headstone; Site of French Military Cemetery, Terny-Sorny;	167
No 5 Civilian Railway Coy, No 1 Gang; railway gang repairing damaged track *(postcards)*	172
Pt E. K. White *(Hull Times)*	173
Pte E. K. White headstone	175
The Kendall brothers *(Hull Times)*	178
Pte P. C. Poole M.M. *(Hull Times)*	180
Pte H. Cox *(courtesy Mrs Ena Underwood)*	182
Mrs Ena Underwood at Ypres November 1999 *(courtesy Mrs Ena Underwood)*	187
Hubert Cox and serving relatives *(postcards)*	188
C.Q.M.S. J. Catterall *(G.C.R. Journal)*; C.Q.M.S. Catterall headstone	201
View of battlefield from Gouzeaucourt New Cemetery	204
Two views of Chapel Hill battlefield	206
Pozières Memorial to the Missing	207
Driver W. Slight headstone	211
Pte T. W. Bramley *(Hull Times)*	213
Forward slopes of hill field near Bois d'Achtmetaal, Haegdoorne	216

Illustrations

View near Ridge Wood	222
Tyne Cot Memorial to the Missing	223
Sapper G. Rhoades, R. E.	225
Pte W. S. Witty *(courtesy Mr Alan Tailby)*	228
Pte W. S. Witty headstone	231
Nettleton War Memorial Cottage	232
Gunner G. W. Rimmington *(Mr Rimmington, Brigg)*	233
Gunner G. Rimmington headstone	236
Pte G. Nicholls *(courtesy Mrs Hastings)*; view Watling Street' of Hélène Ridge	237
View of Bernes near Bernes church	239
Pte C. Braithwaite headstone	242
Prospect Hill Cemetery, Gouy	244
Pioneer C. M. Green headstone	245
Pte A. Reed *(Hull Times)*	251
Sapper F. Burdass, R.E. headstone	254
Sapper E. A. Insley, R.E. headstone	255
Delhi Memorial *(C.W.G.C.)* & E. D. Ffrench Memorial plaque	263
Memorial tablet in St Barnabas Church, Barnetby	271
McAulay family tomb in Aylesby churchyard & Capt F. W. McAulay headstone	278
McAulay Memorial Cottages	279
C.S. Pelham, Lord Worsley *(courtesy Lord Yarborough)*; grave marker crosses	280
Lord Worsley headstone; Household Brigade Memorial, Zandvoorde	287
Lord Worsley's Memorials in Brocklesby Church	287

Diagrams & Drawings

Grimsby Chums postcard *(designed & drawn by Mr R. E. Wrigglesworth)*	18
Drawing based on a sketch drawn 2nd Lt V. J. Gilbert, R.A. *(PRO WO 95/5395)*	258
Diagram of Lord Worsley's burial site *(courtesy Lord Yarborough)*	283

Paintings

Paintings by Stephen Frankish

Soldier	72, 194
Sentry	120, 248

Maps

Maps, except No 1, drawn by Roger Frankish based on trench maps, except for Nos 2, 3, 4, 5, 31 (based on a sketch of The Zhob from 'The Official Account, 3rd Afghan War') & 32.

1 Barnetby-le-Wold in 1908 *(Ordnance Survey courtesy of Grimsby Central Library)*. 3
2 & 3 Sites of the 'Barnetby Boys' Memorials on the Western Front 13,14
4 Position of 2nd KOSB at nightfall 13th October 1914 *(based on sketch, PRO WO 95/1552)* 30
5 Battle of Coronel, 1st November 1914 37
6 The Loos Battlefield, 25th September 1915 55
7 The Bluff – scene of operations of 17th (Northern) Division Feb. 1916 79
8 Area around Fricourt – scene of operations of 17th Division 3rd July 1916 .. 97
9 Area around Bazentin-le-Petit – where 10th Lincolns were 31st July-15th Aug 102
10 Action at le Transloy 23rd October 1916 109
11 Beaucourt-sur-Ancre 114
12 Salient north east of Ypres 128
13 2/4th & 2/5th Lincolns trenches near Villers-Carbonnel March 1917 136
14 Vimy Ridge 144
15 1st Battle of the Scarpe 150
16 Greenland Hill 156
17 Bullecourt 162
18 Terny-Sorny 168
19 Lens 176
20 Battle of Broodseinde 184
21 Chapel Hill 203
22 Villers-Bretonneux 208
23 Gorre 212
24 Haegdoorne 215
25 Ridge Wood 221
26 Area where 7th E. Yorks were in action on 24th August 1918 230
27 Deployment of 287th Siege Battery RGA 26th – 29th August 1918 235
28 Bellenglise, 1/5th Lincolns sector 238
29 Map of Bernes 239
30 Area where 13th D.L.I. attacked from Prospect Hill 5th October 1918 243
31 Area Murgha Kibzai to Fort Sandeman, N.W. Frontier 258
32 Zandvoorde, 30th October 1914 *(based on sketch courtesy Lord Yarborough)* ...283

Appendices

1. Opposing Naval forces at the Battle of Coronel 275
2. Captain Francis Willmer McAulay, R.F.A. (T.F.). 277
3. C. S. Lord Worsley, Lt Royal Horse Guards *(information courtesy Lord Yarborough)*. 281
4. Service documents of L/Cpl G. W. Smith *(National Archives of Canada)*. . . . 288
5. Service documents of Sgt G. W. Thacker *(National Archives of Canada)* 292
6. Roll of Honour 1914 – 1919. 297
7. Barnetby Boys casualties 1914-1919 in chronological order 299
8. Location of Barnetby Boys Memorials 1914-1919 301
9. Barnetby-le-Wold Roll of Honour 1939-1945. 305
10. Location of Barnetby Boys Memorials 1939-1945 306
11. The Memorial plaques in Barnetby Church 308
12. The names and inscriptions on Barnetby War Memorial 310
13. Somerby memorial on lectern, St Margaret's church. 311

Poetry

Poems by Roger Frankish

"Thoughts at Lochnagar Crater on the Somme – 1st July, 1996." 312
"Where poppies grew." 315
"On visiting my Mother's half-Brother's grave…" 316

Introduction
About Barnetby

THE history of Barnetby-le-Wold, nowadays mostly called Barnetby, in the county of North Lincolnshire – previously in Humberside and originally in Lincolnshire, can be traced back to the Anglo-Saxon epoch. Parts of St Mary's Church originate from that period, though the modern roof tiles on the chancel look out of character with the rest of the building. The church tower contains three very old bells believed to have come from Newstead Priory, Cadney, following the dissolution of the monasteries, 1536-1539, by King Henry VIII. They are not rung now, as the bell support structure is not sound enough. The lead font of Norman origin that used to be in St Mary's Church is now in the North Lincolnshire Museum at Scunthorpe.

Barnetby is situated roughly midway between Grimsby and Scunthorpe. Agriculture is one of the main industries though not the main employer here today. The old part of the village centred round the Manor House and farm and incorporated East Street, Old Post Office Lane, Queen's Road, South Street and West Street and then continued on from the present Queen's Road/West Street corner to just past Smithy Lane on St Barnabas Road. With the introduction of the railway in 1848 Barnetby's growth sprang up at the north-western end.

During 1848, the Great Grimsby and Sheffield Junction Railway laid permanent way from Grimsby to Market Rasen that later continued to Lincoln. A new line, running from Barnetby to Gainsborough, was completed and in operation in 1849. By August 1866 a third line, running from Barnetby to Scunthorpe, had opened – built by the Trent, Ancholme and Grimsby Railway. By 1881, Barnetby had its own small locomotive depot. In July 1882, the Trent, Ancholme and Grimsby Railway amalgamated with the Manchester, Sheffield and Lincolnshire Railway.

While Barnetby had grown with the coming of the railways the real expansion began after 1866 with the building of the line to Scunthorpe. With later expansion it became an important junction on the Manchester, Sheffield and

Lincolnshire Railway that amalgamated later with the Great Central Railway (GCR). This narrative is not about the railway but its significance in relation to Barnetby and its menfolk throughout the war will later become apparent.

Barnetby in those days was very different to what it is today. To the north of the railway, on the west side of King's Road, there were no council houses – these having been built shortly after the Second World War; many are now privately owned. Nor were there any bungalows on the other side. Hillside Crescent, a relatively recent addition, was built on the site of the Second World War 'Waafery' which was then in the parish of Melton Ross. The 'Waafery' had been the living quarters for members of the Women's Auxiliary Air Force (WAAF) based at RAF Elsham Wolds. After the war those buildings were used as public accommodation for many years.

Baker's Close and Windsor Way are recent additions – a row of cottages once stood where Baker's Close is now. Branching west off the southern end of King's Road was Railway Street. It ran almost parallel to the railway with small cottages scattered for most of its length on the south side. On the north side, about half way down, was a mill that ground corn into flour and animal feed; originally steam driven, by 1914 it was diesel powered. On the east of the southern end of King's Road was the Maltings, built in 1875 for Truswells of Sheffield: it produced malted barley for the breweries. It was served from the railway by its own sidings for deliveries of barley and fuel, with the finished product leaving the same way; in September 1914 the Maltings was taken over by R. & W. Paul Ltd., of Ipswich. South of the Maltings beyond the railway was the cattle market, until recently the site of Deborah Services, Ltd, and P. T. P. Aerial Platforms. The railway cattle dock facilities were adjacent to the station on the western side of Victoria road.

On the southern side of the railway the houses in Silver Street were relatively new in 1914 as were those situated on the northern side of Victoria Road. The Cuthbert's Avenue, St Mary's Avenue, Walker's Close and the Woodlands developments are all relatively modern. There were no council houses at that time on the eastern side of St Barnabas Road nor were there any in Queen's Road and South Street, although there were some cottages in South Street where the council houses now stand. The bungalows in Marsh Lane and West Street are all fairly new – some built where a cottage and farm buildings had once stood. On both sides of West Street towards the north end were rows of cottages and other buildings – including a butcher's shop and one that later served as a cycle cum radio shop, now demolished and replaced by dwellings.

Numerous shops provided the inhabitants with practically all that they needed for their day-to-day living requirements. These included grocers,

INTRODUCTION

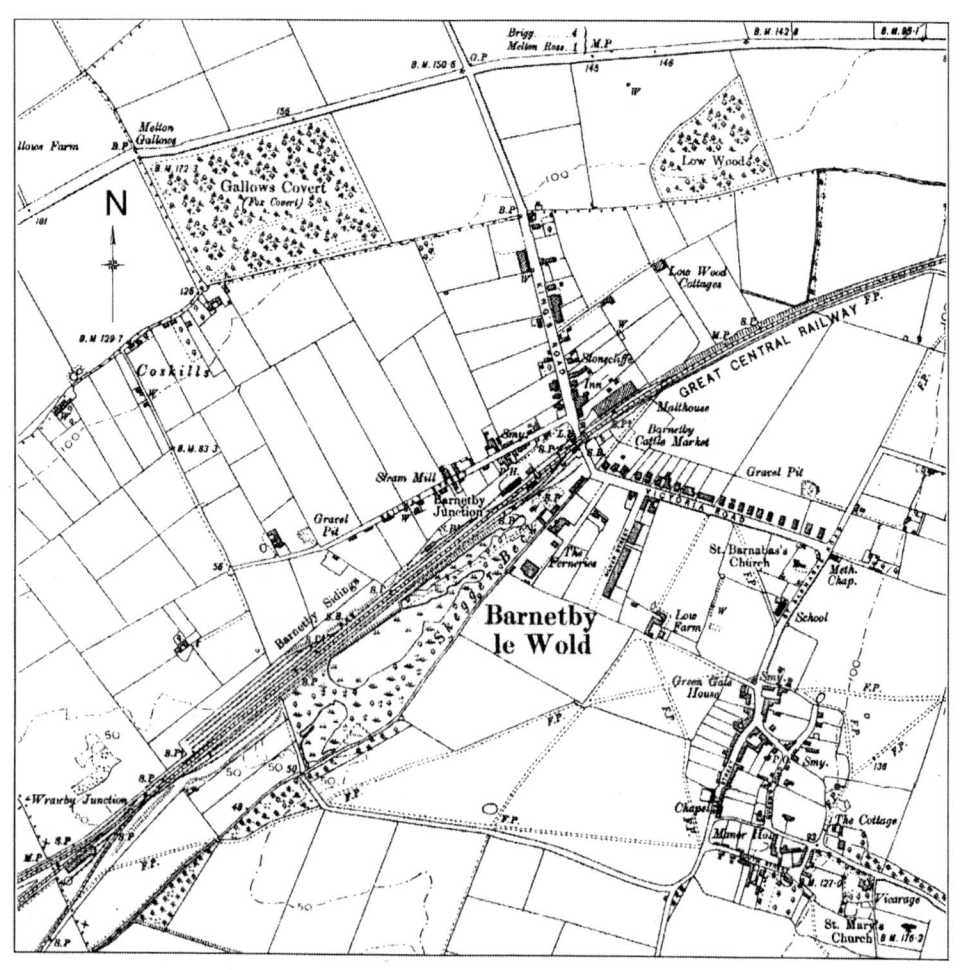

Map 1. *Barnetby-le-Wold in 1908.*   Ordnance Survey

butchers, a baker and a general store all catering for foodstuffs, with fresh milk being available direct from the farms. To attend to the requisites for the outer being was a tailor, a draper, a shoemaker and cobbler and some barbers. Among the other village craftsmen looking after the material side there were builders, carpenters and joiners, blacksmiths and a saddler to name but a few. In the vicinity of the railway station there were two hotels and an inn. A horse-drawn carrier provided for the transportation of goods.

    For spiritual needs the village had a church and two chapels. The church, a temporary wooden building that later became the church hall when the present St Barnabas Church was built, stood on the site now taken up by the new St Barnabas Church Hall and car parking facility. St Mary's Church, which had served the original village surrounding Manor Farm, was in a bad state of repair and not deemed fit for regular use.

Of the two chapels the Primitive Methodist was on the eastern side of St Barnabas Road across from the temporary church at the junction with Victoria Road in what is now the front garden of the Vicarage. The Wesleyan Methodist Chapel was, and still is, in West Street.

The National Day School, built in 1862 and now converted into dwellings, was the seat of learning that many of the Barnetby Boys would have attended. The War Memorial Cross would eventually be erected next to that day school (the day school reference distinguished it from the Sunday school).

Names on stone

In December 1920, when the War Memorial Cross was erected and unveiled, it had no names at all inscribed on it – but more about that later. In late August 1921 a Memorial tablet, inscribed with the names of twenty-five men of Barnetby-le-Wold, was unveiled in St Mary's Church. This tablet is now on the north wall of St Barnabas church.

The War Memorial records the names of thirty men who fell during the Great War but not all were Barnetby men. Included were men from outside the village now known to have worked for the railway at Barnetby Locomotive Depot and some had lodged in Barnetby. This was not at all helpful when it came to having their Memorials traced by the Commonwealth War Graves Commission (CWGC). All I was able to provide to assist identification was a surname, initials, rank, Regiment/Battalion (mostly taken from the War Memorial) a possible year of death and perhaps having an association with Barnetby. Some of the information submitted proved to be incorrect and this did not help matters. The CWGC, however, was very patient with any subsequent enquiries that finally led to all the requested identifications being successfully accomplished. Modern technology, in the form of computerisation, has now simplified and speeded up those proceedings that can now be had from the Internet. This research has shown that the War Memorial has errors relating to some of the men's units. I am certain one name is wrong having traced what I believe to be the correct name by its inclusion on the Roll of Honour.

The original Great War 'Roll of Honour' names one hundred and seventy-four men of Barnetby that enlisted and served with the colours, including the men associated with the village. Of that number thirty-four were killed or subsequently died while still serving. In the column headed 'Our Glorious Dead' thirty-four men are named, but I believe Harry Rhodes is an error. Ernest Insley, named with the survivors in the second column, is recorded as a casualty with the CWGC and also on the memorial tablet in the church, while Harry Rhodes is not. Not all men who enlisted while working at Barnetby Locomotive Depot are

INTRODUCTION

named on the Roll of Honour possibly because they were not Barnetby men nor had need to lodge here. Some men named on the Roll of Honour as having died in the Great War are, for whatever reason, not named on the War Memorial but I have traced them just the same. By comparison the Roll of Honour compiled for the Second World War names one hundred and forty-four men that enlisted of which eleven were killed or subsequently died.

The Memorials

Throughout the text there are references to memorials commemorating men killed or who died from other causes. Memorials are either headstones at graves or 'Memorials to the Missing' naming servicemen who have no known grave. A headstone is engraved with as much information as was known: the man's number (except officers), rank and name, gallantry medals awarded, date of death and age, regimental badge (or national emblem), the regiment's name and a Catholic cross, or Star of David if Jewish, or suitable inscriptions and distinctive markings for Indian faiths and creeds, like Sikhs, Hindus and Muslims, and Chinese nationals. Space at the bottom of the headstone allowed for engraving a small personal family inscription. Occasionally, the cross has been omitted on headstones, usually by family request.

When a Victoria Cross had been awarded an engraving of that device replaces the usual cross on the headstone (similar treatment is given to the rare George Cross recipient of WW2).

Sometimes graves were 'lost' when fighting overran cemeteries made during the war, often by fighting and medical units, when temporary wooden crosses were used (replaced by headstones after the war). A 'lost' grave has a 'special' named memorial, usually in a prominent position away from the main burials, stating 'KNOWN TO BE BURIED IN THIS CEMETERY' or 'BELIEVED TO BE BURIED IN THIS CEMETERY' or 'BURIED ELSEWHERE IN THIS CEMETERY' with 'THEIR GLORY SHALL NOT BE BLOTTED OUT' added if there is no family inscription. For a totally destroyed cemetery, or one with 'lost' graves 'concentrated' into a larger one, a stone placed with the relevant 'special' memorials records the fact that 'THEIR GRAVES ARE NOW LOST' or 'WERE DESTROYED IN BATTLE' and 'THEIR GLORY SHALL NOT BE BLOTTED OUT' and includes information about the original cemetery.

Where it was not possible to identify a body, the headstone is engraved with a cross, with the inscription 'A SOLDIER OF THE GREAT WAR' (or '1939-45 WAR') above the cross and 'KNOWN UNTO GOD' below. As much information as was known is included, e.g. nationality, regiment and rank, date of death and the regimental badge (or national emblem). In 1992, after analysing known data, 'A Lieutenant of the Great War – Irish Guards' whose body lay in St Mary's A.D.S. Cemetery at Haisnes, near Loos, was confirmed as being *Lt John Lockwood Kipling*, Irish Guards, son of Rudyard Kipling; originally named on the Loos Memorial to the Missing, his name has now been removed and inscribed on the headstone. Ironically, Rudyard Kipling, who suggested the phrases for an unidentified body, searched in vain for his son's grave.

'Memorials to the Missing' serve battlefields and areas determined by geographical limits and specific dates and name all the unidentified/not found men in service/regimental seniority. A man's name is listed under his respective military unit in alphabetical order in rank seniority.

Memorials generally relate to a specific battle area and are sited in that area though there are some exceptions. In the main memorials are high walls, bearing panels inscribed with men's names, built round specific cemeteries. This was a compromise as the French objected to the amount of land that separate memorials would take up. However a few separate memorials not forming part of a cemetery were permitted, the Canadian National Memorial on Vimy Ridge, the Menin Gate Memorial, Ypres and the Somme Thiepval Memorial, being fine examples. Names of the missing men of the Commonwealth countries, apart from South Africa, are on national memorials to be found at battle sites particularly associated with that country's exploits.

Anyone wishing to trace a relative's grave/memorial can write to the CWGC at 2 Marlow Road, Maidenhead, Berks., SL6 7DX, giving as much information as possible. A quicker method is via the Internet on the CWGC website, www.cwgc.org, where this information is now available from the Debt of Honour Register. However if information for the site of a previous burial is required this can only be obtained by writing to the CWGC. At one time the CWGC offered a photographic service whereby photographs of graves /memorials, especially those in far countries or countries difficult to access, could be obtained. Unfortunately, whilst I was in the process of obtaining photographs of the WW2 men's graves this photographic service was discontinued. The CWGC also sell a booklet of standard Michelin 1/200,000 scale maps of northern France overprinted with numbered purple dots indicating Cemetery/Memorial locations. The maps cover an area from Ypres, in the north, through to the Somme, to just below Paris in the south.

The Divisions, Brigades and Units that the men belonged to

In the text there are references to the regiments/battalions that the men belonged at the time they were killed, as well as the various brigades and divisions they were with. This can seem somewhat confusing so I will try to simplify things. I will disregard the Armies and Corps as these generally covered large areas and

INTRODUCTION

the make-up of these groups varied greatly depending on what the situation at the time in a particular area demanded.

The division, the largest 'permanent' unit, consisted of three brigades, each one initially having four infantry battalions, and one Pioneer battalion – thirteen battalions in all. When including its other units – cavalry, artillery, engineers, signals and medical, the division totalled just over 19,600 men. The Regular Divisions were numbered 1-8 and 27-29 plus the Guards (as the war progressed non-regular soldiers were sent to regular battalions). The Territorials were numbered 42-69, 74 and 75 and the New Army Divisions, 9-26 and 30-41. By and large brigade numbers can be found by multiplying the divisional number by three thus giving the middle brigade number, e.g. the **21**st Division initially comprised the 62nd, **63**rd and 64th Brigades (does not work with Divisions 1-6). During the war occasionally a brigade was exchanged with one from another division, as was the case of the 63rd Brigade, 21st Division, exchanged with the 110th Brigade, 37th Division. Still confused? Early in 1918 the composition of the United Kingdom brigades was subject to a major change.

There are references in the text to medical units that often made, or began to make, cemeteries simply because soldiers in their care often succumbed to their wounds, or illnesses, and they obviously had to be buried somewhere. These units were often referred to as hospitals and I have used that same expression in the text. (The term hospital, when referring to one in France is probably somewhat misleading. Certainly the work and routine would be what one would expect in a hospital but there the similarity ends – the hospitals in all probability were the Field Ambulances of which every division had three – one per brigade).

Another far better appointed hospital, next down the line from the Field Ambulance, was the Casualty Clearing Station (CCS) with tented accommodation, or, if you were lucky, wooden huts and their equipment in those days could doubtless be best described as basic. Some of those referred to as 'general' hospitals were not much better appointed. Those 'general' or base hospitals were usually situated well behind the lines away from the threat of enemy guns or air attacks. Many were near the Channel coast with easy access to ports for shipping men back to England for possible further treatment in hospitals or for convalescence at home.

During the 1914-18 War, the main areas where the British and Commonwealth forces fought in Belgium and northern France covered an area not much larger than the old county of Lincolnshire (the countryside is also very similar). It makes visits to these areas relatively simple without having to travel large distances. This is where the majority of the 'Barnetby Boys' fought and died, and later on in the text I refer to the various actions, in chronological order, that I *believe* led to their deaths. There I have attempted to describe mainly that part of any action that took place as it involved a man's particular unit and not the whole battle, so the reader must be aware that the action involved many other units.

To the casual visitor to the battlefields it is not immediately apparent how relatively small the areas were where such appalling numbers of soldiers became casualties. It is only when one has either read about a particular area or had it pointed out that the reality begins to sink home. Looking across well-tended fields it is hard to imagine that they were once pockmarked with shell-holes, criss-crossed with trenches and littered with rotting bodies and material debris. Many villages had been reduced to heaps of rubble and woods were a mass of shattered tree stumps. On a quiet, fresh, sunny day how can one visualise the noise, the stench and the mud? Having visited a number of those former battlefields and seen the memorials and numerous cemeteries, I believe I now have a better understanding of the ordeals, for the most part borne ungrudgingly, that those men went through. Today, when counselling is frequently offered at the slightest whim, how many people are aware of the sheer hell and deprivation those men experienced and endured to ensure the freedom we enjoy today? Very few, I suspect. This record might help to redress that. But how did it come about?

1
An idea materializes

DURING the summer of 1986, while returning from the French Charente-Maritime region and making for Boulogne to catch the ferry to Dover, I saw a sign indicating the Military Cemetery at Étaples, near Boulogne. Having time in hand a visit was in order and suffice it to say that I was most impressed by what I saw. What I did not know was that this is the largest British cemetery in France, with 11,436 burials. (The largest CWGC cemetery in the world, Tyne Cot Cemetery at Passchendaele near Ypres in Belgium, has just over 11,900 burials.)

There is however a noticeable difference between the two. Due to the close proximity of many base hospitals the majority of the burials at Étaples are of identified men who died from wounds whilst in care and receiving medical treatment. The burials at Tyne Cot Cemetery, where the vast majority are unidentified, record the struggle of hundreds of unknown men who foundered in, and whose remains were unearthed from, the mud of Flanders.

Every year on Remembrance Sunday, for as long as I can remember, the village men and women have gathered at the War Memorial to remember those who had died in the two World Wars. In the early days I can recall that many of those attending the ceremony were veterans of the Great War, including my father, no doubt there to remember comrades who had been killed. They did not say much but their eyes betrayed the pain and grief that their memories brought back. In Church one year a distraught Mother who had lost a son in the Second World War wept practically throughout the whole service and I was too young then to understand why.

In latter years the numbers of veterans from both wars have dwindled but I remember one elderly Great War soldier, barely able to walk, standing to attention during the Last Post with tears running down his face. At other times I had listened avidly as he talked freely of his war experiences without a visible trace of emotion! At the time I did not have any idea that I would one day set about finding out about the 'Barnetby Boys'. I now realise that an opportunity had been missed as he and other returned First War veterans who I knew are now no longer with us. Their help would have been invaluable.

The real inspiration was initiated on the Remembrance Sunday of 1986. At the wreath laying ceremony at the village War Memorial, in Remembrance of those 'Barnetby Boys' killed in the wars of 1914-18 and 1939-45, the customary reading of the names of the men who had fallen in both World Wars was omitted. Whether this was by accident or design I will never really know but I am inclined to favour accident. Later during the Remembrance Day Service in the Church the Vicar, the *Rev. R. Kenyon*, when making his address asked, 'Who were the Barnetby Boys?' and, basing the sermon around that question, introduced their names in groups throughout the sermon as appropriate.

Of those attending Remembrance Day Services today how many know of the men who fought in those World Wars they are there to remember? In small communities a list of names is read out and for many of those attending those services it is just that – a list of names. Even I only relate to a few men either because their relatives are known to me or, having done research into them and seen their photographs, the mention of their names recalls those photographs.

That question, 'Who were the Barnetby Boys?', in conjunction with having seen all the immaculately kept graves in Étaples Military Cemetery stirred me into finding out something about the men, their memorials and the events that led to their deaths, especially those who were killed during the Great War of 1914-18. To visit their memorials and the battlefields they fought on has been a great help.

Finding information about the 'Barnetby Boys' was perhaps the most difficult part, relying mainly on obituaries in local newspapers *The Grimsby News* and *The Hull and Lincolnshire Times* – on microfilm in Grimsby and Hull libraries respectively. The GCR Journals (hereinafter referred to as the Journal) had information regarding a number of former railwaymen (courtesy of the then GCR Archivist, Mike Fish of Bigby – his grandfather had gone to the Great War from Victoria Road, Barnetby). Dates of birth: unless known (or calculated) the BMD Index format is used, i.e. quarter year and year, e.g. (3)1897 – registered in the 3rd quarter – Jul, Aug, Sep, 1897.

While checking through Army service documents for any of those of the 'Barnetby Boys' I only came across a few as unfortunately a very large proportion of those documents, mainly of soldiers who survived the war and of those who died during the war, were either totally destroyed or very severely damaged by fire and water during the 'Blitz' of London in the Second World War. Those documents that survived and were in a condition sufficient to be salvaged have now been recorded on microfilm, the 'Burnt Records' (WO 363 series), held at the National Archives at Kew. (Records of soldiers who were discharged to pension or medically discharged from the Army during the war are in the WO 364 series of documents at the National Archives.)

I had better luck with Barnetby's two Canadian soldiers; the National Archives of Canada provided photocopies of a number of their service documents. Occasionally a man's relative gave information or provided material that helped to give a more complete picture or confirm points.

Military information has been obtained from unit war diaries (WO 95 series), held in the National Archives at Kew (The Museum of Lincolnshire Life at Lincoln also has typed copies of the Lincolnshire Regiment War Diaries). Regimental histories and numerous reference books, especially 'Soldiers Died in the War, 1914-1919', have been consulted. Other sources include the Imperial War Museum (photographs) and the Ministry of Defence.

With assistance in tracing from the CWGC all of the 'Barnetby Boys' named on the War Memorial have been identified and their memorials located and, since the spring of 1987, all the First World War 'Boys' memorials have been visited except for *E. D. French* (who was really a casualty of the 3rd Afghan War 1919) whose memorial is in Delhi, India.

Almost every CWGC cemetery has a register. The register introduction describes the cemetery development and where applicable includes information about concentration burials from smaller, often remote, cemeteries. In some instances a named unit, or units, used those cemeteries at a certain time. Where this information concurred with data I had about certain Barnetby men I wondered about the possibility of them having been originally buried elsewhere?

The CWGC confirmed that the archival records occasionally showed that men had initially been buried in small cemeteries that were later concentrated into the present larger ones as well as recording locations where men had brought in from individual battlefield graves. This led to more CWGC searches for those Barnetby men, excepting the ones that were buried in cemeteries by medical units, that I believed may have been re-buried. The result is that I now know where a number of men were initially buried, the sites being identifiable by trench map references, some quite near where they had fallen on the battlefield. However, the location of the cemetery where a man is now buried is not necessarily the cemetery nearest to where he was originally buried. These sites have all been visited, as have the 1914-18 battlefield areas where the Barnetby Boys are believed to have been fighting when they were killed.

THE BARNETBY BOYS

In May 1987, when I first went in search of the 'Barnetby Boys' memorials over in France, one place that I had to visit was la Boisselle on the Somme. It was there on 1st July 1916 that the 'Grimsby Chums' first went into battle. Many of the 'Grimsby Chums' would have had similar experiences as regards to 'going over the top' as had my father, who also received his first wound there. Prior to that first visit I had been in touch with Martin Middlebrook, the military historian and author of 'The First Day on the Somme', to whom my father had sent information regarding his experiences of that 1st July 1916. In reply I received the notes that my father had provided. There was no outstanding information in those notes but it was all new to me.

The area where the 'Grimsby Chums' were entrenched near la Boisselle on 1st July 1916 is easy to locate using as a reference a nearby extremely large mine crater called the 'Lochnagar Crater', that is reputed to be the largest hole ever made by man in anger. In 1978, this crater was privately purchased by Englishman Mr Richard Dunning and it is now preserved as a Memorial and looked after by 'The Friends of Lochnagar'. A memorial seat provided by the Grimsby Rotarians and dedicated to the 'Grimsby Chums' was placed at the crater in 1999.

Just before Armistice Day 1998, a soldier's remains were partially exposed close to the rim of Lochnagar Crater at la Boisselle. Personal effects found near the remains gave a clue to the identity of Pte George Nugent, 22nd Battalion Northumberland Fusiliers, killed on 1st July 1916, aged 28 years. Eighty-four years on I attended the service on 1st July 2000, as his remains were buried with full military honours in the nearby Ovillers Military Cemetery. A small wooden cross at Lochnagar Crater now marks the site near where his remains were found.

Meanwhile, the CWGC looks after soldiers' remains as they come to light, often unearthed by farmers. Recently there have been instances of larger numbers: at Monchy-le-Preux in 1996, at Boesinghe near Ypres in 1999, at le Point-du-Jour near Arras in 2001 and at Fromelles in 2008, where research showed that the Germans had buried up to about 400 soldiers in July 1916. Apart from Fromelles they were found in areas being prepared for development. Where a soldier's remains can be identified then efforts are made to trace living relatives prior to re-burial with full military honours in an existing cemetery. At Fromelles a new cemetery has been made for those found there. What sort of a burial would the 'Barnetby Boys' have had I wonder?

Map 2. *Sites of the Barnetby Boys Memorials on the Western Front.*

Map above, and next page, shows where the casualties of the 'Barnetby Boys', of Somerby and other named men occurred on the Western Front and site of their grave/memorial.
H. Cox, *near Reutel, Tyne Cot Memorial Passchendaele;* **C. F. Wilson**, *near Potijze, Vlamertinghe Cemetery;* **W. H. Bell**, *The Bluff, Menin Gate Memorial;* **H. H. Denton**, *near Ridge Wood, Tyne Cot Memorial;* **T. W. Bramley**, *near Haegdoorne, Tyne Cot Memorial;* **G. Hurd**, *near Gorre, Dud Corner Memorial, Loos;* **E. K. White**, *Lens, Nœux-les- Mines Cemetery;* **C. F. Andrew**, **T. Hall** *and* **A. Tweed**, *near Loos, Dud Corner Memorial;* **G. W. Smith**, *on Vimy Ridge, Cabaret Rouge Cemetery;*

Map 3. *G. W. Thacker, on Vimy Ridge, Givenchy Road Canadian Cemetery;* **H. Dawson**, *Greenland Hill near Gavrelle, Chili Trench Cemetery, Gavrelle;* **C. P. Blanchard**, *near Etrun, Haute Avesnes Cemetery;* **W. F. Starkey**, *near Bullecourt, Arras Memorial;* **R. W. Robinson**, *near St Martin-sur-Cojeul, Wancourt British Cemetery;* **G. W. Rimmington**, *near Croisilles, Bac-du-Sud Cemetery;* **F. Thompson**, *near Bienvillers-au-Bois, Warlincourt Halte Cemetery;* **C. Gostelow**, *Beaucourt-sur-Ancre, Ancre Cemetery;* **W. S. Witty**, *near Pozières, Pozières British Cemetery;* **J. W. Lobley**, *near Bazentin-le-Petit, London Cemetery, Longueval;* **J. W. Rapson**, *near Bazentin-le-Petit, Albert Cemetery;* **G. H. Smith**, *near Fricourt, Gordon Dump Cemetery, la Boisselle;* **W. H. Hinchsliff**, *near le Transloy, Thiepval Memorial;* **H. Wright**, *Chapel Hill Heudicourt, Pozières Memorial;* **C. Braithwaite**, *near Gouy, Prospect Hill Cemetery, Gouy;* **G. Nicholls**, *near Bellenglise, Roisel Cemetery;* **W. Slight**, *near le Hamel, Villers-Bretonneux Cemetery;* **W. Blair**, *near Horgny, Thiepval Memorial;* **E. Vessey**, *Terny-Sorny, Vauxbuin French Military Cemetery.*

Other named casualties:
C. S. Pelham Lord Worsley, *at Zandvoorde, Ypres Town Cemetery extension (& The Guards Memorial, Zandvoorde);* **C. Caward**, *Cuinchy, le Touret Memorial;* **Sister E. Andrew**, *Lillers, Lillers Cemetery;* **S. Bowness**, *Lens, Loos Cemetery;* **H. Ward**, *Arras Memorial; C. S. Bott, Feuchy Cemetery;* **F. W. McAulay**, *near Bayencourt/Sailly-au-Bois, Foncquevillers Cemetery and* **A. Carty** *and* **S. H. Pratt** *in Sailly-au-Bois Cemetery and* **A. Mumby-Croft** *in Doullens Cemetery;* **J. K. Adlard**, *Bouzincourt Ridge, Bouzincourt Ridge Cemetery;* **H. Jackson V.C.**, *near Thiepval, A. I. F. Burial Ground, Flers.*

2
1914

Britain, and Lincolnshire, prepares for War

ON the 4th August 1914, when Britain declared war on Germany, orders were immediately transmitted for the mobilisation of the Regular Army, the Reserve Army and the Territorial Force. The Lincolnshire Regiment, having just two regular battalions – the 1st and the 2nd – had only the 1st Battalion, stationed at Portsmouth, immediately available.

The 1st Battalion, being under strength and including men not fully trained, received sufficient reservists on 8th August from the depot at Lincoln to complete the establishment. By 12th August the Battalion was fully mobilised and ready including a reinforcement detail to remain at Portsmouth until required. Meanwhile those men with insufficient training were sent to the 3rd (Reserve) Battalion at Lincoln. On 14th August the 1st Lincolns, part of 9th Brigade, 3rd Division, British Expeditionary Force (BEF), disembarked at le Havre in France from the SS *Norman*. Nine days later their part in the war began in earnest near Mons.

The 2nd Battalion was stationed out in Bermuda at the outbreak of war and, knowing that units of the German High Seas Fleet were at sea, went to readiness in case the enemy attempted sea borne raids or landings. In mid September the Battalion was relieved by the Royal Canadian Regiment and sailed for home on the SS *Canada* via Halifax, Nova Scotia, where the ship joined a trooping convoy that was bringing the 1st Canadian Expeditionary Force Contingent to Britain. On arrival at Devonport, England, the 2nd Lincolns moved to a camp at Hursley Park, near Winchester, and joined the 25th Brigade, 8th Division. Three weeks later, on 5th November, having completed re-equipping and training the 2nd Lincolns embarked onto the SS *Cestrian* at Southampton. The following morning the Battalion landed at Le Havre.

Apart from the Reserves, the only other trained men available at that time were those in the Territorial Force. Although this force was designated primarily for home defence the men could however volunteer for overseas duty if the situation so demanded it. At that time the Lincolnshire Regiment contained two Territorial battalions, the 4th based at Lincoln and the 5th at Grimsby. Towards the end of July 1914 those two units were on annual training at Bridlington and while there, on 2nd August, received orders to return to their respective unit Headquarters to wait in readiness for the expected mobilisation orders. By 10th August both of those units, being up to strength, were designated 'General Service' and the following day set off for their War Station at Belper, Derbyshire, moving on 15th August from there to Luton.

On 15th September the Government called upon all Territorials to volunteer for service overseas and, in response, most Territorial units in Britain signed the voluntary General Service obligation form. Those original Territorial units were referred to as First Line units. Thus the 4th and 5th Lincolns were now entitled the 1/4th and 1/5th Lincolns. Jointly with the 1/4th and 1/5th Leicesters they formed the 138th Brigade of the 46th (N. Midland) Division. In February 1915 the 46th Division set out for France, the 1/4th and 1/5th Lincolns landing at Le Havre.

On 31st August 1914, authorisation was sanctioned to form 2nd Line Territorial Force (Reserve) units and enlistment began in September 1914. With the First Line battalions formed, work then proceeded to establish Second Line units. For the time being the men were to live at home, parading in civilian clothes, until the County Association was able to issue them with clothing and equipment. Men sent from 1st Line units, who had been unwilling to undertake the Imperial Service Obligation or were not medically fit, proved invaluable when it came to training the recruits. In November 1914, clothing was issued to the men but it was a further month before any rifles were provided. When these arrived they were limited to 200 per battalion.

Thus in January 1915, the 2/4th and 2/5th Lincolns were formed at Luton to become part of the 177th Brigade, 59th (2nd N. Midland) Division. (The other two battalions making up the 177th Brigade were the 2/4th and 2/5th Leicesters.) During February 1915, in order to overcome rifle shortages, Japanese rifles and ammunition were supplied. Those rifles were eventually replaced, between November 1915 and March 1916, by MLE Mk III rifles.

In June 1915, drafts began to the 1st Line units out in France. At the same time the home service men were transferred to Provisional units, the Lincolnshire's Provisional unit being the 13th Battalion. In July the 59th Division went to St Albans. During April 1916 the Division moved to Ireland, where the 2/4th and 2/5th Lincolns were on duty at Dublin, from 25th April to 17th May. The remainder of their time in Ireland was spent in war training at the Curragh. In January 1917 the 59th Division returned to Fovant, in England, and in February

1917 it was sent out to France where, by 3rd March, it had concentrated around Méricourt, on the Somme.

In April and June 1915, the 3/5th and 3/4th Battalions respectively came into being and in May 1916 became the 4th and 5th Reserve Battalions based at Grantham. In September 1916 they amalgamated as the 4th Reserve Battalion in the N. Midland Reserve Brigade at Saltfleet. The Territorial Reserve Battalion(s) did not serve overseas.

On 5th August 1914, Parliament approved the increase of 500,000 men for the Army. Two days later recruiting began for 100,000 men to form the first New Army (known as Kitchener's Army or K.I) of six divisions of Service Battalions, numbered 9–14. A few days later recruits forming the 6th Lincolns left Lincoln for Belton Park, Grantham, where training began as part of the 33rd Brigade, 11th (Northern) Division. The 11th Division was eventually destined for the Dardenelles where, on the night of 6th/7th August 1915, the 6th Lincolns landed at Suvla Bay.

On 11th September orders were issued for a Second New Army to be formed. Known as K.II it comprised of six divisions – numbered 15–20. Around 20th September recruits raised in Lincoln, designated as the 7th (Service) Battalion, were despatched to Wool, in Dorset, to start training as part of 51st Brigade, 17th (Northern) Division. On 14th July 1915, the 7th Lincolns landed at Boulogne – bound for Ypres.

On 13th September orders went out authorizing a Third New Army, K.III, to establish the 21st–26th Divisions; and the 8th Battalion was formed. The 8th Lincolns started their initial training at Halton Park near Tring as part of 63rd Brigade, 21st Division. The Battalion moved to Leighton Buzzard for the winter training period, but by the spring of 1915 it was back at Tring. On the night of 10th September the 8th Lincolns sailed from Folkestone for France and next day landed at Boulogne – destination Loos.

The 10th Lincolns, 'Grimsby Chums', was a 'Pals' Battalion that was raised locally, like most of the battalions that eventually formed the New Fourth Army (K.IV: 30th–35th Divisions) and New Fifth Army (K.V: 36th–41st Divisions). The 'Pals' battalions, on being granted War Office approval for their formation, were organized on the understanding that the organizations and towns that had initially raised them were to train, clothe, house and feed them until such time as the Army took over responsibility. The War Office meanwhile met any expenses (after the horrendous 'Pals' losses of July 1916 recruitment of City and Town battalions ceased).

In August 1914 a group of Grimsby Municipal College 'old boys' took the notion to form a school company and approached Captain Stream, their former headmaster, with the idea. At a meeting held on 1st September the 'old boys' decided to go ahead with the idea and present the formation to the 5th Lincolns. Captain Stream, having been in charge of the College Cadet Corps that had been trained up to a high state of efficiency in collaboration with Lieutenant Pratte, offered the College OTC facilities for training. By the end of the first week's training the original fifty odd men had increased to company strength. The company, calling itself the 'Grimsby Chums', was then proffered to the 5th Lincolns only to be told, 'Sorry, we're full up!'

The Mayor, Alderman J. H. Tate, was approached to put the idea of raising a complete battalion to the Town Recruiting Committee. The Committee duly agreed. War Office approval was then sought via Northern Command at York. Affirmation from York to form an infantry battalion at Grimsby was received on 9th September. Thus was born the 10th (Service) Battalion, Lincolnshire Regiment (Grimsby), as it was officially known.

Recruiting commenced almost at once at the Artillery Barracks in Grimsby and two weeks later their strength was about 500. Major G. L. Bennett was in temporary command, his Adjutant being Captain W. A. Vignoles. Non-availability of khaki uniforms caused a minor problem so the men were kitted out in blue serge in the meantime.

The 13th November *Grimsby News* printed a drawing of an escutcheon (left) designed and drawn for the 'Grimsby Chums' by Mr R. E. Wrigglesworth, art master at Grimsby Municipal College. It became familiar to many local families having been printed onto postcards in both blue and brown for the 'Chums' use. I still have one of each type. My father sent one to his sister Amy at Leigh in Lancashire on 24th January 1915, saying *'Thanks for P.C. I like being here very much. What is the weather like at Leigh? It's very wet at GY. – C. R. F.'* (he enlisted on 2nd January 1915. I think '*being here*' refers to the Artillery Barracks where he would possibly have been doing his basic training.)

On 4th December the Battalion went to the new-hutted camp at Brocklesby Park where it trained until 15th June 1915, when a move was made to a camp at Studley Royal near Ripon. The Battalion trained hard there for three months as part of the 101st Brigade, 34th Division. (The other battalions of the 101st Brigade were the 15th and 16th Royal Scots and the 11th Suffolks.) More training took place following further moves – first to Strensall, then to Perham Down.

1914

(Left and below) Recruits for the 10th Lincolns at Brocklesby Park.
Pte Reg. Robinson (hatless) is central in the 2nd row; Pte C. R. Frankish is 2nd from the right. Note two in uniform wearing civilian caps.

On the back of the photo (left) Pte Hubert Cox (my 'uncle') had written: 'Some of boys of E Coy. Just look and see if there is anybody you know'. Pte C. R. Frankish is 4th from the left, 3rd row. The Coy Commander, Captain Frow? (Wroe), is on the extreme right.

A Chums group taken at Brocklesby Park.
Pte Frankish is 2nd from the right, third row.

More 'Chums' at a Brocklesby Park lodge. Pte Frankish is seated directly below the two men in blue on the right.

Another group of Chums at Brocklesby, (Pte Frankish 3rd left, back row).

19

'There's a long, long trail a-winding…' The Grimsby Chums on a route march crossing over the railway bridge at Brocklesby station led by Col Heneage, the C.O. (right) accompanied by Major Cordeaux, 2 i/c. R.S.M. Cheffings is leading the footsloggers. 'Chips', the fox terrier (left) was owned by Cpl John Davey, farmer, of Thornton Curtis.

The end of the column. These are the early route march photographs taken in the spring of 1915. Later photographs at the same location show men marching with rifles. In both photographs, the men are wearing either khaki or blue uniforms or civilian clothes.

10th Lincolns on parade at Brocklesby and not a blue uniform in sight (note fox terrier 'Chips' in front of 5th man from the right.

10th Lincolns marching through Ripon, July 1915, carrying weapons in a relaxed style – not exactly as per the drill book.

In Tents at Strensall.
Pte Frankish arrowed above.

Under canvas at Perham Down...

...where the 34th Divisional Staff had slightly better accommodation.

...before moving to Sutton Veny (and photo left)...

Getting down to serious soldiering on the ranges at Sutton Veny where the aim was to be taught how to shoot – your aim helped!

Pte C. R. Frankish, 10th Lincolns.

An early photograph of Pte Hubert Cox, 10th Lincolns.

Four 'Barnetby Boys?' Pte C. R. Frankish is on the left. The two men in the centre are possibly 'Barnetby Boys' but their names are not known. Pte Hubert Cox is on the right.

The above was among family photographs and although he is not known he looks like the soldier second on the right in the photograph right, or could he be G. H. Smith (see photograph p. 90).

On 10th August 1915, the 10th (Service) Battalion, Lincolnshire Regiment, was officially taken over by the War Office. At the end of September the 10th Lincolns proceeded to Sutton Veny, where the 34th Division was assembling, to complete their training before moving out to France on 4th January 1916.

Many Barnetby men that enlisted, including those associated with the village, were to join into one battalion or other of the Lincolnshire Regiment and I suspect a number joined 'The Chums'. Some men were subsequently transferred to different battalions, regiments even. This has not been helpful when it came to tracing a soldier's background, especially with many Service Record documents having been destroyed or consequently damaged by fire and water in the Blitz during the Second World War. It was only as recently as November 1996 that some service records relating to the First World War became accessible to the public.

It is somewhat ironic that having explained the mobilisation and build-up of the Army, particularly the Lincolnshire battalions and, for most units, their subsequent movements to France that the first Barnetby fatality should be a man serving in the Royal Navy on the other side of the world! (My travels in the Royal Navy took me relatively close to those waters where that Barnetby man had been lost and I had no idea then. I refer to that incident later in this chapter.)

Barnetby level crossing (about 1910). Widening the permanent way from 2 to 4 tracks commenced in 1912. This work, needed to cope with the extra trains carrying coal to Immingham Dock after the Dock opened on Mon. 22nd July 1912, involved replacing the level crossing with a bridge; an underpass (subway) was built to route the road beneath the bridge. (The original bridge was removed and a new bridge put in place over Christmas 2009.) The sign on the building on the right reads 'King's Road'; below that is a post-box.

King's Road Barnetby. Work has not yet started on the subway approach; the heaps look like snow. The old level crossing is on the extreme left with the signal box behind the crossing keeper's house. (see photograph previous page).

The subway almost as it is today. It is not known exactly when the photograph was taken, however the postmark on the postcard is dated 10th June 1915. The railway bridge seen above was replaced by a new bridge on Christmas Day 2009.

In Barnetby, just before the war began, one of the major railway engineering works had finally reached completion namely the road running under the railway lines in King's Road. On the morning of Monday, 25th July, Mr Holloway – the engineer in charge of the project – standing on what was left of the footbridge adjacent to where the level crossing had been, duly declared the underpass (that became known as the 'subway') open to the public.

Staff changes in the August issue of the Journal (presumably for the previous month) included, in the Superintendent's Department at Barnetby, M. Tye taking up an appointment as a porter (he transferred to New Clee as a porter a month later). In the Engineer's Department platelayer G. H. Wobey had transferred to traffic. (Prior to July 1910 the monthly Journal listed few names in the Staff changes. From July 1910 onwards the Staff changes gradually became more and more detailed and by August 1914 they were very comprehensive lists. Unfortunately, for whatever reason, the Staff changes were not published after November 1915; a pity, for they had been a useful source of information.)

On Saturday 3rd August the Barnetby St Mary's football club had held a successful sports and gala in spite of inclement weather. The name of one official, J. Catterall (clerk of the sports course), appears later in this account, as do the names of three of the prize-winners in the sports events, viz C. R. Frankish (winner, 400 yards handicap), Percy Moss (3rd in the same event) and H. Wright (winner of the high jump). Barnetby Prize Silver Band had been in attendance playing a selection of music throughout the afternoon and again in the evening for dancing. It is quite possible that this could have been the last time that the band had the opportunity to turn out at full strength as sooner or later some of its members had left to join the armed forces.

The *Grimsby News* of 7th August had a special page dealing with the outbreak of war. Boxed headlines announced 'England at War with Germany', 'The King appeals to the Nation', 'Commanders appointed for Land and Sea' etc., followed by text like, 'On Tuesday 4th August War was declared on Germany...' etc, leaving no doubt as to the seriousness of the affair.

By the second weekend in August the *Grimsby News* reported that several of the Barnetby reservists had been called up in consequence of the outbreak of war and several young men had already enlisted, thereby ensuring that Barnetby had contributed its share. The womenfolk had also been very busy making clothing for the sick and wounded.

There had also been a water shortage that year and many village wells had begun to dry up. It was still short in the locality towards the end of September (or, as the *Grimsby News* put it, practically a water famine) yet I found no reference in the papers as to exactly when it ended.

The GCR had been having its share of problems with the water shortage inasmuch as its source, the Ballast Hole, was virtually empty. To ensure that the Barnetby locomotive depot had sufficient water for all its engines' needs water had been brought in from Immingham in special trains consisting of an engine and brake wagon plus about seven engine tenders.

By mid March of the following year things were almost normal but even so the GCR, not wanting to rely solely on the Ballast Hole for its water supply, had begun boring for water near the station. Having reached a depth of 150 feet, with no sign of a water bearing strata, the intention was to keep boring to penetrate through the Lincolnshire limestone. Whether the project was eventually successful was not mentioned, but I remember a water tower being there.

By the second week in August news had also become known at home about the plight of Belgian refugees and relief funds were being set up. On Saturday 15th August local workers organised a jumble sale in the village in aid of those refugees and raised £9 for the fund. The Women's Unionist Association announced that it too was working for the same cause. During Sunday's Church service the vicar, the Reverend C. F. Brotherton, made special reference to the war with appropriate hymns and psalms being sung. The Church collection, in aid of the Belgian relief fund, had received a very generous response.

On 18th August the *Grimsby News* published instructions for all men intent on enlisting:

> 'All soldiers who enlist are expected to provide themselves with the following articles: –
> 1 pair of boots, spare boot laces, spare braces, 2 flannel shirts, 2 pairs of worsted socks, toothbrush, razor and case, shaving brush, comb, soap, towel, knife, fork and tablespoon, housewife with buttons, needles and thread. An allowance of 10s. only is made to each man towards the cost of each kit.'

On Sunday 20th September the Band, under the leadership of Mr C. Thompson, had paraded through the village in aid of the Prince of Wales' fund and collected £6 3s. A charitable donation brought this sum up to £7 1s 6d.

On the evening of Monday 21st September an enthusiastic meeting had taken place in the school where a large number had gathered to hear Sir W. A. Gelder, MP, Mr T. J. Bennett, MP and Dr Ffrench speak in support of the call to arms. The need for still further recruits was to be dealt with as a matter of urgency throughout the county. The less accessible places, such as villages, were to hold meetings that would be attended by recruiting sergeants who would give out the necessary enlisting details. The meeting had duly been informed that Barnetby was already doing its share having sent 36 of its sons to enlist some of whom were currently fighting in France while the others were helping to swell the ranks of Kitchener's New Army.

Around this time my grandparents, Thomas and Marian Frankish, wrote to grandfather's younger brother, John West, in Gorham, Ontario County, New York State, USA, stating:

> '...we hope you have had a good harvest. We have had a very good harvest in this country and very fine weather to get it. I see by the papers you have

very good crops in America, which we are pleased to hear as you will be able to send us plenty during this awful war time.

What do you think of old Kaiser Bill and all the awful things he is doing? But I think he will have to suffer for it in the end. Our gallant little army is doing very well against his mighty army. We have sent 36 out of Barnetby to help to keep the Old Flag Flying.

It has been a very trying time here when the war first broke out. Lincolnshire (h)as never seen anything like it before. They shipped so many of the troops from Grimsby. For the first week or two train loads of soldiers, horses, guns and war material of all kinds day and night were passing through.

It has made a great difference here with so many young men going away and what the Railway Company have moved to Immingham where they have built some very big docks. Every thing was in a panic for a little while but they soon quietened down and food got so dear.'

Grandmother added: 'Your letter ought to have been answered before but this dreadful war seems to have upset everything. What a blessing it will be when it's all ended. . . . Barnetby looks very different now to what it used to be now the subway is finished. And there is a new station being built but nearly all the railway men have been moved to Immingham. One time they couldn't build houses fast enough. Now there are several standing empty.'

(The above extracts were from one of two letters sent to me by Deputy Sheriff Steven Mumby of Canandaigua, Ontario County, New York State, USA. Extracts from the second letter, sent to grandfather's cousin George Mumby, great-great-grandfather of Steven Mumby, appear later.)

The Journal for October 1914 produced its first 'List of Great Central Railwaymen who had joined the Colours' up to about 14th September. Included in that list, from The Chief Engineer's Department at Barnetby were: – platelayer F. Baker, light attendant T. W. Allcard and two relayers, A. Tilbrooke and J. Tutty. The Signal Department had provided assistant connector J. W. Worrall; and labourers G. R. Bullyment, G. H. Winterbottom and H. Coney. Shunter J. T. Elsom, a Wrawby man, joined from the Superintendent's Department and engine cleaner A. Moody enlisted from the Chief Mechanical Engineer's (Locomotive) Department.

Joining from the Superintendent's Dept at Immingham were goods guards J. H. Wright and G. H. Smith (the latter had transferred from Barnetby in February). Cleaner S. M. Bowness, a North Kelsey man, went from the

Chief Mechanical Engineer's (Loco.) Dept. Finally, from New Holland Superintendent's Dept, there was goods porter W. H. Scott, newly appointed there in February 1914. ('Supplementary Lists of GC Railwaymen who have joined the Colours' subsequently followed. Occasionally in the Journal there appeared separately a departmental itemization of the total number of GCR employees and the Company agents that had enlisted.)

The first GCR casualty lists, a continuation of the Supplementary Joining lists, appeared in the December 1914 issues of the Journal, naming Prisoners of War, the Missing and the Fatalities, the latter in a black edged box with an appropriate quotation usually poetry but occasionally from the Bible. Subsequent casualty lists included wounded men and, for a brief period, men interned in Holland. (Holland, being neutral, was interning any British serviceman crossing its border following the fall of Antwerp on 10th October 1914. These servicemen were mainly the sailors and Royal Marines of the Royal Naval Division, part of the force that had been defending Antwerp, who were trying to return to England via Holland.)

Meanwhile, no doubt due to the number of railwaymen that had joined up recently, staff changes involving two men at Barnetby Depot had taken place on the railway during September. In the Superintendent's Department, Eastern District, G. H Wilson, a brakesman, had been transferred to Grimsby Docks along with W. Vessey, a porter. Another porter, H. Scott, had been transferred to the Police Department from New Holland. Was he from Barnetby? A man based at Immingham named H. Scott crops up later!

The Barnetby Band had turned out on Sunday 4th October at another venue in order to help raise monies for the Belgian Relief Fund. On this occasion it had marched through the neighbouring villages of Bigby and Somerby. A collection had been made as the band marched through the two villages and had totalled £2 1s; that figure was later rounded up to £2 10s with a generous donation of 9s. The Band's own funds had also received a welcome boost by means of a separate donation of 10s. from Mrs F. Chatterton of Somerby.

The people in the village had assisted in various ways to a number of worthy causes. Round about the middle of October an appeal had been made for new or very slightly worn clothes to be taken to either Mrs Lowish or Mrs Ffrench who were hoping to send a parcel of clothing for the Belgian refugees. Others had been busy since the outbreak of war with the main preoccupation being sewing and knitting garments as contributions to those causes. The Belgian Relief Fund had duly acknowledged receiving 24 hospital shirts, 3 nightshirts, 18 day shirts, 24 pairs of socks and a number of slings and bandages. A very considerable quantity of slings and bandages had also been sent to the 5th Northern Hospital at Leicester. The last beneficiary had been the Lincolnshire Regiment with Mrs Hett having sent 12 fully equipped large kit bags each containing 1 flannel shirt, 2 pairs of socks, 2 large handkerchiefs, a towel, some soap, a pipe and some tobacco. The Mayor of Grimsby had also made an appeal locally for dark blankets, or rugs, for use by the Lincolnshire Regiment now that town had received official confirmation to form the 10th Battalion, known locally as 'The Grimsby Chums'.

The Barnetby Boys go to War

For most of the Barnetby Boys their war, excluding training, had developed from 1915 onwards but there were two incidents in 1914 in relation to the village, one indirectly and the other directly – in that order, to which I now refer.

In 1912, the railway was granted authority for widening the permanent way from Wrawby Junction through to Brocklesby. This work necessitated rebuilding the station here at Barnetby in order to accommodate the two extra tracks. Work on the new station was well in hand when war broke out – one of the contractors being Messers G. A. Pillatt of Nottingham. In the employ of Messers Pillatt was Campbell Caward, a Retford man, who had resided in the village while working here. A former soldier and a reservist he was recalled to the Army upon the mobilization of the Reserves and so 7634 Pte Campbell Caward, 2nd Battalion, King's Own Scottish Borderers (KOSB), went away to war. With him went life long friend 7633 Pte John Marsh, 2nd Battalion, KOSB, (born at Darwen, Lancashire), who, like Campbell, also lived at Retford.

The 2nd Battalion KOSB, in the 13th Brigade, 5th Division of II Corps, was part of the original BEF sent over to France in mid August 1914. On 10th October II Corps, having been rushed up from the Aisne sector to reinforce the French, was in the area of la Bassée on either side of the la Bassée canal, with its 5th Division on the right and 3rd Division on the left, with orders to advance north-eastwards. The situation late on 12th October was that the KOSB, having earlier taken over a 1½-mile length of the line south of the canal from the 1st Norfolks of 15th Brigade, were facing towards Cuinchy. On their right, facing Auchy, were the 2nd Duke of Wellington's and on the left, on the north bank of the canal, the 1st Dorsets of 15th Brigade. Vermelles, some 5 miles to the south and supposedly held by the French, had been taken over by the enemy, the French having reportedly evacuated it at dawn in 'un peu de panique'.

The move started about 5.30 a.m. on 13th October. The 1st Dorsets were soon ahead and by about 10 a.m., having halted east of Givenchy, provided crossfire support. But the 2nd KOSB were unable to advance much more than a couple of hundred yards or so despite the support of one company of 2nd King's Own Yorkshire Light Infantry (KOYLI) sent from Brigade reserve.

The 2nd Duke of Wellington's, on the KOSB's right, were reported to be consolidating so the KOSB duly followed suit. The advance had been subjected to a heavy enemy artillery bombardment around Givenchy with the 1st Dorsets, on the 13th Brigade's left, sustaining very heavy casualties. By mid afternoon the 1st Dorsets, retiring rapidly, were reinforced by a company of KOYLI crossing the canal at Pont Fixe. Soon afterwards a third company of KOYLI went to the assistance of the KOSB. Some units had carried out considerable hand-to-hand fighting throughout the day but by 7p.m. the enemy counter attack had been finally checked. During the night all positions were strengthened. On that day the 2nd KOSB suffered three officers wounded (one of whom died of wounds the following day) and twenty other ranks killed and forty wounded. The KOSB casualties had been mainly from 'D' and 'B' companies on the left. The 1st Dorsets, having been withdrawn to Pont Fixe, had lost 13 Officers killed and more than half the battalion was either killed, wounded or missing.

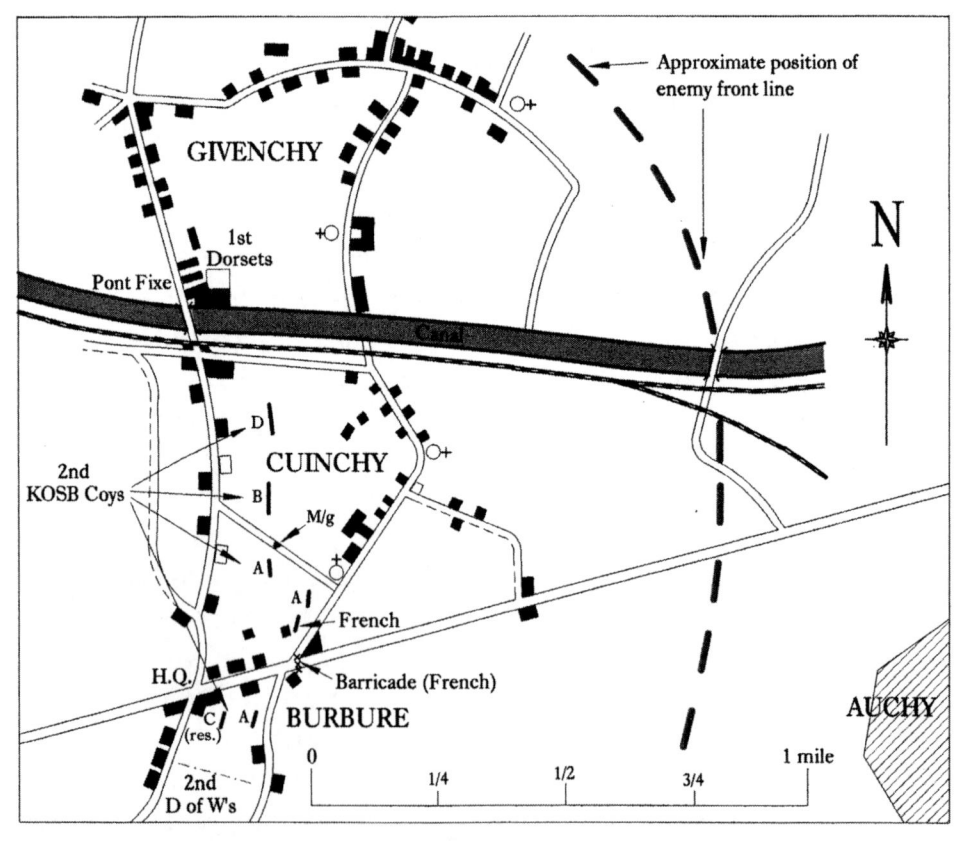

Map 4. *Diagram of position of the 2nd KOSB at nightfall on 13th October 1914. Based on a sketch in the margin of the 2nd KOSB war dairy PRO WO 95/1552*

Woburn Abbey Cemetery, Cuinchy, now occupies a site north of the road approximately where the KOSB had their machine-gun positioned in October 1914, (see map). Oddly there are no KOSB burials there.

Campbell is recorded as being killed in action on 13th October 1914 and John Marsh on the 14th October 1914; neither man has a known grave and both are commemorated by name on panel 15 of the Memorial to the Missing at le Touret. Situated at the eastern end of le Touret Military Cemetery this Memorial forms a loggia surrounding an open rectangular court having three solid walls with a walled colonnade on its east side. It commemorates over 13,000 men who have no known grave who fell in the la Bassée area before 25th September 1915.

Le Touret Military Cemetery and Memorial to the Missing. Campbell is named on the east wall.

Campbell Caward, a native of Retford, Nottinghamshire, had lived with Campbell, his father, in Beck Row, Retford. He was educated at St Saviour's school, Retford, along with his pal John Marsh. Both lads had joined the Army together and served 13 years in the KOSB, seeing service in Egypt, India, Ireland

and South Africa. During a two-year spell in Khartoum both men had met the then chaplain of the Forces, the Rev. A. E. Paxton, who was the Vicar of Retford when war had broken out. Whilst at Khartoum Campbell had picked up an old horse pistol from the battlefield and brought it home as a souvenir. He had been a good rifle shot, having beaten 1,800 competitors to win a marksmanship competition at Cairo.

The Retford Times of 20th November 1914 reported on the sad news that had reached the parents of Campbell Cayward and John Marsh on Friday 13th November that Pte Campbell Caward and Pte John Marsh, King's Own Scottish Borderers, had been killed in action in the trenches in France. (The Grimsby News had a brief obituary to Campbell the following week.)

Although the incident of Campbell's death was mentioned under Barnetby news, he is not named on either the War Memorial or the Roll of Honour. However he had been known well enough in the village sufficient for that report to be included in the local newspaper.

Further to the urgent need for recruits to come forward a scheme had been organised whereby local recruiting agents were being appointed to each district throughout the county. As mentioned earlier recruiting sergeants were to be in attendance at the village meetings.

Arrangements were also being made for local Rolls of Honour to be displayed in all the villages as well as recruiting posters giving out details about terms of service, rates of pay, and how and where to enlist. Other posters called upon volunteers who would be willing to transport prospective recruits to the enrolling stations.

With plenty of activity at home calling upon men to volunteer for active service, the men actually serving at the Front were certainly having their share of activity. The *Grimsby News* of 30th October published a letter from Pte James Baines at the Front (place unknown) to his sister living in Barnetby. A native of Stixwold he had taken up residence in the village. (The May 1914 Journal records that a Barnetby shunter, J. H. Baines, had left the railway service. Previous to that he had been employed as a ground pointsman at Barnetby. Was this the same man?)

> 'October 19th, 1914.
> I was pleased to get your parcel this morning. I have had a dig at both biscuits and 'chocs', they are spanking. I am not on the telegraphy, not much, only to the Germans with my rifle. We have been the last five weeks in the trenches and it is hell. The lads have stuck it and . . . (the next line was illegible). We had seven days raining day and night and had to sleep

in it when we could. We have moved on now and expect to be in the thick of it again. Our retirement was bad enough but we kept our peckers up. I can't tell you half what it is like only I think if the fellows knew at home they would come to fill a few gaps up. We captured about 400 10th of last month. It was warm while it lasted, but they gave in before we had got close enough to use our bayonets.

We are having fairly good weather now and our mails are coming a lot better. Do you know I have answered all your letters, but mine have gone, where I do not know. It was kind of Mrs S to send to me. I sent a P.c. back by return thanking her. You talk about refugees. Well you have seen nothing to what is here, but I think a few more weeks will put a different aspect on affairs. I have told Ed. I wanted pills, Peps for cold, some light overalls for trousers, and woollen waistcoat, but nothing else unless it is two pairs of woollen socks, because we have all to carry and we have enough at present I can tell you. I want you to let me know if you get this safe.

Has Jack Webster come to England? I thought he was coming here, give him my address. I have seen the Stixwold postman, he looks well, he was working round our trenches. You can tell them that 'Jack Johnsons' and 'coal boxes' don't stop our lads and we have no white flags, so if we are captured there will not be many left of us.

Well dear, I will tell you a lot more when I see you, so au revoir for the present.'

('Jack Johnsons' and 'coal boxes' were German 5.9-inch howitzer shells that on bursting emitted clouds of black smoke – also known as 'crumps' from the noise made on exploding.)

Another fatality, the titled son of a well-known local titled family on 30th October 1914, was not forthcoming until January 1915. This interesting story is referred to in the appendix.

Towards the end of October more local railwaymen had enlisted. The November issue of the Journal carried the first 'Supplementary List of GC Railwaymen that had joined the Colours' since the 14th September. Included in that list, from the Chief Mechanical Engineer's Dept at Barnetby, were engine cleaners C. Gostello (*Gostelow?*) and H. L. Partridge and the following firemen: W. H. Bell, S. Lovesay (*Loveday?*), A. Tweed and G. W. Scott. From the Immingham depot: firemen E. Grant, T. Hall and C. F. Andrew and spare driver W. Pretty. Joining from the Barnetby Superintendent's Department was groundpointsman J. Catterall. From Immingham depot: goods guard J. H.

Marrows (not related to Alan in Silver Street) and from Cleethorpes, porter guard W. Denton. Another name listed, possibly that of a Barnetby man, was J. H. Waite a bricklayer at Kirton Lindsey (a *John Waite* is named on the Roll of Honour).

The November issue of the Journal also reported the following staff changes at Barnetby. (Superintendent's Dept, Eastern District): Brakesman G. H. Wilson and porter W. Vessey, were transferred to Grimsby Docks and goods guard A. Kirmond had been transferred to New Holland. (Wilson and Vessey were also mentioned in the October issue.)

The next reported incident involved the Royal Navy and a battle at sea.

The Battle of Coronel, 1st November 1914.

In October 1913, the Admiralty, with Winston Churchill as First Lord, had made plans for a General Test Mobilisation to take place in July 1914, concluding with a Fleet Review at Spithead. Subsequently the First, Second and Reserve Fleets duly assembled including, in the last category, the old armoured cruisers HMSs *Good Hope* and *Monmouth*. At that point, with the political situation in Europe near boiling point and war looking ominous, the Grand Fleet was ordered to its war station at Scapa Flow. As a safeguard against possible blockade and threat to British commerce in the event of hostilities by the German High Seas Fleet and Graf Spee's cruiser squadron the Reserve Fleet was kept mobilised. The Navy was ready.

When war broke out Germany's East Asia cruiser squadron, commanded by Vice-Admiral Graf von Spee, began creating havoc by sinking British merchant shipping. Consisting of five of Germany's older cruisers, similar in speed to their British counterparts but having a far superior armament, this squadron was soon deprived of Pacific bases. Graf Spee being now dependent upon supply ships and colliers was prompted at the beginning of September to despatch *Emden*, his fastest light cruiser, from his force to pursue commerce raiding independently. (*Emden's* exploits caused chaos and tied up numerous allied warships in the search for her. Eventually hunted down and very severely mauled by HMAS *Sydney* on 4th November 1914, *Emden* was driven onto the reefs around the Cocos Islands where she remained – a battered, twisted hulk.)

By mid October, Graf Spee's cruiser force, comprising the armoured cruisers *Scharnhorst* and *Gneisenau* and the light cruisers *Leipzig* and *Nürnberg*, was joined from the South Atlantic by the light cruiser *Dresden* where she had left her consort, *Karlsruhe*, hunting merchantmen.

Dresden conveyed reassuring news to Admiral Graf Spee that a very much inferior British force was in the South Atlantic. With his squadron deprived of bases and heartened by *Dresden's* news Graf Spee adjudged it was the right time to try to return home. Meanwhile Rear-Admiral Sir Christopher Cradock, mindful of what Graf Spee's force could do if it intercepted the Anzac convoys en route to Suez, had ventured into the Pacific with his cruisers to search for the enemy off the west coast of Chile. This left the South Atlantic clear for the commerce raider *Karlsruhe*, now cooperating with the armed liner, *Kronprinz Wilhelm*, to make free with any shipping found in the waters around the West

HMS GOOD HOPE, 1907. Flagship of Rear-Admiral Sir Christopher Craddock. Lost with all hands, 1st November 1914. Armament: 2 x 9.2-inch guns (1 fwd, 1 aft), 16 x 6-inch guns (8 on either side). Clearly seen in this photograph are the secondary armament 6-inch guns. Housed in sponsons (or casemates) on the main deck these were vulnerable to flooding in heavy seas particularly the lower batteries. The gunners' visibility was also seriously affected. Such were the conditions encountered during the Battle of Coronel. (Photo: IWM. Q 21296)

HMS MONMOUTH, at Valparaiso before the Battle of Coronel. Armament: 14 x 6-inch guns (2 twin mountings [1fwd, 1aft] & 10 single mountings). Lost with all hands on 1st November 1914. (Photo: IWM. Q.80707B)

HMS GLASGOW, at Valparaiso before the Battle of Coronel. Armament: 2 x 6-inch, 10 x 4-inch guns. Most modern of the three British cruisers her guns were more sensibly sited. Glasgow's and Leipzig's sighting of each other had initiated 'The Battle of Coronel'. During the battle Glasgow, engaged by Leipzig *and* Dresden, *took five hits but wisely withdrew when she became the attention of four enemy cruisers.* (Photo: IWM. Q.8070A)

SMS SCHARNHORST. (Seine Majestäts Schiff Gneisenau was a sister ship.)
All the main armament (8 x 8.2-inch guns) was at upper deck level. Four guns were mounted in pairs in turrets (1 fwd, 1 aft) with the other four mounted singly on either side, two just forward of the second funnel and two just aft of the third funnel. (The barrels of the port 8.2-inch guns can just be seen in the dark mass below the forward funnel and the third funnel respectively.) When firing a full broadside each ship used 6 of these 8.2-inch guns, a decisive factor at Coronel. The secondary armament (6 x 5.9-inch guns) was mounted singly, three guns on either side. (The port 5.9-inch guns can be clearly seen one deck below the port 8.2-inch gun mountings.) That all guns were mounted well above the waterline was crucial at Coronel. There the accuracy of the gunnery of Scharnhorst and Gneisenau was outstanding, disabling both Good Hope's and Monmouth's forward turrets respectively with their third salvos at a range of seven miles. (Photo: Arthur Renard)

SMS NÜRNBERG after the Battle of Coronel, 1st November, 1914.
SMS Dresden and SMS Leipzig were sister ships. Dresden was armed with 12 x 4.1-inch guns while Leipzig and Nürnberg had 10 x 4.1-inch guns apiece. All guns were mounted singly and were well above the waterline. (Photo: IWM. Q 80704)

Indies. (On 4th November the *Karlsruhe* mysteriously blew-up and sank. For a month the German authorities were unaware of this; once they knew they kept it quiet until March 1915, thus keeping the Royal Navy tied up looking for a nonexistent ship.)

Rear-Admiral Cradock's force consisted of two old armoured cruisers, HMS *Good Hope* (Flagship) and HMS *Monmouth*; the newer light cruiser HMS *Glasgow* and the elderly armed merchant cruiser HMS *Otranto* (maximum speed 18 knots). Attached to this force was the old battleship HMS *Canopus* – heavy in armament, slow in speed. Admiral Cradock had also been told that HMS *Defence*, an armoured cruiser (4 x 9.2-inch and 10 x 7.5-inch guns), would join him from the Mediterranean but her deployment was changed. The Admiralty hoped that when Graf Spee's force was found it would be shadowed until reinforcements arrived if force strength was not in Cradock's favour. The Admiralty's hopes were not conveyed to Admiral Cradock.

On 30th October the German force, heading south some forty miles off Valparaiso, Chile, despatched *Nürnberg* to Valparaiso to pick up mail. Next day, about 250 miles further south, the British light cruiser *Glasgow*, sent to Coronel in Chile to check for important messages, reported intercepting *Leipzig's* radio transmissions. The enemy collier *Santa Isabel* reported *Glasgow's* presence and

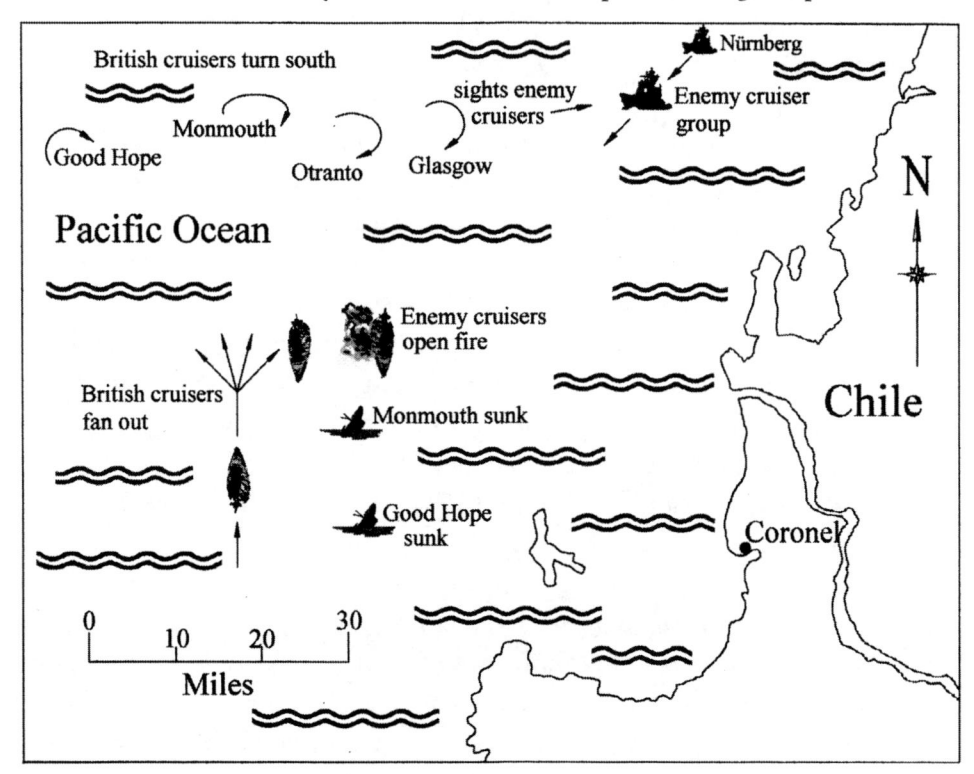

Map 5. *The Battle of Coronel, 1st November 1914.*

Glasgow, ordered to rejoin forthwith, left at 09.00 on 1st November. Until that time neither force had any idea of the actual whereabouts of the other. That morning the British force heard further transmissions from *Leipzig.* With both sides now fully aware of the presence of the other they spread out hopeful of intercepting what each side believed was a single warship.

The British, aware of *Leipzig's* proximity due to transmissions, fanned out left to right: *Good Hope, Monmouth, Otranto* and *Glasgow*. Around 16.30, when approximately 50 miles off Coronel, *Glasgow* sighted a force of enemy cruisers that immediately gave chase. She promptly altered course towards *Monmouth* and *Otranto* and signalled her findings to *Good Hope* on the western edge of the search. Before long all three were heading towards *Good Hope* approaching fast from the west and received orders to alter course and take station on her in preparation for engaging the enemy which, to each side, had now been revealed to be more than just one ship.

By 18.00 the opposing cruiser forces were in battle formation. The lowering sun behind the British lit up the enemy and dazzled his gunners. However the range was far too great for the old British guns, so Admiral Cradock turned his cruisers towards the enemy to decrease the range. Meanwhile the enemy, with enough sea room to manoeuvre in, simply turned away and kept out of range. The British force by now was only too well aware of the superior strength of the adversary and was without *Canopus,* delayed with engine problems 300 miles to the south.

To the east the enemy, having the landmass behind him, had merged into the twilight and seemed to be closing. To the west the red afterglow of the setting sun lit up the British force like a fiery omen. Shortly after 19.00 the enemy opened fire at a range of 12,000 yards with devastating effect. The British cruisers replied, their inferior weapons no match against those of its enemy.

Scharnhorst's 8.2-inch guns quickly registered hits on *Good Hope*, disabling her forward 9.2-inch gun. *Monmouth* was not long in receiving a similar terrible treatment from *Gneisenau. Scharnhorst* inflicted dreadful punishment on *Good Hope* unrelentingly, slowing her down, her foredeck ablaze. In order that the secondary armament could be brought into action, the British again steered towards the enemy to close the range, but Graf Spee simply kept that to the advantage of his 5.9-inch guns. Shortly after 19.40 *Good Hope,* in a seemingly final desperate and futile manoeuvre, again turned towards the enemy and *Scharnhorst,* thinking she was about to fire torpedoes, turned away, leaving a crippled *Good Hope* virtually stopped, afire. Ten minutes later, blazing and drifting helpless in the water, an explosion ripped through her and her flaming hulk drifted away into the night, never to be seen again.

Meanwhile *Monmouth*, having been continuously pounded by *Gneisenau's* 8.2-inch and 5.9-inch guns, eventually swung out of line well afire aft, listing to port and taking in water forward – her days as a fighting unit finished.

Of the remaining three British ships the *Otranto*, being ordered early on to break off the engagement, had left the area; *Glasgow*, being unable to offer any assistance to *Monmouth*, set off south to warn the old battleship *Canopus* that was coming north to join them, leaving *Monmouth*, on fire, listing to port and down by the bows, limping slowly towards the Chilean coast. Around 21.00 *Nürnberg*, steaming down hard from Valparaiso, on coming across the stricken *Monmouth* with her colours still flying, immediately opened fire and sank her. No survivors were ever recovered from either *Monmouth* or *Good Hope*.

Back at home a fortnight later news received disclosed the loss of HMS *Good Hope* in a naval engagement in the Pacific Ocean but, ever fearful of the tragic outcome, there was still no official news to relieve the awful anxiety and terrible suspense felt by their loved ones particularly the wife and parents of…

RFR/PO/B/2165 Able Seaman Herbert Bull, HMS Good Hope, aged 30.

Able Seaman *Herbert Bull*, the son of Thomas and Emily Bull, was born at Retford, Notts., on 9th October 1884. When the family came to Barnetby has not been ascertained but the father, a railway labourer, probably came as a result of a railway transfer. Herbert had been employed as an errand boy prior to enlisting in the Royal Navy. On 9th October 1902, Recruit 215077 Herbert Bull joined HMS *Ganges*, at Harwich, on a 12-year engagement. After serving 5 years in a number of ships (HMS *Minotaur, Duke of Wellington, Bellona, Firequeen, Mars* and *Hermione*), including time in foreign waters, he applied for discharge by purchase. Approved on 17th April 1907, subject to joining the Royal Fleet Reserve (RFR), his subsequent discharge 'to Shore for RFR' became effective on 27th April 1907 and on 28th April 1907 he joined the RFR Portsmouth, Class B Reserve, Number 2165. In 1911, Herbert was working as a skilled labourer (painter) in H M Dockyard Portsmouth, lodging at 14 Northbrook Street, Landport. On 14th October 1913, while living at 33 Hall Street, Landport, he had married Mabel Spence, 27, of 50 Hawke St, Portsea, in the Queen Street Weslyan Church Hall, Portsea.

A/B H. Bull

Prior to 1914 HMS *Good Hope,* being considered too old for any further use, had been taken out of commission. In July 1914 a practice Mobilisation replaced the summer manœuvres: among the ships brought back into service was *Good Hope* – manned mainly by reservists. On 13th July 1914 Herbert joined HMS *Good Hope* for eleven days training, as part of his annual RFR commitment, followed by five days in HMS *Victory* (RN Barracks, Portsmouth). On ending shakedown training manœuvres with hostilities being imminent orders were received to prepare for war. Herbert duly received draft orders on 31st July 1914 to join HMS *Good Hope,* shortly to join the Fourth Cruiser Squadron on the West Indies station taking over from HMS *Suffolk* the duties of Flagship for Rear-Admiral Sir Christopher Cradock.

Herbert was amongst those lost at sea on that fateful 1st November 1914 day. In his service history (ADM188/377) the final entry for *Good Hope* in the column headed, 'If Discharged, Whither, and for what Cause', simply records: 'D.D' (Discharged Dead); a note below that, N.P. 2788/14, reads, 'D. D. 1 Nov 1914. Lost when HMS *Good Hope* sunk in action off Chilean Coast'.

The names of 827 men out of the 891 lost from *Good Hope* at the 'Battle of Coronel' are recorded in the Portsmouth Naval Memorial Register, 'of those Officers and Men of the Navies of the Commonwealth, who fell in the war, who have no other grave than the sea.'

The Portsmouth Naval Memorial, on the seaward edge of Southsea Common overlooking the Solent, commemorates 9,666 names in total. The section of the Memorial commemorating Coronel and other 1914 battles is inscribed with 1,917 names including, on Panel 2, Able Seaman *Herbert Bull*. His name is also on the family headstone in St. Mary's Churchyard, Barnetby.

This was the second tragic blow that had been dealt out to the Bull family that year for in July they had lost their second son James, aged 27 years. Just prior to his untimely death James had been employed on building the new subway under the railway lines here in Barnetby. For whatever reason he changed his job, took up work with Messers Logan and Hemingway at Gunness and started work with his new employer on Wednesday 1st July. That day the weather was exceedingly hot and James had complained of not feeling well but carried on working. As he left work for dinner he collapsed and died two hours later without regaining consciousness.

On Saturday 21st November the marriage took place in St Barnabas Church between Miss Mandy Hanks Denton, daughter of Mr and Mrs F. Denton and Pte William John Ponting, the only son of Mr and Mrs Ponting of Gloucester. The Reverend C. F. Brotherton presided over the ceremony. The wedding had been brought forward at short notice because the groom was anticipating leaving for the Front at any time. Attached to the East Yorkshire Yeomanry he had been granted a brief leave for the occasion. After the ceremony the couple had their

Portsmouth Naval Memorial to the Missing at the seaward edge of Southsea Common. Herbert Bull is named on the second memorial panel from the left beneath the left lion.

wedding breakfast at the bride's parent's house in Victoria Road before departing on their honeymoon in London. Now the Denton family had three soldier sons and one soldier son-in-law.

The following afternoon the vicar had officiated at a special children's service held in the Church in aid of the Belgian relief fund with the proceeds of the collection, £1 12s 6d, being donated to that cause. The service had ended with the children displaying Union flags during the singing of the National Anthem.

On Tuesday 24th November the Women's Adult School had met in the Co-Op rooms for a musical social evening listening to a selection of records on a gramophone kindly lent for the occasion by Mr Wilson. The event, in aid of the Belgian relief fund, had raised 15s.

The next night a whist drive had taken place in the schoolroom inaugurated by Misses Lowish and Ffrench in aid of obtaining comforts for soldiers and sailors. Refreshments had been served in the interval and the event had made a total of £2 10s 9d.

At the end of November the *Grimsby News* had given out news of further local aid to the war effort with the residents at the Wold having contributed blankets, mufflers, socks, belts and other useful items. These had duly been received by the working committee and sent on as comforts for soldiers serving at the Front.

Only one Barnetby railwayman had joined the colours during the month and that was platelayer Fred Lansley. He had joined the 111th Company, Royal Engineers Railway Troops. Labourer G. R. Bullyment, who enlisted at the beginning of the war, had been returned to duty in the Engineer's Department at Barnetby. No reason was given.

Also during November various railway staff promotions and transfers had taken place at Barnetby. In the Engineer's Dept, Leicester District, platelayer T. Coupland had been promoted to sub-ganger following the retirement of sub-ganger G. Holt. F. Goodrich, a stores deliverer in the Stores Superintendent's Dept, had been transferred to Grimsby Docks as an officeman and New Holland officeman F. Westoby had been transferred to Barnetby to take up stores deliverer's duties. In the Superintendent's Dept, Eastern District, W. H. Mumby, a junior clerk, had been transferred to Ulceby and shunter W. Gostelow had left the service.

The month's final news item reported Pte Caward killed in action (as mentioned earlier).

What now follows, although it has no connection with Barnetby, has been included purely out of interest as the sequel to the Battle of Coronel.

The Battle of the Falkland Islands.

While the Battle of Coronel was the first major defeat the Royal Navy had suffered in more than a hundred years, and by an essentially non-seafaring nation at that, it was in truth a humiliating blow for the greatest sea power of the time. The Royal Navy, hoping to redress the situation, dispatched the battle cruisers *Invincible* and *Inflexible*, under Vice-Admiral Sir Frederick Doveton Sturdee, down to the South Atlantic. There they were reinforced by three armoured cruisers: *Carnarvon*, *Cornwall* and *Kent*; two light cruisers: *Glasgow* and *Bristol*, and the armed merchant cruiser *Macedonia*. Throughout the 7th/8th December 1914 this fleet was busy coaling at Port Stanley and Port William in East Falkland – the inner harbour entrance protected by *Canopus*, deliberately grounded. *Kent* and *Macedonia*, detailed as guard ships, covered the entrance beyond the outer harbour.

For some unknown reason on 8th December, having ventured with his fleet into the South Atlantic (presumably now on his way home), Vice-Admiral Graf von Spee chose to attack the Falkland Islands.

Shortly before 08.00 this fleet, along with its three attendant colliers, was approaching East Falkland from the south-west. By 09.00 *Gneisenau*, detailed with *Nürnberg* to carry out this attack, was drawing near to Port Stanley when her lookouts caught sight of the masts of a number of large warships in the outer harbour and reported them to Admiral Graf Spee, in Scharnhorst, as being those of large cruisers. A gunnery observer on East Falkland with a telephone link to Canopus had sighted the enemy ships and through Canopus had raised the alarm. Presently Gneisenau's lookouts saw tripod masts indicating the presence of two larger warships – mistakenly opined as Canopus type. Undeterred Gneisenau pressed on only to find Kent beyond the outer harbour and sought to cut her off but received such a shock when Canopus opened fire on her that she altered course away.

Graf Spee, keen to avoid engaging Canopus-type battleships, immediately ordered his ships out of the area to the south-east. With the enemy's proximity now obvious, Vice-Admiral Sturdee ordered his ships to be ready for sea without delay. By 10.00 *Glasgow* was steaming out of Port William and before long all the remaining ships, except *Bristol* and *Macedonia*, were strung out astern of her. The chase was now on and the British ships were slowly, but surely, closing on the enemy. For once the weather was ideal and the notoriously stormy South Atlantic remarkably calm. On *Gneisenau* the identification errors became very quickly apparent as two 28-knot battle cruisers (8 x 12-inch guns apiece) bore down on them.

Shortly before 13.00 *Inflexible* opened fire on the *Leipzig* – the shells pitching short. But further ranging shots showed the range to be still slowly closing. About 13.20 Admiral Graf Spee ordered his light cruisers to make a dash for freedom while he made ready for action against the British battle cruisers. Soon after this all the British armoured cruisers (except *Carnarvon*) and *Glasgow* set off in pursuit of the breakaway enemy light cruisers. This was soon to be followed by a typical big ship broadside battle.

The outcome was inevitable, for the German armoured cruisers' 8.2-inch guns were no match against the 12-inch guns of the larger, faster British battle cruisers. Similarly the 4.1-inch guns of the German light cruisers could not match the British cruisers' 6-inch guns. It was like the Battle of Coronel in reverse, but not before the enemy had given a good account of himself. That the battle lasted so long was largely due to the initial inaccurate shooting by the British ships caused by the smoke from their own funnels obscuring their gunners' view.

The finale began at 16.17 with the sinking of *Sharnhorst* by *Invincible*. *Gneisenau*'s fate was sealed at 18.00 by the combined firepower of *Inflexible*, *Invincible* and *Carnarvon*. Of the enemy's light cruisers – *Nürnberg* was sunk by *Kent* at 19.27 and *Leipzig*, mortally crippled by the guns of *Cornwall* and *Glasgow*, sank at 21.23. *Dresden* successfully eluded the chasing cruisers, having slipped away about 17.00, and made good her escape back into the Pacific. Of the three colliers – at 19.53 the *Baden* was caught and sunk by *Bristol*, assisted by *Macedonia*; at 21.30 the *Santa Isabel* was also sunk by *Bristol* (their crews having been taken off first) while *Seydlitz*, the third, escaped. Thus ended the Battle of the Falkland Islands. Coronel had been avenged.

The *Dresden*, continually seeking refuge among the inlets along the Chilean coastline, was hunted down relentlessly. On 14th March 1915, after a number of narrow escapes, *Kent* and *Glasgow* finally found her in Cumberland Bay at Más a Tierra, in the Juan Fernández Island group, where her Captain scuttled her after putting his crew ashore.

With the removal of the last of Graf Spee's raiders from the scene merchant shipping felt that it was once again relatively safe to sail the high seas. (It is interesting to note that two Royal Navy ships of the Task Force sent to the Falkland Islands in 1982 bore the same names as those involved in the 1914 Battle of The Falkland Islands, namely H.M.S. Invincible (through-deck aircraft carrier) and H.M.S. Glasgow (Type 42 destroyer).

There was nothing further in the way of news relating to Barnetby Boys at the Front for the remainder of the year apart from the 15th December newspapers reporting the first detailed account of the Battle of Coronel, as witnessed first-hand by an officer serving in HMS *Glasgow*.

At home there had been one final fund raising effort in aid of Belgian relief in the run up to the festive season when the Primitive Methodist and Weslyan chapels' members' joined forces to sing Christmas carols around the village on two evenings and collected £1 15s in the process. This sum was duly handed over to Lady Doughty for the Belgian relief fund.

A few more railwaymen had enlisted during the month. From the Chief Engineer's Dept at Barnetby went relayers F. Langley and R. W. Parker and labourer P. Cox. (From Immingham depot platelayer W. Briggs had joined 112th Company, Royal Engineers Railway Troops. Was this William Briggs, RE, of Barnetby, referred to later, I wonder?)

On the railway final staff changes for the year had taken place. In the Engineer's Dept, Signal Dept, connector H. H. Goodhand had been transferred from Sheffield to Barnetby and Barnetby signal linesman J. White had retired from the Company. In the Superintendent's Department, Eastern District, signal cleaner J. W. Turner had been transferred as a signalman over to Edwinstow. At the Immingham depot shunter A. Denton had left the service. Could this be Arthur Denton?

Christmas had arrived and passed, all hopes that the war would be over by Christmas having long since faded, and the war continued on unabated into the New Year.

3
1915

BY the end of 1914 the British Expeditionary Force (BEF) – 160,000 strong in 1914, having suffered a savage mauling, had very few of the original regular army men left. These men had been experts in the use of the .303-inch Enfield rifle, probably too expert for their own good, for it had proved to be very much a one sided contest when matching skilled rifle firepower against that of the numerous machine-guns that the enemy used.

The war on the Western Front, having started off in 1914 as a war of movement, had now settled down to a static state of trench warfare. But not before 'The Contemptible Little Army' had severely upset the enemy's plans of a speedy end to the war with some outstanding rearguard actions during the retreat from Mons, in southern Belgium, to south of the river Marne close to Paris. There, during the first week in September, the enemy was held.

The following week it was the Allies turn to go on the offensive, pushing the enemy back as far as the river Aisne, where he became firmly entrenched. The French saw that the answer to this problem lay in trying to outflank the enemy on his western flank. The enemy then decided that a change of battlefield was called for with the Flanders plain in mind. The British read this as a move to deny them use of the Channel ports resulting in what is now called 'The race to the sea' with both sides making moves to the north. Things finally ground to a halt during the third week in November, but not before the British had put up a stubborn resistance to defend Ypres at all costs. At the beginning of 1915 it was stalemate with both sides firmly entrenched for the winter planning moves to break the deadlock.

On 8th January my grandparents, T. and M. Frankish wrote a letter to my grandfather's cousin George Mumby in Canandaigua, Ontario County, New York State, USA, stating:

'...the 2 girls are very well and so is the boy. He is a soldier at present helping his country in this awful war, but we hope and trust that he will come home again alright. ...you would not (k)now Barnetby now it (h)as altered so much. So many new houses built and a new station and the old crossing done away with and a bridge over the road.'

(The 2 girls were Ethel and Amy Frankish; the boy – Charles Frankish, my father.)

The Journal for February had references to three Barnetby railwaymen. Assistant timber loader W. E. Lee, from the Railway Transport Department at Barnetby had enlisted. The first Barnetby man named in the railway casualty lists was 5650 Pte A. Tilbrooke, 1st Battalion Suffolk Regiment, invalided home to Barnetby suffering from rheumatism and frostbites. He had been a relayer at Barnetby before enlisting. Finally, brakesman H. Rhodes, in the Superintendent's Dept at Immingham, had left the railway service. He had been a shunter at Barnetby and transferred to Immingham around October 1911 (the 1911 census refers to a Harry Rhodes, age 23, GCR shunter, born at Stallingborough, living with wife Lilly in Barnetby).

By June 1912 he had been promoted from shunter to brakesman and in November 1913 had been promoted at Immingham from brakesman to goods guard. Had he left the railway in order to enlist? There is certainly no mention of him in the Journal supplementary lists of those joining the colours. However I did find two newspaper references to a Pte H. Rhodes but is it the same man? The inclusion of his name among the fatalities on the Roll of Honour is something of a puzzle.

The March Journal lists a G. W. Insley (no grade given) as having enlisted. He had been employed at Grimsby Docks. That name also crops up later on.

During March three special Lenten services had been held in the Church, conducted by The Rev. J. S. Swan (Rector of Somerby), the Rev. Canon Quirk (Vicar of Great Coates) and the Rev. J. E. Walker (Vicar of Ulceby), when special Intercessional prayers had been said on behalf of soldiers and sailors.

The April Journal lists railwayman labourer G. R. Bullyment as having been transferred to Sheffield from the Engineer's Signal Department at Barnetby (in November of the previous year he had been returned from the Army to his railway duties at Barnetby).

Some form of Roll of Honour had by now been created and put on display in the village. First mention of this Roll was in a brief report in the *Grimsby News* of 9th April. This merely stated that another from Barnetby's Roll of Honour had fallen a victim and gave the information that J. W. Smith had been seriously wounded and was at that time lying in Dublin Castle.

The following evening a concert in aid of Belgian soldiers, organized by the Barnetby Adult School, had taken place in the schoolrooms. This involved the 'Chums' battalion from Brocklesby Park who had been responsible for rendering a splendid concert programme under the arrangement of Pte Barnett. About 50 other 'Chums' had also been in attendance and had equally enjoyed the dancing until midnight after the concert. Mrs Lowish had kindly provided refreshments at what had been a thoroughly enjoyable evening's entertainment that had raised £10 for the fund after £1 7s had been deducted for expenses.

A Catechism Festival had been held in the Church on Sunday 25th April during which the Sunday School children had been presented with their prizes. One enterprising youngster had unselfishly forfeited his prize so that its value could be donated to the Belgian relief fund.

Regarding railway men who enlisted during April I found no names that were positively identifiable as Barnetby men but the name W. Stainton caught my attention. This man had been employed as an extra porter in the Railway Transport Establishment Portmaster's Department on Grimsby Docks. Could this have been Barnetby man William Stainton?

There had however been a few railway staff changes at Barnetby. In the Superintendent's Department porter W. Vessey had been transferred from Grimsby Docks depot to Barnetby as a shunter. Another man appointed as shunter at Barnetby was leading shunter J. Wilford, also from Grimsby Docks, while C. Green, a Barnetby shunter, had been transferred in the same role to Grimsby Docks. (Was this Charles Meysey Green, who I now believe to have been a GCR employee? The only reference to C. M. Green was in the June 1909 issue of the Journal when a man of that name was transferred as a clerk from Wombwell to Cleethorpes Pier.) In the Engineer's Dept, labourer W. Grant had left the service.

The *Grimsby News* of 21st May published a brief report about a project that had been undertaken during the previous three months by Miss Lowish, ably assisted by Miss Ffrench and Mr A. Havercroft, for the benefit of wounded servicemen. During that period they had collected, on average, 93 eggs per week from around the parish that had amounted to 1,116 eggs being sent to the local Red Cross hospital. They also received money donations amounting to 12s. Through the newspaper those three collectors had asked that their gratefulness be made known to all the generous respondents to their work.

More charitable work had been undertaken the following week by members of the Girl's Friendly Society. On Wednesday 26th May they had held a Café Chantant in the school where one room had been set aside for an exhibition of handicrafts. This well attended function had raised the sum of £8 1s 1d. From that total the Church building fund received £5 while Queen Mary's fund had benefited from the remaining £3 1s 1d.

On Monday 24th May an event took place in the village involving soldiers from the recently formed 'Grimsby Chums' that were at the time undergoing training in Brocklesby Park. This event, held in a field owned by Mr H. Robinson, was the second annual fete and sports meeting organized in support of the Great Central Railwaymen's Medical Aid Fund. The band and drums of the 'Chums', the 10th (Service) Battalion, Lincolnshire Regiment (by kind permission of their Colonel, the Hon. G. E. Heneage), started off the proceedings by marching through the village. This had the desired result of gathering a large crowd to the field drawn by their stirring martial music. The band, under the baton of Sgt N. S. Killoran, had then played a splendid selection of music throughout the afternoon.

Apart from the usual side shows there had been a full programme of sports events under the direction of Mr H. Kitchen. Khaki was evident at this field fete with the 'Grimsby Chums' from Brocklesby Park well represented in the sports events. The sports and competition results were as follows (three names without rank in the men's events may have been civilians):

100yds H/cap: 1, Pte C. Frankish; 2, J. Andrews. 400yds H/cap: 1, Pte C. Frankish; 2, J. Andrews. Obstacle race: 1, Cpl A. Shepherdson; 2, Pte J. Davey. Band race: Cpl A. Weaver. 150yds for soldiers: 1, Cpl A. Weaver; 2, Pte Bateman. High jump: 1, H. Clayton; 2, Pte C. Frankish. Tug of War: H. Feirn's team beat a team of 'Chums'.
Ladies events: Ladies' egg and spoon race: 1, Miss D. Partridge; 2, Mrs Girdham. Ladies' musical chairs: 1, Miss Lockwood; 2, Miss C. Smith.
Boys' races: (5 to 7 years): 1, Harry Smith; 2, L. Parrott. (7 to 8 years): 1, C. Peart; 2, William Cook. (10 to 12 years): 1, William Peart; 2, Reginald Hall. (13 to 15 years): 1, Kenneth White; 2, George Baker.
Girls' races: (5 to 7 years): 1, E. Brader; 2, Emma Peart. (8 to 9 years): 1, Jessie Battersby; 2, Mabel Slowen. (10 to 12 years): 1, A. Cook; 2, Ethel Smith. (12 to 15 years): 1, Gertie Cook; 2, Nellie Wardle.
Novelty and other events: Potato race: 1, Pte J. Davey; 2, J. Andrews. Sack race: 1, J. Braithwaite; 2, Pte J. Davey. Chain measuring: 1, W. Cuthbert; 2, J. Bates. Pig competition: A. Batton. Wheelbarrow competition: G. Johnson. Gents musical chairs: 1, H. Nelson; 2, Harry Allison. Hidden treasure: R. Hall. Baby show: 1, Mrs Ashton's child; 2, Mrs Rowson's child.

Later that evening, to round off the celebrations, there had been dancing to the music of the 'Grimsby Chums' band.

The Journal for June recorded that three more railwaymen from Barnetby had enlisted. From the Chief Mechanical Engineer's (Loco) Dept there had been firemen E. Hutchinson and W. Overton and from the Chief Engineer's Dept labourer W. Holt.

Only one staff change was listed in the Journal for July. Porter shunter H. Farrow had transferred from Healing to the Superintendent's Dept at Barnetby to take up shunter duties. The following month W. Harness left the railway service after having worked at Barnetby as a platelayer in the Engineer's Dept.

Three more railwaymen working at Barnetby had enlisted during July. In the Resident Engineer's Office there had been draughtsman J. Mawson and in the Engineer's Dept there had been navvies C. Bellamy and H. Frow. The Engineer's Signal Dept had also lost a man with the death of oiler F. Turner.

Around this time outside employees of the GCR, on account that they could not be spared from the railway for military service, were issued with badges (shown right). The object of this was to prevent such workers being accosted by well-meaning, but ignorant persons, who were in the habit of handing out white feathers to anyone they thought to be shirking military duty.

With the war having taken workmen away from the railways there had been a shortage of manpower in certain departments. A news report of 23rd July 1915, records that a lady porter (unnamed) had taken up employment at Barnetby station. A month later the *Grimsby News* of 24th September informed its readers that two lady porters were now currently being employed there. (A few months' earlier names of newly appointed female staff began to appear in the Journal but none are mentioned appertaining to Barnetby.) And the railway was not the only employer to suffer from the manpower shortage. The same newspaper told of the first local postwoman (also unnamed) beginning work in the village.

Eggs for wounded soldiers was again a topic in the 27th August *Grimsby News*. This time it was the turn of the Barnetby schoolchildren to be in the news having, since 18th May, provided 749 eggs for the wounded soldiers. That same cause had also benefited from an additional 2,000 eggs that had been collected in the village. The British Farmers Red Cross Society had also received a welcome contribution of £41 from the farmers of the parish.

Eggs were again in the news with the Primitive Methodist Society having held an Egg and Flower Service, on Sunday 22nd August, when many gifts of both those items had been received and during the service children had read out the messages attached to the eggs and flowers. Those eggs and flowers, along with part of the collection, were sent to the hospitals at Lincoln, Leicester and Nottingham where some of the local wounded soldiers were having treatment.

During August two Barnetby railwaymen had received awards from the Sir Edward Watkin Meritorious Conduct Fund, that had been created by the late Sir Edward Watkin, Bart, MP and administered by the Trustees, Sir Sam Fay, general manager, and Mr Oliver S. Holt, the secretary of the Company. They were among a group of men who had been rewarded in recognition of conspicuous acts of merit performed by the Company's staff during 1914. The recipients were carpenter G. M. Meggitt and acting permanent way inspector R. Vessey, both from the Engineer's Department in Barnetby. In addition R. Vessey had also been awarded a Certificate of Merit for courageous conduct, the citation for which read as follows:

> ACTING PERMANENT WAY INSPECTOR R. VESSEY, BARNETBY. At the imminent risk to his life, Vessey, on the 15th July, was the means of preventing an aged man from being knocked down and run over at Grimsby Town. The 10.25 a.m. Down Main Line Passenger train Cleethorpes to Manchester was standing in the station, when the man attempted to cross in front of the engine, which fouled the foot crossing, obviously unaware of the approach of a passenger train on the Up road. With commendable presence of mind, Vessey rushed to the man and pulled him almost from under the wheels, holding him in the 'six-foot' until the passenger train had got clear.

To round off the railway news for August there were staff promotions and transfers within the Superintendent's Dept at Barnetby. Brakesmen W. Cawkwell and H. Dawson were promoted to goods guards. (H. (Henry) Dawson, became a brakesman around January 1911, having previously been a shunter at Barnetby. Commonly known as Harry, he was the brother of Hugh and Jesse.) Shunters G. H. Frow and C. B. Hunsley both became brakesmen. T. Britt, a signal cleaner and lighter, became a shunter; G. E. Robinson, who had been employed as a ground pointsman, also took up duties as a shunter.

Back to the war, reports had begun to come in of soldiers who had been casualties at the Front. I found it very time consuming scanning the casualty lists for recognisable names. It was more productive to look in local news, which often gave more information even though it usually appeared later, as in the case of the 17th September *Grimsby News*, which carried a brief local item stating that two Barnetby men had been wounded. One man being treated for his wounds in a Leicester hospital was 240355 Pte Walter Scott, 1/5th Lincolns, a former New Holland goods porter, who had been in France since February.

The other man, former Immingham goods guard 12736 Pte H. Wright, 7th Lincolns, whose parents had been notified of his wounding, was in a hospital at Faversham recovering from his wounds. The *Hull Times* of 18th September was slightly more explicit when it added that Pte Wright had been wounded in the head by shrapnel.

At the time both the 1/5th and 7th Lincolns were in the Ypres sector, carrying out trench duties as 'old hands', the 1/5th having received instruction in trench warfare duties during March. Similarly, towards the end of July, the 7th Battalion had its trench initiation training partially under the wing of its Territorial cousins in the 138th Brigade, 46th Division.

Neither battalion had had it easy in those first few months at the Front. The trenches initially taken over by the 1/5th Lincolns in particular had been in a terrible condition. In the first six months the 1/5th Lincolns had lost 43 other ranks killed, 7 officers and 217 men were wounded and 4 missing. The 7th Lincolns, having only been there for just over three months, had lost 1 officer died of wounds, 2 officers wounded, 21 other ranks killed and 108 wounded.

During September the railway staff promotions and transfers at Barnetby were as follows. The Engineer's Dept promoted relayer G. Dale to relaying ganger. In the Superintendent's Dept, there was a general change round; brakesman W. E. White became a goods guard and shunter J. Wilford became a brakesman; shunter W. Sickler was promoted to goods guard while porter E. Quickfall and ground pointsman S. Chadwick took over the duties of shunters.

Two weeks later the papers were announcing news of a major battle being fought on the Western Front in France.

The Battle of Loos, 25th September – 8th October 1915, (that part of the action appertaining to the 8th Lincolns)

In September 1914 the 8th Battalion Lincolnshire Regiment (formed at Lincoln) along with 8th Somerset Light Infantry, 12th West Yorkshire, and 10th York and Lancaster battalions constituted the 63rd Brigade, 21st Division (the 21st Division's three brigades were the 62nd, 63rd and 64th). This newly formed division of Kitchener men landed in France between 7th and 11th September 1915 to concentrate near Watten, the 8th Lincolns going to Bayenghem; they were straight out of training in England and inexperienced in warfare.

The general Allied situation, especially in Russia, and France insisting on an attack to assist their operational plans forced the British to adopt Loos. The battle opened later than proposed on 25th September using First Army, under Gen. Sir D. Haig, with insufficient forces on open, flat, adverse ground between the la Bassée Canal in the north and Lens in the south that offered little cover for the assaulting troops. (First Army was made up of: I Corps – 2nd, 7th, 9th and 28th Infantry Divisions; IV Corps – 1st, 15th and 47th Infantry Divisions and 3rd Cavalry Division; with XI Corps (general reserve) under control of Sir John French, Commander-in-Chief (C-in-C), comprising the Cavalry Corps (1st, 2nd and 3rd Cavalry Divisions – the 3rd allotted to 1st Army), the newly formed Guards Division and the two novice Kitchener Divisions – the 21st and 24th. The general reserve, at first kept too far back, was eventually moved nearer at Haig's requests but, unbeknown to him, not for his immediate use should the opportunity arise.)

On the night of 20th/21st September the 21st Division began to march, in stages, to the front, the 8th Lincolns proceeding via Racquingham, Norrent-Fontes (both stops in bivouacs) and Cauchy-à-la-Tour – this stop being spent in billets. In the early hours of 25th September the 8th Lincolns ended up cold and wet to bivouac about 1½ mile west of Nœux-les-Mines. The noise from the British guns in action near Loos, new to these men, interrupted their sleep – the battle had begun. Here the 8th Lincolns and 8th Somersets were warned to prepare for moving up to the firing line. For that move forward the 8th Lincolns would have the 8th Somersets on their right and the 24th Division on their left.

Starting at 5 a.m. IV Corps, operating south of the Vermelles–Hulluch road with all its Divisions in the line and no reserves, had overrun the enemy trenches west of Loos at very heavy cost and pushed on east of the Lens–la Bassée road to reach Bois Hugo; reserves were urgently needed to sustain the momentum: only the general reserve under C-in-C's control were available. The urgent need for those reserves resulted in the controversial late decision to release the raw, untried troops of the newly arrived 21st and 24th Divisions to the front under First Army control.

Mid morning of the 25th, and still raining, the 8th Lincolns set off towards Vermelles on roads that were so crammed with a diversity of traffic – supply wagons, ambulances, prisoners and wounded – as to limit all movement to a snail's pace. Resting east of Nœux-les-Mines the Battalion came under shell-fire from enemy long-range artillery targeting a nearby heavy battery. Later that afternoon Vermelles was reached; from there, the 8th Lincolns, increasingly becoming aware they were nearing the forward battle zone, headed for Loos.

By late afternoon the 8th Lincolns (and the 63rd Brigade) had reached Fosse No. 7 (a coal pit) where they halted, the men being soaked through, hungry and utterly tired out from carrying full equipment including extra rations and rain-sodden great coats. At this time some of the 15th Division were relieved here. Three hours later at 8 p.m., on orders to advance, the men headed off for the Loos – Hulluch road, then beyond to the Lens – la Bassée road, with their ultimate goal being Annay, about 6 km. east of Loos.

The 8th Lincolns and 8th Somersets, their start delayed by the crowded road, set off across country while the 12th West Yorks and 10th York and Lancaster detoured by road. On the 21st Division's left the 8th Lincolns, stumbling on in the darkness, shortly crossed the old British front line then the shattered enemy front-line trenches and shell-torn ground beyond. It must have been a very rude introduction to men as yet unacquainted with warfare as they tripped and stumbled over numerous dead and dying. About 11 p.m., after crossing the last old enemy trench line, the 8th Lincolns' men lay down and waited for the remaining troops to catch up with them.

On the 8th Lincolns right, meanwhile, two support companies of the 8th Somersets lost direction and ended up amongst the 46th Brigade on Hill 70. At about midnight of the 25th the 63rd Brigade, having resumed the advance, came under machine-gun fire thought to be from Chalk Pit Wood. After A Company of the 8th Lincolns had cleared the wood, sustaining heavy losses in doing so, D Coy, in support, subsequently formed up some fifty yards north of Chalk Pit Wood and then pressed on over the Lens – la Bassée road where some partly dug trenches were found. They set about getting organised there and began improving those trenches.

By 26th September three Lincolns companies were dug in on the south side of the west end of Bois Hugo with a fourth in reserve on the north side. About 300 yards from the road on the wood's north side the 12th West Yorks formed a north-south line with one company in reserve in rear. A little further north the 10th York and Lancaster had a north-south line about 100 yards in from the road but with no unit in touch on the left. The two Somersets companies were in the area of Chalk Pit Wood and the 63rd Brigade HQ was in a house near the Chalk Pit at the wood's eastern end. The enemy line extended northeast from Hill 70 past Bois Hugo's eastern edge.

Soon after 8 a.m. the Lincolns, on Bois Hugo's southern side, opened effective fire on the enemy seen on Hill 70. The enemy thereupon retaliated with shrapnel shell causing fifty or so casualties. Then the Brigade received orders to attack the enemy to the east of its position. The Lincolns made headway for about 700 yards but due to lack of support were duly pushed back nearly half that distance. The enemy meanwhile subjected the area to shell-fire while his troops worked their way through Bois Hugo from the east, eventually breaking out to attack the Lincolns to the south and the West Yorks to the north. Both the Lincolns and the West Yorks were forced to retire through the wood to their support trenches but due to the congestion many took shelter in trenches on the western side of the Lens – la Bassée road. In a subsequent counter-attack the Lincolns re-took part of Bois Hugo only to be driven out again by the enemy who now held all the wood and the Lincolns and West Yorks front line trenches. Those men occupying the support trenches held out a little longer until the enemy worked a machine- gun through the wood and brought it to bear in enfilade upon them. This, in combination with an assault, shortly forced the men holding the support trenches to retire.

By the 27th September the 63rd Brigade had withdrawn in small groups to the old enemy front-line trenches. In the early hours of 27th September the 8th Lincolns, having been relieved by a Guards battalion, moved back to Noyelles-les- Vermelles from where, on 28th September, they moved north to Linghem. The Battalion later moved by stages to the Borre – Strazeele area before going to a quieter sector of the front line near Armentières.

The two New Army Divisions that made up the general reserve, the 21st (including the 8th Lincolns) and 24th, had certainly had a rough baptism of fire. Most novice Divisions spent a short time in a relatively quiet sector learning the ropes and acclimatizing to warfare. These two New Army Divisions were quite literally thrown in at the deep end having been inadequately briefed with no real idea about their task and had had no time to familiarize themselves with the terrain. The initial positioning of the reserves, the late move nearer to the front and late release to the front to come under First Army control and who was to blame, caused a further deepening of the rift between Sir John French, the C-in-C, and Sir Douglas Haig, Commander First Army.

The 8th Lincolns war diary records very little for the 25th September and nothing for the 26th/ 27th, apart from a brief report, annotated Appendix 1, written by Acting Company Sergeant Major C. Lower, 3 Coy and Acting Company Sergeant Major F. W. Brown, 4 Coy, on account of all the officers having become casualties. That report (from WO 95/2158) follows:

> Vermelles. 25th, 6 p.m.:
>
> On the night of 25th September our battalion left the road leading to Loos and formed lines of platoons of fours. After a short advance we halted for three hours. We then advanced in echelon formation over the trenches. After advancing for about three hours, in short stages, we halted for a short time and then moved in the direction of Hill 70. We dug ourselves in during the night. It was now daybreak. Major Storer came to us and said 'All is well'. The advance will commence at 11 a.m. In the meantime we were under heavy shell and rifle fire.

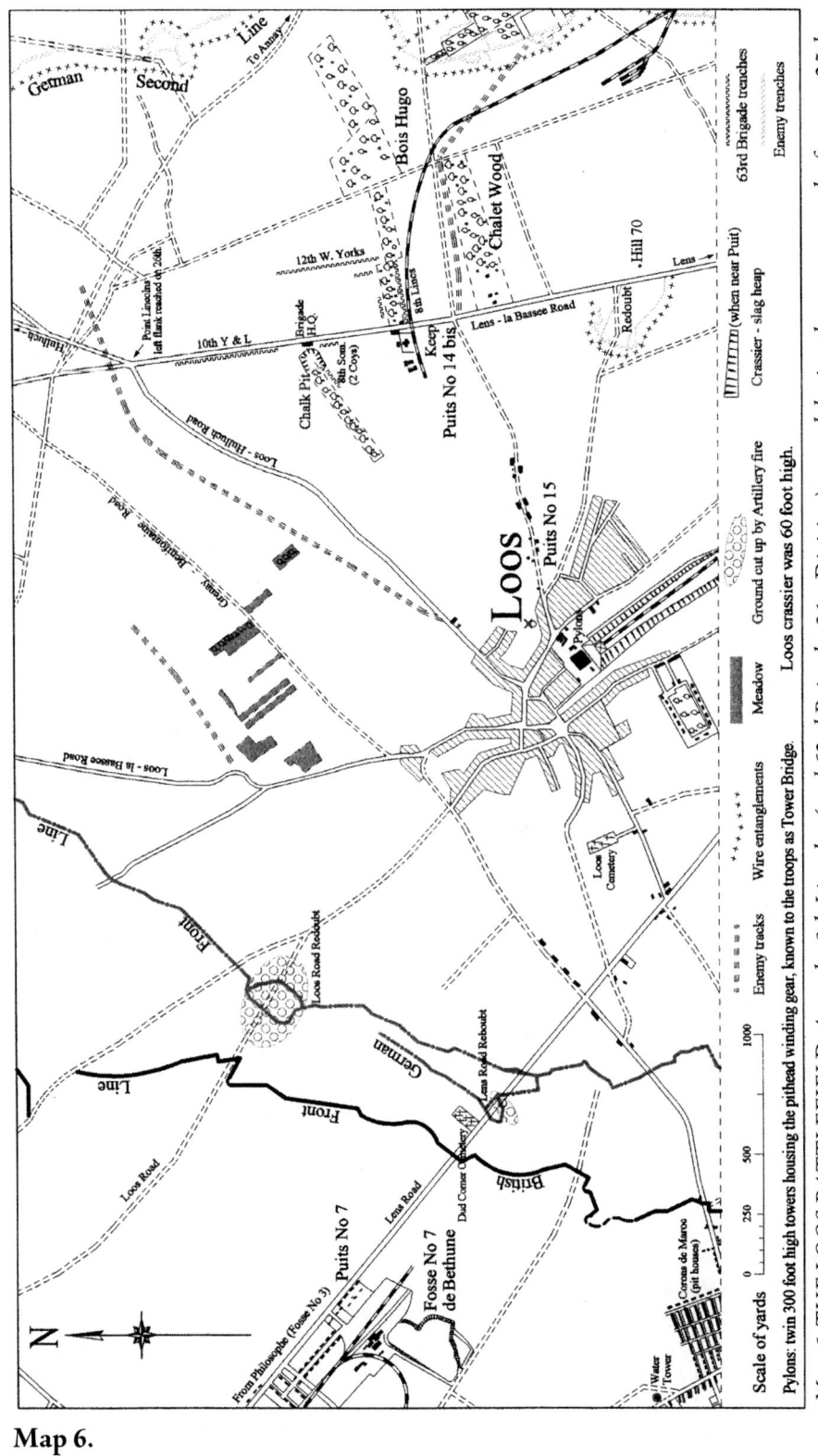

1915

Map 6. THE LOOS BATTLEFIELD. Area the 8th Lincolns (and 63rd Brigade, 21st Division) crossed during the move up to the front on 25th September 1915. N.B. Dud Corner Cemetery (incorporating Loos Memorial to the Missing) was built after the war on a site where four Officers and one Private were buried during hostilities. The remainder, almost 2,000, was concentrated into it from smaller cemeteries and isolated positions. Over half of these burials are unidentified soldiers.

Map 6.

A panoramic view of the area where the 8th Lincolns first went into action. The chalk pit is still in use but Chalk Pit Wood no longer exists. Puits No 14 bis is disused but the building housing the winding gear still remains. It is called now Ancienne Fosse No 14 bis. The western end of Bois Hugo is now part of Lens airfield. The building in front of Chalet Wood is a Crematorium. Hill 70 and Hill 70 Redoubt are just off the right-hand edge of the photograph.

Another panoramic view of the wide-open area the 8th Lincolns crossed during the attack on positions in Bois Hugo.

We then advanced meeting great numbers of the enemy. A short retirement took place the battalion making a new line, of men composed of various units, about 400 yards in rear of our first position. We advanced again under the command of the nearest officer. By this time a great number of our officers had become casualties. The men continued to fight with the units to which they had become attached. On the 27th we were relieved by a unit of Guards.

(The subsequent reorganisation and advance by mixed units after the retirement had taken place might explain an event in connection with L/Sgt T. Hall – see later).

In its very first action the raw, untried 8th Battalion, Lincolnshire Regiment, was left with a terribly high casualty list. Twelve officers, including the Commanding Officer, had been killed or had died of wounds, four were wounded and six missing. Among the other ranks one hundred and forty-eight had been killed, or had died of wounds, and three hundred and twenty-three men were either wounded or missing.

Where Chalk Pit Wood was there is now a quarry. Some of Bois Hugo still remains as the Parc des Cytises; a runway running approximately NNE starts in its southwestern corner, with a few buildings of the Aérodrome de Lens-Bénifontaine to the east, while the E – W runway passes through the northeastern corner of the wood. The area south of Bois Hugo and east of Chalet Wood is now given over to Hypermarkets (*Centre Commercial Lens 2*). On the northern slope of what was Hill 70 is a *Centre Infantile*. (One might be forgiven for thinking of

Hill 70 as a vast hill towering high above the rest of the terrain, but in reality it was merely the highest point in the area around Loos, apart from coal pit spoil heaps, in what is gently undulating countryside; with being a higher point meant it did have commanding views over the rest of the terrain and it was the enemy who held it.)

The 9th October *Hull Times* had a brief article with photographs, about three of the Denton boys namely Ernest, Walter and Arthur, with mention of Ernest's gassing and a note to say that Pte Arthur Denton, 7th Manchesters, had last been heard of in hospital in Malta.

W. Denton.

Pte W. Denton.

Pte Ernest Denton, 8th Lincolns, reported as having been gassed, was in Broadstairs hospital. Seven 'pals' who joined up with him were all right but seven others were missing and thus far their relatives had received no official notice. It went onto say there was a great deal of anxiety and uncertainty felt in the village regarding the fate of a number of young soldiers in the 8th Lincolns. It appeared they had been in severe fighting around la Bassée, resulting in a glorious victory for the English, but that the cost was not yet realised.

Pte A. Denton.

Fourteen young men from the village had taken part in the fight and to date there is information only as to half that number. The seven missing Barnetby Boys' names were given as: – Sgt A. Tweed, Sgt T. Hall, Cpl F. Robinson and Ptes Andrews, Grant, Pretty, and Scott.

Pte Ernest Denton, writing home from Broadstairs hospital said,

We were in the fight for Hill 70. On Saturday and Sunday we marched straight into action in pouring rain, the Germans shelling us all the time...

The Germans attacked in the night, but we repulsed them and attacked again in the morning. This time we were in for it.... We were fighting the Prussian Guards, and they haven't the pluck of a cat. They will shoot you down till you get a few yards away from them, and then throw down their arms and ask for mercy... A shell exploded near me and threw me into the air, and I hurt my back when I dropped, and I was very lucky to get off so easy... I got separated from the Barnetby Boys, so don't know how they fared.'

Further information in Walter Denton's letter home, of 30th September, said,

> ...'I don't know any more news of the other boys, only four got back. Arthur Tweed, Tom Hall, Fred Robinson, Ernest Grant, William Pretty, George Scott, Charles Andrews and Joseph Chivers are all missing... I have heard Fred Robinson is wounded and gone to hospital, but am not certain'.

The *Grimsby News* of 22nd October reported that Sgt A Tweed, Cpl Fred Robinson and Pte Jim Worrall, 8th Battalion Lincolnshire Regiment, were being held prisoners of war at the Kriegsgefangenschwendung at Munster, in Germany. The item then went on to mention that Pte William Pretty and Pte Ernest Grant were reported wounded and progressing favourably. The *Hull Times* of 6th November ran three brief articles, two complete with photographs, of three men still missing. One, with a photograph of Sgt Hall of Saxby, said he was one of the missing Barnetby lads who had suffered at Loos and then went on to disclose that two other Barnetby men both from the 8th Lincolns, Pte Andrew and Pte Tweedie, were also listed as missing. The second item, also with a photograph, related to Mr and Mrs C. Andrews having received official information that their son Pte C. Andrews, 8th Lincolns, was acknowledged as missing since September 25th. The third item 'expressed anxiety over Pte Charles Andrews of *1/5th* Lincolns, missing since 25th September!'

The Journal for December named four 'Barnetby Boys' in the casualty lists: – <u>Missing</u>: 12539 Sgt T. Hall, Lincolns (a spare fireman from the Chief Mechanical Engineer's Dept at *Grimsby*!) <u>Prisoners of war</u>: 12540 Pte W. Pretty, Lincolns (a spare engine driver from the Chief Mechanical Engineer's Dept at Immingham), 12340 Pte G. Scott, Lincolns (a fireman from the Chief Mechanical Engineer's Dept at Barnetby) and Pte J. W. Worrall, Lincolns (an assistant connector in the Engineer's Dept at Barnetby), the latter being held in a prisoner of war camp in Westphalia.

Back to news home, on Sunday afternoon, 3rd October, the 34th half yearly Catechism Festival had been held in St Barnabas Church. At that service 30 Sunday School children had been presented with their prizes. On this occasion 17 had volunteered to donate the value of their prize towards the Belgian relief fund. This had been handed to them in an envelope at the prize giving which afterwards they subsequently returned to the vicar, the Rev. C. F. Brotherton.

Sometime during October W. Needham left the railway service where he had worked as a platelayer in the Engineer's Dept here at Barnetby. For whatever reason there were no further railway staff changes listed in the Journal after November 1915.

A fortnight later the Adult School had held its Harvest Festival in the Co-Op rooms. There the collection had amounted to £2 10s and this amount, as promised, was made up to £5 by the Ladies Adult School to go towards the purchase of a motor ambulance that was to be presented by the Lincolnshire Adult Schools to the Red Cross Motor Ambulance.

On Saturday 6th November the wedding took place in St Barnabas Church, Barnetby, between Miss Dorothy Partridge, eldest daughter of Councillor and Mrs Partridge, of Melton Villas, King's Road, Barnetby, and Mr Percy Blanchard, only son of Mr and Mrs C. Blanchard, also of King's Road. After the wedding the newlyweds went off to Bradford for their honeymoon.

The 26th November *Grimsby News* gave a brief account of what the village had done in the way of providing comforts for the soldiers since November of last year. Many of the garments and comforts had been made or procured by the villagers and sent to either Mrs Lowish or Mrs Ffrench who had then forwarded them at various times to Admiral C. E. Buckle (for the North Seas Fleet); to the Belgian soldiers' fund and to the Lincolnshire Regiment.

The total number of articles sent from Barnetby amounted to 382. Included among that total were 106 pairs of socks, 70 mufflers, 17 shirts, 12 pairs of steering gloves, 32 pairs of mittens, 11 helmets, 100 sandbags and 24 packets of cigarettes.

A parcel of clothing had also been sent to the Hon. Mrs Nelthorpe of Scawby for the aid of the Belgian refugees. It was also hoped to put into effect a scheme whereby fresh fruit and vegetables could be collected and sent to the Navy each week. In order to collect the items a bag had been provided at Mr W. Smith's grocery store in Queen's Road in which the said fresh provisions could be deposited.

On 26th and 27th November the *Grimsby News* and the *Hull Times* respectively carried brief reports about local men. The former newspaper told how during the previous two or three weeks a number of married men, employees of the GCR, had been enlisted under Lord Derby's scheme and they would be called up in their class as and when required. Several single young men who had joined the colours and were currently undergoing training were William Lobley, who had enlisted into the colours from the railway, Percy Poole and Ernest Fish. (The 'Derby Scheme' was the compulsory call-up of all fit men of military age starting with single men first. Inevitably many young men throughout the country simply got married in order to delay their call-up date. It also brought an end to voluntary enlistment.)

The *Grimsby News* briefly related that a Barnetby man at the front, Pte Walter Denton, had been wounded. The *Hull Times* reported that Mr and Mrs Denton had received a letter from their son Walter saying that he was in a hospital in France with a thigh wound (12515 Pte Walter Denton, 8th Lincolns, had been a guard at Cleethorpes). Their son Ernest, also a Private in the 8th Lincolns, (previously reported as having been gassed at Loos and in Broadstairs hospital), was now at Deal making progress. The next paragraph gave an idea as to the severity of the conditions that those men were then undergoing in France: 'Pte H. L. Partridge, 7th Lincolns, (an engine cleaner in the Chief Mechanical Engineer's Dept at Barnetby), was in a hospital in France suffering from frostbite'.

Only one railwayman, other than W. Lobley, is believed to have enlisted during November that being S. Witty, who had worked as a chainman on the Resident Engineer's staff at Barnetby.

On Friday evening 26th November a meeting had been held in the school to set up a fund to provide comforts for soldiers. Mr J. B. Vickers had proposed 'That a continuous War Fund be raised by a weekly collection in the village to be used for comforts of our local soldiers primarily and any surplus for soldiers and sailors generally.' The motion was carried unanimously and a committee was duly elected comprising of Mr Foster, Mr Naylor, Mrs Lowish, Mrs Brotherton, Mrs Ffrench and Mrs Overton, with power to add to their number if that later became necessary.

One of the first immediate objects of the committee would be to provide the five local lads who were being held as prisoners of war in Germany with bread from Switzerland. Up to that time two or three local ladies had defrayed the cost of providing that sustenance for the previous two months. Mr Foster then launched the War Fund off the ground by making a very generous donation of £5 5s Now that the War Fund was officially an ongoing concern the Barnetby branch of the Women's Unionist Association put their weight behind the new scheme with a subscription of £4 4s. Further support had come from Mr J. Manders and Mrs Danby (Brigg) who each made a contribution of £1 1s. The meeting ended with a vote of thanks to all those who had given the fund such a good start.

Still with home news, Mr and Mrs Thomas Worrall, of Railway Street, told how they had three sons serving with the colours.

The 4th December *Hull Times* had a small article, with two unnamed photographs, about those three sons who had all enlisted on the declaration of war. Their eldest son, Jim, 8th Lincolns, having been captured at Loos, was in a prisoner of war camp near Munster in Germany. Joe, the second son, serving with the King's Own Light Infantry (*should it be* King's Own *Yorkshire* L.I?) had been in the trenches in France and since been in hospital for an operation – at the time of the article he was at home on short leave. Arthur, their third son, having joined the North Lancashire Light Infantry *(should this also read KOYLI? - see later)* had received severe wounds to his chest and mouth but made a sufficient recovery to return to his regimental headquarters.

PATRIOTIC BARNETBY FAMILY

Staying with news from home, on Wednesday 8th December, a 'Patriotic Whist Drive' had been held in the schoolroom organised by Miss de St Croix assisted by a willing team of helpers. This fund raising event was on behalf of all the local lads who at that time were being held by the enemy as prisoners of war. Many residents of the village had been very generous in providing the refreshments during the evening and also with donating the prizes. Mrs Peart, Miss Esme Stringfellow, Dr E. D. Ffrench, and Messers E. Cuthbert, J. Havercroft, J. R. Manders, J. Mudd, W. Slowens, William Turner, J. B. & E. Vickers, and J. Wells had kindly given these latter items. The event had raised the sum of £11 12s 4d towards providing comforts for the prisoners and later, after a parcel had been forwarded to each of the 'Boys' known to be held as prisoners of war, the balance was handed over to the new found village War Fund.

I think that by now most people in the village would go through those casualty lists in the newspapers in the hope of not seeing any familiar names mentioned. Whether those casualty lists appeared before, or after, families had received official notification is not clear but I am inclined to believe that in a lot of cases the casualty list would be the first information that a family would have. Sometimes more distressing information may initially have been received from a soldier who had been a personal friend, or senior NCO, of the casualty while another informant may not necessarily have had any connection whatsoever with the man concerned. This latter example may have been the situation in which Mrs Hall had received a letter with the sad news concerning her son…

12539 Lance Sergeant Thomas Hall, 8th Battalion. Lincolnshire Regiment

Thomas Hall, born and brought up in Saxby-all-Saints, was the son of George and Sarah Ann Hall. By the age of 13 (1901 census) he was working locally as a farm labourer. He later worked on the railway, living in Barnetby with his sister Mrs E. Girdham. In the 1911 census Thomas was a boarder in the George

Eaton household at 1 Silver Street. The late Mrs Allison, of Queen's Road, remembered him living in the village. Prior to enlisting at Grimsby he had been employed as an engine fireman at Immingham. His niece, the late Miss Mary Girdham, of 71 Victoria Road Barnetby, was unable to offer any further family information.

A newspaper report of 10th December 1915 gave the depressing news that Sgt T. Hall, 8th Lincolns, had been killed in action (believe aged 27 years). It went on to say that his mother had received a letter from a Private T. Reach, of the 2nd Battalion Welsh Regiment, offering her his condolences, as well as returning Thomas' cap, badge and some photographs.

L/Sgt T. Hall.

Private Reach paid a glowing tribute to Thomas' bravery in the letter he wrote to Thomas' mother saying that,

> *'He died fighting to the last and in the centre of his men, dead Germans all round him. He was a brave soldier and I think that had he lived through that fearful battle he would have won distinction'.*

(Had L/Sgt Hall been one of those soldiers in that new line comprising of men from various units under control of the nearest officer?)

The 2nd Battalion, Welsh Regiment, (3rd Brigade, 1st Division), had earlier been on the left of the 21st Division's sector so there is the possibility that Thomas had become attached to them (see the C.S.M.s' report, pp. 54/56.) I believe that he was the first Barnetby soldier to have been unofficially reported as 'killed in action'. He is also named on the GCR memorial at Sheffield.

Thomas' name is rightly mentioned on the Saxby Memorial for 1914-18 war. That memorial, in the form of a marble tablet, is mounted on the north wall of the nave in Saxby-All-Saints Church. His name is one of seven from that village who fell in action during the Great War.

(*A 11736 Pte Thomas Reach, 2nd Battalion Welsh Regiment, is listed in 'Soldiers Died in the War 1914-19.' A native of Govan, Lanarkshire, who had enlisted at Merthyr, he was killed in action on 18th July 1916. Thomas Reach has no known grave and is commemorated by name on the Thiepval Memorial to the Missing, on the Somme. The name Reach was not listed under any of the other Welsh Regiment battalions.*)

One Brigg family must have had many anxious moments regarding a son reported missing at the battle of Loos. It was September 1916 when news eventually came through of...

12514 Lance Sergeant Arthur Tweed, 8th Battalion, Lincolnshire Regiment.

On 23rd September, 1916, a brief item in the *Hull Times*, complete with a photograph, stated that 'Sgt. A. Tweed, missing since 26th September 1915, is now reported as killed in action.' The Journal of November 1916 simply lists him as being killed in action.

About the same time as the above information became known Arthur's parents received the following letter from Mr F. F. Partridge of Barnetby: –

'It has fallen to my lot, on behalf of the enginemen and firemen stationed at Barnetby, the most painful duty of conveying to you and your family the feelings of deepest sympathy in your sad visitation. Sad indeed it is to lose one of our loved ones; but let us hope and trust that it will be a grain of comfort to you and yours that your dear son, Arthur, was held in the greatest esteem and respect by those who were daily in touch with him during his civilian life. In fact he was one of the best; also as a soldier (one who volunteered at first to do his bit for King and Country) may it in the years to come be some pride and satisfaction to know that Arthur gave his life for the benefit of others in this terrible war. Truly he has made a noble sacrifice, a lesson to many others that have not had the pluck and courage to do'.

Arthur Tweed, the son of George and Lavinia Tweed of 35, Engine Street, Brigg, was born in Alkborough (3)1887. The 1901 census records the family (including three younger sisters and a younger brother) living at 3 Forrester Street, Brigg, with 13-year-old Arthur working as a cattle stockman. He later worked on the railway as a fireman at Barnetby Locomotive Depot and had lodged in the village prior to enlisting into the Army at Grimsby. He was probably encouraged to do so by the fact that his elder brother, Samuel, was at the time serving with the 1/5th Lincolns.

L/Sgt A. Tweed.

The 1911 census shows Arthur living in Engine Street, Brigg, with his parents, a younger brother George Harold and three sisters. The *Grimsby News* of 22nd October 1915 and the *Hull Times* of 23rd October both referred to Sgt A. Tweed, 8th Lincolns, as a prisoner of war at Munster in Germany! Unless there was another Sgt A. Tweed with the 8th Lincolns at that time this does not ring true!

Sgt Tweed is named on Brigg War Memorial (front left hand tablet) and Roll of Honour in St John's Church, and the GCR Memorial at the Holiday Inn

Royal Victoria Hotel, Sheffield. For some years the GCR Memorial was at the Sheffield Wicker Arches before being moved back to within yards of its original 1922 site. A relative of Arthur (his father's brother) is Mr H. D. Tweed, of 26 Woodbine Avenue, Brigg. Little else is known about Arthur except that he was among those men who were killed in action at the Battle of Loos on 26th September 1915, aged 28 years.

The third soldier, named on Barnetby Roll of Honour but not on the War Memorial, also known to have been killed at Loos, is...

12540 Private Charles Frederick Andrew, 8th Battalion, Lincolnshire Regiment.

Charles Frederick Andrew, born at Wrawby (4)1892, was the son of Charles and Charlotte Andrew of Wrawby, Brigg, Lincs. The 1911 census lists him living at home in Wrawby and his occupation given as engine cleaner. Before enlisting at Grimsby he had been employed as a GCR fireman at Immingham.

A brief news report of 6th November 1915, said that Charles' parents had now received official confirmation of him as 'missing since 25th September'. That brief item used the name *Andrews* and gave his parents address as *Wrawby Lane, Barnetby*! (On making the initial enquiry to the CWGC I used the name *Andrews* and that bore no fruit. The location of Wrawby Lane, Barnetby, is a mystery.)

Pte C. F. Andrew.

'Soldiers Died in the War, Lincolnshire Regiment' records a Pte 12540, Charles Frederick Andrew, 8th Battalion and a subsequent enquiry to the CWGC using that information produced the required result. (The Lincolnshire Regiment Roll of Honour of the 8th Battalion, also records the name as Andrew.) Charles Andrew was killed in action on 26th September 1915, aged 23 years.

His name is commemorated on the Memorial Tablet in the Church of St Mary the Virgin, Wrawby, and not on Barnetby War Memorial although the name Charles *Andrews* is included on Barnetby Roll of Honour. Most newspaper reports referred to him as *Andrews;* the Journal used both Andrew and Andrews and the GCR Memorial in Sheffield records the name C. F. Andrews. The CWGC use Andrew so I am satisfied *Andrews* is a spelling mistake.

None of the above three men have a known grave and all are commemorated on the Loos Memorial to the Missing (Panel 32). The memorial is situated on the N43, Lens Road, about 150 yards NW of a former enemy strongpoint – the Lens Road Redoubt. 1000 yards away to the NE was another former strongpoint

– the Loos Road Redoubt. An elevated view of the battlefield can be seen from the top of the left-hand pavilion that forms the front of the Loos memorial.

The memorial, serving an area from the river Lys south to a line east and west of Grenay (just to the north of Lens), forms the side and back walls of the Dud Corner Cemetery, Loos-en-Gohelle, where 1,785 officers and men are buried. The memorial panels name 20,712 officers and men whose graves are not known, and commemorate those who fell in actions dating from the first day of the Battle of Loos (25th September 1915), through to the Armistice.

Another Wrawby man, 1741 L/Cpl John Thomas ELSOM, 1/5th Lincolns, is also named on that same panel. He was killed in the action at the Hohenzollern Redoubt, a couple of miles north of Loos, on 13th October 1915. Before enlisting he had worked on the railway as a shunter in the Traffic Dept at Barnetby. The first reference that I found to J. T. Elsom was in the Journal of January 1913. He had been a lad porter at Thorne and been promoted and transferred to Hexthorpe as assistant shunter. The Journal of November 1913 then records his transfer as assistant shunter from Hexthorpe (Northern District) to Barnetby (Eastern District). He is named on the GCR Memorial at Sheffield.

The Loos Memorial to the Missing and Dud Corner Cemetery. The panel bearing the names of the Barnetby Boys is immediately to the left of the break in the wall between the two trees on the left.

Also named on Wrawby's Memorial Plaque is Sister Ellen Andrew. Born at Gedney Dyke, Lincolnshire 1.1.1886, the daughter of Hannah Leeson (formerly Andrew) of Wrawby and the late Frederick Andrew, but thought not related to C. F. Andrew. The 1901 census refers to Ellen *Andrews*, 15, b. Sutton St James (near Gedney Dyke), living at Barnetby in the house of Dr Ffrench as a domestic nurse. The 1911 census lists Ellen *Andrews,* born Gedney Dyke, working as a nurse living at the Leicester Hospital. She joined the Territorial Nursing Service (TFNS) on 26th August 1914; Sister Ellen Andrew was attached to the 58th (West Riding) Casualty Clearing Station based at Lillers in northern France. Awarded ARRC medal (Associate of the Royal Red Cross – Royal Red Cross, 2nd Class).

Sister Ellen Andrew was killed in an enemy air raid on Lillers on 21st March 1918, age 32 years and is buried in Lillers Communal Cemetery, Plot V, Row A, Grave 15. The inscription on her headstone reads, *'Thy purpose Lord we cannot see but all is well that's done by Thee.'*

CWGC Cemeteries are unique in their layout and Lillers is no exception. The plot in which Ellen Andrew lies consists of two rows of burials, all Officers, laid at right angles to the other plots and with the space between the headstones planted with flowers. A Major David Nelson, V.C., RFA, is buried immediately behind Sister Andrew and Cpl W. R. Cotter, V.C., East Kent Regiment (The Buffs) is in the front row of the adjacent 'standard' plot.

Headstone of Sister Ellen Andrew, ARRC, in Lillers Communal Cemetery. She was killed on 21st March 1918 in an air raid on the 58th (West Riding) Casualty Clearing Station based at Lillers.

Panels 28-34 on the Loos Memorial to the Missing bearing the names of Barnetby men. Pte George Hurd, The King's Liverpool Regiment, is named on Panel 28, the left hand panel; The Lincolnshire Regiment missing are named on Panels 31-34; L/Sgt T. Hall, L/Sgt A. Tweed and Pte C.F. Andrew are named on Panel 32, the right hand panel before the break in the wall.

The Great Central Railway Memorial (Great War 1914-1918) at the Royal Victoria Holiday Inn, Victoria Station Road, Sheffield, following re-dedication on 11th November 2003 after renovation and relocation to its near original site from the Wicker Arches.

THE BARNETBY BOYS

On 6th December Cpl Henry Lowish, 1/1st Lincolnshire Yeomanry had written a letter to his parents from the Middle East extracts from which follow:

North Midland Mounted Brigade,
Forces in Egypt,
'Somewhere on the Desert'

Monday Dec. 6th 1915

Dearest Mother & Father,
Very many thanks for all the nice letters & papers you have sent me since I have been out here. I received your last mail a week last Sunday Nov. 28th which I was very delighted to get… as a letter from home is worth its weight in gold out here. Also a paper is worth nearly everything, as we get to know no news whatsoever of the outside world, except by papers which we get sent from England. The last lot of papers you sent me where in great request, especially the Lincoln Chronicle with the account of our adventure in it. It was read by nearly everyone in the Regiment. (*See Chapter entitled 1917 for further information.*)

You will be surprised to hear that we have left Alexandria & are now out on the edge of the desert, about one hundred miles south of Cairo. We came on here by train from Alexandria last Wednesday night Dec. 1st., left Alexandria eleven o'clock at night & arrived at our destination nine o'clock next morning. We are camped about six miles from a station & we have a light railway runs up to camp from the small town where the station is, so we are not so badly situated. The whole of our Brigade are now here altogether.

I often see Jack Southwell & Bert Glasier who are in the next tents to ours. They were at Cairo for a week before they came here & said the Pyramids were a wonderful sight. There are a few round here but not very large ones. One side of our camp is open to the desert. Sand for miles & miles as far as you can see. It is rather hilly in some places – other parts it is flat as a pancake.

We go out on to the desert every day scouting & patrolling but have seen nothing but sand up to now. Except occasionally we see some wild dogs; also a caravan coming across the desert which is composed mostly of camels which do most of the work round here, as well as mules, donkeys & Egyptian cattle which are more like buffaloes than anything. Our horses were terrified at the sight of the camels at first, but are now getting more used to them. On our way here Sgt Drury's horse 'Travelling Maid' (which Mr Tomlinson used to have & which he raced) shied at one & fell into a large dike on the roadside & had great difficulty in getting it out, being assisted by the natives.

The other side of our camp is all fertile land which is irrigated for miles round from the canals which are connected with the Nile & the water is all pumped onto the land by large waterwheels. They grow some wonderful fine crops about here, chiefly maize, sugar cane, cotton seed, date palms also barley is grown in some parts but not of very good quality. We feed our horses with it & bran, which is more like sawdust. They also get some very bad hay, more like hedge sidings. They also get a certain amount of green stuff, very much like lucerne.

Our worst trouble here is in getting any water. We are only allowed about a pint a day which we have to use both for washing & drinking purposes. All the water has to be specially filtered before it can be even used for washing purposes & it has to be boiled & filtered before we can drink it. It is supposed to contain several injurious ingredients so we have to be very careful what we use. I find the shaving paste that I brought with me very useful out here. Should be very pleased if you would send me a couple more tubes of it when you next write, also a little chocolate would be greatly appreciated. We have only had one payday up to now since we left England, and most of the fellows are now spent up & have been for several days. I am very thankful to say that I have a little in hand yet, that which you so kindly sent me before I left. I find it most useful, as we have a canteen here & can buy almost anything in the way of food. I buy most of mine, as we are not fed too well. You can get a good supper of liver, bacon, eggs, a tea for 4 piastres which equals ten pence in English money, which is very reasonable. We can also get oranges, dates & figs here for very little, so we might be a lot worse off than we are now. Shall not mind if we are here until the end of the war.

There are several tribes round about here who are expected to cause some trouble before long & we are here to keep them in order. There is one tribe somewhere about this quarter, which is said to be equipped with arms & ammunition also guns etc. & they are under the pay of Germany & are said to have German officers in command of them. They are a good long way from here at present & where they are, they are said to be nearly run out of food & provisions & they are expected to make a raid on the more fertile land which is irrigated & where there is plenty of food to be got. So we are stationed here to stop them from raiding.....

I had a very nice time in Alexandria & was very sad to leave. Ted Davey, Pepper & myself saw Mrs Lang several times. Last Sunday we were there she took us out to see some of the sights. We went to see the Nuzhah Gardens which were simply magnificent, very similar to the Zoological Gardens in London. All kinds of animals & birds & some most beautiful palms, trees & shrubs of all descriptions… I am pleased to say that Harold & myself are both well….

I must now close as it the mail is just leaving. Hoping you will receive this letter safely, also the letters & cards, which I sent you from Alexandria. Again thanking you all very much for all your kind letters you have sent me. Hoping you are all well & that you will have a good time this Christmas. Wishing you all at Barnetby a Merry Christmas & a Happier & more Prosperous New Year. Hoping the war will soon come to an end & that we may all be saved to enjoy next Xmas at home in Old England.

Best of love from your loving son,

Henry.

PS, I am enclosing some cards which I wrote while on board ship & could not get them posted before now. Please deliver them. H. L.

(NB. The punctuation and paragraph layout is mine. I think Henry used many commas and few paragraphs to save space. Each sheet of paper that Henry wrote on has a small hole in one corner. Were they intended for another use?! R.F.)

On Thursday 9th December the Women's Adult School had held a Patriotic sale of work in the Co-Op Rooms that had brought in £7 1s 6d, of which £2 10s was sent to the Lincolnshire Adult Schools for the Red Cross Motor Ambulance fund and a donation of £4 10s made to the newly set-up village war fund.

Occasionally, when men were wounded, it may have been the soldiers themselves who first gave out the news to their families. Was that the case with Pte C.W. Holt? The newspapers of 10th/11th December had reported that Mr and Mrs Holt had received a letter from their son Pte C.W. Holt, 2nd Lincolns, saying that he had been slightly wounded in the knee and was now progressing favourably. He then went on to say,

'If all the young fellows would come I think the war would soon be over'.

Back here in the village on Tuesday 14th December the War Fund committee, having taken advantage of the local Fat Stock Show, had organized a 'flag day' in the cattle market. Small flags had been sold and the event had realised £6 6s for the local war fund. On that same day Pte A. Worrall, King's Own Yorkshire Light Infantry (KOYLI), having been at home on leave after being wounded, had returned to duty in France. The following day (Wednesday 15th December),

1915

Mrs Rose Thacker, the youngest daughter of Mrs Maddison, had returned home to Barnetby from Indian Head, Saskatchewan, in Canada – where she resided – having followed her husband, Sgt George Wm Thacker. He was over here in England doing training with the 32nd Battalion Saskatchewan Rifles, Canadian Expeditionary Force. When interviewed she had said that very little news of the war ever reached them at Indian Head.

A tragic news item that same week related to a Mrs Mary Ann Starkey, a widow, whose son William was serving with the 2/4th York and Lancaster Regiment. On Sunday 12th December Mrs Starkey, when going into an outhouse at her home in King's Road, Barnetby, came across the body of Mr Burgess, a railway guard who lodged with her. Mr Burgess, a bachelor from Hyde in Lancashire, had lived in the village for roughly twenty years and had appeared to be in very good health.

An inquest into the incident was held on the afternoon of Tuesday 14th December in the Temperance Hotel, Barnetby (the building that was once the Temperance Hotel still exists in Railway Street as dwelling houses numbered 9 and 11 almost opposite the bandroom). The foreman of the jury was Mr Meggitt, of the Maltings, Barnetby, and the GCR representative was Mr F. Patman, the District Superintendent at Grimsby.

At the inquest Mrs Starkey had affirmed that around mid-day Mr Burgess had come downstairs complaining of head pains and had gone out. P.C. Hall said that he had visited the outhouse and found Mr Burgess dead. Dr Ffrench, having known the deceased for twenty years and had last treated him in January for a dislocated hip, stated that he had suffered an extensive haemorrhage of the brain. The inquest had returned a verdict of 'Death from natural causes'. Little could Mrs Starkey know of the further anxiety and distress that the future held for her.

The 31st December *Grimsby News* carried a report of the first month's work of the new War Fund. The committee had duly announced that to date the sum of £52 10 2d had been obtained. The bulk of this sum had been made up of subscriptions that amounted to £40 4s 2d (including £9 9s 4d – the balance of the 8th December whist drive proceeds after deducting the cost of making up and sending parcels to each of the five prisoners of war). The remainder came from the proceeds of the Flag Day (£6 6s) and three weeks' house-to-house collections (£6).

The War Fund had also made payments to various organisations that were assisting in the War effort. £1 16s went to pay for the bread supply to the five prisoners of war and £2 4s 10d had been spent on purchasing wool to make socks and other knitted woollen articles. The YMCA and Serbian Relief Fund had each been sent a donation of £5 and one of £2 had been made to the Lincolnshire branch of the Red Cross, leaving a balance in hand of £36 9s 4d. The committee had acknowledged the donation of £4 4s from the Barnetby Women's Unionist Association and one of £4 10s which had been the proceeds from the sale of work held on 9th December by the members of the Women's Adult School. Finally a vote of thanks had been given to Mrs Charnley, Miss de Ste Croix, and others for their contribution in assisting the local lads who were held as prisoners of war in Germany.

So 1915 had drawn to a close with the village folk having made positive moves to look after the comforts of their soldiers and sailors knowing that their services would certainly be required in the New Year.

4
1916

THE war which at the outset was, according to the popular belief, 'going to be over by Christmas 1914' and had already seen a second Christmas come and go, now moved on into 1916. With Christmas having just been celebrated the soldiers out at the Front had not been forgotten and were appreciative of the comforts they received. During the first week of the year Miss Esme Stringfellow had received in acknowledgement of gifts of mittens and eggs two letters and a post card from soldiers in France. The wounded soldiers that had received the eggs said how much they were appreciated after so much beef and biscuits in the trenches (not to mention plum and apple jam, which a Grimsby newspaper understandably didn't, seeing that Tickler's of Grimsby (*T. G. Tickler, Ltd*) made the plum and apple jam).

A few men had been lucky enough to be at home for Christmas or the New Year and no doubt they were thankful for the change from the monotony of trench diet. On Tuesday 11th January Pte Walter Denton, 8th Lincolns, had returned to the front having been at home on short leave; a few days later L/Cpl Fred Thompson (bandmaster), 1/5th Lincolns, was due to return to his regimental HQ on Sunday 16th when his leave here expired. What would now be the thoughts of those men who had been at home on leave and just returned, or were soon to return, to duty? What would 1916 hold in store for those 'Barnetby Boys?'

At the end of January the War Fund Committee, at their monthly meeting, reported that it had £48 3s 6d in hand and on the strength of that had decided to send a parcel to each of the local soldiers who at that time were at the front. These were prepared ready for dispatch during the first week in February. Towards the end of January the villagers had been busy in providing comforts for those soldiers interned in prisoner of war camps thereby enabling Mrs Fish and Mrs Partridge to send parcels out to five of the local lads who were being held as prisoners of war. Cpl Fred. Robinson and Pte William Worrall had both promptly replied on receiving their boxes of food and socks saying that they had arrived in good condition.

Concerning recruiting it is not known how many men enlisted during the month. The Journal for January 1916 lists two Barnetby railway employees as having enlisted into the colours. They were C. H. Cox, who had been a clerk on the staff of the Resident Engineer and W. Lobley, a bricklayer in the Chief Engineer's Dept but it is known from newspaper reports that W. Lobley was undergoing training at the latter end of November 1915.

Word came through during the month about the fate of 12350 Pte E. Grant, 8th Lincolns, a former fireman in the Chief Mechanical Engineer's Dept at Immingham, who had fought at the battle of Loos. He was now known to be a prisoner of war in Germany. There can be little doubt that his family had welcomed this most reassuring news.

The Journal for January listed one fatality: 1741 Pte J. T. Elsom, 5th Lincolns, a former shunter from the Traffic Dept at Barnetby; he was a Wrawby man.

Ever mindful of the need to keep funds coming in for the various organisations that assisted servicemen Miss Maggie Robinson and Mrs R. Smith had arranged a very successful evenings entertainment on Wednesday 2nd February in the form of a concert and dance in the schoolroom. There a small band of artistes from Barton-upon-Humber had entertained a crowded and appreciative audience. This effort, on behalf of the Red Cross and the local war fund, had realised the sum of £13 16s 9d of which the war fund received £6 8s 6d.

In the meanwhile, men were still continuing to come home on leave to see their families. L/Cpl Jack Marrows, 8th Lincolns, having been on leave at the end of January, had returned to duty on Wednesday 9th February. The first reference about Jack was in the May 1911 Journal. As a lad porter at Claxby and Usselby, he had been transferred to North Kelsey as a porter. In August of that year he moved to New Clee as a porter and in November came to Barnetby to take up shunting duties. In February 1912 he was appointed brakesman at Barnetby and the following November became a goods guard. Transferred to Immingham in that capacity in March 1914 he remained there until joining the colours around October of that year.

The other soldier, Pte George Smith, had recently arrived home for a short break from the rigours of Army life. (Was this George *Herbert* Smith, 7th Lincolns, or George *William* Smith, who had recently arrived in England from Canada with his regiment?)

By mid February news from another satisfied parcel recipient had been passed on to the village war fund committee. Pte George Scott, 8th Lincolns, had written a letter home to say that he had received splendid parcels from a Mrs Lovegrove of Wooton Grange and from Mrs Fish and Mrs Partridge of Barnetby and that these ladies have his heartfelt thanks. George had earlier been reported missing but latterly it became known that he was safe, albeit as a prisoner of war and had been as such for the last five months. The village war fund committee would no doubt be very pleased that the parcels they had sent out to the village lads held as prisoners of war were reaching their various destinations safely and that their efforts were very much appreciated by the recipients.

Towards the end of the month the Adult School announced that for the period 1914-15 they had raised a total of £29 2s for various causes of which £4 10s had gone to the local war fund and that they had also sent a parcel to each of the five Prisoners of War.

The war fund committee, having earlier sent out a parcel to every local soldier on active service had subsequently received letters of thanks from nineteen of them, namely: Tom Allcard, J(?) Allison, Harry Bell, J. Briggs, Hubert Cox, Walter Denton, Harold Freestone, Cyril Gostelow, John Kirkbright (or Kirkbride?), Fred Lansley, Stephen Loveday, Tom Parrott, Ernest Pearte, Reg. Robinson, W. Stephenson, Walter Scott, Fred Vessey, John Waite and Arthur Worrall. The committee had also decided to send a batch of parcels for each of the local soldiers who were currently undergoing training.

The Journal for February named just two Barnetby men in the list of wounded. One was 655 Pte G. Winterbottom, Lincolns, a former labourer in the Engineer's Dept at Barnetby, the other being 12515 Pte W. Denton, 8th Lincolns, a former guard in the Cleethorpes Traffic Dept. It had just one local name listed as missing namely: 12540 Pte C. F. Andrews, Lincolns, a former fireman at Immingham (the latter two men are mentioned in the previous chapter).

News of a more serious nature concerning another Barnetby Boy had been contained in North Kelsey reports of 25/26th February. Headed: FALLEN HERO / LOCAL GUNNER KILLED the items offered widespread sympathy to Mr and Mrs Bell and family who had, on the evening of Monday 21st February, received news from Private Harry Partridge of Barnetby of the death in France of his chum and their son...

12654 Private William Henry Bell, 7th Battalion, Lincolnshire Regiment.

William Henry 'Harry' Bell the second son of George and Betsy Bell, of 'Elmsfield Villa' in North Kelsey, Lincolnshire, was born in North Kelsey (3)1887 where his father was a local Methodist preacher. Harry had been a scholar at the North

Kelsey Council School and on leaving school, like many men from outlying villages, had worked for the Great Central Railway. Harry was at Barnetby locomotive depot as an engine fireman. The 1911 census shows him boarding with Thomas Maitson's household at 37 Silver Street: his occupation given as a railway engine stoker. The late David Baker of 69 Silver Street, Barnetby, whose father had been an engine driver, thought that Harry had at one time been a fireman for his father.

At 28 years of age Harry had been cheerful and generous. He was associated with the Methodist Church and had taken a lively interest in the Adult School and in social questions. It was no doubt due to Harry's Methodist upbringing that a few years earlier, largely through his efforts, he had been instrumental in setting up here in Barnetby a successful branch of the Independent Order of Rechabites Friendly Society. In September 1914 Harry left the railway to join the army enlisting at Grimsby for the 7th Battalion, Lincolnshire Regiment.

The 7th Battalion, Lincolnshire Regiment – raised at Lincoln in September 1914, with the 7th Borders, 8th South Staffords and 10th Sherwood Foresters (Notts and Derby) formed the 51st Infantry Brigade, 17th (Northern) Division). Having landed at Boulogne on 14th July 1915, the 7th Lincolns began making their way towards Ypres where they were due to commence rudimentary training in the conduct of trench warfare. There the battalion learnt the ropes from 'old hands' in the 138th Brigade, 46th (North Midland) Division, the brigade that the 1/4th and 1/5th Lincolns were part of.

On 14th August, after this initiation into trench life, the 7th Lincolns moved into the front line manning trenches at Voormezeele. From the end of September until the year end the battalion remained in the Ypres sector. There, during November, the men had occupied trenches that were knee-deep in water with the result that many were soon to become victims of a new enemy – trench foot! Because of the severity of the conditions in those trenches duty tours in December were limited to forty-eight hours.

In January 1916 the 7th Lincolns were relieved and in February, after rest and training, went into trenches in V Corps, Second Army area at the 'Bluff' – less than two miles due east of Voormezeele. The local operation referred to next was carried out only by the 17th Division. The 'Bluff', a small natural area of steeply rising ground north of the Ypres - Comines Canal, extended to a man-made stretch of high ground that formed a long tree-fringed bank, 20–30 ft high, on the north bank of the canal. This high ground consisted of the debris excavated when making the cutting to take the canal through the ridge. It was an important piece of high ground that the enemy had not been completely dislodged from.

1916

On 7th February the 7th Lincolns relieved the 2nd Suffolks (76th Brigade, 3rd Division) holding the line from the Bluff to the left of Trench 32. The next day the 17th Division took over the 3rd Division sector from St Eloi, on the right, to the Ypres-Comines railway. Things were fairly quiet on the 8th February and the day after with no enemy shelling. On the 10th February the support and communication trenches were subjected to heavy shrapnel shell-fire that was quickly silenced by a response from our own artillery. Early next morning, 11th February, enemy miners broke into one of the British mining galleries on the left of Trench 29. The British mining officer there shot one German whose head appeared through the hole and then exploded a camouflet (counter-mine) that blew in the enemy gallery.

The remaining stint that the 7th Lincolns spent in those trenches was relatively quiet, apart from the Battalion bombers being active during the day – throwing 102 bombs into the enemy's trenches – who thankfully did not retaliate. The 10th Sherwood Foresters relieved the 7th Lincolns on 13th February. After relief the Battalion A, C and HQ companies – less three platoons – went to a rest camp while the remainder relieved the 10th Sherwoods in reserve in the Kingsway Dugouts.

The enemy put an end to this quiet spell at 3.30 p.m. on the 14th February. The whole area was subjected to a gun and mortar bombardment followed by firing off three mines on that section of the Bluff near the canal held by the 10th Lancashire Fusiliers of 52nd Brigade with the 10th Sherwoods of 51st Brigade on their left. Meanwhile those 7th Lincolns in the rest camp received 'Stand-to' orders and later details, having moved to the General HQ line, on receiving orders from the 51st Brigade HQ, went down to their Battalion HQ at the Bluff.

The enemy then put in an assault on the trenches and by 6.10 p.m., having broken into them and frequently fighting hand-to-hand, began making progress northwards. At 6.30 p.m. the 7th Lincolns in reserve on the debris bank sent companies to support the 8th S. Staffords and at 7.15 p.m. those companies remaining were sent up in support of the 10th Sherwoods. By 11 p.m. the details from the rest camp had arrived and were attached to the 7th Borders.

That night C Coy took part in two unsuccessful counter-attacks on the enemy in New Year Trench. The situation on the 15th February was that the enemy held the trenches from the top of the Bluff north as far as the Ravine, while the support lines were in our possession.

The 7th Lincolns (except for D Coy attached to the 8th S. Staffords), on being relieved by 7th East Yorks during the day, moved back to the debris bank until late evening when the Brigade carried out an all night bombing attack on the enemy trenches. This involved the 7th Lincolns assisted by the

6th Dorsets and 7th E. Yorks. The enemy replied to this with heavy shell-fire causing casualties among the bombers and their supply and support parties. By morning the enemy, in spite of reports to the contrary, was still managing to hang on to all that it had gained on the 14th February. The 7th Lincolns held onto their positions throughout the day until relieved in the early hours of the 17th February when they moved back 8 km. due west to the base camp east-south-east of Reningelst where they spent the next two days.

The fighting at the Bluff, 14th-17th February, had cost the 7th Lincolns one officer killed and seven wounded; twenty-five other ranks killed, seventy-one wounded and three missing. Among those casualties was 12654 Private William Henry Bell, D Coy, 7th Battalion Lincolnshire Regiment, killed in action on 15th February 1916, aged 28 years. He has no known grave and is commemorated on panel 21 of the Menin Gate Memorial to the Missing at Ypres, Belgium, one of four such memorials in Flanders (the name of another North Kelsey man, 15440 Pte Herbert Fawcett, 6th Battalion, Lincolnshire Regiment, killed in action on 8th June 1917, is recorded on that same panel). In Spoilbank Cemetery, adjacent to the former Kingsway spoilbank at the Bluff, there is a headstone to 'A soldier of the Great War, Lincolnshire Regiment, Known unto God.' That unnamed soldier might even be Harry Bell!

In the Flanders area, from Langemarck south to Messines and from Poperinghe east to Dadizeele, there are 137 cemeteries that contain the graves of 40,000 unidentified soldiers. These and 50,000 other soldiers who died in the Ypres Salient whose graves are not known or marked, are commemorated on four Memorials to the Missing in Belgian Flanders.

The Menin Gate Memorial, Ypres, records the names of 54,896 officers and men who were killed, or died, dating from 1914 up to 15th August 1917. Nightly at 8 p.m., since the spring of 1929 (except during the German occupation of Ypres in World War Two), traffic through the Menin Gate is brought to a halt while buglers of the Ypres Fire Brigade sound the Last Post. To witness this brief ceremony is a very moving experience.

The newspapers of 25th/26th February announcing the death of Harry Bell mentioned his parents having received two letters of condolence from men of the battalion at the Front. One letter, from Barnetby man Private Harry Partridge, 7th Lincolns, related:

> 'Dear Mr and Mrs Bell,
> We as the greatest of friends are very sorry to express to you that your son W. H. Bell was killed while doing his duty for his country on the 15th February.

1916

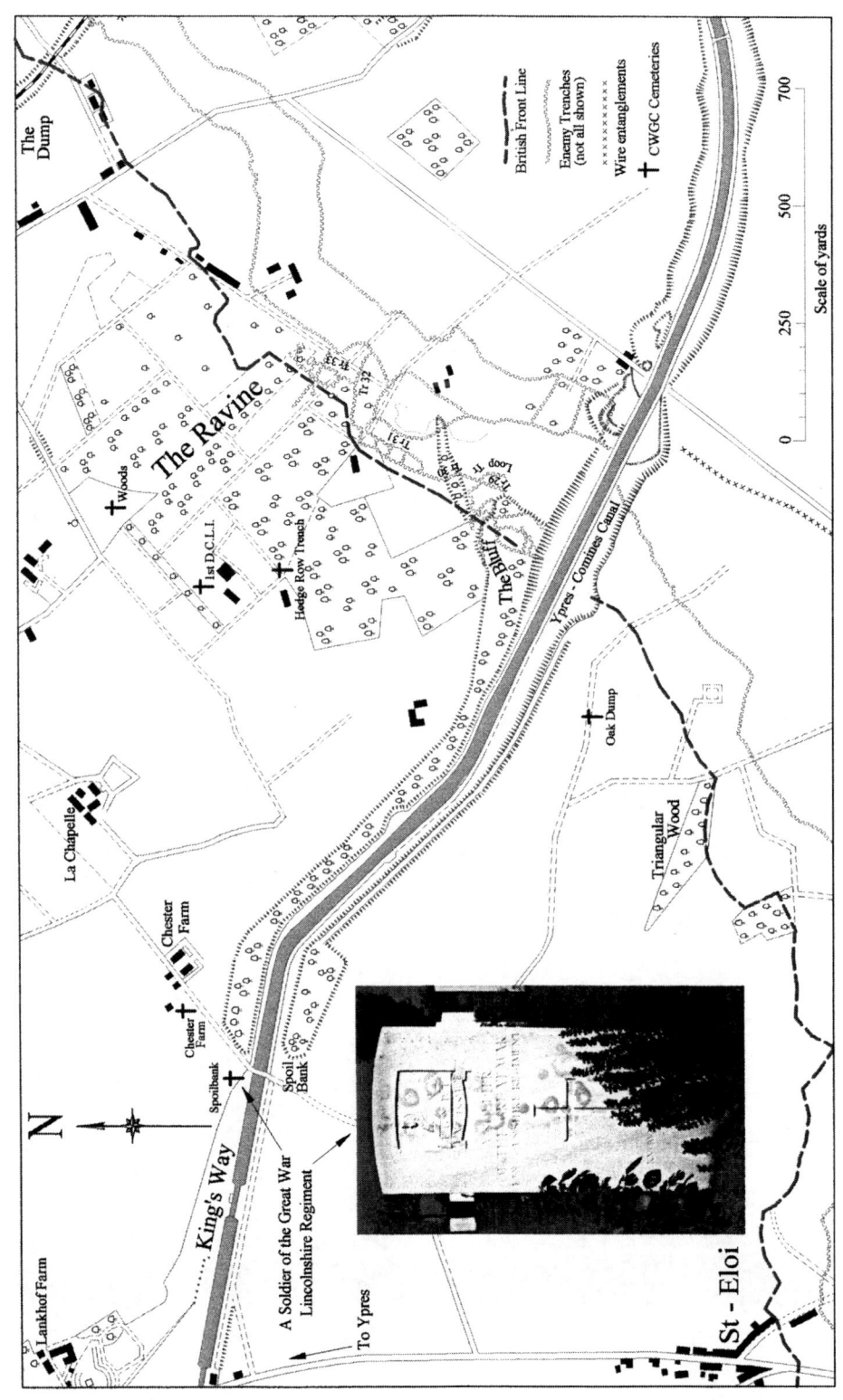

Map 7.

Menin Gate Memorial to the Missing, Ypres. The panels bearing the names of the missing from the Lincolnshire Regiment are accessed through the archway on the right leading to another archway…

…and steps leading to the right hand side of the memorial. The Lincolnshire Regiment missing are named on the panels above the steps to the left of the wreaths (the left hand half of the right hand photograph.

I am sure he suffered no pain, he was killed outright and died happy like all good soldiers do. He was one of the very best of soldiers that has ever entered France, he always took things with a good heart no matter how hard they were. He will be missed by his machine-gun section and not only by them but by the whole Battalion. There was one thing, Harry knew his work well, he was always ready and willing to do anything to help his mates and no other could have done what he had to do better than he. All of us offer our deepest sympathy in your sad bereavement.'

The other letter, from 2nd Lieutenant Bott, Machine-Gun Officer of the 7th Lincolns, said,

'I am very sorry to have unpleasant news to tell you. The battalion had been in a fight a few days ago, during which time your son helped a wounded man to the dressing station and returned to his dug-out. A shell fell on the dug-out and crushed him. I offer you my deepest sympathy and say that he died doing his duty well.
Yours sincerely,
C. S. Bott, 2nd Lt, MGO.'

(*Sadly, 2nd Lt Charles Stuart Bott, Lincolns, was killed in action on 17th April 1917. The son of the Rev. W. E. Bott and Mrs Bott, of Partney Rectory, Spilsby, Lincs., he was born at Osmaston, Derby. He is buried in Feuchy British Cemetery, Plot I, Row A, Grave 4.*)

One of Harry Bell's friends was Sidney Bowness, the son of James and Julia Bowness, of West End Farm, North Kelsey, who had been employed on the railway as an engine cleaner at Immingham. He had joined the 1/5th Lincolns, was promoted to corporal and whilst holding that rank was awarded the Military Medal and was subsequently promoted to sergeant. He was killed in action, aged 23, on 19th June 1917, during the fighting in Cite de Riaumont in the suburbs of Lens. 240179 Sgt Sidney Bowness, 1/5th Lincolns, was initially buried in Caldron Military Cemetery (after Caldron Trench), near to where he fell, and he is now buried in Loos British Cemetery, France, plot XIX, row A, grave 25. (Caldron Military Cemetery no longer exists, its burials having been concentrated into other Cemeteries – see map p.176. A bungalow now stands on the site once occupied by the Cemetery.)

Harry is named on Barnetby Memorial, the GCR Memorial at Sheffield, the Memorial Tablet in North Kelsey Methodist Chapel, the War Memorial

Lt Bott, Machine-Gun Officer, 7th Lincolns, buried in Feuchy British Cemetery.

Harry Bell's friend Sgt Sidney Bowness, MM buried in Loos British Cemetery.

A bungalow now stands on the site in Lens once occupied by Cauldron Military Cemetery where Sgt Bowness was originally buried.

in North Kelsey Cemetery and the headstone of his sister Mary's grave in that Cemetery, where an inscription reads:

'also Harry their son (George and Betsy Bell) who was killed in action in France Feb 15th, 1916 age 28 yrs. Greater love hath no man than this, that a man lay down his life for his friends'.

Harry Bell's Memorial Plaque was latterly held by his late sister-in-law, Mrs G. Bell, of Homelea, High Street, North Kelsey, who passed away in the summer of 1997.

View of the high ground held by the enemy at the Bluff, taken from a point on the road SE of the Bluff About 200 yards NE from the Canal, looking roughly NW. The white line indicates the approximate position of the enemy front line trenches. More enemy trenches occupied the foreground (see Map 7).

Today the Bluff is a quiet, peaceful, recreational area. The area on and around the Bluff itself, known as the Palingbeek Provinciaal Domein, is used for recreational walking that seems to be quite a popular pastime. Facility wise there is car parking at the eastern end of the Bluff with a bar/restaurant nearby. There is little to see of the old Ypres-Comines canal itself, other than some evidence of a lock gate, a stretch of stagnant water filling up with dank vegetation and a cobbled path, possibly the old towpath, which is now used for recreational walks. The footpath on the Kingsway, on the spoilbank at the western end of the Palingbeek Provinciaal Domein, goes all the way back into Ypres.

The real give-away that the Bluff had once been a battlefield is the proximity of six CWGC Cemeteries. To the north there are three: – 1st DCLI, Hedge Row

Trench and Woods. Woods Cemetery – the northerly of the three – is near to the western end of the Ravine (in Molenbos). South of the old Ypres-Comines canal there is Oak Dump Cemetery, bounded on three sides by a golf course and by a road on the northern side. At the western end of the walking area near the road are Chester Farm and Spoilbank Cemeteries.

A newspaper report of 3rd/4th March is somewhat baffling. It related to a number of local GCR platelayers of which a gang of ten had consented to go across to France subject to their medical fitness. Nine had been passed fit and were due to leave for the Front a few weeks later. However I did not find any more news relating to it during the following two or three months, although another article on the same subject did come to light a year later but I am not sure whether it concerned the same men or not.

At the beginning of the month two fund raising events had been put on in the school. The first event, during the afternoon of Saturday 4th March (held then because of lighting restrictions), was a concert organised and presented by the Church of England Scholars that was well attended and received with the proceeds, £4 4s 3d, being split between the Sunday School and local war fund. The other, that had taken place on the evening of Wednesday 8th March, had involved the Primitive Methodist Chapel holding an 'At Home' in which the funds raised, £10 14s, were equally shared between the local war fund and the Primitive Methodist's new organ fund. (The PM Chapel is now no more, having become the victim of subsidence. It had stood in what is now the front garden of the present new Vicarage at the junction of Victoria Road and St Barnabas Road. When it was eventually demolished many of the bricks were used in building the extension to the cottage at No.7 Smithy Lane, Barnetby.)

Reports of men wounded continued to come in. On 10th/11th March the newspapers reported on how Mrs H. Walker had received a letter from a lieutenant of the 10th Lincolns announcing that *'her son, 1290 Pte Harold Freestone, had been wounded in the head but no details were to hand'*. His mother would doubtless be anxiously hoping that Harold's wound would prove not to be serious. (On 24th February the 10th Lincolns had 'gone solo' for the first time in the trenches having taken over a sector of the front line near Bois Grenier. By the end of the month the 'Chums' had sustained casualties of 4 killed and 5 wounded. It is quite possible one of those casualties was Harold Freestone.) Another casualty, Pte Walter Denton, 8th Lincolns, had written a letter to his parents informing them that he had been wounded for the second time and was in hospital recovering from an operation on his knee. (About that time the 8th Lincolns had been carrying out periods of trench duty at Houplines, in the Armentieres sector, interspersed with relief periods in billets in Armentieres itself.)

A 17th March casualty report listed the fate of another Barnetby Boy, Sgt Thomas Hall, of Saxby-all-Saints. These reports simply gave elementary facts that were generally, but not always, listed by Regiment/Battalion in date order of the Official Report under brief sub-headings: *Previously missing – now killed: Lincolnshire Regiment, 8th Battalion: 12539 Sgt T. Hall.*

By the end of the third week in March the War Fund Committee had dispatched a further forty parcels to local soldiers. One local lady had been busy shirt making having just completed her thirtieth for the Fund. The gift parcels that had earlier been sent to soldiers at the front were now known to have reached their destinations safely. The local papers printed extracts from a letter typical of those that had been sent to the local war fund committee, in acknowledgement and grateful appreciation of the contents of the 'Tommies' Parcels' that had been received. The following letter is the combination of those extracts.

'7th Battalion Lincolnshire Regiment,
Dear Madam,

Just a line in answer to parcel received on the 22nd last month from the Barnetby War Fund, also for which I am very grateful as I was in the trenches when it arrived and had to be out all night. The tablets were very useful seeing we were having snow and rain every night. I managed to have a hot drink for myself and men about midnight and they wish to send their thanks to the workers of the fund for the benefit they received from you. Along with myself they enjoyed a hot drink. The parcels you send out are enjoyed by all who receive them, because they contain just what Tommy likes, and needs, every day. Please excuse my being so long in answering it, we have not been able to get letters off for a few days and I have written as early as possible. Please accept my good wishes for the prosperity of your fund and heartfelt thanks to the workers who are doing such good work for the lads out here.

Believe me to be yours sincerely,
G. H. Smith.'

At the end of the month the Grimsby News reported the shelling of the SS Mercian by a surfaced U-boat on 3rd November 1915 in the Mediterranean. At the time the Mercian was conveying the Lincolnshire Yeomanry, including Sgt Henry Lowish, out to Egypt. The report included a message from the Army Council praising the conduct of the Lincolnshire Yeomanry during the attack.

Also at the end of the month two more local lads had been home on a short leave, namely QMS Robert Parrott of the Army Service Corps and Private Fred

Vessey, of the 8th Lincolns. Robert Parrott, a reservist at the outbreak of war, had been recalled to the colours since when he had been in France practically the whole time. Fred Vessey had been out in France since September 1915 and had taken part in the battle of Loos.

The Journal for April lists two men as having joined the colours both having worked at Immingham as clerks in the Chief Mechanical Engineer's Dept. They were W. H. Hinchsliffe and J. W. Rapson, both Barnetby men. The final entry in relation to Barnetby, in the 'Killed in Action' list, named former fireman 12654 Pte W. H. Bell, Lincolns.

During May there was little war news appertaining to the village. Several 18-year-old young men (unnamed) had been called up that required their staying at the Lincoln depot for a few days while they underwent medical examinations. On completion they all returned home to await further instructions.

SS Mercian was again in the news during the second week in May. On that occasion it was the ship's skipper, Captain C. J. Walker, who had been in the limelight when he had been presented with a silver salver by the families of the men of the Lincolnshire Yeomanry at a ceremony held at Lincoln.

The May Journal names just two Barnetby men as having enlisted. From the Electrical Engineer's Dept there was F. Gee, an apprentice linesman and from the Resident Engineer's Staff at Barnetby clerk C. H. Cox. (C. H. Cox, also mentioned in January's Journal as having enlisted, is not listed on Barnetby Roll of Honour so possibly he was not from Barnetby. The CWGC have records of 6 men named C. H. Cox and as that name is not on the GCR Memorial at Sheffield I believe he is not one of the six and survived the war.) The 'Wounded' list named former Cleethorpes porter guard 12515 Pte W. Denton, 8th Lincolns, as being at Boulogne (his second casualty). Finally, named in the 'Killed in Action' list was former Immingham fireman, 12539 Sgt T. Hall, 8th Lincolns. He had previously been listed as 'missing' in the December 1915 issue of the Journal.

A brief article in the *Grimsby News* of 2nd June announced that Capt. F. W. McAulay, Royal Field Artillery (RFA), of Aylesby, had been killed in action on 21st May. Although not from or connected with Barnetby I have included an article about this man in the appendix as there is at Aylesby an unusual, but practical, memorial to his memory; Aylesby is also where my mother was born. Her brother, John Kirk Adlard – killed at Bouzincourt Ridge on the Somme, March 1918, is named on the memorial tablet in St. Lawrence's Church, Aylesby (his son Harry Adlard, of Barton-upon-Humber, was killed during WW 2 at Imphal, in India, in April 1944).

The papers of 2nd/3rd June gave news of Pte Harry Partridge, 7th Lincolns, the only son of Councillor F. F. and Mrs Partridge. Prior to the war Harry had been employed by the GCR and had joined the colours in September 1914. After completing nineteen months of training he had then gone out to France, arriving there on 15th July 1915, his 18th birthday. Since then he had seen a great deal of heavy fighting and had been very lucky in not having received any injuries. At the time of the item Harry had been at home on his first leave from 'Somewhere in France' and had been looking remarkably well.

In the first week in June the War Fund Committee held a meeting and reported on the first six months of being in existence. Throughout that time it had raised £120 19s 4d of which £50 3s 4d was by way of weekly house-to-house collections in the village and New Barnetby, with the balance coming from subscriptions, etc. During that time the Committee had seen to it that the five local lads who were prisoners of war had been regularly supplied with bread through the agency at Berne in Switzerland. In that first six months a total of 43 pairs of socks, 17 shirts, 20 scarves, 9 pairs of mittens and 200 sandbags had been included with the items making up the 135 parcels sent out to the soldiers and prisoner's of war. Other war charity organisations had shared £22 by way of donations, which had left the War Fund with a balance in hand of £45. Finally the Committee had expressed its gratitude to all those that had helped out in any way.

Two weeks later on 23rd/24th June the local papers gave out the news that Pte Reg. Robinson of the Lincolns (Grimsby Chums) had received wounds from shrapnel in the head and thigh in the fighting at Albert, near Arras. He was currently being treated in Whitchurch Hospital, near Cardiff. Oddly, Reg.'s niece, Mrs June Manning, cannot recall her aunt ever mentioning that Reg. had been in that Cardiff hospital.

Following the fighting of 1st July, the opening of the Somme Offensive, three further casualties were reported. On 14th/15th July it was stated that Private Hubert 'Bert' Cox had been seriously wounded with shrapnel in the back and head and had received bullet wounds in each shoulder. The *Grimsby News* then disclosed that 'Ted' Hutchinson had been *'wounded in the foot'*, while the *Hull Times* said, *'it had no news of Ted Hutchinson, a married man with three children'*. The third casualty was Pte C. Frankish, who had been wounded in the left arm but not too badly (my father, Pte 1216 Charles Robert Frankish, 10th Battalion, Lincolnshire Regiment – see items below).

My father, detailed as an 'orderly man' on the morning of 1st July, had commenced his day going to the field kitchens in Bécourt Wood in a 10th Lincolns working party.

There they had collected the Battalion breakfast and taken it to the men in the trenches.

'Breakfast at 5 a.m. then our platoon (a carrying party) collected our loads of small arms ammunition (SAA), Mills and trench mortar bombs, and moved up to the front line'.

The 10th Lincolns trenches were roughly south of la Boisselle village. About 200 yards in front of the extreme left of their front was a strongpoint, the Schwaben Höhe Redoubt, and the nearest point that the Lincolns front line trenches were to the enemy front line. East of Schwaben Höhe, No Man's Land increased in depth to about 500 yards on the extreme right of the 10th Lincolns front. In front of that redoubt the British 179th and 185th Tunnelling Companies had prepared a mine charged with 60,000 lbs of ammonal. Due to the proximity of this mine the 10th Lincolns assembled for the attack in trenches in rear of their front line. Two minutes after the mine had been detonated the 'Chums' left their assembly positions to advance across No Man's Land in a north-eastward direction past the redoubt's southern edge. They did not get far.

My father later wrote of his experiences on that 1st July day, 1916:

'It seemed a long wait until 7.28 a.m. when the mine went up. *(The resultant 'hole' is now privately owned and preserved as a memorial called 'Lochnagar Crater'.)* I remember the ground shaking like a jelly. We had been told that the advance would be a walk over, as the trenches had been destroyed, and most of the troops killed but we knew this was not true, as several times before the attack we had shown our dummy troops over the parapet, (tunics filled with straw and wearing gas masks and tin hats). The reply was a terrific hail of machine-gun and rifle fire. We had also been told that most of the German guns had been spotted, but would not be knocked out until early morning on July 1st, too late to be replaced. This all seemed to be wishful thinking, to judge by the barrage we had to face. In addition to our 'Battle order', we also carried extra S.A.A., extra food, two Mills grenades, empty sand bags and either a pick or a shovel, as we had to help consolidate the trenches when we got to them.

After what seemed an endless wait (two minutes), we went over the top into the churned mud of No Man's Land. The small arms and shell-fire was very heavy. I had not gone far when a bullet struck my equipment and spun me round like a top, but I was none the worse. It was very hard going, with the weight we had to carry, the mud and the shell torn ground (I was also carrying two trench mortar bombs in a sandbag).

About half way to the German trenches I received a terrific blow on my left forearm. I collapsed into the nearest shell hole, my arm quite useless, apparently broken. I lay for some time in the shell hole wondering what to do next. After a time I decided to try and get back to our front line, going a few yards at a time, from shell hole to shell hole, being sniped at all the time. After losing my direction several times I arrived back at our front trench. I made my way down to a First Aid Post, had a dressing put on my arm and was given a 'shot'. Then by road transport to No. 102 Field Ambulance Station to enjoy the best sleep I had had for months'.

Thus had ended my father's involvement in the fighting at the beginning of that fateful Somme offensive. I knew none of this at all until I received the information from Mr Martin Middlebrook, of Boston, a military historian and author. With my father's name being amongst the acknowledgements list in Mr Middlebrook's book, *The First Day on the Somme*, for having provided material during the book research I was curious to know what his contribution had been. Even my mother had not been aware that my father had been wounded in the arm.

(A witness to that mine explosion was 2nd Lt Cecil Lewis, a pilot in the R.F.C. Being on patrol over la Boisselle on 1st July but warned to stay clear of that immediate area at Zero hour he quite literally had a bird's eye view of the mine going up. He died in January 1997, aged 98 – in those days the survival time for a pilot in the R.F.C. was reckoned to be about three weeks!)

The 10th Lincolns had gone into that battle with a fighting strength of just over 840 and came out of that first day of the Somme offensive with slightly above 180 killed, or subsequently died of wounds, out of a casualty list of just over 500. Considering those casualties the Barnetby Boys came through relatively unscathed with just wounded among their number.

In the appendix to the battalion war diary, PRO WO 95/2457, there appears the following letter addressed to the 'Chums' Commanding Officer:

10th Bn, July 5th, 1916
Dear Colonel Cordeaux,
    Will you please express to your Battalion my admiration of their fearless conduct in the Battle on July 1st. Having to start further back than the two right Battalions they had to bear the brunt of the full force of the machine-gun fire during their advance across the Sausage Valley, they never wavered but pressed forward, but their ranks were too thin, as their casualties show, to gain their final objective though they got well into the German lines and assisted in holding for 2 days the exposed left flank which became the pivot of the successful advance of the Divisions on our right. No troops could

have done better and it was no fault of theirs that they did not reach their allotted objective.

Yours Sincerely,

R.C. Gore. (Brig. Gen.) Cmdg 101st Inf. Bde.

During the second week of the month the Women's Adult school announced that they had raised more than £40 over the last eighteen months for various war charities. This was a quite creditable achievement considering that other village organisations were also carrying out similar fund raising activities occasionally for the same beneficiaries.

The 22nd July *Hull Times* announced that Pte Reg. Robinson, 10th Lincolns, who had been wounded during June and then hospitalised at Cardiff, was at home on ten days leave.

The following week the Hull Times of 29th July ran a separate piece announcing that: on Thursday, (27th July), Mrs Emma Smith, formerly of Barnetby, who now resides with her daughter at New Holland, Lincs, received the sad intelligence, that among those killed in action on 3rd July, was her son...

12577 L/Cpl George Herbert Smith, 7th Battalion, Lincolnshire Regiment

George Herbert Smith, the second of three sons of Emma Smith of 2 Manchester Square, New Holland, Lincolnshire and the late Luke Smith, was born in Barnetby (1)1887. He enlisted at Grimsby on 3rd September 1914 along with the rush to join the colours during the first month of the war and had spent twelve months in France.

In 1911 George was living with his widowed mother, brother William and sister Eliza in King's Road and employed by the GCR as a signal fitter. His name first appears in the January 1912 Journal when, as a labourer in the Engineer's Dept at Barnetby, he was transferred as a shunter to Traffic. The April 1913 issue records his promotion at Barnetby to brakesman. By November 1913 he had been promoted to goods guard in which category, by March 1914, he was transferred from Barnetby to the Immingham Depot (Traffic). His enlistment to the colours is recorded in the October 1914 Journal. The September 1916 Journal records his name amongst those 'killed in action'.

L/Cpl G. H. Smith.

George, 29 years old, was highly respected in the village. Back in March he had written to the War Fund committee to thank them for the 'Tommies' parcels'. Much sympathy had been felt for his mother who already had two sons serving. Charles, the eldest, was in Canada at the outbreak of war and, having enlisted into the Canadian Army, had come over to France 'to do his bit' for the homeland. At the time of the report he was in a convalescent home at Epsom having been shot in the chest.

William, the youngest son, had also been seriously wounded in the chest whilst serving with the Coldstream Guards and was likely to receive his discharge from the Army. (Charles' and William's names are recorded on the Barnetby Roll of Honour.)

12577 L/Cpl George Herbert Smith, 7th Lincolns, was killed on 3rd July 1916, aged 29 years. He was buried in Gordon Dump Cemetery,

G. H. Smith headstone.

Ovillers-la-Boiselle, at map reference 57d,.X.15.c.3.5. The burial site was originally in the Cemetery front right quarter a few yards in from an old lane, now disappeared through disuse, that led to the Cemetery front entrance on the south-eastern side. George's grave became lost and there is now a 'Special Memorial' to him by the rear wall, B23, 'Believed to be buried in this Cemetery'.

Some of the 'Special Memorials' along the rear wall of Gordon Dump Cemetery. L/Cpl George Smith's 'Special Memorial' headstone, B23, 'Believed to be buried in the cemetery' is 4th from the right.

The personal inscription on George's headstone reads: *'A longing look, a silent tear, keeps his memory ever dear'*.

Gordon Dump Cemetery is now accessed from the la Boiselle – Contalmaison road by a grassed path across a field. The cemetery was initially made by fighting units after 10th July 1916 and when closed in September 1916 contained 95 graves, mainly Australian soldiers. After the Armistice it was increased by incorporating 3 existing graves and concentrating 1,543 from the surrounding battlefields. 1,052 graves are of unidentified soldiers, some being identified by rank, regiment or both. There are 34 'Special Memorials' to men 'Known to be buried' or 'Believed to be buried' there, six of the latter being men of the Lincolnshire Regiment.

The 7th Lincolns were last recorded here as being in action near Ypres at the Bluff. That had been captured by the enemy on 14th February and taken from him again on 2nd March in an action also involving the 7th Lincolns. Relieved on 3rd March, after a short rest, the 7th Lincolns went back in the front line on 19th March at Armentieres. From about mid May until 11th June the 7th Lincolns, with other units of the brigade, were in training at Hellebrouck, near St. Omer, whence it moved down to the Somme, to Allonville, north east of Amiens. For the next two weeks the battalion trained and provided working parties to assist with the preparations in the build-up for the Somme Offensive. On 30th June the 7th Lincolns left Allonville bound for Morlancourt in readiness for the forthcoming battle.

On 1st July the 51st Brigade, XV Corps, Fourth Army, was in Divisional Reserve until nightfall when it relieved 50th Brigade in the front line near Fricourt, the 7th Lincolns taking over from 6th Dorsets, with orders to clear the enemy out of Fricourt the following morning. Intelligence gathered from prisoners captured early on in the forenoon of 2nd July, indicated that the enemy was pulling out of Fricourt and the 51st Brigade was ordered to take Fricourt and then press on up to Fricourt Farm (8th South Staffords) and Fricourt Wood (7th Lincolns). While the 7th Lincolns headed for Fricourt Wood and the 8th South Staffords towards Fricourt Farm, fresh orders were received to push on towards the railway to make contact with the 21st Division on the left and the 7th Division on the right.

The 7th Lincolns, having been subjected to machine-gun fire from the wood whilst on the edge of Fricourt, stayed amongst the village ruins until a reconnaissance of the wood showed it to be clear. The battalion then pushed on and were through the wood (in reality a park with trees) by mid afternoon. By late afternoon the 8th South Staffords had reached Fricourt Farm and Lozenge Alley and the 7th Lincolns were on the northern and north-eastern side of

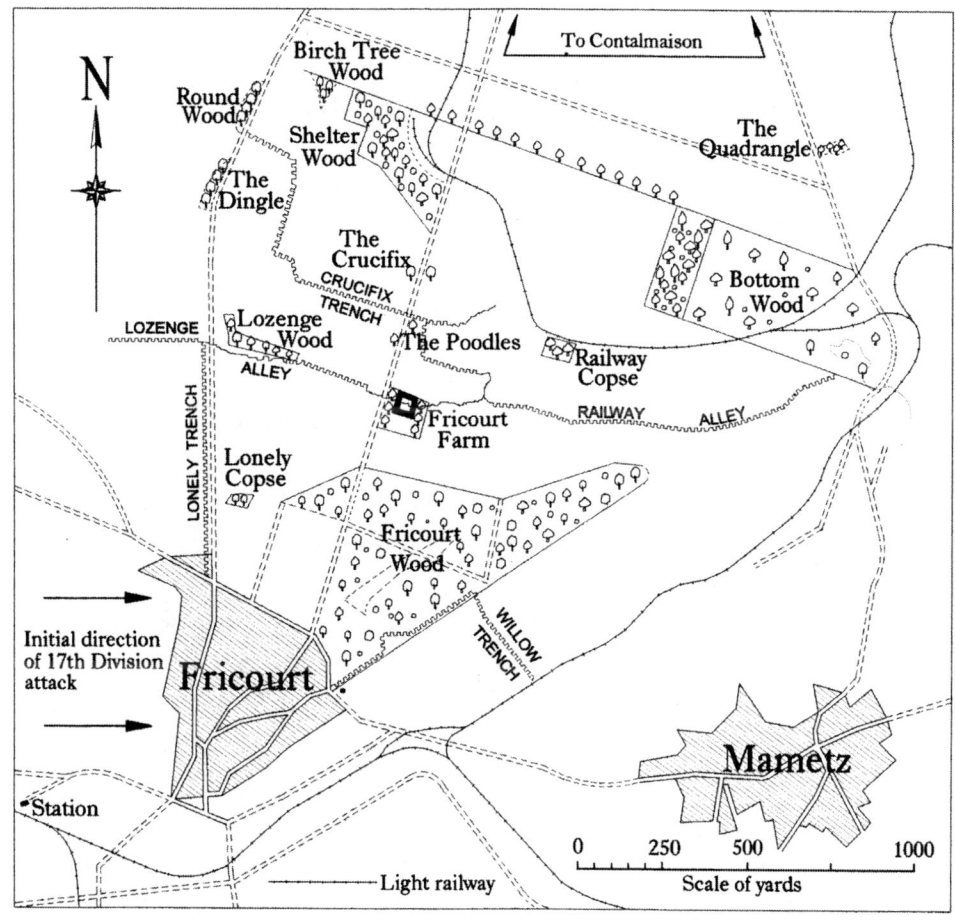

Map 8. *Fricourt.*

Fricourt Wood, except for one platoon and the machine-guns who were in support in Willow Trench along with the 10th Notts and Derby (Sherwood Foresters). On the following morning, 3rd July, the 17th, 21st and 34th Divisions resumed the attack at 9 a.m. In the 51st Brigade the 7th Borders and 10th Sherwoods advanced onto Railway Alley while the 7th Lincolns, having sent their bombers from Fricourt Farm into the northern end of Crucifix Trench, attacked Crucifix Trench with the 8th South Staffords without a preliminary artillery barrage.

The 7th Lincolns, on seeing their bombers making progress down the trench, rushed out from Fricourt Wood with the 8th South Staffords on their left and despite being subjected to rifle and machine-gun pushed on towards Crucifix Trench. The enemy, on attempting to fall back to Shelter Wood, ran into the Lincolns' bombers and were driven back towards the advancing South Staffords and surrendered.

By early afternoon the 10th Sherwoods had taken Railway Copse assisted by detachments of the 7th Lincolns and 8th South Staffords. It had been a good day's work for the 17th Division. It had achieved all its objectives, taken over nine hundred prisoners, a large amount of stores, a couple of field guns and eleven machine-guns; of this the 7th Lincolns had captured a quantity of stores, the two field guns and two machine-guns. The casualty toll of the 7th Lincolns was four officers and thirty other ranks killed; six officers and nearly one hundred and sixty other ranks either wounded or missing. The following day the 7th Lincolns consolidated their positions in Railway Alley being very frequently subjected to enemy shelling whilst doing so and on the night of 4th/5th July, on being relieved by the South Staffords, went into billets at Ville (-sur-Ancre) to reorganise and refit.

The soldiers at the Front continued to be thought of by the people here at home with the Womens' Adult School having been busy putting together and despatching 60 half-crown parcels to local soldiers (making a total of £7 10s). (The half-crown was a coin that had the value of two shillings and six pence, or 12½ p. in today's money, and it represented 2½ days pay for a private.)

Still with the *Hull Times* of 29th July, that paper gave further news about Pte Harold Freeston of the Grimsby Chums. Previously reported as having been wounded in the head without any details being given this latest item, although still not going into detail, did give a hint by reporting that Harold's progress had been satisfactory and he was now convalescing although his sight was not yet properly restored. At the time of that report Harold was at home on leave and the local correspondent thought he was looking remarkably well considering the extent of his wounds.

The last local item for that week gave out news of Sgt Sidney Tillbrook(e) who was at home on six days leave. Sgt Tillbrook had previously seen service in the South African War and presumably he had been on the reserve list with him having been recalled to the colours on the outbreak of war. Sgt Tillbrook had been a bomber (regiment not stated but recorded in the February 1915 issue of the Journal as being 1st Suffolk) before being wounded and invalided home from France and was currently stationed in England.

A final item in the 29th July *Hull Times* reminded one that life threatening situations were not just the lot of men in war zones. On Friday 28th July a potentially life endangering incident had happened to fifteen year old Nellie Elsom when she had accidentally swallowed a gooseberry which lodged in her throat. Her mother had managed to move the obstruction from her daughter's windpipe with her fingers until such time as the doctor arrived although he was unable to extract it there and then. The obstructive gooseberry was later successfully removed under anæsthetic and the girl was said to be progressing favourably.

During the week ending 5th August Pte Jesse Dawson, who was shortly due to go out to France, had been at home on short leave as had Pte W. Smith, who was then training with the Lincolns. (Which W. Smith: Walter or William? A further identification problem is also posed by Pte A. Robinson, of whom, according to the Roll of Honour, there were three that had a Christian name beginning with A – Albert, Albert and Arthur!)

During the same week the Broughton family must have been very relieved when their son, Pte William Broughton, returned home after a brief training period in the Army to help his father in the family business on Government work for an indefinite period.

The *Grimsby News* of 4th August had a brief obituary for the late L/Cpl G. H. Smith who had been killed in action on the Somme on 3rd July.

More sad news relating to a Barnetby soldier was in the *Grimsby News* of 4th August and the *Hull Times* of 5th August. Both papers announced that Mr and Mrs Thomas Worrall had just received intelligence about their youngest son Arthur who was in the machine-gun section of the KOYLI. This disclosure, from Arthur's section sergeant, informed them that he had been killed in action during the recent Somme offensive. In a letter to Arthur's parents his section sergeant, Sgt Brookes, had told them,

> 'He was a true and brave soldier and stuck to his gun to the last. He will be sadly missed by everyone who knew him amongst the gunners'.

Arthur, a former GCR employee, had joined the colours on the outbreak of war. In the October 1914 Journal his employment is listed as a connector's labourer in the Signal Dept of the Chief Engineer's Dept at Sheffield. Just a few months prior to the announcement above being made he had been at home on leave after having been wounded. The newspaper reports ended expressing sympathy to the grieving parents who had two other sons serving with the colours, William, held as a prisoner of war in Germany, and Joe, serving 'in France'.

There then came an announcement in the papers of 18th/19th August giving further news of Arthur, saying that,

> 'Mr and Mrs Thomas Worrall, who had received news three weeks ago that their son, Pte A. Worrall, KOYLI, had been killed, have this week received a card from him stating that he is a prisoner of war at Dulmen in Westphalia'.

What profound relief all those in the Worrall household must surely have felt when that gratifying news reached them, specially as it had come from Arthur himself, telling them he was alive and safe even though he was a prisoner of war? (The September issue of the Journal also had Pte 145 A. Worrall, Yorkshire Light Infantry listed as being 'killed in action'. The October issue duly listed him as a 'prisoner of war' with a note stating that he had previously been shown as 'killed in action'.)

It makes one wonder how many other families were to be put into similar predicaments by receiving such distressing and unfounded news that would later prove to be incorrect. In this instance the information, such as it was, had seemingly come from an unofficial source. That therefore seems to imply that only official sources were the ones to be believed, but, as events will prove, even the official source would, on at least one occasion here in Barnetby, be found to be alarmingly wrong.

In a lighter vein the Barnetby Band had announced its intention to raise money by means of a collection whilst playing music for dancing. The proceeds from the event were to be jointly split between the Band and the village War Fund. The event, programmed for the evening of Saturday 19th August, was to be held in the paddock in rear of the Railway Inn in King's Road.

Unfortunately, the anticipated pleasant evening of music and dancing was marred by the intervention of inclement weather that quite literally put a damper on the event with rain having made the grass too wet for any dancing. Nevertheless the Band had honoured the musical part of the bargain by entertaining those hopefuls who had turned up for the dancing to a programme of selections. The collection made from this somewhat depleted audience had realised the small amount of 10s. 2d. The sum of 7s. 6d. was handed over to the War Fund to help with the purchase of comforts for the local soldiers. The proceeds from the Band's previous fund raising effort had been used to buy tobacco and cigarettes for those same local soldiers, when a total of 64 parcels had been sent out.

Another brief item accompanying a small photograph spoke for itself with the headline BARNETBY MAN RECOMMENDED FOR DCM.

The Insley family would doubtless have felt very proud with the write-up that appeared in the local newspapers announcing that their son, Cpl George W. Insley, 2nd Lincolns RFA(?), had been recommended for a gallantry award. Before hostilities broke out he had been employed as a blacksmith with the GCR and

Cpl G. W. Insley.

joined the colours on the outbreak of war. Corporal Insley had spent a very considerable time out in France and two weeks earlier during the heavy fighting there he had successfully opened an enemy fuse thereby saving the lives of many of his pals though he did not escape injuries himself. This action left him with a severely shattered left hand and arm. Corporal Insley was mentioned in despatches for this deed and has duly been recommended for the award of the Distinguished Conduct Medal, (DCM). As a result of those injuries he was currently undergoing treatment in the Military Hospital at Birmingham.

(Although Cpl Insley may have been recommended for the award I believe it was not sanctioned. His name is not in the National Archives DCM index. The Medal Index card for Cpl Insley, who had served in both the Field and Garrison arms of the Royal Artillery as 1268 Gunner, RFA; 313654 Wheel Corporal, RGA (TF) and 801587 Corporal, RFA, gave his medal entitlement as the Victory and War Medals with no reference either to Mention in Despatches. (Had the DCM been awarded the index would have referred to Corporal Insley, DCM.) A check of the listing under Royal Artillery in the DCM register book, held by the Imperial War Museum, recording all the DCM's awarded during the Great War had the same negative result.)

But while the news of the gallantry recommendation and a postcard from a 'lost' son would have brought joy to some families other families had received less welcome news. During August Mr and Mrs J. Rapson, of 29 Milner Road, Long Eaton, Derby, had received the sad news announcing the death in France of their son...

21575 Pte John Wilfred Rapson, 10th Battalion, Lincolnshire Regiment

John Wilfred Rapson was the eldest son of John Henry and Louisa Rapson of Long Eaton, Derby, and his untimely death came as a staggering blow to his family to whom he had been a dutiful son. (John's father, a Sergeant in the 1st Battalion, Notts and Derbys Regiment, having done nine month's active service, in May 1915 had been wounded in fighting at Aubers Ridge and in April 1916 had been invalided home and subsequently discharged from the Army.)

By all accounts John had not spent very much time in Long Eaton where he had been a member of the local Zion Church Sunday School in his earlier years. Having left Long Eaton to take up a railway career, John had joined the GCR in April 1909 and became a clerk in the Locomotive Running Department at Immingham. By 1911 the Rapson family and their four sons and two daughters had moved to Barnetby and were living in King's Road (the *Grimsby News,* 26th May 1911, records that J. H. Rapson, John's father – a GCR railway wagon builder, had been successful in gaining a certificate and bronze badge in an examination and open exhibition for handicrafts held in London under the auspices of the National Association of Fretworkers. He was also appointed a handicraft judge for the district). John was well liked in Barnetby having had a large circle of friends and had led a full life taking a keen interest in village activity.

John was a member of the Church of England. He had put his 'clerking' skills to a very good use by instructing the Adult School in shorthand where his loss was acutely felt. Being fond of outdoor sports of all forms, he had been secretary to both the cricket and the football clubs (the *Grimsby News* of 6th September 1912 recorded his election as assistant secretary to the Barnetby St Mary's football club when it had re-formed after a season's rest).

Upon the outbreak of war John had joined the R.F.A. but being in the employ of the GCR, that protested he was indispensable to the railway, he had been claimed back. He subsequently re-enlisted at Grimsby on 1st December 1915 into the 3rd Battalion, Lincolnshire Regiment. His address at attestation was 111 Spring St, Immingham; his age was given as 22 years 53 days (calculated birth date: 9th October 1893); his mother, Louisa Rapson, was named next of kin.

Pte J. W. Rapson.

John joined the colours on 21st February 1916 (the *Long Eaton Advertiser* records that he was called up on 20th February). After completing his initial training John was drafted out to France on 28th June 1916 from where, on 12th July 1916, he was sent to join the 10th Lincolns at Hennencourt where the 10th Lincolns and the other 101st Brigade units, having been relieved on 4th July after taking heavy losses at la Boisselle, were in that area refitting with training taking place in the area around Bresle.

The 10th Lincolns, in need of replacements after an almost sixty percent loss in strength in the first few days of the Somme fighting, received drafts of men at that time. The Regimental history relates that the replacement drafts received by the battalion included men from various regimental units, as well as a few Lincolns, many of whom were third-line Territorials who had only had about three months of training.

Meanwhile on 7th July the 34th Division had undergone a brief reorganisation. Following the losses sustained on the first three days of July 1916 it had had its 102nd and 103rd Brigades and Pioneer battalion temporarily replaced, until 21st August, by the 111th and 112th Brigades of the 37th Division including the Pioneers. It was with those two brigades that the 34th Division returned briefly to the Somme fighting during mid July.

On 31st July the 101st Brigade rejoined the 34th Division when it went back into the line in the area around the Bazentins. Fighting was still in progress, as the 101st Brigade took over the sector east of Bazentin Wood to High Wood exclusive. The 10th Lincolns took over trenches northeast and southwest of Bazentin-le-Petit Wood (the 101st Brigade War Diary (WO 95/2455) records that the line on 31st July ran from the Bazentin-le-Petit – Martinpuich Road (A) to about S.3.c.9.5. (B); 16th Royal Scots on the right and 11th Suffolks on the left; 2 Coys 10th Lincolns in close support about the cemetery and 2 Coys in the Old German Line south of Bazentin-le-Petit Wood. On 3rd August the 111th Brigade, having been in support in Mametz Wood, took over the right half of the sector – see map 9, p 102.)

On 4th August the 10th Lincolns relieved the 11th Suffolks in the front line and support line trenches north-east of Bazentin-le-Petit. Whilst there the 15th Royal Scots launched a bombing attack at 9.15 p.m. on the enemy part of Intermediate Trench assisted by details of the 10th Lincolns. However a very fierce enemy artillery barrage during the 10th Lincolns advance thwarted their co-operation attempt as a result of which the attack was not successful.

On 6th August the 101st Brigade, on being relieved in the line by the 112th Brigade (in reserve at Bécourt Wood), moved back into trenches west of Mametz Wood – the 10th Lincolns going to a trench between Shelter Wood and Bottom Wood.

Those six days of duty in the line had cost the 10th Lincolns in excess of 200 casualties with twenty-four killed and at least one hundred and seventy-six wounded.

I do not know when John was actually wounded as the War Diary of the 10th Lincolns (WO 95/2457) only briefly states, '1st August, 10th Battalion in occupation of trenches north-east and south-west of Wood. Shell-fire, more particularly from High Wood, at times very heavy.' But it is quite probable it was there during that six-day period that Pte 21575 John Wilfred Rapson, aged 23 years was mortally wounded.

What has been recorded in various accounts are the terrible conditions that greeted the men when they took over the front line with dead bodies and bits of bodies from the previous fortnight's fighting strewn about everywhere and the awful stench of putrefaction that emanated from them!

I believe John died in a Field Ambulance Unit at Albert having been mortally wounded, at Bazentin-le-Petit, during the Battle of Pozières Ridge. Two dates are recorded for his death. The CWGC use 3rd August 1916 and record the battalion and regiment as the 3rd Lincolns, the home-based Lincolnshire reserve battalion that trained and dispatched drafts to its overseas battalions. 'Soldiers Died in the War' record: '10th Lincolns, died of wounds, 5-8-16'.) John's service documents (among the 'Burnt Records', WO 363/R0834) record: GSW fctd? (*fractured*?) skull 5-8-16 (by memo); died 5-8-16. When John's parents wrote to the military authorities in September 1921 enquiring after his medals they stated 5th August 1916 as the date of death!

21575 Pte John Wilfred Rapson is buried in Albert Communal Cemetery Extension, plot I, row M, grave 37, where the personal inscription on his headstone reads, *'He was loved by all'*.

Fighting units and Field Ambulances used Albert Cemetery Extension for burials from August 1915 until November 1916, more particularly so during and after September 1916 when various Field Ambulances were concentrated about Albert. From November 1916, the 5th Casualty Clearing Station used it for two months. Except for four burials in March 1918, it was out of use between March 1917 and the end of August 1918, when the 18th Division made Plot II. It now contains 863 burials including 23 men killed during the Second World War and one CWGC employee. This Cemetery is typical of those used for burials by medical units in that it has only 12 unidentified graves.

J. W. Rapson headstone.

Not long after receiving John's few personal effects on 23rd November 1916 his mother wrote to the military authorities stating that his wristwatch strap and gold ring were missing. She was certain he had them when he was wounded.

John left brothers Harold, George H., Alfred and Leonard and sisters Mrs Christine Wilson, of Immingham, and Olive May Rapson.

Shortly after this the Lobley family, of West Street, received sad news about their son...

1560 Cpl James Willie Lobley, 10th Battalion, Lincolnshire Regiment.

James Willie Lobley (born at Wrawby (3)1893) was the son of William and Sarah Jane Lobley of West Street, Barnetby. The 1911 census shows James, as the eldest of five children, employed as bricklayer's apprentice. He had been a bricklayer in the Great Central Railway Chief Engineer's Department at Barnetby Locomotive Depot prior to signing up at Brigg in November 1915 ('Soldiers Died in the War' list his place of residence as Lincoln). James went out to France in July 1916 and was killed in action on 15th August 1916, aged 23 years (the local newspapers, 8th/9th September, reported that he was killed in action on 14th August).

In order to join the colours James had to undergo an operation from which he had made a good recovery. He had been a great favourite with his officers and rapidly gained his stripes. Captain Kennington, James' commanding officer, had sent James' parents a letter of condolence and, in offering his condolences, had testified to his ability and cheerfulness when in trying circumstances and that he had been a good non-commissioned officer of more than ordinary merit.

J. W. Lobley.

During the first two weeks in August the actions of the 34th Division were concentrated around Intermediate Trench that was peculiar inasmuch as the enemy held the western part of the same trench! All attempts by the 34th Division while they were in that sector to remove the enemy from Intermediate Trench were unsuccessful even though the dividing barricade was on occasions successfully moved. Unfortunately the 10th Lincolns war diary records very little in the way of any battalion activity round about that time.

On 6th August the 10th Lincolns, on being relieved in the front and support lines at Bazantin-le-Petit, moved to a trench between Shelter Wood and Bottom Wood west of Mametz Wood from where, on 10th August, they moved into trenches and bivouacs at Bécourt Wood and relieved the 11th Suffolks. That day the 10th Lincolns, along with 15th Royal Scots, received notice that they would be attached to, and come under orders of, 111th Brigade on 11th August when the 101st Brigade relieved the 111th Brigade.

When the 111th Brigade relieved the 112th Brigade on 13th August the 10th Lincolns relieved the 8th East Lancashires, 112th Brigade, and took over support trenches in Mametz Wood. The next day they relieved the 11th Royal Warwicks, 112th Brigade, in 500 yards of trench running east and west 200 yards north of Bazantin-le-Petit and facing 300 yards of Intermediate Line being tenaciously held by the Germans.

The war diary entry for 15th August mainly concerns the state of the trenches that the 10th Lincolns had taken over. 'The trenches were in a very bad condition in the close support line being much blown in and with many unburied dead lying about.' No casualties are recorded.

The final chapter of the 10th Lincolns fighting during the 1916 Somme battle closed at Bazentin-le-Petit on 15th August on being relieved by the 1st Battalion Cameron Highlanders, 1st Brigade, 1st Division. On relief they went into bivouac at Bécourt leaving the area later that day and moving north to Armentières. From there, on 29th August, the 10th Lincolns went into the line at Bois Grenier where they had first taken over the front line at the end of February, after initial trench instruction, not long after the Battalion arrived in France.

Cpl James Willie Lobley was originally buried near to where the 10th Lincolns had been entrenched at Bazentin-le-Petit at map reference 57c.S.8.b.55.85. He is now buried in London Cemetery and Extension, High Wood, at Longueval, in plot VIII, row D, grave 10.

The original London Cemetery dates from 18th September 1916 when the 47th (London) Division (hence the name) commenced the burial of 47 men in a large shell hole and later added 54 other graves. This original plot is to the left of

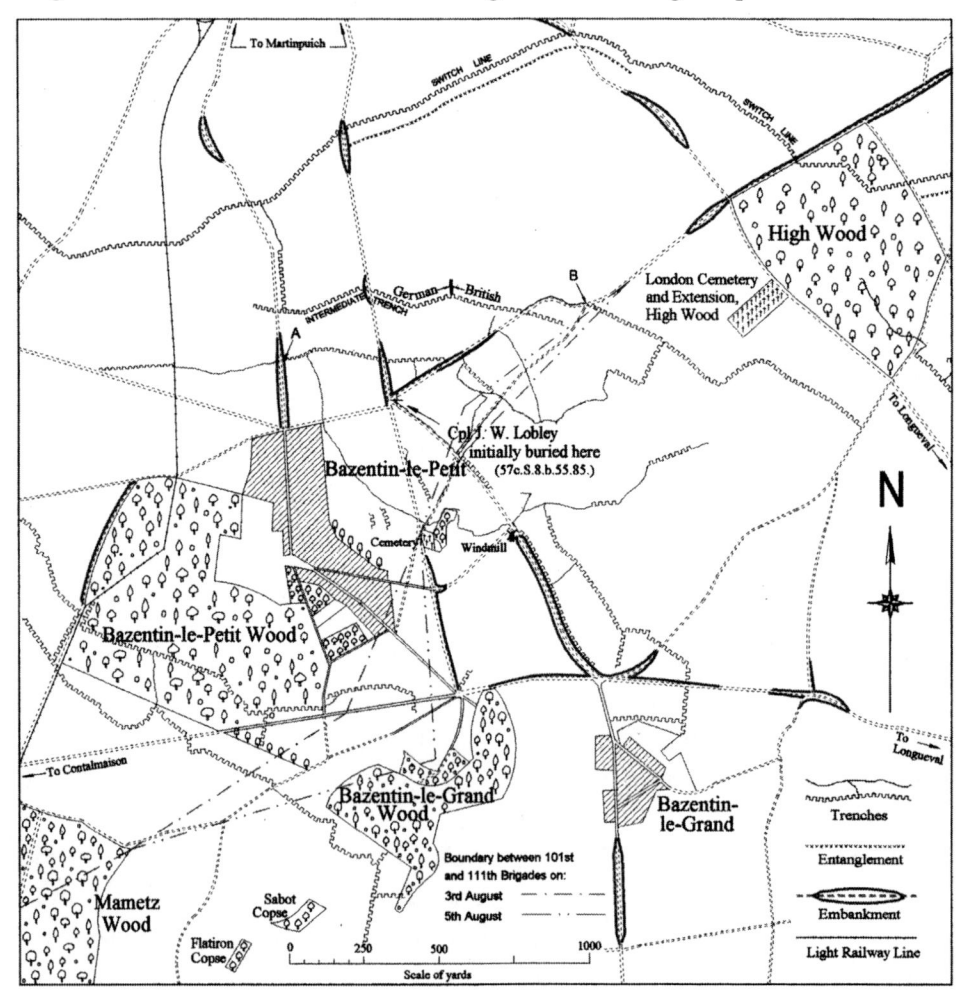

Map 9. *Bazentin–le-Petit.*

the entrance gate. Work on the Extension began after the Armistice, with burials from battlefield clearances, until the Second World War interrupted this in 1939. Burials recommenced after 1945 when almost 900 clearances were brought in from the First War battlefields and 165 Second World War casualties were also buried there. The cemetery, the third largest on the Somme, now contains a total of 3870 graves (3335 of those are men from the United Kingdom) of which 3114 are of unidentified soldiers.

The initial burial site of Cpl J.W. Lobley is to the right of the top of the farm implement. He now rests in London Cemetery, High Wood, Longueval, seen above the car in front of the wood in the background.

A line drawn from Cpl Lobley's grave (2nd from left) to the RHE of Bazentin-le-Petit Wood leads to his original burial site.

A private memorial. Lochnagar Crater and Memorial Cross – la Boisselle, Somme.

The Anglo-French Somme Monument and the British Memorial to the Missing at Thiepval.

During the Battle of Pozières Ridge the 10th Lincolns had been fighting in and around Bazentin-le-Petit from the end of July to mid August and I believe that is possibly when and where my father received the second wound that put him out of the war. In his notes he says,

> *'I returned to the Somme fighting later but after only four days I was severely wounded and my active service days were over'.*

On a postcard sent to my father by his sister Amy while he was in the Belmont hospital in Liverpool she had written,

> *'Friday – A letter came back here this morning from France that Mother sent to you on the 30th July. Not taken long has it.'*

(Unfortunately the stamp had been removed and the postmark with it.)

The Casualty List (*Grimsby News* 18th August) had briefly stated, 'Pte C. R. Frankish, Lincolns – wounded'. That would seem to put the time of his wounding to about 4th August seeing as the 10th Lincolns had been in a rear area refitting from 7th – 30th July and had gone back into the line on 31st July. Then only four days after returning to the fighting he received his second wound. His discharge certificate after serving 1 year and 54 days with the colours with the 6th Battalion, Leicestershire Regiment, during WW 2, dated 19th December 1940, states that he was 'Permanently unfit for any form of Military Service' and written into the section headed 'marks or scars' is the notation, 'GSW (gunshot wound), left hip'. (Apparently debris from that old wound had been making its presence felt, hence the discharge).

So within six weeks Barnetby had added three more names to its Roll of Honour. On Sunday 3rd September the Rev C. F. Brotherton had conducted a very impressive memorial service for those three most recent fallen soldiers, Corporals G. H. Smith and J. W. Lobley and Private J. W. Rapson, in St. Mary's Church. Similar memorial services had also been held for them in the Primitive and Wesleyan Chapels.

On that very same day Pte Percy Moss was wounded in both legs. Mr and Mrs Moss were informed of his having received his wounds during the heavy fighting on 3rd September and that he was in a hospital in France. This had been reported on the 15th/16th September when the Casualty List in the *Grimsby News* had again briefly stated, 'Pte C. R. Frankish, Lincolns – wounded.' (This appears to have been the normal practice for the Official Lists were often updated and thus the original names would be included along with those that had come to light later appertaining to a particular date.)

About that time some villagers were beginning to become a little apprehensive as to the possibility of air raids with the residents of Silver Street having decided to establish a system of patrols for those who wished to be notified in case of an air raid. Those forming the patrols were to work in pairs, remaining on guard for an agreed time, and in the event of the likelihood of a raid those wishing to be notified would be knocked up. (No further reports on this were found.)

Towards the end of September fund raisers had been out in force around the village making house-to-house collections in aid of the Star and Garter Fund. The collections, effected by Miss and Master Brotherton, Miss M. Meggitt, Miss Fish, Mrs Henson and others, had collected between them the sum of £6 5s for that fund.

The September 1916 Journal had three entries referring to Barnetby men. The first related to 1432 Pte E. Hutchinson, 10th Lincolns, a former fireman at Barnetby, who was in a hospital at Salford after having been wounded. The other entries related to two men reported as 'killed in action', which have already been dealt with, namely: 145 Pte A. Worrall, KOYLI, and 12577 L/Cpl G. H. Smith, 7th Lincolns.

Early in October Bert Cox, who had been wounded on 1st July in the Somme fighting, had been back home for a spell of ten days' well-earned leave. Considering the extent of his recent wounding he appeared to have made a very good recovery and was looking remarkably well.

Towards the month's end Pte Percy Moss, who had been wounded in both legs a few weeks earlier, had also been at home on leave and was making a slow recovery.

The next 'Barnetby Boys' fatality is in the chronological order of it occurring though it was to be a long time before it was officially announced and concerned…

21682 Pte William Henry Hinchsliff, 2nd Battalion, Lincolnshire Regiment

William Henry Hinchsliff, born in Barnetby (3)1890, was the only son of Charles and Lucy Hinchsliff and husband of Caroline Mary Hinchsliff (nee Marsden, born at Burringham, Lincs., (3) 1889) of 50 Kesteven Street, Lincoln, who he had married (4) 1915. The *Grimsby News* of 22nd August 1912 mentions that H. Hinchsliff had been appointed vice captain to the newly reformed Barnetby St Mary's football club.

In 1911 William had been employed by the GCR as a clerk and before joining the colours at Grimsby in February 1916 had been in the Chief Mechanical

Engineers Dept at Immingham. Following his enlistment William had received a short period of training and had then been drafted out to France where he was unfortunately killed in action on the 23rd October 1916.

The 8th Division (that included the 2nd Lincolns, 25th Brigade), following the severe losses incurred during the first four days of the 1st July Somme Offensive, had been sent to the relatively quiet Loos area. Back on the Somme the British advance during the October 1916 fighting had been very painfully slow. By mid October the 8th Division had been ordered back to the Somme. The 2nd Lincolns returned there on 16th October to Méaulte, south of Albert. On 19th October, a day of rain, the 2nd Lincolns were on their way from Méaulte to trenches near Lesbœufs, via Trônes Wood, where the conditions were absolutely abominable with water and mud everywhere. There the 8th Division was to relieve the 6th Division.

The 25th Brigade took over Gusty and Misty Trenches; the 23rd Brigade was on its right and the 24th Brigade on its left. During the night of 19th/20th October the 2nd Lincolns relieved the 8th Bedfords (16th Brigade, 6th Division), and took over the right sector of 25th Brigade's front line that formed a salient in the enemy line facing Zenith and Eclipse Trenches.

Between the 20th and 22nd October, with an improvement in the weather, both sides had been actively pounding each other's positions with artillery. The British artillery activity was part of a preliminary bombardment in preparation for an assault towards le Transloy now the weather was more favourable. The attack, to be carried out by XIV Corps (4th and 8th Divisions), was in co-operation with a French attempt to take Saillisel on the dominating high ground on their right. Apart from assisting the French the purpose of the operation was to make way for a later assault on le Transloy by gaining ground within striking distance of that village.

The 8th Division's objectives were as follows: 23rd Brigade was to capture Zenith and Orion Trenches and set up a line past them; 25th Brigade was to take the rest of Zenith Trench and advance the line to the right to meet up with that of 23rd Brigade's and, on the left, establish a line from the Eclipse/Zenith junction through to Misty Trench; 24th Brigade, with its right sector well advanced, was to have its left battalion take Mild Trench and straighten the line towards its right sector.

The 2nd Lincolns, in entirely inadequate trenches (6th Division troops had not improved on them very much on account of enemy activity and rain impeding their efforts), prepared for the attack on the enemy positions in Zenith trench. The attack was initially timed for 11.30 a.m. on 23rd October but was postponed until 2.30 p.m. because of fog. The 2nd Lincolns were to go into the attack using W and Z companies as the two front line assault companies, W being on the right and Z on the left, leaving its X and Y companies in support.

At zero hour, and keeping close up to the creeping barrage, the assault went ahead in four lines with the 2nd Middlesex, 23rd Brigade, on the 2nd Lincolns right and the 2nd Rifle Brigade, 25th Brigade, on the left, and initially all went well. Earlier the enemy had been seen attempting to get back into Eclipse Trench from Zenith Trench but Zenith had been so badly damaged by the British bombardment that it had become blocked up and was consequently fairly crammed with enemy troops. That part of Zenith Trench was opposite the advancing line of Lincolns and an enemy officer, determined that his men should stand and fight, climbed up onto the parapet and ran along it encouraging them to stand on the trench fire-step. The resultant rapid rifle-fire stopped the Lincolns' attack in its tracks with heavy losses. The second wave had that rifle-fire and machine-gun fire to contend with and never reached Zenith Trench either.

The 2nd Middlesex, 23rd Brigade, plus a few Lincolns of W and Y companies on their right, was the sole unit of those mentioned above to reach its objective, the 2nd Rifle Brigade having fared no better with their assault than the 2nd Lincolns. On the extreme left the 2nd East Lancashire (24th Brigade) took Mild Trench but failed to straighten the line out to their right. At 5 p.m. the 2nd Lincolns were collected and moved back to Rose Trench in Brigade support. An attack that night on Zenith Trench by 1st R. Irish Rifles and 2nd R. Berks (25th Brigade) also failed, hampered by rain. A later attack planned for 8th Division on 25th October was postponed due to continuing rain. The Division was relieved between 29th/31st October by 17th Division (its 7th Borders and 7th Lincolns (51st Brigade) took Zenith Trench on 2nd November).

Beside the Guedecourt – Beaulencourt road, in an area of land approximately in line with Zenith Trench and near where Mild and Stormy Trenches once met, a Newfoundland 'Caribou' Memorial overlooks the fields where the le Transloy action took place. However, the view towards le Transloy from the former Zenith Trench position is interrupted by two main transport routes, the A1 *Autoroute du Nord* and the high-speed railway *Ligne TGV,* that run side by side slightly to the west of the alignment of the former Castor and Pollux Trench positions.

The 2nd Lincolns, having gone into that action with sixteen officers and four hundred and seventy men, had lost a total of thirteen officers and two hundred and seventy-two men. Of the officer casualties five had been killed, eight wounded and two had subsequently died from their wounds, whilst among the casualties of the men twenty-three had been killed, one hundred and twenty-nine wounded and one hundred and twenty were missing.

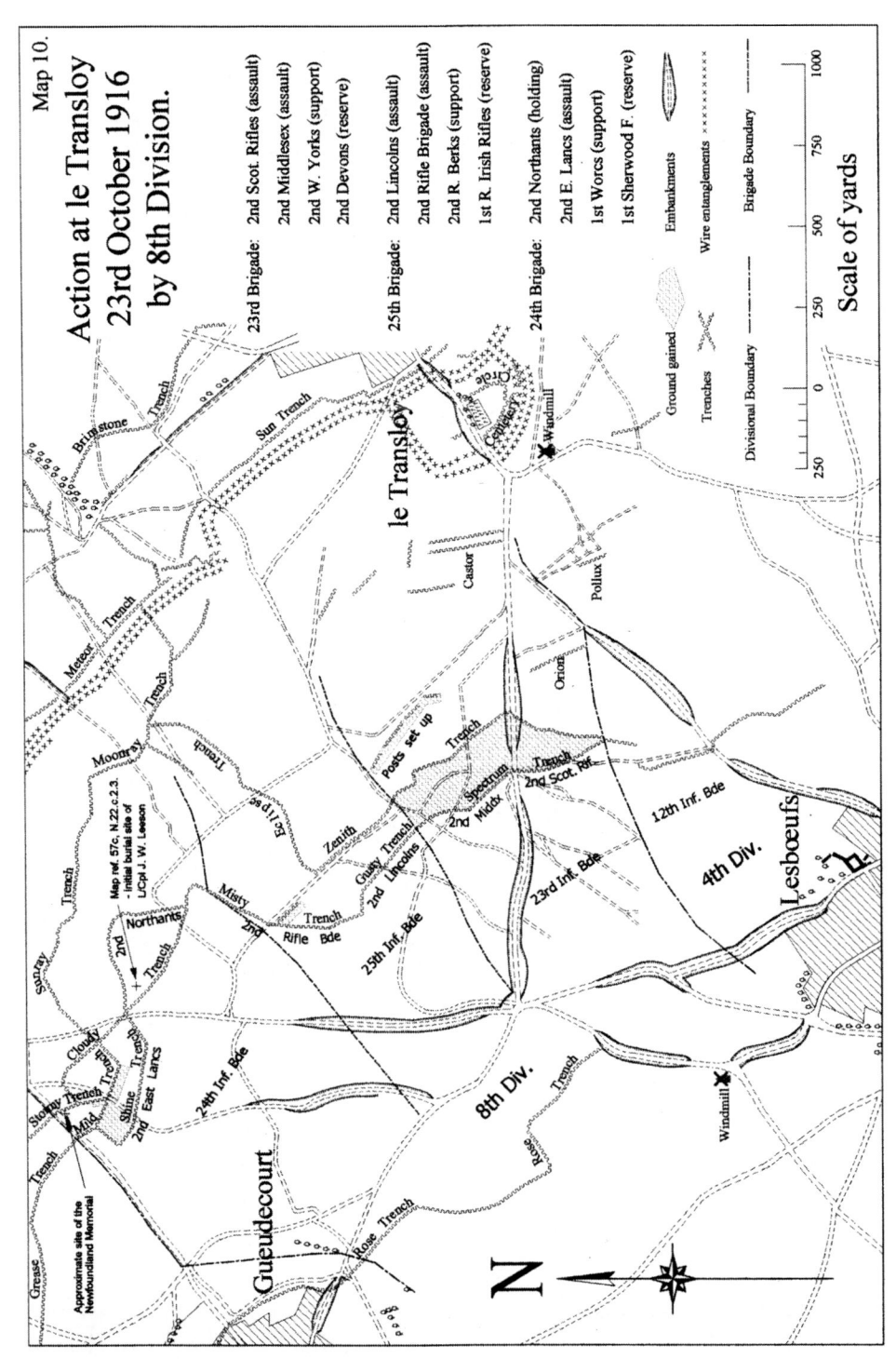

Map 10. *le Transloy.*

Pte William Henry Hinchsliff, aged 26 years, was killed in action that 23rd October day 1916. William, who has no known grave, is commemorated by name on the Somme Memorial to the Missing at Thiepval, Pier 1, Face C. He is also named on the headstone of his parent's grave in St Mary's Churchyard, Barnetby and the GCR Memorial at Sheffield. (A number of unknown Lincolns killed that same day are buried in Bancourt British Cemetery, possibly removed there from Cloudy Trench Cemetery or other battlefield cemeteries in the vicinity used at that time.)

Another 2nd Lincolns man also killed that day was 22847 L/Cpl John William Leeson, of Brigg, aged 29, father of Mrs Edna Wells, of Barnetby. Originally buried on the battlefield at map reference 57c, N.22c.2.3., in what was probably Cloudy Trench Cemetery, he was later re-buried in Bancourt British Cemetery (Plot III, Row L, Grave 11), approximately 4 km. east of Bapaume.

The Thiepval Memorial, the CWGC's largest, commemorates the names of 73,350 men from the United Kingdom (the figure varies as bodies are found and identified) and 850 South Africans, who fell in the Somme area before 21st March 1918. Thiepval Memorial is also the Anglo-French Somme Memorial, indicated by the French Tricolour and the British Union Flag, which occasionally fly from the Memorial top. This symbol of Anglo-French cooperation extends to the Cemetery at the rear of the Memorial, which contains the graves of 300 British and 300 French unknown soldiers. There the inscription on the base of the Cross of Sacrifice reads, *'That the World may remember the sacrifice of the two and a half million dead here have been laid side by side soldiers of France and of the British Empire in eternal comradeship.'*

About the end of October/beginning of November a local girl, Miss Baldwin, had the misfortune of having been injured in an accident whilst engaged on essential war work. She had been employed on the manufacture of munitions at a factory in Gainsborough when the mishap occurred that had taken her thumb off and she had been returned to her home.

The October Journal listed two clerks from Barnetby Traffic Dept as having enlisted, namely Robert Baxter and W. Richardson. (The former is on the Roll of Honour the latter is not.) A. Worrall, previously shown as 'killed' in September's Journal, was named as a Prisoner of War.

During November Pte C. R. Frankish, my father, was at home on leave but making a slow recovery following his second wounding on the Somme. At some time following this wounding in the left hip my father had been hospitalised at Belmont Military Hospital, Liverpool, and whilst there had the good fortune of receiving regular visits from his sister Amy who at that time was living at Leigh in Lancashire. It is not known how long he was in hospital, but postmarks on

Pte C. R. Frankish with his sister Amy. The two vertical bars on his left cuff are wound stripes. His cap badge is that of the Notts and Derby Regiment (No 79814). At some stage he also had a Labour Corps number, 239514. These two numbers are on the cover of his Soldier's Small Book (Army Form B 50) but nothing is written in the book to explain them!

some of the postcards he received from his sister date from 7th September to 6th October 1916. There is also mention of a second hospital on one postcard and my mother had spoken of his having been at Fazakerley, Lancashire. I do not know whether the reference on that postcard is to the Fazakerley hospital, but by all accounts his sister thought *'Belmont was splendid compared to the other place'.*

Sometime during the week ending 18th November the Co-Op management had organised a whist drive that was held on the Co-Op premises in aid of the Barnetby War Fund. Messers Vickers senior and junior, Mr Carter, Mr Williamson and the Co-Op staff had donated the prizes. There had been a good attendance at this social occasion but unfortunately the amount raised had not been mentioned in the paper.

The next report of that same week stated that Pte Langley, who had been working in France over 12 months with the GCR relaying gang, and Pte Hugh Dawson, Pte Maurice Allison and L/Cpl Thomas Rowe were now on leave. When their leave was completed Pte Dawson and Pte Allison were due to leave 'for somewhere abroad.' Presumably the GCR relaying gang reference is attributed to Pte Langley (this is confusing as the Journal refers to a relayer F. Langley and platelayer F. Lansley! Are they one and the same person? F. Lansley is recorded as joining the RE Railway Troops 111th Coy. Is that the aforementioned GCR relaying gang?) I do not think this refers to the report of 3rd/4th March mentioned earlier.

That same 18th November newspaper also wrote briefly about Mrs F. Barnett. At that time she was living with her parents Mr and Mrs J. Overton, having recently received news that her husband, Sgt Fred Barnett of the Light Trench Mortar Battery – no regiment given – had been wounded but she had not been given any details.

A group of Railway Troops of 111th Coy, RE. Sapper F. Lansley is somewhere in the picture. Unfortunately the only recognisable person is Lt S. E. Fay, son of the Chairman of the GCR. At one time S.E. Fay, as part of the training of a higher grade railway clerk, had been at Brigg. All men of the 111th Coy Railway Troops, RE, (below) were formerly employed by the GCR.

At Applepie Camp, Longmoor, February 1915, before leaving for 'somewhere in Flanders'.

Far worse information though was shortly to come to another Barnetby family for on the morning of 25th November Mr and Mrs F. Gostelow received sad news of their son...

12513 Pte Cyril Gostelow, 8th Battalion, Lincolnshire Regiment

Cyril Gostelow, born in Barnetby (1)1897, was the youngest son of Frederick and Alice Gostelow of Queen's Road, Barnetby. In 1911 the family were living at Post Office Lane with Cyril employed as a day boy farm labourer. A bright young fellow in his late teens Cyril had been employed by the GCR as an engine cleaner at Barnetby Locomotive Depot. He had signed on immediately on the declaration of war and from the time of being drafted abroad in August 1915 had not had any home leave for at least fifteen months. He was killed in action on 15th November 1916, aged 19 years.

The 8th Lincolns, (63rd Brigade, 21st Division), having previously been deployed up in the Armentières area, where they remained until the end of March 1916, had then moved down to the Somme area for the July offensive. There, on 1st July, the opening of the 1916 Somme offensive, the part of the 8th Lincolns in the fighting was in support of the 63rd Brigade attack towards Fricourt. The 8th Lincolns remained in that area until relieved on 4th July when they moved down to Dernancourt.

From there the 63rd Brigade moved to Talmas, between Amiens and Doullens, and by 7th July had been transferred to 37th Division having been exchanged with its 110th Brigade.

Save for relieving the 1/5th Lincolns at Gommecourt on 10th/11th July the 8th Lincolns took no further part in any action on the Somme until 13th-18th November – the Battle of the Ancre. By then the 63rd Brigade had moved to the area Léalvillers/Acheux.

On 12th November the battalion marched from Lucheaux and billeted in tents in Acheux Wood and remained encamped there all the next day, during which time other units of V Corps carried out attacks on German positions north of the Ancre.

During the evening of 14th November the 8th Lincolns, preparatory to the 63rd Brigade's (37th Division) relief of units of the 63rd (Royal Naval) Division later that night, marched to a camp near Martinsart. The 63rd (Royal Naval) Division, having successfully captured positions in and around Beaucourt-sur-l'Ancre, was duly relieved that night and the 8th Lincolns took over parts of those positions taken by the 63rd Division on the day previous including some of Beaucourt village. The enemy subjected those Beaucourt positions to continual shelling all the next day (see map 11).

On 15th November, Pte Cyril Gostelow died in the presence of his friend Pte John Waite, also of the 8th Lincolns, having received mortal wounds in his chest possibly as a result of that continuous enemy shell-fire.

The 8th Lincolns were in action on 15th November but no details are given apart from a reference to patrols being sent out at night. The 63rd Brigade, with sending patrols out at night, had slowly gained ground and on reaching Muck and Railway Trenches found them to be deserted. By the 18th the Lincolns had

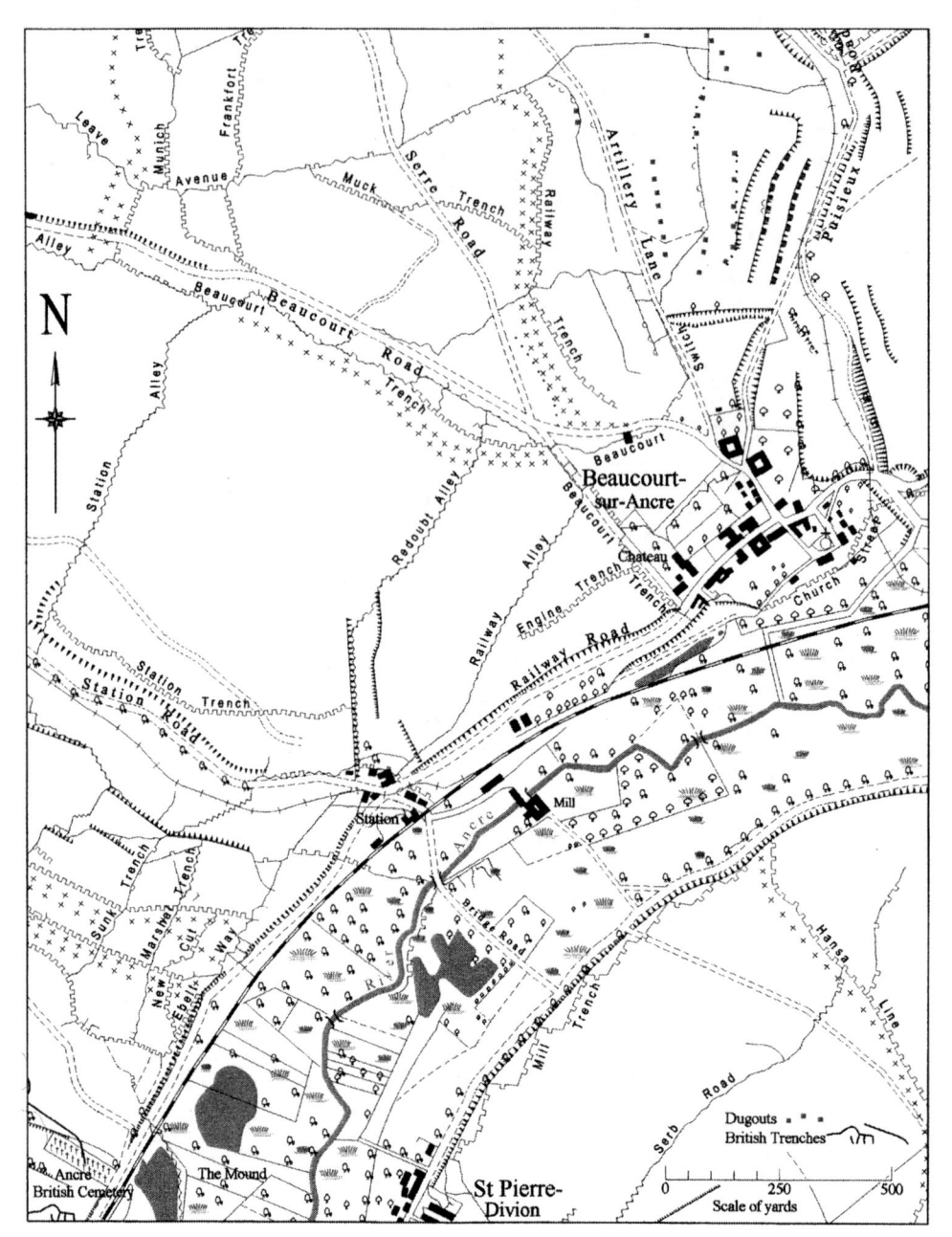

Map 11. *Beaucourt-sur-Ancre.*

established posts in Muck Trench, along with units from 111th Brigade, but did not participate in the attack by 63rd Brigade.

The battalion remained in those trenches until 20th November in truly dreadful winter weather conditions of rain and snow. Very heavy shelling had pulverised trenches and the ground surrounding them into a mass of glutinous mud. The 8th Lincolns were in reserve throughout the 21st/22nd November and on 23rd November they took over the trenches at Beaumont-Hamel until the 26th November when they were relieved by the 1/21st Battalion London Regiment and moved to Mailly-Maillet to begin the necessary reorganisation to accommodate and train the newly arrived draft.

The 8th Lincolns casualties for the period 14th-20th November were 2 officers wounded and 1 missing; 14 other ranks killed, 115 wounded, 8 missing and 35 evacuated sick.

Pte Cyril Gostelow, killed in action on 15th November 1916, was among the early burials in Ancre River No. 1 British Cemetery at Beaumont-Hamel. It then contained 517 graves, mainly of men of the 36th (Ulster) Division killed in July 1916 and the 63rd (Royal Naval) Division, of which many preferred the name Royal Naval Division to the Army title of 63rd Division. After the war when the Cemetery was enlarged and seven small battlefield Cemeteries from the area were closed and duly brought in making a total of 2,497 graves, mostly 1916 deaths, the name changed to Ancre British Cemetery.

C. Gostelow headstone.

The Cemetery, sitting atop a high bank at the side of the Hamel – Beaucourt road, is almost hidden from view. The clue to its presence is the name on the bank retaining wall by the entrance. The left bank of the Cemetery was once in No-Man's-Land having been a forward trench from which, on 13th November, 1916, men of the 63rd Division launched their attack on enemy positions in and around Beaucourt.

Cyril Gostelow's headstone in Ancre Cemetery (plot 3, row B, grave 55) has a personal inscription that reads, 'Jesus Saviour Pilot Me'. On my first visit to the Cemetery I read the inscription and it struck me as unusual but gave it no further thought until the summer of 1999 when asked to choose a hymn for the village 'Songs of Praise' service. I came across, 'Jesus Saviour, pilot me', by Hopper Edward (1818-88) in a hymnbook. It struck me as being a most suitable and apt choice and what a meaningful little hymn it is:

Jesus, Saviour, pilot me
Over life's tempestuous sea;
Unknown waves before me roll,

Hiding rock and treacherous shoal;
Chart and compass come from Thee:
Jesus, Saviour, pilot me.

As a mother stills her child,
Thou canst hush the ocean wild;
Boisterous waves obey Thy will,
When Thou say'st to them, 'Be still!'.
Wondrous Sovereign of the sea,
Jesus, Saviour, pilot me.

When at last I near the shore,
And the fearful breakers roar
'Twixt me and the peaceful rest,
Then, while leaning on Thy breast,
May I hear Thee say to me,
'Fear not, I will pilot thee.'

Was this Cyril's, or his family's, favourite hymn and with it having a nautical reference was the family aware that many of the original burials in that cemetery were sailors and Royal Marines of the Naval Division? I will never know the actual reason why those four simple words were chosen but the hymn was selected for the 'Barnetby Songs of Praise – 2000' and sung as a special tribute dedicated to Cyril and the 'Barnetby Boys'.

Although the Journal Supplementary List of GC Railwaymen who joined the Colours does not refer to Cyril being killed in action his name is on the GCR Memorial, Sheffield. In St Mary's Churchyard the headstone of the family grave also bears his name and the following inscription, *'In a land far distant, nobly he did his duty – but the sacrifice was great.'*

Towards the end of November several more ladies of the village had taken up war work. Miss Ffrench had gone to Lady Sheffield's Hospital at Normanby, having volunteered to become a Red Cross nurse. Seven others had commenced employment locally around the 20th of the month when they were engaged to take on various duties in the Maltings.

Around that time there had been a number of soldiers billeted in the locality and it was felt that a suitable venue should be provided for them where they could have the means to amuse themselves by indulging in all manner of indoor games during their off-duty hours. To that end the Co-Operative stores management assented to open their rooms to them for four nights every week where they would be able to pursue those activities. For those wishing to spend a little

Pte Cyril Gostelow's headstone, central in the third row, surrounded by at least nine headstones of 63rd (Royal Naval) Division personnel.

View of Ancre British Cemetery looking towards the entrance: beyond is the Ancre Valley with the Thiepval Ridge on the horizon. Among the trees on the horizon is the Ulster Tower Memorial. (1,250 metres in rear of the cemetery is the Newfoundland Memorial Park.)

time writing to their families and loved ones a quiet room was provided where, thanks to some kind assistance from Mrs Lowish, free writing material was made available for their use.

The November Journal named three Barnetby men in the Killed in Action list, all of whom have been mentioned previously. They were J. W. Rapson, A. Tweed and J. W. Lobley. There was also a brief obituary to J. W. Rapson, complete with a photograph of him.

The newspapers of 1st/2nd December that reported Cyril Gostelow's death had added a small paragraph at the end saying that Pte J. Waite, who was with Cyril when he died, was suffering from trench fever in a French hospital. (Trench fever was a highly acute infectious disease transmitted by that verminous scourge of the trenches – the louse. It was unknown in civil communities, and thereby the medical profession, but became prevalent during the war in the extremely unsanitary conditions that prevailed in the trenches.)

With Christmas approaching the men of the village at war were uppermost in people's minds. Families would no doubt have been making private arrangements for their menfolk's welfare, but organisations too thought of their associates, such as the Primitive Methodist Christian Endeavour that sent all of its members who were then serving with the forces small parcels for Christmas.

While most of the village folk would be busy making preparations for the approaching festivities of Christmas the Hinchsliff family, already anxious with having heard nothing at all of their son Henry for six weeks, received the depressing notification that he was missing – a sure damper for their Christmas.

The Saturday 22nd/23rd December editions of the papers contained a short report of the first annual statement of the receipts and expenditure of the Barnetby War Fund for the year ending 30th November last. The receipts from subscriptions etc. came to £91 1s 2½d; the weekly house-to-house collections realised £96 14s 3d making a total of £187 15s 5½d. On the expenditure side £31 had gone to the YMCA of which £16 had been specially raised or subscribed for that purpose. £12 had been presented to the Red Cross including the sum of £5 purposely raised for that cause. Donations amounting to £5 each had been made to the hospitals at Grimsby and Lincoln and the Serbian Relief Fund. The cost of providing bread for the prisoners of war came to £16 1s. The purchase of materials for parcels to be sent out to the soldiers, plus the postage, had come to £55 18s 0½d. The cost of the shirting and wool had totalled £16 4s 10½d and material for making sandbags £1 15s 9d, making a total of £148 9s 8d. That had left the fund with a balance in hand of £39 5s 9½d.

In addition to the parcels of food, and the like, the following articles had also been sent out to the soldiers: 38 shirts, 61 pairs of socks, 9 pairs of mittens and 24 scarves. There had also been mention of the contribution that the village had made towards the National Egg Collection Scheme for wounded soldiers in that 44,280 eggs had been sent in from the Barnetby depot, with the village having supplied 5,463 eggs and contributed £9 6s 6d. The school children had

Pte C. R. Frankish convalescing at Barnetby in 1916 (late) or 1917. The venue is possibly at the photographer's house. His cap badge is that of the Notts. & Derby Regiment.
Photo: E. Waby, Barnetby

sent 2,673 eggs and £2 4s in money. So all in all the War Fund had had a fairly successful year and the village could rightly feel proud of its achievements.

1916 was fast approaching the year-end. The war that had begun in August 1914 and 'would be over by Christmas' of that year was not due to be finished this Christmas either. What would the future hold? Would it be brought to an end during 1917?

5
1917

THE third Christmas of the Great War had just been observed and had passed on into history with no sign of an end to the conflict anywhere in sight. The opposing armies in France and Flanders were still facing each other across narrow strips of ground commonly known as No Man's Land. From their trenches each side did little more than to observe the other's positions for any movement and signs of unusual activity. Apart from the intermittent raids on the other's positions interspersed with sporadic harassing artillery fire, both sides had waged a constant battle against a common enemy – the winter weather. That enemy when mobilized could muster three formidable weapons – intense cold, wind and rain. In its various combinations when coupled with a rain-induced concoction – mud, it made any work extremely arduous and the existence of the troops in those conditions one of considerable acute discomfort.

Shortly after the New Year had begun a report appeared in the local press giving out that another member of the Denton family had been wounded. This time Herbert was the unlucky one. 'Bert', having been wounded in the left forearm, after receiving treatment in a hospital in France was said to be progressing favourably. That report, under the sub-heading of 'A NOBLE SACRIFICE', went on to state that Bert had consented to give an infusion of his own blood to save the life of an officer. Bert was the third of four sons who had joined up but Ernest, who had been severely gassed in 1915, had since received his discharge from the Army. The Denton's also had a soldier son-in-law in their family with Pte William Ponting having married their daughter Mandy just over two years ago.

On Saturday 13th January a man well known in the district, Private A.W. Robinson, RMLI, eldest son of Mr and Mrs G. Robinson, married Miss H.E. Moore of Lowestoft in St Margaret's Church of that parish. Private Robinson, having volunteered his services upon the outbreak of war, was currently serving in HMS —. Before enlisting A. W. Robinson had been a power signal lineman's labourer at Immingham. His name first appears in the Journal in November 1912 when he was appointed as a locking fitter's labourer in the Signal Dept at Barnetby. In May 1914 he was transferred as a labourer to the Signal Dept at Grimsby Docks; the October 1914 Journal then records his transfer as a Signal Dept labourer from Grimsby Docks to Immingham.

Fund raising got off to a good start in the New Year on the evening of Wednesday 17th January with a concert in the school, organised by Mrs Lowish, in aid of the War Fund and the Prisoner of War Fund. A well-known group of Scunthorpe singers had freely given of their services to put on a musical entertainment. The concert had gone down well with the audience and had been a highly successful venture for the promoters having raised £11 10s. All credit and thanks were due to Mrs Lowish for all the hard work she had put into arranging the event.

Throughout January the War Fund Committee had similarly been busy, having by the fourth week already made up and despatched 67 parcels since the beginning of the year with more having been prepared ready to be sent out before the end of the month.

Near the end of the month, during a meeting of the Independent Order of Rechabites, condolences had been offered to Mrs Emma Smith following the death of a very willing and active member of that Order, her son, Brother G. H. Smith. The reader will recall that he had been killed in action on 3rd July 1916, during the early days of the Somme offensive.

W. Borrell, a porter at Scawby, is named in the Journal of January 1917 as having enlisted. The Barnetby Roll of Honour lists a William Borrill. The name is spelt differently but I am left wondering is it the same man? The Journal also records two men 'killed in action'. (Both men's details have already been dealt with.) Fireman 12540 Pte C. F. Andrews, Lincolns (previously reported missing) and clerk 21682 Pte W. H. Hinchcliffe, 3rd Lincs, both from Immingham Depot. Again there are spelling differences adding weight to the previous question.

February began with a mixture of village news. Gunner Henry Stephenson was home on leave from abroad. Doubtless the Stephenson family were pleased to see him safely home if only briefly. Two soldiers at home at the beginning of the month were Corporal Charles P. Blanchard of the Dispatch Riders and 'Bert' Denton, recently promoted to Lance Corporal, home for three weeks no doubt to recuperate from his recent wounding in France.

Word had also arrived home that Henry Lowish had been promoted to Sergeant. At the time Henry was serving with the Lincolnshire Yeomanry in the Middle East having been out there since the end of November 1915. He was currently convalescing after having recently come down with fever and been treated in a Cairo hospital.

Henry Martin Lowish was born at the Manor, Barnetby, on Tuesday 17th November 1891. I do not know when Henry joined the Yeomanry but he had written a postcard to his parents from the annual camp at Belton Park, near Grantham, in 1911. At that camp he had participated in and won the recruit's one-mile horse race. Henry also attended the training camps at Louth, Grimsthorpe and Riseholme.

When HM King George V officially opened the Immingham Docks on 22nd July 1912, Henry had been on parade in B Squadron, 1/1st Lincolnshire Yeomanry, as part of King George V's mounted escort.

Following mobilisation on 4th August 1914, the Regiment moved to Norfolk, part of the North Midland Mounted Brigade, 1st Mounted Division. Near the end of October the Regiment embarked in the SS Mercian at Southampton. On 27th October 1915 SS Mercian, the troopship taking the Lincolnshire Yeomanry out to the Middle East, got under way – destination Salonica.

Sergeant 1380 Henry Lowish.

Henry's first experience with fighting was in the western Mediterranean on 3rd November 1915. Not long after the SS Mercian left Gibraltar she was shelled by a surfaced U-boat causing 103 casualties to the men and their horses, including some killed. I remember Henry telling me of that encounter and showing me a framed picture of the Mercian and newspaper cuttings recounting the skirmish.

Initially, the Lincolnshire Yeomanry had been bound for Salonica, but en route the ship was diverted to Egypt. Intelligence had unearthed a Turkish plan to attack the Suez Canal from Sinai while the Sennussi Arabs attacked Egypt from the Western Desert.

The North Midlands Mounted Brigade (originally 1/1st Lincolnshire, 1/1st Leicestershire and 1/1st Staffordshire Yeomanry) took only the Lincolnshire and Staffordshire Yeomanry to Egypt where the 1/1st East Riding of Yorkshire Yeomanry joined them. Henry spent most of his wartime service in Egypt and Palestine with the Lincolnshire Yeomanry. In Egypt, April 1916, the North Midlands Mounted Brigade became the 22nd Mounted Brigade then operating with the Western Frontier Force. In February 1917, when the Brigade moved to Palestine, it became a unit of the Anzac Mounted Division. In July 1917 the Brigade formed part of the Yeomanry Mounted Division (Desert Mounted Corps) that included the Anzac and Australian cavalry. On 7th April 1918 the Regiment along with 1/1st East Riding Yeomanry (both now dismounted) left the 22nd Mounted Brigade to form 'D' Battalion, Machine Gun Corps and remained out in Palestine until May 1918. (Henry's service number in the Machine Gun Corps was 55024.)

As such they went to France having left their horses in Palestine for Indian Cavalry units that had arrived dismounted from France. In France they were trained as machine-gunners to become part of 102nd (Lincolnshire and East Riding Yeomanry) Battalion, Machine Gun Corps. Thus did the one-time mounted Lincolnshire Yeomen finish their war service as horse-less machine-gunners in First Army on the Western Front.

On 21st May 1924, Henry attended the unveiling of the Cavalry War Memorial in Hyde Park. He later donated his Yeomanry dress uniform to the Lincoln Museum of Lincolnshire Life.

At the end of January rather alarming news had been received by the Thompson family when they were informed that their son, L/Cpl F. Thompson (Bandsman), 1/5th Lincolns, had sustained serious injuries as the result of an accident in France. From the initial information received by the Thompson's it appeared that while he was in the course of taking down some buildings they had collapsed and fallen on him causing injuries to his back and legs. As a result of this he was being treated for his injuries in a hospital in France. About a week later, following on from that earlier report, worse information arrived when the Thompson family received the tragic news they must undoubtedly have dreaded ever receiving concerning their son…

1037 L/Cpl Frederick Thompson, 1/5th Battalion, Lincolnshire Regiment.

Moses and Mrs Julia Thompson received the grievously devastating news that their son *L/Cpl Frederick Thompson*, aged 34? (born at Barnetby (2)1881), had passed away in a hospital in France on 3rd February 1917 following fatal injuries he had received to his back and legs in an accident in France. That accident had occurred whilst Fred was procuring firewood from an old building. Tragically, the building's roof had collapsed and fallen onto him.

Fred had been apprenticed to his father as a shoemaker. In 1911 Fred was working as a machine-operating labourer in a Gainsborough engineering works, lodging at 11 Old Dispensary Buildings, Little Church Lane, Gainsborough. It is recorded that he enlisted at Gainsborough and lived at South Cockerington,

Lincolnshire. He was serving in France within six months of the commencement of hostilities. A member of Barnetby Band, a newspaper referred to him as Bandsman L/Cpl F. Thompson but was this with regard to the Battalion Band or Barnetby Band?

When the 1/5th Lincolns, 138th Brigade, 46th Division, first arrived in France in February 1915, they were used initially in the areas around Ypres and Kemmel. During mid October the Battalion had participated in the action around the Hohenzollern Redoubt, south of la Bassée, from where in, November, it moved to Neuve Chapelle, whilst most of December had been spent in the vicinity of St Omer. In January 1916 the 46th Division went out to Egypt but only for a very short spell as it was suddenly ordered back to France in February and by 10th March it had moved near to Souchez relieving French troops – the 1/5th Lincolns being at Villers-au-Bois.

During April the 1/5th Lincolns were in a sector north of Arras before moving in May to the Foncquevillers/Gommecourt area where they were at the opening of the Somme offensive in July 1916. There, around midnight on 1st/2nd July, they took part in an aborted attack on enemy positions at Gommecourt. The Battalion remained in that general sector right through the autumn and on into the winter where, during January and February, it alternately manned the line trenches around Foncquevillers with the 1/4th Lincolns.

Those trenches, being full of water, made life almost unbearable for men off duty as often they had nowhere dry to sleep – except on the firing steps out in the open. There is reference in the Battalion War Diary (WO 95/2690) to 'water being above the thighs in places especially near *Colchester Street* – gumboots issued.' Some portions of their trenches became so uninhabitable that they had been secured with wire and left empty. By all accounts more time was being spent fighting the elements than the enemy but eventually, by sheer dogged hard work, those trenches were pumped out and cleared up to be made usable once more.

When the accident occurred to L/Cpl Frederick Thompson is unclear. On 22nd January, on being relieved by the 1/4th Lincolns, the 1/5th Lincolns went to Bienvillers-au-Bois, 3 km. north of Foncquevillers, in Brigade reserve. They remained there until 26th January when they relieved the 1/4th Lincolns in the line between Hannescamps and Foncquevillers. The 138th Brigade War Diary casualty return from 1/5th Lincolns for January 1917 shows one other rank wounded on 23rd January and one on 31st January. The 23rd January seems the more likely date when the mishap happened given that the newspapers reported the accident on 3rd February. That makes the whereabouts of the accident most likely to have been in the Bienvillers area while the battalion was in Brigade reserve; there the pressures would be somewhat relaxed with time perhaps to go out foraging for firewood. But that is pure conjecture. Is it any wonder then that L/Cpl Thompson went in search of firewood after existing in those diabolical conditions?

L/Cpl F. Thompson is buried in plot IV, row G, grave 11 of Warlincourt Halte British Cemetery, Saulty. His headstone inscription reads: 'God's Will Be Done'.

Between June 1916 and June 1917 four Casualty Clearing Stations used the Cemetery for burials and in May/June 1918, Field Ambulances. After the Armistice fifty-six graves from three from small Cemeteries used by Field Ambulance units – la Herlière, Courturelle and Gaudiempré, were concentrated into it, bringing the total of burials to 1,295, including 29 German prisoners buried there. As those Cemeteries were within 2–3 km. of Saulty, and with Gaudiempré being the nearest to Foncquevillers, I asked the CWGC if there was a record of previous burial for Fred in one. Unfortunately, the CWGC did not have documentation for concentration of graves into Warlincourt Halte Cemetery.

L/Cpl F. Thompson headstone.

As No 20 and No 43 Casualty Clearing Stations were using that Cemetery at the time Fred died I am confident one of those was the hospital referred to in the information his family received.

Initially, research into this project was carried out solely for the 'Barnetby Boys'. But I later decided to include a Somerby man named on a headstone in Somerby churchyard especially as I had not come across a memorial at Somerby. Then in February 1999 a parishioner pointed out a postcard sized tarnished brass memorial plaque, attached by a narrow brass strip to the rear of the lectern, bearing three names (see photos, Appendix 13). Information found relating to those three men is now included in chronological order.

The first man named on the Memorial Plaque in Somerby Church is…

50168 Lance Corporal Charles Frederick Wilson, 16th Battalion Sherwood Foresters (Notts and Derby Regiment)

Lance Corporal Charles Frederick Wilson, the son of Charles and Annie Elizabeth Wilson, of The Beeches, Burnham, Barton-on-Humber, was born at Irby (4, 1893). In 1911 the family was living at Somerby where Charles worked as a wagoner on a farm. He enlisted at Caistor and resided at Barton – little else is known. He died on 6th February 1917, and is buried in Vlamertinghe Military Cemetery, Ypres (Plot V, Row H, Grave 2). His headstone inscription reads, *'In remembrance of a dear son and brother'.*

1st January 1917 saw the 16th Battalion Sherwood Foresters, part of 117th Brigade, 39th Division, in the Ypres Salient in the right sub sector of the Brigade line north of Ypres, roughly 1½ miles north-west of St Jean, and in the support billets on the canal bank (Yser Canal) and in the Chateau des Trios Tours (750 yards west of Brielen). On 13th January Christmas boxes, provided by the people of Derby, were handed out to the men. The following day substantial enemy activity blew in Ealing Communication Trench resulting in considerable delay with the battalion's relief later that day by the 14th Royal Welsh Fusiliers. After relief the battalion proceeded to 'B' Camp, just north of Brandhoek, near Poperinghe.

On 16th January the battalion celebrated a belated Christmas Day at 'B' Camp with Christmas fare provided for all ranks and next day most of the battalion attended a concert in a Church Army hut near 'B' Camp. 57 other ranks joined the battalion from base on 23rd January and a further 72 men joined on 25th January. Later that day the battalion relieved the 17th Sherwood Foresters as left support battalion on the Canal Bank at Kaaie (just north of Ypres) in the Wieltje sector. The 16th Sherwood Foresters War Diary (WO 95/2587) records the weather as extremely cold – the Yser Canal was frozen – and the men had to contend with a biting east wind and snow. Up until the battalion relieved the 17th Sherwood Foresters in the line on 30th January, in the left Wieltje section, time in support had been fairly quiet with only one man being wounded with a rifle bullet whilst on a wiring party the previous day. The relief had been carried out without incident.

Throughout the night of 1st February enemy machine-guns were very active and during this activity raided the 14th Hampshire's positions on the 16th Sherwood Forester's right. After relief by the 1/1st Hertfordshire Regiment on 4th February three companies went into support in Ypres and one went to Dragoon Farm, 400 yards south of Potijze. Next day the 16th Sherwood Foresters relieved the 16th Rifle Brigade in the left sub sector of the line, at Railway Wood, where enemy snipers were more active than usual.

C. F. Wilson headstone.

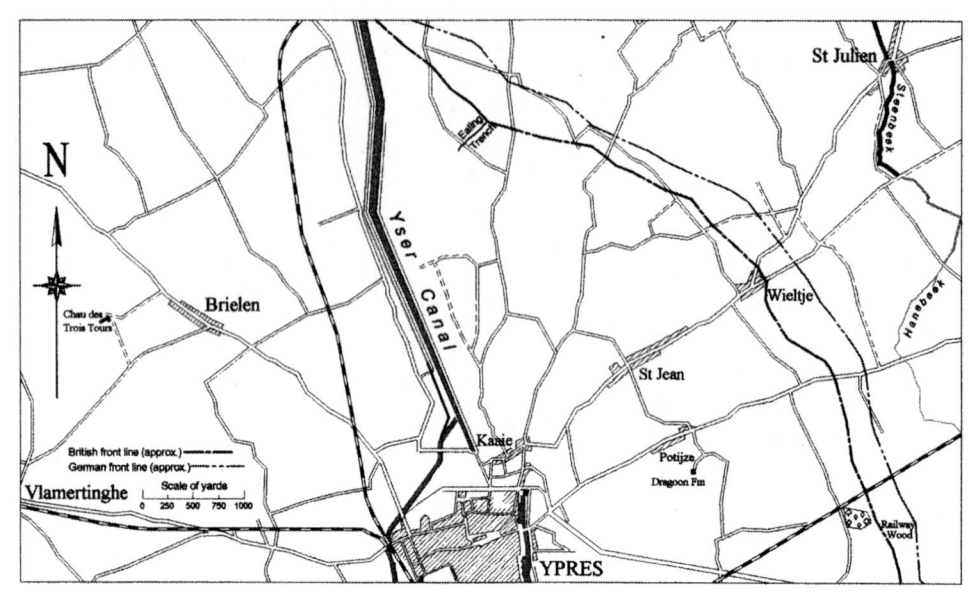

Map 12.

But it was not all one-sided for the 16th Sherwood's snipers claimed two enemy who were seen to fall. On 7th February the battalion was relieved by 16th Rifle Brigade and went to Ypres, leaving one company at Dragoon Farm. British artillery had been in action all day wire cutting in the sector; during the evening the battalion Light Trench Mortars registered on the enemy wire and throughout the night of the 6th the battalion Lewis gunners played on the gaps cut in the wire. The battalion War Diary records casualties of one man killed and two wounded. Apart from referring to a man wounded on 29th January those were the only other casualties recorded up to 7th February so presumably the fatal casualty was L/Cpl C. F. Wilson. His Service Documents appear to have been burnt.

French troops operating in Belgium during 1914 started Vlamertinghe Military Cemetery. Field Ambulances and fighting troops used it, looking after it carefully, until June 1917 when the adjacent land was required for a Military Railway and extension of the cemetery was prohibited. From then on the burials there were few. The cemetery contains a high number of Territorial graves particularly those from Lancashire units. During the early part of 1917 the 55th Division had a particular liking for this cemetery and endeavoured to bring in its dead from the front for burial. Units also took care to bury side by side those of their own that had fallen around the same time. There are also three German graves and a number of burials from the 1939-45 War. With a total of 1164 burials only 18 of those are of unidentified soldiers.

Fund raising continued to be on going with a whist drive held in the Co-Op rooms on the evening of Wednesday 14th February 'to provide amusements for soldiers!' as one newspaper put it. Another newspaper specified it was for the provision of books and games etc., for the RFC. On this occasion Mrs Lowish, Mr Wood and Mr E. Vickers had donated the prizes with the refreshments also being provided by Mrs Lowish. Whist was once very popular and competitive whist drives were a regular occurrence in the village but it appears to have died a natural death.

At the annual meeting of the Women's Adult School a record of their achievements during 1916 had been presented showing that quite considerable assistance had been given to various causes. In all £6 15s had been contributed towards providing parcels for local soldiers; the YMCA had received £4, the Waifs and Strays £1 10s, and the sum of £1 had been given to each of the following – Lincoln Hospital, Grimsby Hospital and the Motor Ambulance. Miss Harriet Wilson had duly won the attendance prize having attended on 36 out of a possible 37 occasions.

By the end of the month more of Barnetby's soldiers had been home on leave. Sapper William Percival was on a six-day leave after having only latterly completed a brief training period with the Royal Engineers. He had been described as looking remarkably well, to use a seemingly standard phrase of the time. Pte John Waite had been at home on sick leave recovering from trench foot after having received treatment in a hospital. Two other men seen around the village about that time and no doubt enjoying a well-earned rest from the dangers of the trenches were Pte Jesse Dawson and Pte Bert Cox.

The Journal for February 1917 carried one or two items of local interest. First there was mention of S. M. Bowness of North Kelsey, a former engine cleaner from Immingham Dept, having won the Military Medal. The next brief item related to 1434 Pte R. Bilton, E. Yorks, a platelayer in the Engineers Dept at Barnetby, who had been wounded and was currently in hospital at Liverpool. (His name is not on the Roll of Honour for Barnetby so presumably he lived in one of the outlying villages.) The final item concerned 'The Lord Charles Beresford Appeal' for smokes for wounded soldiers and sailors. The report gave details of the amount collected courtesy of Gorton Locomotive Running Dept, GCR. Out of a total of £48 8s 2d, Immingham, including Grimsby and Barnetby, had contributed £7 8s.

Another Dawson, Hugh, was mentioned in the papers the following week but the item had been very difficult to read even with magnification (the condition of some papers when they were recorded on microfilm was often very poor). The 10th March issue of the *Hull Times* was a case in point with one word in the report being almost obliterated (I've put what I think the word was but I could easily be wrong.) Pte Hugh Dawson of the Lincolns, who had been in France, was now in hospital suffering from . . . *measles*? It was definitely not trench fever for the item went on to report Pte W. Smith as having been hospitalised suffering from that complaint. (The village Roll of Honour bears the names of two W. Smiths in the returned servicemen's columns, Walter and William, so which one is being referred to here is anybody's guess!)

The local papers for the week ending 24th March had more village news than usual. Firstly they mentioned that Cpl Charles Percy Blanchard, of the Motor Dispatch Riders, who had only been married just over sixteen months ago, had been at home on leave and left for the front to return to duty. There then followed two heart-rending items, one very brief but its simple message was nonetheless tragic, that would bring distressing sadness to two more Barnetby families that had a soldier brother and a soldier son on active service somewhere over in France.

Earlier that week Mr and Mrs J. Holt, of Railway Street, had been recipients of grave news concerning Mrs Holt's brother...

443323 Lance Corporal George William Smith, 54th (Kootenay) Battalion, (2nd Central Ontario Regiment), Canadian Infantry.

George William Smith was born at Barnetby on 3rd September 1873. He was the son of the late John and Ann Smith. George was two years old when his mother died and it fell upon Harriet, his sister (later Mrs Holt, of Railway Street, Barnetby – his next of kin), to bring him up. No mean task for a youngster.

As soon as he was old enough George joined the Army and served for a total of 9 years and 335 days in the Royal Field Artillery as 78458 Driver G. W. Smith. Nearly all his Army time had been spent at Woolwich and Aldershot until he went on the Reserve List. George was recalled to the colours when hostilities broke out in South Africa and saw service there during the Boer War. His medals indicate participation in the following campaigns whilst out there: King's South Africa Medal 1901-1902, with bars S. A. 1901 and S. A. 1902; Queen's South Africa Medal 1899-1902, with bars for Tugela Heights, Orange Free State, Transvaal, Laing's Nek and Relief of Ladysmith.

L.Cpl G. W. Smith.

1917

ATTESTATION PAPER.

No. 443323 DUPLICATE
Folio.

CANADIAN OVER-SEAS EXPEDITIONARY FORCE.

QUESTIONS TO BE PUT BEFORE ATTESTATION. (ANSWERS)

1. What is your name? — George William Smith
2. In what Town, Township or Parish, and in what Country were you born? — Barnsley, Lincolnshire, England
3. What is the name of your next-of-kin? — Mrs George Smith
4. What is the address of your next-of-kin? — Barnsby, England
5. What is the date of your birth? — 3rd September 1875
6. What is your Trade or Calling? — Labourer
7. Are you married? — No
8. Are you willing to be vaccinated or re-vaccinated? — Yes
9. Do you now belong to the Active Militia? — No
10. Have you ever served in any Military Force? If so, state particulars of former Service. — Royal Field Artillery 9 yrs 335 days with colors
11. Do you understand the nature and terms of your engagement? — Yes
12. Are you willing to be attested to serve in the CANADIAN OVER-SEAS EXPEDITIONARY FORCE? — Yes

G. Wm. Smith (Signature of Man)
_____ (Signature of Witness)

DECLARATION TO BE MADE BY MAN ON ATTESTATION.

I, George William Smith, do solemnly declare that the above answers made by me to the above questions are true, and that I am willing to fulfil the engagements by me now made, and I hereby engage and agree to serve in the Canadian Over-Seas Expeditionary Force, and to be attached to any arm of the service therein, for the term of one year, or during the war now existing between Great Britain and Germany should that war last longer than one year, and for six months after the termination of that war provided His Majesty should so long require my services, or until legally discharged.

Date May 24th 1915   G. Wm. Smith (Signature of Recruit)
_____ (Signature of Witness)

OATH TO BE TAKEN BY MAN ON ATTESTATION.

I, George William Smith, do make Oath, that I will be faithful and bear true Allegiance to His Majesty King George the Fifth, His Heirs and Successors, and that I will as in duty bound honestly and faithfully defend His Majesty, His Heirs and Successors, in Person, Crown and Dignity, against all enemies, and will observe and obey all orders of His Majesty, His Heirs and Successors, and of all the Generals and Officers set over me. So help me God.

Date May 24th 1915   G. Wm. Smith (Signature of Recruit)
_____ (Signature of Witness)

CERTIFICATE OF MAGISTRATE.

The Recruit above-named was cautioned by me that if he made any false answer to any of the above questions he would be liable to be punished as provided in the Army Act.
The above questions were then read to the Recruit in my presence.
I have taken care that he understands each question, and that his answer to each question has been duly entered as replied to, and the said Recruit has made and signed the declaration and taken the oath before me, at Vernon Camp this __ day of Aug 1915.

W. J. Waterman (Signature of Justice)

I certify that the above is a true copy of the Attestation of the above-named Recruit.

C. Hungerford Pollen (Approving Officer)

Attestation Paper, G. W. Smith. (See Appendix for further documents)

George, put on the reserve list on leaving the Army, returned to Barnetby to live with his sister and worked on the GCR for two years. On leaving the railway he emigrated to Canada and worked as a labourer living in huts in the backwoods, presumably in the area near where, on 24th May 1915, he enlisted into the Canadian Over-Seas Expeditionary Force (CEF), at Vernon Camp. Vernon, in British Colombia, is situated roughly midway between Calgary and Vancouver in the foothills of the Selkirk Mountains to the west of the Rocky Mountains.

During the ten years spent in the backwoods George did all his own cooking, housework and washing. On enlistment he joined D Company of the 54th (Kootenay) Battalion, 2nd Central Ontario Regiment, CEF (Kootenay refers to the lake and river of that name located south east of Vernon in the Selkirk Mountains). George trained as a 'bomber', indicating that his primary weapon in an attack was a Mills bomb, and after seven months training was posted overseas.

On 2nd December 1915 the SS *Saxonia* arrived in England with a contingent of Canadian soldiers. While in England George spent some time at Bramshott from where, in mid May 1916, he took six days leave. On 12th August 1916, George went with his regiment to France. Upon arrival the 54th Battalion became part of 11th Brigade, 4th Canadian Division, Canadian Corps that relieved the 3rd Canadian Division, on 10th October 1916, in the area around Courcelette on the Somme front. Near the end of October 1916 the Canadian Corps was withdrawn from the Somme front – except for the 4th Canadian Division; it was transferred to II Corps and remained with that Corps until the end of the Somme battle on 18th November 1916.

The Canadian Corps, except for the 4th Canadian Division, on having been withdrawn from the Somme towards the end of October 1916 had moved to the Souchez sector of the front north of Arras. It was there, near the end of November 1916, that the 4th Canadian Division rejoined it. Preparations were well in hand there for the allied offensive of the following year, with their objective being to attain the Vimy Heights. On 23rd January 1917, during all these preparations, George was promoted to Lance Corporal. As a prelude to the actual storming of the Vimy Heights the Canadians harried the enemy with trench raids that were not always on a small scale. The largest raid, on the night of 28th February/1st March, involved 1,700 troops from four battalions of the 4th Canadian Division, 54th and 75th (11th Brigade); 72nd and 73rd (12th Brigade) and was aimed at Hill 145 – the highest point of the ridge on which the Canadian National Memorial now stands – the object being to destroy the enemy defences and gain information. The 2nd Canadian Division, on the right, was to co-operate with a smoke barrage.

1917

In preparation for the raid 'lunch baskets' (gas cylinders) were placed in Snargate Trench from 19th to 26th February. On 24th February the 54th Battalion carried out practice attacks at Berthonval Wood (Bois l'Abbé) some 1.5 km west of the Arras – Bethune road. Next day the 54th and 75th Battalions of 11th Brigade went into the line, the 54th relieving the 87th Battalion in the right sub-sector with the 75th relieving the 102nd Battalion to their left. The disposition of the 54th Battalion Companies was as follows: A, plus details, remained in the Music Hall Line; C were positioned from Lassalle Avenue to 200 yards south of Cavalier Trench; D from there to 50 yards north of Central Avenue with B in support in Cavalier Tunnel. To their right was the Canadian 22nd Battalion (5th Brigade, 2nd Canadian Division).

Originally planned for the night of 26th February, the raid was initially postponed for 24 hours due to the wind direction being unfavourable. On the 27th an inter–company relief took place in the 54th Battalion with A and B relieving D (to Cavalier Tunnel) and C (to Music Hall Line). It was a quiet day and night and the weather fine, but the wind was again unfavourable. It was not until the early hours of 1st March that conditions were considered suitable for gas to be discharged and the signal for the raid sent off.

At 3 a.m. on 1st March, prior to the raid going in at 5.40 a.m., tear gas was discharged towards the enemy lines on the 11th and 12th Brigade fronts. Then the wind changed direction blowing the gas back towards their own lines causing chaos among the troops waiting to move up. The enemy, apparently unaffected by the gas but alerted by the commotion and aware that something was afoot, retaliated with gas shells and machine-gun fire. A second discharge of gas (poison) scheduled for 4.45 a.m. was cancelled due to the adverse wind conditions. At 5.05 a.m. the troops left the assembly trenches and moved up to No Man's Land virtually unopposed. As they deployed into No Man's Land they were subjected to heavy machine-gun and rifle fire but despite that the assault went ahead on schedule at 5.40 a.m. Although some troops managed to enter the enemy lines most of the raiders' advance was held up by substantial uncut wire and faced with that they had no option but to retire. Three-quarters of an hour after the start of the raid the survivors were back in their own lines – the raid had failed hopelessly.

That raid had cost the Canadians over 680 casualties in killed and wounded, including the officers commanding the 54th and 75th battalions (both killed). Apart from the enemy having exacted a heavy toll on the raiders the 54th Battalion had also suffered casualties from friendly artillery 'shorts' on its left and centre. Of the 54th Battalion's 15 officers and 390 other ranks that took part in that raid 6 officers were killed (the CO, Lt-Colonel A. H. G. Kemball,

CB, DSO, contrary to orders left the front line trench to re-organise and lead his men following the chaos after the wind changed) and 7 wounded; 77 other ranks were killed, 126 wounded and 10 were missing. Attempts to retrieve the wounded that night were abandoned due to enemy vigilance.

Next day the Canadian 87th Battalion relieved the 54th. During the night a party of scouts and volunteers, venturing out into No Man's Land, managed to bring in several bodies. An armistice set up for the following day, 3rd March, enabled each side to clear its dead from No Man's Land. On that occasion the enemy carried those Canadians that reached its lines into the middle of No Man's Land for retrieval. Making full use of this armistice to bring in dead comrades for burial the 54th Battalion successfully recovered 43 bodies. They were taken to Villers Station Cemetery, Villers-au-Bois, near the HQ of the 4th Canadian Division, for burial.

A similar arrangement for 4th March was cancelled but during the night a 54th Battalion burial party did manage to bury several bodies in No Man's Land under cover of darkness. An entry on George's record sheet reads, 'killed in action, 1-3-1917'; he was 44 years old. I believe George was killed on that raid and was among those originally buried on the battlefield on the night of 4th March, on the western approach to the ridge, about 760 yards south west of Hill 145.

The map reference of George's initial burial site, 44a.S.21b.10.35, locates it roughly 50 yards outside the entrance to the Canadian Cemetery No. 2, situated in the Canadian Memorial Park on Vimy Ridge.

George was re-buried in Cabaret Rouge British Cemetery, Souchez, plot 14, row D, grave 14, over a mile to the west. Originally a small cemetery of 470 graves begun in March 1916 by British troops, it was used until August 1917 (chiefly by the Canadian Corps and 47th (London) Division), then intermittently until September 1918. It is now the second largest CWGC Cemetery in France (7,661 burials), increased after the Armistice by concentrating isolated graves from the Arras battlefields, and many small cemeteries in the Nord and Pas de Calais areas into it. (Note: the headstone, right, has no cross.)

George's niece, Mrs Joyce Brumpton of King's Road, Barnetby, kindly loaned the photograph of George as well as producing his South African Campaign

G. W. Smith headstone.

medals and a document that had been sent to Mrs Harriet Holt from the Adjutant General, Canadian Militia, in Ottawa.

The other brief item mentioned earlier concerned a youth of 19...

202866 Pte Walter Blair, 2/4th Battalion. Lincolnshire Regiment.

Walter Blair, born in Brigg in (3)1897, was the son of George and Mary E. Blair of 75, Town Street, Hemsworth, Wakefield; his parents had lived in Barnetby (at Crosskills – 1901 census) for twenty years before moving to Wakefield. (The CWGC refer to the son of Mrs Sharman, formerly Blair, and of the late George Blair of 2, Barnsley Road Estate, Hemsworth, Pontefract). In 1911 Walter was living with his widowed mother and five siblings in the household of Joseph Barnett at Rookery Farm, Barnetby, where he worked as a farm lad.

Pte W. Blair.

Walter had enlisted at Brigg in November 1916 joining the 2/4th Lincolns – a Territorial unit. He had been on active service about two weeks when he was killed in action on 9th March 1917, aged 19 years. Captain Harold Ward, an officer with his battalion, wrote to Walter's parents, saying,

> 'On behalf of the company I am writing to offer you our deepest sympathy in the loss of your son. He was a good soldier, and having paid the great sacrifice by giving his life for his country he leaves a void in the hearts of his comrades. He was killed by a 'fish-tail shell' whilst on duty in the first line and he met his end without pain. We are sorry such a loss has to come to you, but the fact that he died a noble death will take away the sting of loss'.

(What is a 'fish-tail shell'? – the 2/5th Lincolns War Diary also mentions it. The Imperial War Museum's dictionaries of military terms and slang expressions do not refer to it. The term may have been one not in common use. A plausible explanation is that the 'fish-tail' was the fins of a low velocity projectile, like a mortar bomb, and that the said projectile was not a 'shell' at all.)

At the end of February the 2/4th Lincolns, 177th Brigade, 59th Division, on arrival in France moved to Bayonvillers, east of Amiens, leaving there on 4th March for Foucaucourt en route for their first spell of front line duty albeit in a fairly quiet sector south of the river Somme.

The 2/4th Lincolns sector was at the bottom of a shallow depression in an almost flat area compared to the British 1916 area north of the river Somme.

Although signs of trenches are not apparent on the ground the area where the 2/4th Lincolns were entrenched is easy to find from a map, with a minor road bisecting the 2/5th Lincolns trench line and a couple of farm tracks cutting across the 2/4th Lincolns trench line. The enemy had the higher ground to the east.

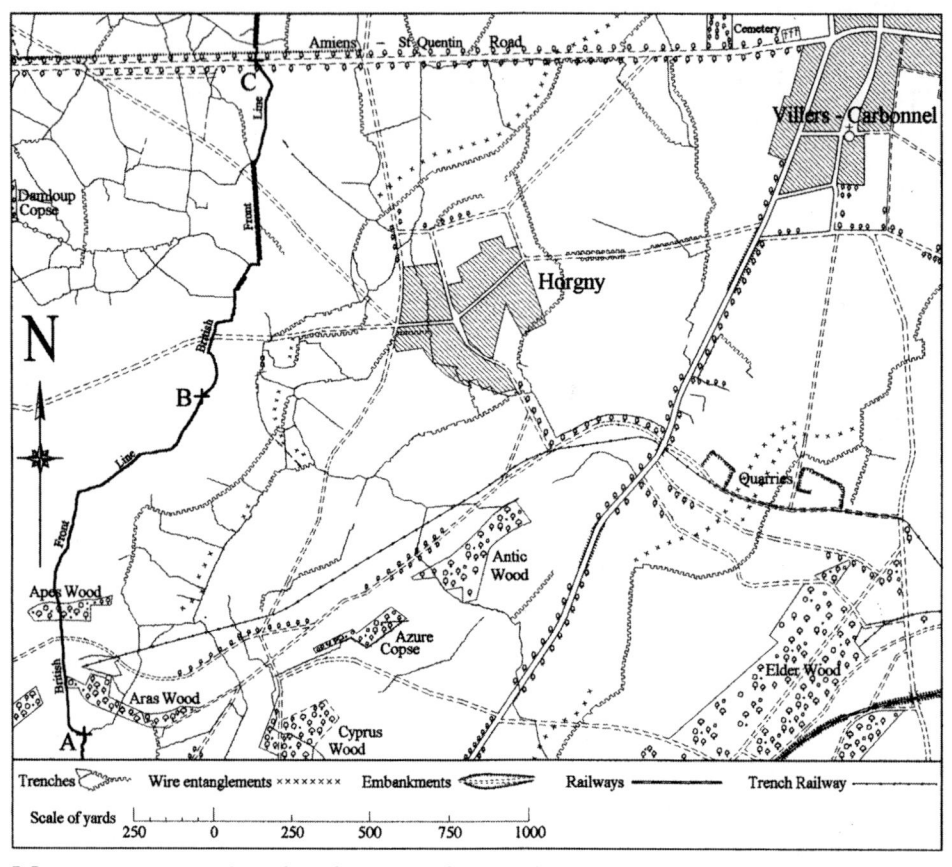

Map 13. *Position of 2/4th and 2/5 Lincolns trenches near Villers – Carbonnel. The 2/4th line ran from A (T4c.8.6.) – B (N34d.5.5.); the 2/5th from B (N34d.5.5.) – C (N28d.9.4).*

At 4.45 p.m. 6th March the 2/4th Lincolns left Foucaucourt to march the five miles to the left sub sector of the old French front line trenches to relieve the 5th Yorks and arrived there just before 11 p.m. The 177th Brigade front line sub sector was from map reference N28d.9.4. (just off the Amiens – St Quentin Road) to T4c.8.6. (about 1500 yards ESE from Berny-en-Santerre). There the 2/4th Lincolns took over the right of the line, from N34d.5.5., where the Companies deployed: A right, B centre, D left, with C in support, each less one platoon forming the battalion composite reserve. The relief was duly completed without any casualties being sustained. The following day 2/5th Lincolns took over the left of the line. They had taken over some old French trenches, which were in very poor condition – mainly from mud and water, and here the 2/5th Lincolns record there had been occasion to dig men out of the mud.

The battalion War Diary (WO 95/3023) does not record very much at all for that period – I even had to refer to the 2/5th Lincolns and the 177th Brigade War Diaries (WO 95/3024 and 3022 respectively) for the trench position map references – but it did contain one rather unusual entry. The 7th March for the 2/4th Lincolns, in the left sub sector, had been a relatively quiet day apart from one man being injured in a gunshot accident and, between 5-6 p.m., some heavy artillery firing to the north – about eight miles away. The 8th March was likewise a fairly quiet day with essential work being carried out on communication trenches and dugouts and a note made of any wind direction changes (presumably as a check against a possible gas attack). Now follows the unusual entry – normally only officers are named. Two men had been wounded by artillery fire and one of the casualties, Pte 2900 Blair, subsequently died. (Is the service number correct? The CWGC have checked all service numbers 2900 but none of the seven casualties recorded are called Blair. Were 2nd Line Territorials given new service numbers? – see W. F. Starkey.)

The next day was similarly a quiet day except for the headquarters being shelled at round about 2.30 p.m. and the unit on their left being shelled with gas shell. By contrast 10th March was a day of considerably more enemy artillery activity, including trench mortars, with the inevitable retaliation by their own artillery. Then a change of wind direction from the north west to the south caused a thaw to set in with the result that the trenches were soon in a very bad state again. The day following was also one with a marked amount of enemy artillery activity; later that day the battalion was relieved by the 2/4th Leicesters and moved back into support in trenches at Belloy-en-Santerre some 2 km to the NNW.

On 16th March the enemy withdrew from his front line and moved back into the newly prepared defensive system – the Hindenburg Line. In the Regimental History it is recorded that the 2/4th Lincolns had sustained a total of seven casualties by the middle of the month as a result of shell-fire or rifle-grenades.

Pte Walter Blair has no known grave and is commemorated by name on the Memorial to the Missing at Thiepval, pier 1, face C. I think Walter would have been buried somewhere near to the 2/4th Lincolns position and that his grave was subsequently destroyed or its marker lost, or became illegible, in the very heavy fighting in that region in the spring and summer of 1918.

(Capt (Major) Harold Ward, 2/4th Lincolns attached 2/5th Lincolns, writer of the letter to Walter's parents, was killed just over a year later, on 21st March 1918, age 31. While serving as a Captain he was mentioned in dispatches. Harold, son of the

late Mr and Mrs William Ward, of Sycamore Terrace, York, and husband of L Marion Ward, of 24 Gladstone Terrace, Grantham, has no known grave and is commemorated by name on the Arras Memorial to the Missing.)

Both the Grimsby News and the Hull Times of 23rd/24th March had reported briefly on the following item concerning a number of GCR platelayers.

'Several platelayers on the GCR who some time ago volunteered for railway work in France, have left to take up their work there. Mr.Charnley has also gone with them'.

In a local news item on 3rd March 1916, I had noted a brief paragraph on that subject and I wondered if this was the follow up to that item? Those men were: – Padmore, Vessey, Clark, Parkinson, Welton, Smith, Cox and Calver and locking fitter Mr Charnley. The article does not convey much information to the reader but presumably at the time many of the villagers would be aware what it was all about. There was a sequel to it later on in the year and a fuller explanation will be given at the appropriate time.

During the last week in March a meeting chaired by Dr Ffrench had been held in the school with a view to forming a section of the Brigg Volunteer Training Corps. Lt T. Cliff of the Brigg Company had talked in great detail about the Volunteer Training Corps and conditions of service while Sgt Glover had spoken on the advantage of joining. By the end of the meeting a number had given their names as Volunteers.

Due to the need for ever more men at the front they were now being conscripted into war service. At the beginning of April several young ladies from the village had stepped into the breach caused by this conscription when they commenced employment as painters on the GCR taking on the work that had previously been carried out by men.

News continued to come from France of local men being in hospital for one reason or another. Mr and Mrs Footitt had received information that their son Amos, a private in the Lincolns, had been injured in early April in a transport related accident. He had apparently been run over by a transport (*type not specified*) and received serious injuries to both legs and apart from information that he was 'progressing favourably' there were no more details as yet available.

At the end of the month Pte John Waite, who in December 1916 had been hospitalised suffering from trench fever, was now home on leave after having been out in France since 1915. About that same time Mr and Mrs Poole had received news that their son Pte Percy Poole, of the Lincolns, had been wounded in the left shoulder during recent fighting in France and was in a hospital receiving treatment. Mr & Mrs E. Rowe, headmaster and headmistress respectively at Barnetby school, had received similar information at the beginning of the following month with news that their son L/Cpl Thomas Rowe, also of the Lincolns, was being treated for a fracture of the left forearm in a Chichester hospital where his progress was favourable.

As a result of the meeting held towards the end of March a section of the Volunteer Training Corps had been formed here in Barnetby during the third week in April and had begun training at Low Farm. However the weather had not been kind to that first meeting with the result that only about a dozen lads had turned up. Nevertheless those lads who had managed to turn up had received drill instruction from Master Dudley Ffrench under the discerning eye of a former Lincolnshire Yeoman Mr H. M. Webb. Whether or not the unit continued to function is not known as no further mention of it was found in either the *Grimsby News* or the *Hull Times*.

Then a spate of tragedies hit the village and will be referred to in the order they occurred and not in the order they were reported. (The *Grimsby News* reported all of them on 11th May, while the *Hull Times* reported two on the 5th May and two on the 12th May).

On 8th May Mrs Rose Thacker received the wretched news from the War Office that amongst the men killed in action on 9th April was her husband...

426356 Sgt George William Thacker, 102nd Battalion. (2nd Central Ontario Regiment), Canadian Infantry.

George William Thacker, the son of David and Sarah A. Thacker, of East Stockwith, in Lincolnshire, was born there on Wednesday 21st July 1880. At some stage after leaving school George joined the Army and served for thirteen years and three months with the 1st Battalion Durham Light Infantry as 71737 L/Cpl G. Thacker. He was on active service in South Africa during the Boer War campaign for which he received the awards of the Queens South Africa Medal and 3 Bars: Transvaal, S.A. 1901 and S.A. 1902.

I believe that George Thacker may at one time have been an employee of the GCR. The Journal of November 1910 records that a porter-shunter G. W. Thacker had been transferred from Dovecliffe (Northern District) to Barnetby (Eastern District) to take up duties of a shunter. (Dovecliffe, near Barnsley, was on the Barnsley to Sheffield line.) In December 1911 the Journal recorded that Barnetby shunter, J. W. Thacker, was transferred to Grimsby Docks as a shunter. In October 1912 shunter J. W. Thacker, Grimsby Docks, was promoted to leading shunter. (In March 1913, J. W. Thacker again appears as having been promoted to leading shunter at Grimsby Docks! The next rung up the promotion ladder, judging by other entries, is from leading shunter to brakesman.) The final entry, in August 1913, records that brakesman G. W.

ATTESTATION PAPER.

CANADIAN OVER-SEAS EXPEDITIONARY FORCE.

No. 416356

QUESTIONS TO BE PUT BEFORE ATTESTATION.
(ANSWERS)

1. What is your name? — George William Thacker
2. In what Town, Township or Parish, and in what Country were you born? — East Stockworth, Lincolnshire, Eng.
3. What is the name of your next-of-kin? — Mrs. William Thacker (Wife)
4. What is the address of your next-of-kin? — Ind. Head, Sask.
5. What is the date of your birth? — 21st July 1880
6. What is your Trade or Calling? — Labourer
7. Are you married? — Yes
8. Are you willing to be vaccinated or re-vaccinated? — Yes
9. Do you now belong to the Active Militia? — No
10. Have you ever served in any Military Force? — 124th D.L.S.
11. Do you understand the nature and terms of your engagement? — Yes
12. Are you willing to be attested to serve in the Canadian Over-Seas Expeditionary Force? — Yes

Signed G. W. Thacker (Signature of Man).
Signed E. H. Hill (Signature of Witness).

DECLARATION TO BE MADE BY MAN ON ATTESTATION.

I, George William Thacker, do solemnly declare that the above answers made by me to the above questions are true, and that I am willing to fulfil the engagements by me now made, and I hereby engage and agree to serve in the Canadian Over-Seas Expeditionary Force, and to be attached to any arm of the service therein, for the term of one year, or during the war now existing between Great Britain and Germany should that war last longer than one year, and for six months after the termination of that war provided His Majesty should so long require my services, or until legally discharged.

Signed G. W. Thacker (Signature of Recruit)
Date January 13th 1915. Signed E. H. Hill (Signature of Witness)

OATH TO BE TAKEN BY MAN ON ATTESTATION.

I, George William Thacker, do make Oath, that I will be faithful and bear true Allegiance to His Majesty King George the Fifth, His Heirs and Successors, and that I will as in duty bound honestly and faithfully defend His Majesty, His Heirs and Successors, in Person, Crown and Dignity, against all enemies, and will observe and obey all orders of His Majesty, His Heirs and Successors, and of all the Generals and Officers set over me. So help me God.

Signed G. W. Thacker (Signature of Recruit)
Date 13th January 1915 Signed E. H. Hill (Signature of Witness)

CERTIFICATE OF MAGISTRATE.

The Recruit above-named was cautioned by me that if he made any false answer to any of the above questions he would be liable to be punished as provided in the Army Act.
The above questions were then read to the Recruit in my presence.
I have taken care that he understands each question, and that his answer to each question has been duly entered as replied to, and the said Recruit has made and signed the declaration and taken the oath before me, at Regina, Sask this 13th day of January 1915.

(Signed) M. Fegan (Signature of Justice)

I certify that the above is a true copy of the Attestation of the above-named Recruit.

(Signed) Herbert Snell (Approving Officer)
Lieut.-Col Cmdg. 46th Battalion C. E. F.

Attestation G. W. Thacker.

Thacker, Grimsby Docks, left the service. I think the initial J. is a mistake, as is the promotion entry for March 1913. Age wise it is possible that if George had initially joined the Durhams as a boy soldier he would have left about 1909-10. Finally, did George emigrate to Canada in 1913?

Having married Rose, the youngest daughter of Mr and Mrs Maddison of West Street, Barnetby, late in 1911, George and his wife subsequently emigrated to Canada and set up home at Indian Head in Saskatchewan (about 40 miles east of Regina) where he worked as a labourer. After the declaration of war on Germany George, like many former British citizens that had emigrated to Canada, volunteered his services and was enlisted into the 46th Battalion, Canadian Expeditionary Force, at Regina, Saskatchewan, on 13th January 1915. (By early 1916 roughly two thirds of all men serving with the Canadian Expeditionary Force were British immigrants.)

After arriving in England George went to Shorncliffe, near Folkestone, on 13th September 1915 where he joined the 32nd Reserve Battalion, Canadian Infantry. On 18th February 1916, he was promoted to Sergeant. His wife Rose had also returned to England and from 1st November 1916 her address is shown as being in West Street, Barnetby. From 27th February 1922 Mrs Thacker's address was No 8 Saunders Street, West Marsh, Grimsby (the *Hull Times* of 19th May 1917 printed a brief report – with photograph, right).

Sgt G. W. Thacker.

On 27th November 1916, George was sent to France to join the 102nd Battalion (2nd Central Ontario Regiment), Canadian Infantry, (11th Brigade, 4th Canadian Division).

By the middle of March 1917 the enemy had withdrawn his forces eastwards to the Hindenburg Line – a newly prepared defensive system running from Arras in the north to the Aisne valley, north-west of Reims, in the south.

Subsequently, the Allies moved towards this line, their speed being exceedingly slowed due to the enemy causing wholesale destruction in towns and villages that he passed through, laying waste to anything that would delay the British advance. Houses were demolished, trees were felled across roads and the roads themselves, particularly at cross roads, were mined. There were some instances of wells being fouled and the soldiers had to be very wary of 'souvenirs' for many objects that were collected as trophies had been booby-trapped.

Meanwhile the British High Command, with plans for the next offensive in Flanders, had not reckoned with Lloyd George – head of the new British government – who favoured the plan of the French General Nivelle and ordered the British Commanders to comply. Thus once again British plans had to be modified to suit the French and hence on 9th April the British opened the Arras offensive as a prelude to the main French one on 16th April on the Aisne.

It was originally planned as a diversionary action, aimed at deterring the enemy from diverting reinforcements from the British sector while the main French offensive went ahead further south. It had to be prolonged to keep the heat off the French – in turmoil, with its Armies in disarray, rocked with mutinies – and turned into a savage full-blooded battle.

In the north the Canadians had been busy preparing an assault using its four divisions on the Vimy Ridge, a few miles north of Arras. In their rear massed artillery had begun a three-week wire-cutting programme prior to bombardments to blast the enemy off the ridge commencing five days before the attacks went in. Beneath the ridge itself were numerous caves and much work had been done constructing tunnels linking up these caves. Tunnelling was also carried out to the assembly trenches on the western approaches to the ridge in the hope of keeping their assaulting troops under cover right up to the last minute. (There was a similar system of caves beneath Arras and tunnels were likewise dug from there out to the assembly trenches – some hitherto lesser known ones were explored during the Spring of 1997 by French archaeologists, revealing information about the troops that had once occupied them.)

The 4th Canadian Division, allotted the task of capturing Hill 145 at the northern end of the ridge, used two brigades for the assault – 11th Brigade (102nd Battalion right, 87th Battalion left) on the right and 12th Brigade on the left. Hill 145, the highest point and dominant feature on the ridge, being a miniature enemy fortress was going to be a hard nut to crack. Some 250 yards lower on the western slope, in the path of 87th Battalion's attack, was the heavily defended enemy second line 'Batter Trench'. The Officer Commanding the 87th Battalion did not want this bombarded as he wished to use it when captured and won the Divisional Commander's approval against the better judgement of the Artillery advisers. This was to cause serious problems for his men.

On 3rd April the 87th and 102nd Battalions, 11th Canadian Brigade, left St Lawrence Camp, where they had been training since 28th March, to relieve the 54th and 75th Battalions in the Berthonval Sector. A and C Companies of 102nd Battalion went to Cavalier Trench; D, with the HQ Company, went into the Music Hall Line and C was in Wood. For the next few days the Brigade was employed digging and repairing front line trenches hampered by mud and water.

The 102nd Battalion War Diary (WO 95/3093) records that wire-cutting by the artillery commenced at 1.30 p.m. on 6th April and was active thereafter which brought enemy artillery retaliation in the Zouave Valley. Meanwhile preparations were being progressed for the move to the forward areas and the subsequent offensive. News was also received that the offensive had been postponed 24 hours. The following day, D Company moved up from Music Hall Line to the Tottenham Caves; the Medical officer and his staff went to Cavalier Trench and the Brigade HQ moved to Tottenham Tunnel. Throughout the day the enemy artillery was very active. During the early hours of 8th April liquid fire and gas was to be used against the enemy positions. Since the wind conditions were unsuitable for gas to be released only liquid fire was discharged with some effect. It was also noted that a new type of wire-cutting shell was being used. During the morning the 102nd Battalion received orders to move its HQ to Cavalier Tunnel before noon.

Unfortunately for the men of 11th Brigade in the assembly trenches it had been decided not to issue hot soup at 8.30 p.m. – the night was considered too bright and the distribution likely to attract fire. At 9 p.m. the battalions moved off to their assembly positions. To cover any noise during the move the 11th Brigade Light Trench Mortar Battery fired intermittently throughout the night. By 11.30 p.m. the 11th Brigade battalions were reported to be in position and resting. At 2 a.m. the 102nd Battalion sent a message to the guns saying that reports had been received of one 18-pounder firing persistently short. 11th Brigade recorded that the 54th Battalion received casualties in the assembly trenches resulting from 18-pounder 'shorts'.

At 5.30 a.m. on 9th April the attack commenced. In a cold drizzle, with occasional sleet and snow flurries, the Canadians left their assembly positions to advance behind the creeping barrage. Along most of the ridge the attack was going well. Many of the defensive positions had been totally wrecked except on the 4th Division front where the occupants of Batter Trench, not having been 'battered' by request of 87th Battalion's CO, opened up with machine-guns on the Canadians as they left their assembly positions, inflicting terrible damage especially on the 87th Battalion. By 6.10 a.m. enemy artillery was also subjecting the Zouave Valley to heavy shelling.

Initially the attack went well for 102nd Battalion. At 7.40 a.m. the 3rd line of trenches were reported as gained and in need of consolidation but things were not going too well on the right.; but their reports were not getting through to Brigade HQ. What 11th Brigade was aware of was that the right of 12th Brigade, on its left, was held up. The 54th Battalion, in support of the 102nd, having passed through the 102nd's positions also reported objectives reached, posts established and positions being consolidated. At 8.10 a.m. the 102nd's D Company reported that an enemy strongpoint on the left of Broadmarsh Crater

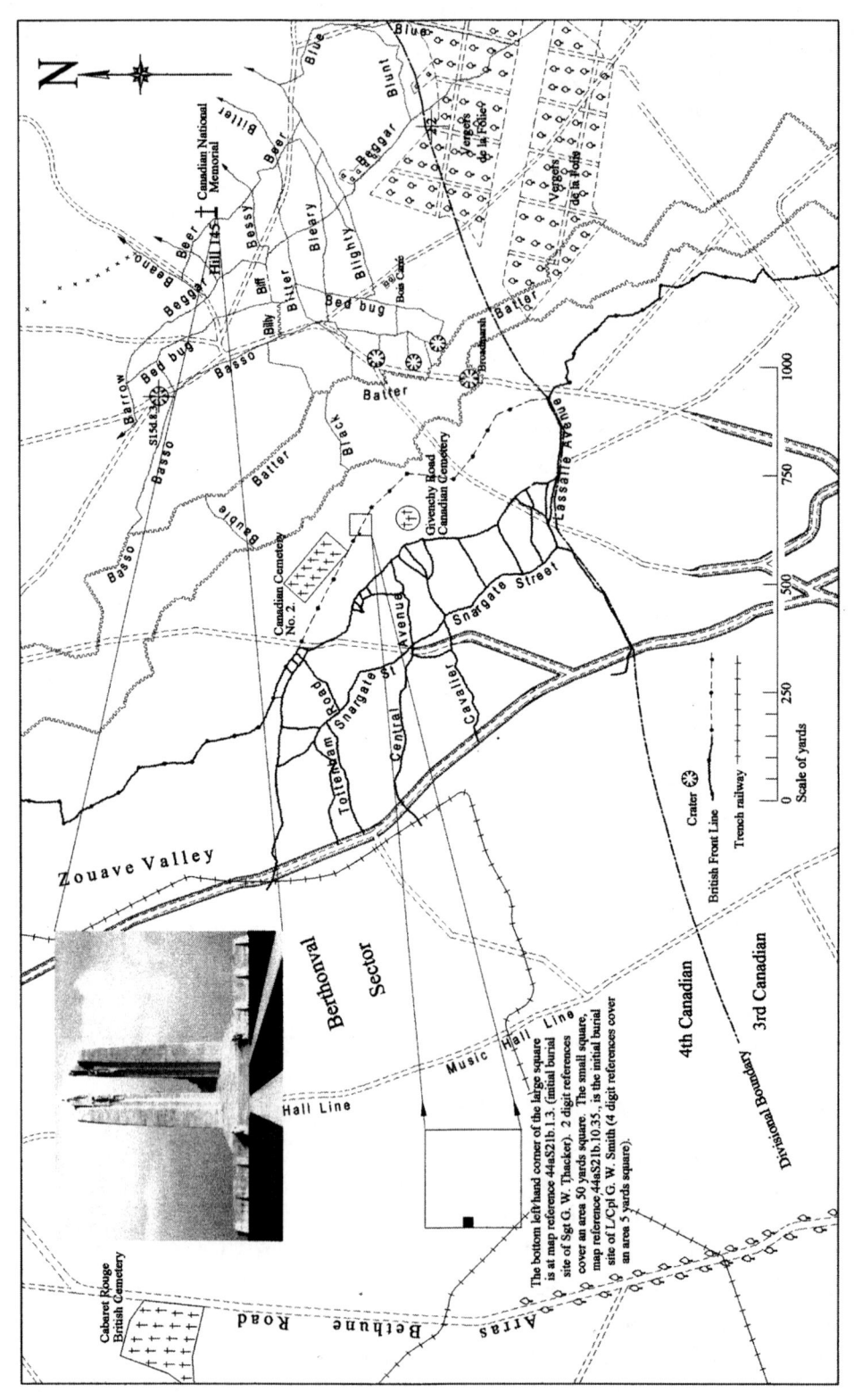

Map 14. *Vimy Ridge.*

had been captured and No 2 Strongpoint established. However, elsewhere enemy snipers on Hill 145 were causing serious problems.

Meanwhile things were not going well for the 54th Battalion. Having been forced to fall back they were assisting the 102nd Battalion in maintaining their hold of the trenches they had captured. By 9 a.m. the 102nd Battalion had consolidated Bed Bug Trench but their left flank was not covered due to the 87th Battalion not having reached their objectives. A party of 75th Battalion in support had reached Basso Trench but had been counterattacked by the enemy. To assist with that situation 4 Lewis guns had been sent up from Brigade. Further problems were caused due to delays bringing ammunition up as the ammunition parties were being subjected to heavy sniping. The 54th Battalion was also falling back on the right.

Before long the advance of the 4th Division was almost at a standstill with enfilading fire coming from 'The Pimple' – another high point about a mile to the north – this setback causing problems on its right flank for the 42nd Battalion (7th Brigade, 3rd Division). The War Diary of 42nd Battalion (WO 95/3886), records that at 8.15 a.m. the Battalion had received reports that the left battalion was being held up and this was the first indication that all was not well with the Division on the left. The left flank then pushed out patrols in an attempt to make contact with 4th Division and reported that sniping and rifle-fire from the left and Hill145 was very severe. By 10.15 a. m. the 42nd Battalion was aware that the 87th Battalion, on the left of the 54th, were held up and that the 102nd were in the process of consolidating their positions in Beggar Trench with their flank being at the junction of Beggar and Blunt Trenches.

At 10.54 a.m. the 42nd Battalion informed the 54th that their left flank was in advance of Blunt and Blue Trenches and asked the 54th if they could push forward to that point and that the 42nd were willing to cooperate. But as already stated the right of the 54th Battalion was having problems. Subsequently the 42nd Battalion, in order to protect its left flank, had by 11.30 a.m. created a defensive line along the left flank from positions already gained. This meant that Princess Patricia's Canadian Light Infantry, on their right, had to extend their frontal coverage to the left due to the 42nd Battalion's extended line.

During the afternoon the 10th Brigade was brought up as reinforcements for the battered remnants of 11th Brigade. By mid afternoon it was reported that machine-gun fire from Hill 145 had ceased. Meanwhile arrangements had been made for a barrage to be put onto Batter Trench at 4.30 p.m. between Bauble and Black. Things were still not going well for the 54th Battalion as it reported at 6 p.m. that its line in Beggar Trench, from to point 200 yards north of Blunt to 50 yards north of Bleary, was being threatened and it was not in touch with the left battalions.

Help was at hand. The 85th Battalion, Divisional Reserve, were to attack the troublesome Batter Trench in the left sub-sector of 11th Brigade front. The 85th Battalion advanced without an artillery barrage and initially the depleted occupants of Batter Trench exacted a terrible toll upon them but the 85th men doggedly pressed on and the enemy retreated. The 102nd Battalion recorded this attack at 6.30 p.m. and added, 'Hill 145 taken, and to a large extent sniping ceased'. At 8.10 p.m. 11th Brigade received a message from 4th Division ordering that the Beggar line was to be made good, including Hill 145 and the crater and road junction at S.15d.8.3., and it was to join up with 12th Brigade on the left. Gradually the enemy was cleared from the hill but it was not fully consolidated until the following morning. Further south the Canadian attack had gone well. Except for 'The Pimple' – taken on 12th April, the Canadians now held Vimy Ridge.

To show for their efforts the 102nd Battalion had captured 119 prisoners, 1 'minenwerfer', 4 in number 4" bomb throwers and 2 Maxim machine-guns but at a very heavy cost – 4 officers killed, 2 died of wounds and 9 wounded; of the other ranks: 113 were killed, 6 died of wounds, 180 were wounded and 17 missing. Listed among those killed that day was Sgt George Thacker. He was initially buried on the battlefield on the western approach to the ridge some 750 yards south west of Hill 145 (about 100 yards from the assembly line) and between 70 and 120 yards from Givenchy Road Canadian Cemetery, where he is now buried.

(Sgt Thacker and L/Cpl Smith were originally buried in the same 50 yard square area about 100 yards north of Givench Road Canadian Cemetery and 50 yards from the entrance to the Canadian Cemetery No. 2. The CWGC record the burial site of Sgt Thacker as a two figure map grid reference, 44a.S.21b.1.3. [50 yard square], while L/Cpl Smith's burial site has a four figure grid reference, 44a.S.21b.10.35. [5 yard square]).

Givenchy Road Cemetery, Neuville-St-Vaast, is a small Cemetery containing the graves of 111 Canadian soldiers – including two unidentified – who fell between 9th and 13th April 1917.

Sgt G. W. Thacker is buried there in plot A, grave 30 (see photo next page). Givenchy Road Cemetery is one of two Cemeteries on Vimy Ridge situated in the Canadian Memorial Park – a preserved battlefield with mine craters, shell holes, trenches and a vast network of tunnels and galleries. A number of these tunnels and galleries are open to the public with guided tours given by Canadian students. Standing on the highest point of Hill 145 is the Canadian Memorial

G. W. Smith's initial burial site was roughly near the base of the nearest thin tree in the bottom right quarter of the photograph. G. W. Thacker was buried in a 50 yard square that extended from there to the front, left and rear. He is now buried in Givenchy Road Canadian Cemetery, seen through the trees in the left background.

The Givenchy Road Canadian Cemetery, Canadian National Memorial Park, Vimy Ridge. Note the shell-holes in the foreground of both photographs.

to the Missing. This magnificent monument, together with the second larger Canadian No. 2 Cemetery and a Memorial to the French Moroccan troops, completes the park. The main Calais – Paris autoroute now runs along the western slope of Vimy Ridge more or less following what was once the British front line. Visiting the park in June 1995 I met a student who came from of, all places, Indian Head!

The 11th May paper also reported the sad news that yet another lad had made the supreme sacrifice for King and Country. Mr and Mrs Robert Robinson had received word on Friday 27th April that amongst those killed in action on the 11th April, was their son...

Sgt G. W. Thacker's grave.

1353 Pte Reginald Walter Robinson, 1st Battalion Lincolnshire Regiment

Reginald 'Reg.' Walter Robinson was the only son of Robert and Ann E. Robinson of 11 (now 79), Victoria Road, Barnetby. He was baptised at Barnetby on 8th April 1894. Reg. had been apprenticed as a butcher to Mr Edwin Cuthbert in his premises in Queen's Road where, until recently, Vic. Bowness had his shop and workshops. Reg. enlisted into the Lincolnshire Regiment on 2nd February 1915 at Brigg. His age at attestation was 20 years 331 days (calculated date of birth: 8th March 1894). It is on record that Reg. had a snake tattooed on his right forearm. He joined the 10th Battalion, Lincolnshire Regiment, on 9th January 1916. He is on a photograph with the 'Grimsby Chums' in Brocklesby Park.

In early May 1916 the 10th Lincolns left Bois Grenier for the Somme. On 11th May they were at Franvillers and on 21st May moved to Dernancourt where two companies went into Brigade reserve at Bécourt, (A, C & H.Q. Coys at Bécourt Château.) On 26th May the 10th Lincolns relieved the 11th Suffolks in the right sub-sector front line trenches at Dernancourt. For the rest of the month the 10th Lincolns and 11th Suffolks interchanged line trench duties at Dernancourt and posts at Bécourt Château. Relieved in the line at Dernancourt by the 21st Northumberland Fusiliers on 1st June the 10th Lincolns moved on to Bresle.

Pte R. W. Robinson.

A news report of 23rd June 1916 said Reg. had received shrapnel wounds to the head and thigh in the fighting near Albert in June. The battalion war diary does not record any casualties during May – June. But his service documents (WO 363/R453 –'Burnt Records') show that Reg. was wounded on 26th May 1916. The somewhat indistinct casualty report appears to read: GSW (gun shot wound) I, II, III, and also GSW head. The medical unit, the 36th CCS (Casualty Clearing Station), was at that time at Heilly about 10 km. to the SW of Albert. The next unit entry by '1st Aust. Gen. Hosp.' reads: 'to hospital in England'.

Reg. spent some months in Whitchurch hospital, near Cardiff, before returning to duty in France (5th September 1916?) and that is possibly when he was transferred to the 1st Lincolns ('D' Company). The newspapers said 'he had not long been returned to France' before he was in action with the 1st Lincolns that led to his death. That action, the '1st Battle of the Scarpe, 9th-14th April 1917', was part of the Battles of Arras, 1917, 9th April–11th May, an attempt to breach the new heavily fortified German defensive system – the formidable Hindenburg Line.

The attack by the 64th Brigade on 9th April on part of the Hindenburg Line between the Sensee and Cojeul rivers, with 1st Lincolns in support east of Boiry Becquerelle, had only been a partial success except on the brigade left. Prior to the attack the 64th Brigade had dug assembly trenches on each side of the sunken road east of Hénin sur Cojeul (see Map 15, p. 150).

10th April saw the 1st Lincolns ordered to the Croisilles–Henin road area in support of an attack by the 10th Yorks on part of the Hindenburg Line that the 9th KOYLI had failed to take the previous day with the object of joining up with the front line trenches already taken by the 64th Brigade. This was cancelled and the 1st Lincolns were ordered to relieve the 64th Brigade (1st E. Yorks, 15th DLI and 10th KOYLI) in part of the line previously taken, from roughly T.5.a.3.4. (A) on the right to about T.4b.9.8. (B) – a frontage of some 500 yards? – and the sunken road in T.4.a & b, where two companies of 10th KOYLI were in reserve.

Enemy artillery in the meantime had driven the 64th Brigade out of their trenches and the 1st Lincolns were subsequently ordered to occupy the 64th Brigade assembly trenches. Having occupied the assembly trenches in the evening the 1st Lincolns received verbal instructions to dig a new assembly trench 400 yards north-east of and parallel to the 64th Brigade assembly trench and join the one being dug by 10th Yorks. This was in preparation for a new attack next day, 11th April, on the Hindenburg Line by the 62nd and 110th Brigades of the 21st Division. (62nd Brigade consisted of 12th & 13th Northumberland Fusiliers, 10th Yorks 'Green Howards' and 1st Lincolns). During this time the 1st Lincolns patrols made touch with 110th Brigade on the right and 'A' company relieved the two 10th KOYLI companies in the sunken road T.4.a & b. About 3 a.m. the attack orders were received; the first objective was the enemy front line between T.5.a.5.3. (A1) and T. 4.b.9.9. (B1) with the second objective the enemy second line between points T.5.a.7.7. (A2) and N.35.c.1½.7. (B2). On their left the 10th Yorks were to attack the front line between B1 – C1 with their second objective the enemy second line between B2 – C2.

Early on the morning of 11th April patrols of the enemy line by both attacking battalions had found it to be protected by thick wire with very few gaps; the enemy was also alert and active. The British barrage commenced at 5.38 a.m. with zero hour for the infantry at 6 a.m. At zero hour the attack went ahead with the 110th Brigade on the 1st Lincolns right, the 10th Yorks on the left and 12th

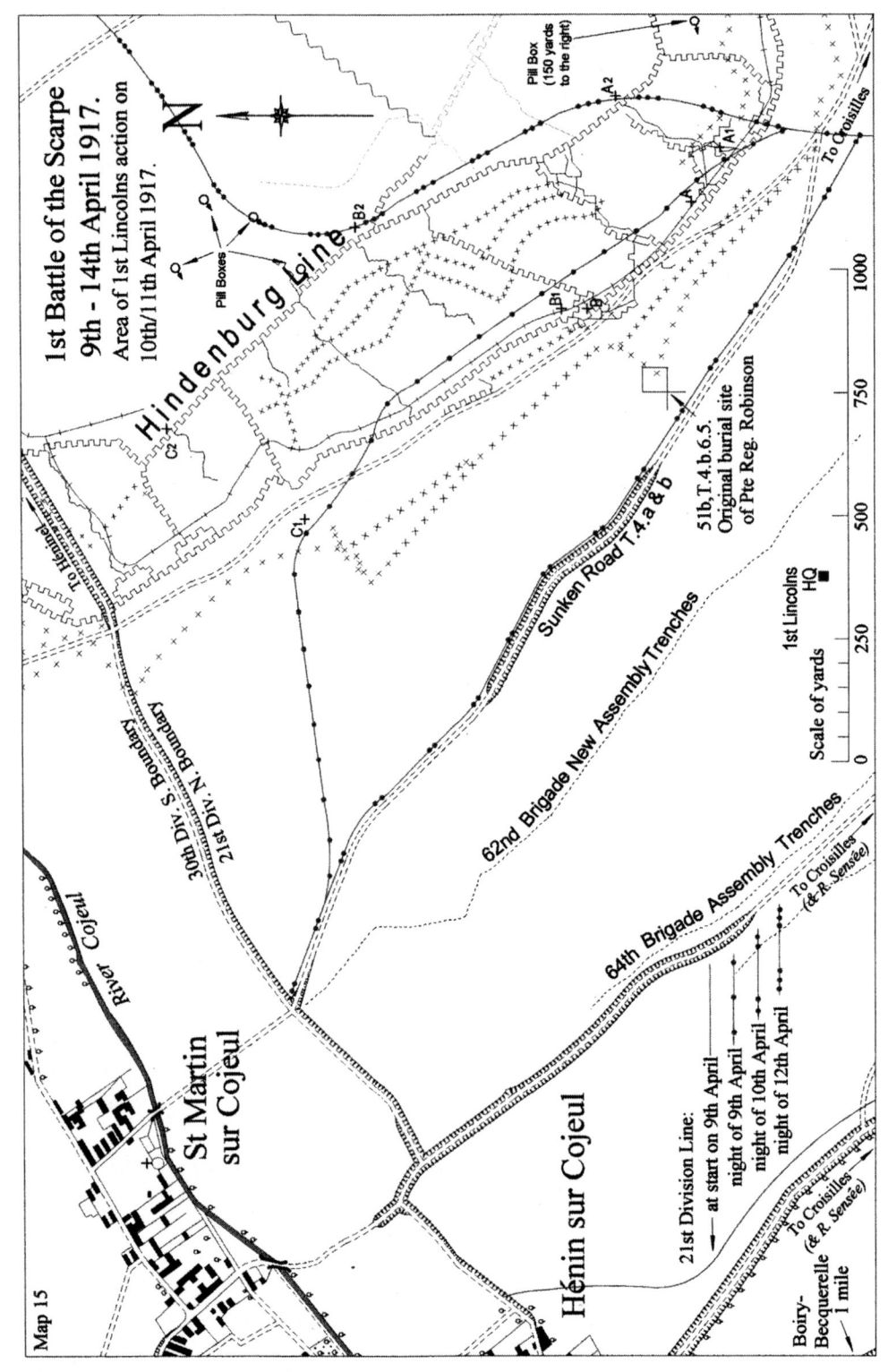

Map 15. *Henin sur Cojeul*

and 13th Northumberland Fusiliers in support and reserve. Little opposition was met until the wire was reached whereat fierce machine-gun crossfire, and frontal fire aimed at gaps in the wire, from concrete gun-emplacements caused heavy casualties and halted the assault. (Concrete emplacements (pillboxes) can still be seen today – four facing the 10th Yorks front (three in the SW quarter of N.35.a; one at N.35.c.0½.9.) and one at T.5.b.3.4. It is possible they are the ones referred to.

Concrete emplacement – pillbox – on the Hindenburg Line at N.35.c.0½.9 near Héninel. Another two can be seen in the field (N.35.a.3.3. – arrowed left – and N.35.a.2½.1. – arrowed right. Arrowed central in the background is the CWGC Bootham and Cherisy Road East Cemetery.

The men who reached the wire opened fire on the enemy snipers and machine-guns. In an effort to silence those machine-guns over a hundred rifle grenades were fired from a nearby communication trench; these proved ineffective. Although a Stokes mortar was brought up to the communication trench it was considered impractical to use it with men still being inside the wire and would probably be ineffective against the concrete machine-gun emplacements. The men were duly withdrawn in order that a fresh bombardment on the wire could begin for an attack the next day. By early evening all units had returned to their original starting positions.

That evening the 12th and 13th Northumberland Fusiliers relieved the 1st Lincolns and 10th Yorks respectively, the 1st Lincolns moving back to the Croisilles - Henin road in support. By then it was snowing hard. During the night the wounded were brought in. The following morning the part of the line attacked by 62nd Brigade was evacuated by the enemy and occupied by the 1st

Lincolns. The 1st Lincolns losses for the 1st Battle of the Scarpe were one officer, sixteen NCOs and thirty-two privates killed, six officers, twenty-eight NCOs and seventry-three privates wounded, one NCO and fourteen privates missing.

The Lincolns buried their dead, including Pte Reg. Robinson, aged 23 and his original burial place, map reference 51b.T.4b.6.5., was near to the area of the 1st Lincolns attack on the Hindenburg Line. Twenty-two NCOs and men who fell on the 11th April were buried on the battlefield in the 'Lincolns Cemetery' at St Martin-sur-Cojeul and it is quite possible that Reg. was initially in this 'Lincolns Cemetery' (unfortunately the CWGC records do not include a map reference for the 'Lincolns Cemetery'.) This cemetery was among those that were concentrated into Wancourt British Cemetery. At the Armistice Wancourt Cemetery held 410 graves. That number was later increased to 1,839 burials after concentration into it from small cemeteries and battlefield graves, of which 827 are unidentified. Special Memorials record the names of 76 men known, or believed, to be buried among the unknowns, and of 20 men who were buried in Signal Trench Cemetery, Heninel, their graves having been destroyed in later battles (22 surviving graves were subsequently moved into Wancourt Cemetery).

R. W. Robinson headstone.

Of the unidentified men, 237 are from the United Kingdom, 24 are from Canada and 566 are unknown by name and unit. As a result of this concentration of burials from the Lincolns Cemetery at St Martin-sur-Cojeul and other small cemeteries in that area 1353 Pte R. W. Robinson, 1st Battalion Lincolnshire Regiment, is now buried in Wancourt British Cemetery, plot VII, row B, grave 29.

On the evening of Sunday 20th May a Memorial Service for Reg. was held in Barnetby West Street Wesleyan Chapel. During the service of special hymns and prayers the preacher, Mr Jetson of Grimsby, gave a very touching address. On 5th November 1917 his family received Reg.'s few personal effects – 2 letters, 5 cards and 3 photographs (his medals arrived later). Known relatives: Mrs June Manning of Ferneries Lane, Barnetby, who provided Reg.'s photograph and some information, and her daughter Mary and family.

Only just over a month earlier Mrs Dorothy Blanchard had no doubt been enjoying the time spent with her husband, at home on embarkation leave, when on Tuesday 1st May she received the sad information that on 23rd April a bursting shell had killed her husband...

194926 Corporal Charles Percy Blanchard, 'R' Corps Signals Company, Royal Engineers

Cpl C. P. Blanchard.

Charles Percy Blanchard, the only son of Charles and Sally Blanchard was born at Barnetby (3)1891 and in 1911 was living with his parents in Barnetby, working as a tailor in his father's business. In (4)1915 he married Dorothy Partridge, 20 (b. Barnetby (4)1895) and lived at Melton Villa, Barnetby. He enlisted at Brigg in August 1916 and became a Motor Dispatch Rider in 'R' (i.e. XVII) Corps Signals Company, Royal Engineers. In March 1917 he had been on home leave from France, where he had served just one month, only to return and receive mortal wounds on 23rd April 1917. In St Mary's Churchyard, Barnetby, his parents' grave headstone bears his name, aged 25 years.

For 'The 2nd Battle of the Scarpe', 23rd/24th April 1917, XVII Corps used the 37th and 51st Divisions and the 103rd Brigade of the 34th Division. XVII Corps war diary (WO 96/947) of 23rd April 1917 records: 'At Etrun. Work continued on forward route from Arras'.

The prearranged attack took place at 4.45 a.m. on a nine mile front from Croisilles to Gavrelle and certain objectives were gained. The Corps communications were subject to hostile shell-fire'. It is quite likely as not that Cpl Blanchard was a victim of the hostile shell-fire given that he was wounded while delivering dispatches near Etrun on 23rd April 1917, a small village about three miles north-west from Arras and died of his wounds that day, aged 24.

After the incident Mrs C. P. Blanchard received a letter from Charles' sergeant telling of her husband's death and informing her that Charles had died almost instantaneously. The

C. P. Blanchard headstone.

letter went on to relate that, '... *from the moment he arrived among them he was well liked by everybody. He always did his work well and no matter what inconvenience he was put to or what trouble came his way he never grumbled'.*

Charles Percy Blanchard is buried near Etrun in Haute Avesnes British Cemetery (plot C, grave 27). The inscription on his headstone reads, 'Loved by all'.

The 51st Highland Division started the cemetery in July 1916 and was used by Divisional Field Ambulances in the area. It holds one hundred and fifty-one burials including three Canadians, seven South Africans, one Indian Labourer, thirteen Chinese Labour Corps members and eight German prisoners of war. Also buried there is local man 27126 Pte Frank Beacock, 1st Battalion, The King's Own (Royal Lancaster Regiment), formerly 19359, Lincolnshire Regiment. Frank, son of George and Eliza Beacock of Cottage Lane, Wrawby (born (1) 1896 at South Ferriby, Lincolnsire), died of wounds on 12th April 1917, aged 21 years and is named on the War memorial at South Ferriby.

The paper of 11th May contained the final tragic item of Barnetby news, received by his family on Monday 7th May, that killed in action on 28th April and also leaving behind a young widow to mourn his loss was …

27435 Private Hugh Dawson, 8th Battalion, Lincolnshire Regiment

Hugh Dawson, husband of Harriet of Railway Street, Barnetby was the fourth son of Thomas and Elizabeth Dawson of Barnetby. In (2) 1915 Hugh married Harriet Eaton (b. at Elsham (1) 1880) and enlisted at Grimsby on 3rd June 1916 when his address was given as 4 Alfred St, Alexander Rd, Grimsby. His next of kin was named as Mrs Harriet Dawson, wife, c/o Mrs Eaton, Railway St, Barnetby. Hugh's age on attestation was stated as 28 years 170 days (calculated date of birth: 19th December 1887). Other named members of his family were: mother, Elizabeth, of West St; brothers: Thomas S. 44, of Pilot Station, Eden, NSW, Australia; Edward 42, of Woodhouse, Sheffield; Henry 39, Jesse 23 and sister Mrs Elizabeth Moss 38, all of St Barnabas Road.

Not much else is known about Hugh. In 1901, aged 13, he was working as a joiners labourer. In 1911 Hugh, a bricklayer, was living with his brother-in-law George William Moss in West Street. He had played cricket for the Barnetby village team and at the cricket club AGM held in April 1911 it was recorded that he headed the bowling averages. He was also appointed vice captain for the coming season. (Other familiar names mentioned at that AGM included H. Freeston, secretary; with H. Denton, A. and W. Smith and W. Worrall being appointed to the committee.) On Wednesday 28th February 1912, Hugh, in company with Albert Smith entrained at Barnetby for Liverpool en route for Alberta, in Canada, sailing from Liverpool on Friday 1st March. Many friends and relatives had gathered at the station to give the pair a good send-off and to wish them good luck. I do not know when Hugh returned home or if Albert Smith did.

Hugh was posted overseas on 9th August 1916. In February 1917 he received medical treatment for his legs (unable to decipher the medical terminology).

1917

On 7th March 1917 he was admitted to hospital at St Omer. From an earlier report in the *Hull Times*, that in places was almost illegible, I had deduced that Hugh was suffering from … *measles*? His service records confirmed my deduction with an entry stating that his complaint had been German measles! He was discharged back to his unit on 2nd April 1917. The next entry records Hugh as being killed in action on 28th April 1917, age 29.

Four months later Hugh's widow received what few personal belongings her husband had. She was awarded a pension of 13s. 9d. per week with effect from 19th November 1917 and in due course received his Scroll and Memorial Plaque.

The 8th Lincolns, as far as it concerns the Barnetby Boys, were last in action in November 1916 at Beaumont-Hamel on the Somme. Shortly afterwards the Battalion received a large draft of men to replace the losses it had incurred and went into training. At the end of February the Battalion was in the 37th Division training area at Neuville-au-Cornet some 30 km west of Arras. (The 63rd Brigade was originally part of the 21st Division but, on 7th July 1916, after the initial July Somme fighting, it was exchanged with 110th Brigade of the 37th Division).

The 8th Lincolns were next in action near Monchy-le-Preux during 'The First Battle of the Scarpe, 9th-14th April' (part of 'The Battles of Arras, 1917', the ongoing offensive agreed on to assist the French in their operations down on the Aisne). After the battle the 8th Lincolns were withdrawn to various locations and ended up at Montenescourt some 6 miles west of Arras. On 20th April the 8th Lincolns left Montenescourt for the front and moved to an area between Rœux and Gavrelle, some three miles further north from their last action at Monchy-le-Preux, in readiness for 'The Second Battle of the Scarpe, 23rd-24th April'. There they took up support positions in Hazard and Hudson Trenches that ran SW–NE some 250 and 500 yards respectively west of Hyderabad Work (Hyderabad Redoubt – see Map 16).

During the 'Second Battle of the Scarpe' the 8th Lincolns (63rd Brigade, 37th Division) were part of the 37th Division attack towards Greenland Hill and the Plouvain – Gavrelle road in support of the 10th York and Lancaster (left-front battalion). Starting at 4.45 a.m. on 23rd April the 8th Lincolns (left support battalion) soon passed through the 10th York and Lancaster – held up by the barrage – and after clearing some fifty to sixty enemy from part of Chili Trench at H.12.b.3.8. had occupied that and the southern end of Candia Trench. Both battalions continued to advance towards the road and by noon had established a line between Chili Trench and the road. The enemy retaliated with a counter attack from Greenland Hill but this was broken up by rifle and machine-gun fire.

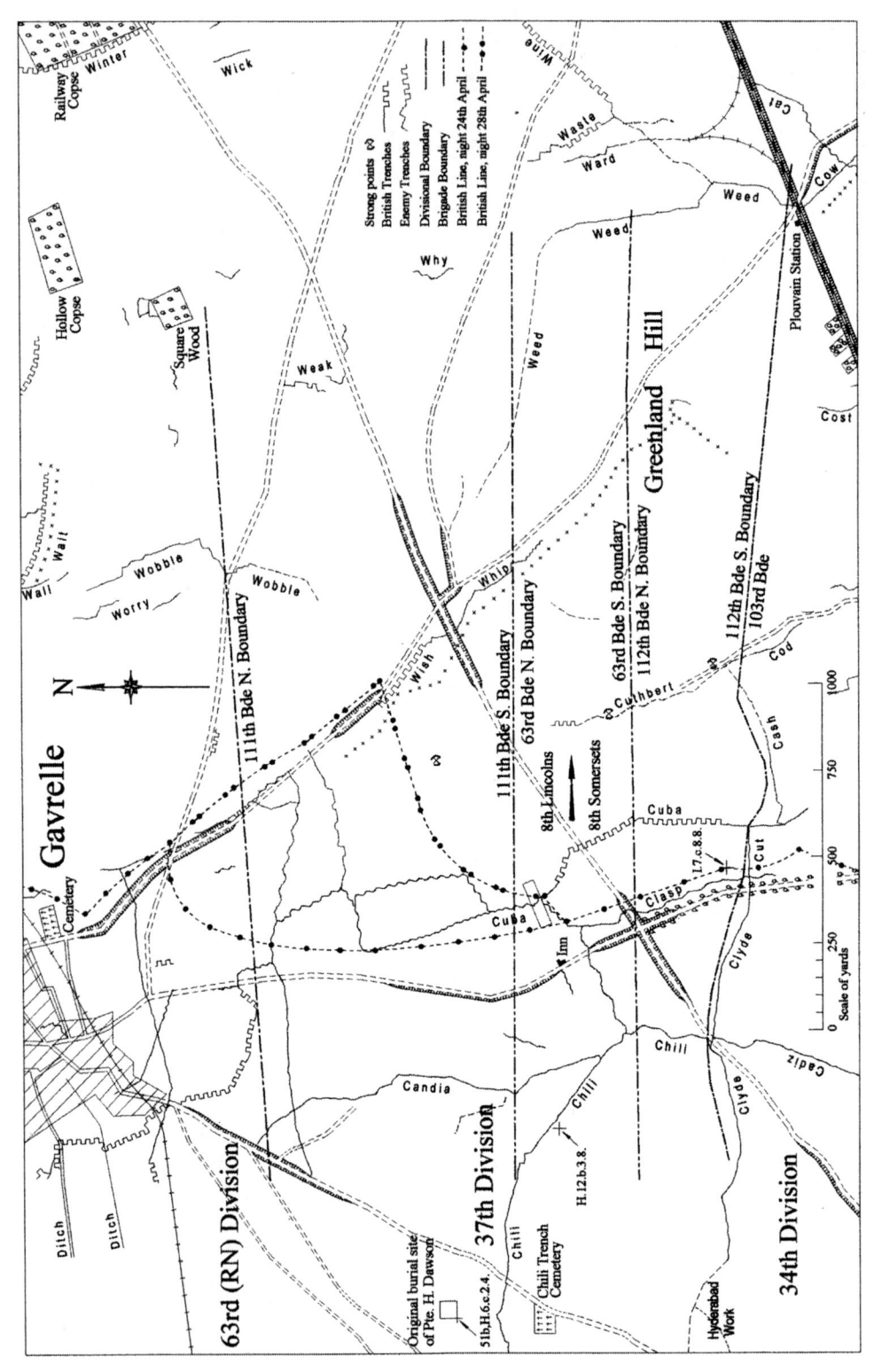

Map 16.

In the 'Battle of Arleux' 28th-29th April, the objective of the 37th Division was to take Greenland Hill, between Plouvain and Gavrelle. For this attack the 63rd Brigade, in the centre, was to take the German Cuthbert Trench. The 37th Division's 112th Brigade was on the right and 111th on the left. The 63rd Brigade was to assemble in Cuba Trench with the 8th Somerset on the right and the 8th Lincolns on the left, zero hour for the attack being timed for 4.25 a.m. When the attack commenced direction in the centre was lost, due to the darkness and the smoke from the barrage, and most of the attacking troops went left past Cuthbert Trench resulting in Whip and Wish trenches being mistakenly attacked for Cuthbert Trench.

Both battalions continued to push forward in small groups from shell-hole to shell-hole and between 2 p.m. and 3 p.m. were positioned about 50 yards east of the road between the Inn and the crossroads where they dug in. By nightfall a line was established with the remainder of the 63rd Brigade about the road from the Inn to map reference I.7.c.8.8. The 8th Lincolns were then withdrawn to Chili and Candia Trenches in support.

The majority of the battalions went way beyond these trenches; past Why and Weak almost to Railway Copse, taking prisoners in doing so which were subsequently recaptured by the enemy, supposedly in the vicinity of Weed Trench, as they were sent back.

Some troops even reached Wick Trench. Realizing the attack had gone wrong small groups began working back to Whip Trench and others to a line about 300yards east of Cuthbert Trench – still occupied in part by a few enemy troops- where they dug in and remained for the rest of the day. Small parties continued to work back to Whip Trench throughout the night and to the line east of Cuthbert Trench. Those troops that had reached

H. Dawson headstone.

Cuthbert Trench, being unsupported, eventually returned and evening saw the Brigade back where it had started.

This action cost the 8th Lincolns two hundred and ninety-six casualties of which twenty-two other ranks were killed, one hundred and sixty-four were wounded and one hundred and five missing. On 29th April the Battalion was withdrawn to Arras, where it rested, before being taken by bus to Beaufort where it arrived on 30th April. The 8th Lincolns war diary merely states that they were part of the attack on the left of the Brigade front and gives the numbers killed.

The actions of 23rd – 24th April and this latter had reduced the battalion in strength by four hundred and twenty-seven other ranks.

Pte Hugh Dawson is buried in Chili Trench Cemetery, Gavrelle (plot B, grave 19). The inscription on his headstone reads 'Peace perfect peace.' The cemetery is near to where the action had taken place, with Hugh having previously been buried nearby on the battlefield at map reference 51b,H.6.c.2.4. that was perhaps the original Chili Trench Cemetery before the present one was laid out at or near the same site?

Chili Trench Cemetery, Gavrelle. Hugh Dawson's grave is approximately central in the photograph – next but one from the seat by the wall. He was originally buried in the field beyond the Cemetery roughly mid way between the Cemetery and the clump of tall trees seen half right on the skyline.

Looking towards Chili Trench Cemetery from the direction of Gavrelle through the approximate position of Hugh Dawson's original burial site (arrowed). The spire of Rœux Church is on the left skyline and the Seaforth Highlander's Memorial on the right skyline.

The cemetery derives its name from the proximity of a trench called Chili Avenue and was made chiefly by units of the 37th Division in April and May 1917. It contains the graves of one hundred and ninety-six United Kingdom soldiers, of which seventeen are unidentified, and includes one burial from the 1939–45 war. At first glance the cemetery seems far too large for the number of burials there although the relatively large grassed frontal area possibly contains graves destroyed by shellfire as represented by the eighty-six special memorials along the cemetery front and side walls. Some of these markers can be seen in the photograph on the previous page.

It is relatively easy to determine the positions of Whip, Wish, Why, Weak and Weed trenches and Railway Copse where there is a small wood. Cuthbert Trench is more difficult for its location is now the intersection of the main A1/A26 AutoRoute that obstructs the view between Greenland Hill and Chili Trench Cemetery. A better view can be had from the high ground to the south-west of Chili Trench Cemetery where the high bank-top of the road running behind Sunken Road Cemetery affords an uninterrupted view looking towards Greenland Hill. Just down the road from that Cemetery is a monument to the Seaforth Highlanders.

The construction of modern developments across battlefields, such as AutoRoutes and the TGV high-speed train lines, which often run parallel to the AutoRoutes, must have caused problems for the contractors in not knowing quite what they might unearth. In June 2000, a grave containing the remains of 19 British soldiers, initially believed to be mainly 10th Lincolns, was unearthed on an industrial development at le Point du Jour, about 1½ miles due west of Chili Trench Cemetery. Military cemeteries and monuments apart, the occasional samples of 'iron harvest' (unexploded ammunition and pieces of exploded shells) that can still be seen lying around emphasise the fact that a conflict had taken place thereabouts.

After the deaths of four village lads during April, it was perhaps very much a relief for four families to have their sons home on leave knowing at least that they were safe and well. During the second week in May Gunner Robert Allison of the RFA was back in the fold for a short spell as was Pte Charles Maddison, Lincolns, who had been in training for some months.

During the week ending 26th May two more men were home on leave, both having been in hospital for some time. Pte Maurice Allison, Lincolns, (related to Robert Allison?) had been suffering from shell shock but was reported as looking fit and well again; Sgt Fred Barnett, of the Lincolns Trench Mortar Battery, had been seriously wounded on 6th November 1916 and been in hospital since that time. He was now convalesced and progressing favourably but perhaps not quite looking forward to Monday 28th May, when he was due to return to his unit.

In December 1915, Mrs Mary Ann Starkey had had the distress of finding Mr Burgess, her lodger, dead in an outhouse at her home. Previous to that her husband had died after a prolonged illness on Wednesday 14th February 1912, age 54 years. Now even more anxiety was to be her lot with having not heard any definite word of her son, missing more than three weeks; neither had he been seen by any of his 'pals' over that period. It was going to be a very trying time indeed for that poor woman for she was to endure that suspense and anxiety for more than a year before official news arrived regarding the fate of her son...

202688 Private William Foster Starkey, 2/4th Battalion, York and Lancaster Regiment (Hallamshire, T. F.)

William Foster Starkey, son of Mary Ann Starkey (of Kings Road, Barnetby) and the late Frederick John Starkey (buried in St Mary's Churchyard 17th February 1912, William in attendance), was born at Barton in December 1883. In 1891 the family were living at Barrow on Humber. In 1911 Water, a grocer's assistant, was lodging with Joshua Henry Bernans at 3 Seed Hill, Huddersfield. On 11th November 1915, single, aged 31 years 11 months, a grocer's assistant living at 223 Ecclesfield Road, Sheffield, he enlisted at Sheffield into 'The Hallamshires', the local Territorial Force of The York and Lancaster Regiment, and given the service number 5258 (changed on 24th April 1916 to 202688). Placed on the reserve list after attestation he was subsequently called to join the 2/4th Battalion York and Lancaster Regiment on 18th March 1916. On 13th January 1917 the battalion sailed for Le Havre, France.

By 15th January 1917 all units of the 62nd (2/West Riding) Division had arrived in France. The newly formed 2/4th 'Hallamshire' Battalion, York and Lancaster Regiment, was part of the 187th Brigade along with 2/5th York and Lancaster, 2/4th KOYLI and 2/5th KOYLI.

By the third week in February, after receiving rudimentary instruction on trench duties interspersed with providing fatigue parties employed on railway work, the battalion went into the line near Beaumont-Hamel on the Somme. From there the 62nd Division was initially in pursuit of the enemy during his retreat to the Hindenburg Line, but en route was taken out of the line with orders to provide working parties for road and railway repairs. At the beginning of April the 187th Brigade took over front line duties in the St.Léger - Gommiecourt area near Bullecourt.

On 11th April, in conjunction with the Arras offensive of 1st and 3rd Armies to the north, the 4th Australian Division and 62nd Division (5th Army) mounted an attack on the Hindenburg Line at Bullecourt. It had only limited success. The 62nd Division spent the rest of the month engaged in trench warfare and preparing for a further attempt on that formidable enemy line.

1917

The 3rd Battle of the Scarpe (3rd-4th May 1917) was part of The Battles of Arras, 1917, the ongoing offensive against the Hindenburg Line. From 3rd-17th May 5th Army, using three British divisions (7th, 58th and 62nd) of V Corps and three Australian divisions of 1 Anzac Corps, carried out a flanking action to that offensive – the Battle of Bullecourt.

The 62nd Division, in its first battle action, was to capture Bullecourt (185th Brigade) and part of the Hindenburg Line and support line to the north-west (186th and 187th Brigades), then take Hendecourt and make defensive positions from Hendecourt up to the Hindenburg Line with the 187th Brigade, on the left flank, taking up defensive positions around the cemetery to the north west of Hendecourt. The 2/4th Yorks and Lancs, on the Brigade right, were to take the Hindenburg Line first line (A Coy right, C Coy left) and second line trenches (B Coy right, D Coy left). On their left the 2/5th Yorks and Lancs were to take the front and support lines and set up strong points and bombing blocks. The 2/5th KOYLI were to form the defensive left flank with 2/4th KOYLI, less six platoons, held to reinforce as necessary (see Map 17 overleaf).

The white line is the approximate position of the taped start line. The white arrows indicate the wire in front of first line trenches. The chalk beyond is possibly the second line. The white dot near the railway is the approximate position of Battalion H.Q. with the First Aid Post about 50 yards in rear. Note the shell holes. In the foreground is the Croisilles – Ecoust St Mein Road. Photo IWM.

Late on the night of 2nd May, having assembled on the Croisilles – Ecoust St. Mein road, the 2/4th Yorks and Lancs were taken to the start line (marked from U19d.6.45 – U26b.3.8. with white tape) incurring a few casualties on the way. At 3.45 a.m. on 3rd May the assault went ahead behind the barrage covering the half mile advance to the enemy trenches. In poor light, made worse by dust and smoke, the leading waves of the 2/4th Yorks and Lancs managed to reach the enemy first line trench and took up positions in and around it. However the following waves of the 2/4th Yorks and Lancs had their formations broken when the left battalion of 186th Brigade lost direction and came across their front between the 4th and 5th waves.

Despite the confusion many pressed on to reach the second line trench and, being unable to take it as the enemy was there in strength, took up positions

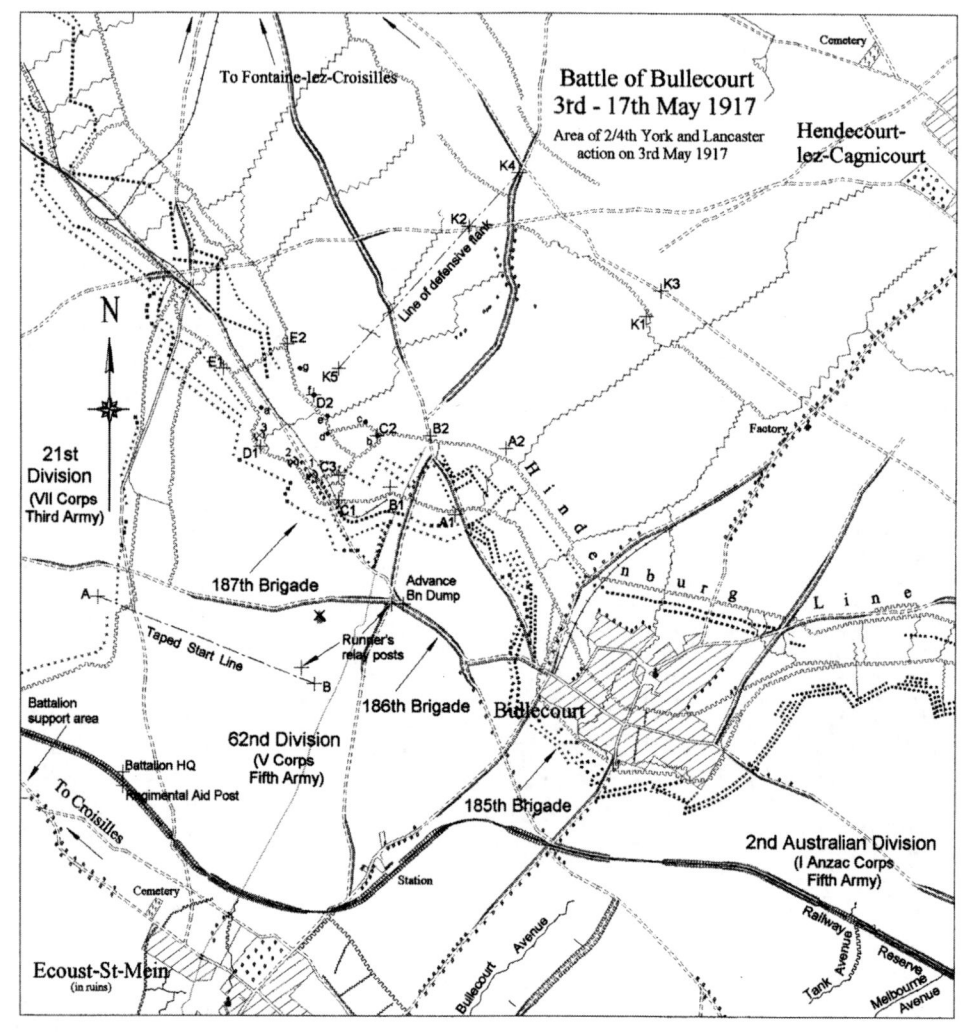

Map 17.

nearby. Orders were then issued to withdraw and reorganize, some 2/4th Yorks and Lancs duly returning to the railway cutting.

At 9 a.m. the Brigade Major arrived at the railway cutting with orders to form up for a second attack. About 70 2/4th Yorks and Lancs formed up with 2/4th and 2/5th KOYLI but their attack was broken up by machine-gun and shell-fire and the men took up positions in shell holes. Battalion headquarters (at U25b.8.1.) was unaware of this situation due to problems in getting messages back. Meanwhile the men hung on to their positions taking casualties in doing so.

At 4p.m., due to the difficulty of reinforcing positions, Brigade ordered the 2/4th Yorks and Lancs to pull back to the railway cutting in rear of posts set up by the 2/5th Yorks and Lancs. On completion the 2/4th Yorks and Lancs went into support near the Ecoust-Croisilles road, and remained there until 4 p.m. on 4th May, then moved back to a camp near Mory Copse.

The 187 Brigade summed up the whole attack 'as a failure and a costly failure' (PRO WO 95/3088). The 2/4th Yorks and Lancs casualties were: 3 officers killed, 4 wounded, 1 missing; 6 other ranks killed, 18 missing (believed killed), 130 wounded, 18 wounded and missing and 57 missing. William was initially recorded as missing during this battle on 3rd May 1917, aged 34.

A newspaper report of 25th May 1917 stated that Mrs Starkey was anxious, having had news that her son had been reported missing for three weeks. It was announced on 21st June 1918, that Mrs Starkey had received news notifying that her son William, reported missing since 3rd May 1917, was killed in action on or about that time. A month later Mrs Starkey replied stating that having had official notification of William's death if any of her son's personal effects had been received she would like them returned, especially his (w)rist watch. In June 1919 Mrs Starkey filled in and signed a statement of next of kin, witnessed by the Vicar of Melton Ross, entitling her to be issued with the Scroll and Memorial Plaque of her late son.

William has no known grave and is commemorated by name on the Arras Memorial to the Missing (Bay 8), at the Faubourg d'Amiens Cemetery, Arras. The memorial names 35,698 officers and men from only the United Kingdom, New Zealand and South Africa, serving the area from Loos (exclusive) to Berles-au-Bois (except for the Battle of Cambrai 1917). Placed centrally on the memorial walls are the 1,149 names of all officers and men of Great Britain and the Dominions, belonging or attached to the Royal Naval Air Service, the Royal Flying Corps and the Royal Air Force, who fell on the whole Western Front. The Air Forces Memorial stands within the Arras Memorial. The Cemetery contains 2,652 British burials.

Part of the Arras Memorial to the Missing, Faubourg d'Amiens Cemetery, Arras. Pte Starkey's name is on the bay on the right. The Air Forces Memorial, a globe surmounted on a pillar, is to the right of centre.

Neil Wilkin of Barnetby had an uncle, 242293 Pte Fred. Wilkin, 2/6th West Yorks, killed in action at Bullecourt on 11th April 1917. He is named on the Arras Memorial (2/6th West Yorks were in 185th Brigade, 62nd Division). Fred Wilkin has no known grave but Neil is fairly certain of the location where his uncle was believed killed from information stated in the battalion war diary. Although this cannot be confirmed all known facts point to a precise spot that is readily identifiable, there being a Chapel (Oratory) built on the spot but I do not think that is significant.

A few hundred yards from the Faubourg d'Amiens Memorial, at the Citadel, is a tragic memorial – the Mur des Fusilées. Plaques sited on the moat walls commemorate members of the French Resistance executed there by the Gestapo during the Second World War. A white post at the far end of the moat marks the execution site. I have also seen memorials in village cemeteries to Resistance executions. The grim word 'Fusilée' tells its own tragic story.

Mur des Fusillées at Arras. Over 200 plaques line the moat walls.

A stone post marks the site of the execution post.

Sad news came to a young Owmby family when they received distressing information of their husband and father…

77473 Gunner Ernest Vessey, 160th Siege Battery, Royal Garrison Artillery.

Ernest Vessey, born on 20th November 1889 at Risby Moor, Walesby, Lincolnshire, was the fifth of six sons of Joseph and Sarah Ann Vessey (he had two sisters). The 1901 census shows Ernest was living with the family at Searby (his parents were living at 55 Silver Street, Barnetby in 1919). Ernest had married Ethel Ester Lacey on 25th November 1914; they had one son, John Thomas, born on 9th February 1915 and lived at Owmby, near Grasby.

Ernest, a farm horseman, enlisted at Market Rasen on 12th December 1915 and on the following day was placed on the reserve list. Posted as a Gunner on 26th April 1916 on 6th June 1916 he joined the 160th Battery, RGA. His time with the BEF dates from 18th September 1916. Ernest was accidentally killed on 3rd May 1917 and is buried in the French National Cemetery at Vauxbuin, in plot III, row B, grave 7. This cemetery is roughly 4-km south-west of Soissons.

There are 4,803 French burials, 9,568 German and 280 British, including one English woman, Mrs Gartside-Tipping, Croix-de-Guerre (France) – (daughter of Lady Pilkington and widow of a Lt Commander (RN), she died on 6th March, 1917, while serving as a voluntary canteen worker for French soldiers and is buried in the same row as Ernest.) A tall hedge separates the French and British burials from the German Military section in the cemetery.

Pte E. Vessey.

Introductory notes in the cemetery register name burial grounds that had had graves transferred into Vauxbuin. One, Terny-Sorny French Military Cemetery, contained the graves of 365 French soldiers, and two RGA Gunners who died there in May 1917 – indicating that Ernest had been buried there. The CWGC affirmed his burial at Terny-Sorny, and transfer into the Vauxbuin Cemetery in 1924, along with 75180 Gunner William Thomas Parker, RGA, of Rushden, Northamptonshire. Ernest's burial at Terny-Sorny was subsequently verified in his Service Documents (WO 363/V69) that are among the 'Burnt Records' that had recently been recorded on microfilm and are now held at the National Archives at Kew.

Ernest had initially been buried at map reference Soissons 33.(1:20,000) 183.65 x 303.5 in Terny-Sorny Military Cemetery, sited at the north-east end of the village. When I first visited Terny-Sorny, which is roughly 9 km north of Soissons, I had not acquired that map. My initial enquiries in the village as to the location of the former cemetery drew a blank. At the school cum Marie (town hall) the Mayor's wife, and others who joined in (the mums were by then bringing their children back to school after lunch), was adamant there had been no Military Cemetery there and gave me locations of French Cemeteries in the surrounding district. Having written proof I maintained I was right. Eventually, one lady suggested telephoning the oldest inhabitant – an elderly man. I was in luck for he was just old enough to remember where the cemetery had been. I was taken to see him and the site was duly pointed out to me.

There still remained the question of what the 160th Siege Battery was doing in that area in April/May 1917 in what was then French Army territory. It transpires that the Battery had been attached to, and was working with, the French Army from 4th April to 9th May 1917.

The 160th Siege Battery, RGA, consisting of 4 in number 6" Howitzers (26 cwt), went to the Western Front on 18th September 1916 joining the LI. Heavy Artillery Group (HAG) until 23rd September 1916 when it was transferred to the V. HAG. It transferred to the LXIX. HAG on 26th September and rejoined the V. HAG on 9th February 1917. From 21st March to 24th May 1917 the Battery was independent of the V. HAG having been detached to XXIV. HAG along with the 176th, 207th and 255th Siege Batteries, all 6" Howitzers, for use by the French Army.

At the end of March 1917 the 160th Siege Battery was in the Ypres area. On 1st April the Battery moved to Abeele where it entrained. The train left for Villers-Cotterêts the following day arriving there on 4th April. After unloading its guns and lorries the Battery proceeded by road to Soissons. At 9 a.m. on 6th April an advance party left Soissons bound for Terny-Sorny to prepare gun

1917

Vauxbuin French Military Cemetery. The hedge dividing the British and French burials from the German burials casts the dark shadow at the left edge.

The French Military Cemetery at Terny-Sorny (above)...

...had previously been sited near to the road in the field seen in the middle ground of the above photograph (approximately in front of the houses seen centre and right).

positions (no map reference given), the battery personnel arriving at 11 p.m. (the XXIV. HAG Batteries were emplaced in the deep valley between Terny-Sorny and Margival 3 km to the ESE and probably in the area about 1.4 km from Terny-Sorny where the terrain, following an initial steep descent, levelled out (preferable, to avoid hauling heavy guns up steep embankments) some 700 m south of Sorny for about 900 m towards Margival – see Map 18 below, lower right hand corner, map ref. 184.7 x 302.8). Preparation of the gun positions continued the next day with the guns arriving at 5 p.m.; during the day the road near to the Battery position was subject to bombardment.

On 8th April the 160th Battery carried out a registration shoot on the northwest corner of a rectangular wood southeast of Moisy farm (roughly 6,000 yards away in an east-northeasterly direction). From then on the Battery carried out regular shoots until 2nd May when No. 3 gun accidentally burst, wounding 1 officer and six other ranks and killing 2 other ranks (as the date of death is registered as 3rd May I believe these two soldiers died of wounds). The Battery left Terny-Sorny on 8th May bound for Soissons and thence by road to Compiègne. Later the 160th Battery joined X Corps Heavy Artillery.

'Soldiers Died in the War' lists both Ernest Vessey and W. T. Parker as having died of wounds. It is possible that a French Army field hospital had been located in the area and had made the military cemetery, with Ernest and W. T. Parker being among their casualties and subsequent burials. On my next visit to

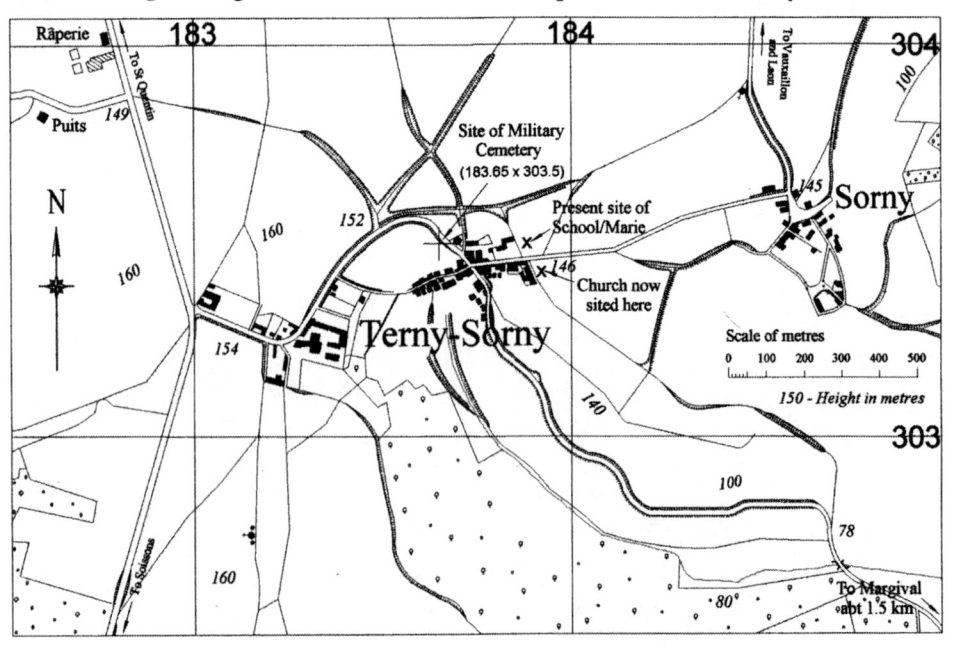

Map 18. *Terny-Sorny French Military Cemetery at ref. 183.65 x 303.5 (based on map dated 1918).*

Terny-Sorny I was lucky enough to meet the Mayor who took me to see a village resident, presumably the local historian. After explaining the reason for my visit I was shown a collection of documents relating to the war in that area, including a postcard photograph of the French Military Cemetery in Terny-Sorny taken during the war. This same gentleman confirmed the location of the Cemetery and I also think he was rather surprised that I had a copy of a French military map (PRO WO 297/5283) of that area dated 1918!

Positive identification of Ernest was confused by the CWGC also offering an Ernest Luke Vessey, 6th Lincolns, from Lincolnshire, named on the Helles Memorial, Gallipoli. Having seen an Owmby reference; been told that his parents lived in Silver Street and that Ernest Vessey is named on the memorial plaque in St Nicholas' Church, Searby-cum-Owmby, convinced me that I had the right man. This was confirmed by his Service Documents (which has his birth place as Wyham, while the 1891 Risby census states Walesby and the 1901 Searby census states Risby!).

While little has come to light about Ernest's life at home some satisfaction has been gained in finding out how he died and the reason for being in the French sector. The visits to Terny-Sorny were fruitful and enlightening. The only other information gleaned is that Ernest's name is on a carved wooden Roll of Honour in Grasby village hall. (He is named on the Barnetby Roll of Honour.) Known relatives include Mr Ernest Vessey, Mrs Wyn Vessey and Mrs Karen Havercroft. Ernest (Snip) of St Mary's Avenue, Barnetby, says he was named after his uncle. His father, Harold of 34 Victoria Road – renumbered 29 in the 1960's, was an elder brother; Ernest's other brothers were: William, Albert, Joseph, Harold and Walter. Walter, who lived at Low Wood Cottage, was the father-in-law of Mrs Wyn Vessey and grandfather of her daughter, Mrs Karen Havercroft. Ernest's two sisters were Mrs Gertrude Rose and Miss Rose Emily Vessey.

On 17th September 1917 Ernest's widow, Mrs Ethel Vessey, who had earlier been notified of his accidental death, received his few personal effects. Among those was a silver cigarette case containing locks of hair. His widow was awarded a pension of 18 s. 9 d. per week for herself and one child effective from 19th November 1917. On 30th September 1921 she received Ernest's British War Medal and Victory Medal. Her address was given as: The Lodge, Holton-le-Moor.

Back in Barnetby, two more soldiers had been on leave at the end of May. Pte John Waite, who was with Cyril Gostelow when he died, had been sampling home comforts for a while before returning to the Western Front. Pte W. Smith, of the Lincolns, who had been convalescing after receiving hospital treatment for some months suffering from shell shock, had been home on ten days sick leave.

A brief item under the sub-heading 'CARD OF HONOUR' followed this – an unusual award term that I also came across in the Journal. 'It is with pride that the inhabitants of the village learn that Pte P.C. Poole, of the Lincolnshire Regiment, has been awarded a 'card of honour' for displaying remarkable pluck and determination and doing good work in carrying messages, and showing a keen devotion to duty near Arras between April 9th & 14th. He has been slightly wounded, but has recovered sufficiently to rejoin his battalion again. He is the eldest son of Mr and Mrs R. Poole. This is the second distinction gained in the village, the first being the DCM gained by Corporal G. W. Insley in May, 1916, who by his quick handling of a German fuse saved the lives of many of his comrades. He has since been transferred and is now a gunner'. (See p. 97.)

The October 1915 Journal mentioned that Pte J. W. Ellerby, 1st Lincolns, a former assistant timber loader at Ulceby and son of timber loader A. Ellerby, had received a card from Major-General Haldane, his Divisional Commander. 'Your Commanding Officer and Brigade Commander have informed me that you distinguished yourself in the field on the 16th June, 1915. I have read their report with much pleasure.'

The Journal for May 1917 provided two brief items. The first gave out that C. Bell, a junior clerk in the Traffic Dept at Barnetby, had enlisted. The second concerned a former Signal Dept labourer at Barnetby, 655 Pte G. H. Winterbottom, Lincolns, who had enlisted at the outbreak of war and been wounded early in 1916. He had received his discharge from the Army and had also left the railway service.

Two more soldiers were home on leave at the beginning of June. Pte A. Robinson, of the Lincolns, who was in training had been on leave during the first week to visit his invalid brother and Pte William Baker had just 'been on leave'.

The following week a news report on the meeting of the Independent Order of Rechabites stated that the Order had sent a message of sympathy to Mrs Blair following the death of her son Walter, killed in action, who was an officer in that tent at the time of his enlistment.

During the third week in June Pte Alfred Frow's sister, had received word from her brother in the Lincolns saying he had been wounded again, for the third time.

L/Cpl Thomas Rowe, Lincolnshire Regiment, who some time ago had been wounded in the left forearm, was at home on sick leave during the last week in June, looking fit and well again. Quartermaster-Sergeant Thomas Allcard, RAMC, at home on leave for ten days, had also been seen going about the village around that time.

The War Fund committee had been busy again preparing parcels for the men in the forces. They were hoping in the near future to dispatch between 90 and 100 parcels out to the Boys wherever they were serving.

More fund raising had been going on, this time organised by the Ladies' Adult School. They had held a sale of work and useful articles on the evening of Saturday 23rd June in the grounds of the Manor House, kindly lent for the occasion by Mrs Lowish. The Barnetby Band had very generously given their services, playing selections during the evening. In a competition to assess the weight of a cake two men, Mr E. Vickers and Mr Cowling, had both guessed the weight to within half-an-ounce, so the cake was divided between them. The proceeds of the evening had realised a total of £7 12s, with £5 1s 10d coming from the sale of work; 8s 2d. from the cake competition and the remaining £2 2s having been donated. The effort had been in aid of the Adult School and the Roll of Honour. The Roll of Honour at that time had 127 names on it and was shortly to be erected on the Co-operative Stores premises in Victoria Road.

You may recall that back in May Gunner Robert Allison of the RFA had been home on leave; now news had come to the village, 30th June, that he had been wounded in both legs, though not seriously, through the bursting of a gun (the wounding item gave his unit as the Royal Garrison Artillery (RGA)! N.B: This is probably not the same bursting gun that killed Ernest Vessey.)

The final article of 30th June gave notice of a much more serious wounding when it announced that Pte 'Kit' White of the Lincolns was very seriously ill in a hospital in France.

One newspaper article in the last week of June concerned GCR employees returning from France to resume their ordinary duties. I had hoped the Journal might have had an explanatory item on that but there were only two photographs of the Civilian Railway Companies, one depicting the 'Gangers' of No. 5 Company and the other No. 5 Company, No. 4 Gang. (From the 'Gangers' photograph I have identified the Ganger in charge of No. 5 Company, No. 1 Gang.)

Now follows an article relating to the above paragraph about a little known aspect of the Great War that affected a small group of railwaymen from the village.

An Unsatisfactory Experiment

Back in March a small group of village GCR employees had gone to France to work on rebuilding the railways, where their expertise was desperately needed. This brought to mind two family First World War photographs I had come across that at the time did not make sense. Having since found three items in the *Grimsby News* about Barnetby GCR employees I began to understand what the photographs referred to. One, a 'Carte Postal', shows a group of thirty relatively old men, wearing armbands, with a central figure holding an upside-down tea tray on which is chalked, 'No. 5 Railway Civilian Company No. 1 Gang.' On the back is written, *'Dear Mother, Just sending a photo will write a letter later. With love to all, Harry'*.

No. 5 Railway Civilian Company, No. 1 Gang. Harry Cox is fourth left, middle row. Ganger W. C. Statham from Grimsby Docks is holding the tray.

The second photograph (below) shows a R.E. gang repairing damaged railway tracks – possibly in northern France. I wondered if there was any connection between the two, as by then I had a good idea who Harry was. The newspaper article of March this year stated, 'that the following had left for France: Padmore, Vessey, Clark, Parkinson, Welton, Smith, Cox and Calver, also locking fitter Mr. Charnley'. Harry was Harry Cox, who later became Uncle Harry on marrying my Father's eldest sister Ethel.

Three months later the 29th June newspaper carried the following heading – 'GCR Employees Return'. Then a brief note to say that, 'a number of employees of the GCR, including platelayers, labourers and locking fitters, who volunteered for a period of railway work in France, have this week returned home, and for the present resumed their ordinary duties'. But why were they returned home after working just three months out in France?

I subsequently enquired on the subject to the Royal Engineers museum at Chatham. The reply was to the effect that in the spring of 1917 an experiment was carried out engaging civilian expert railway platelayers in eight companies under a civilian railway official. As the experiment was not giving satisfactory results the engagement at the three-month end was not renewed. That knocked on the head the thought that the railwaymen had been put into uniform and absorbed into the RE's, that notion coming from the second photograph. The answer about that photograph was found in an item dated November 23rd, 1917, saying, 'Mr. Cox's eldest son was about to join the colours'. It did not say what he was joining but I know that he served in the Royal Engineers as 169074 Sapper Harry Cox, RE. Presumably he is on the photograph showing RE's repairing damaged track, possibly the small stocky man standing astride a broken rail slightly right of centre. Why else the photograph?

An item of 6th July announced that L/Cpl Fred Maxted of the Royal Field Artillery was at home on ten days leave, his first leave for twenty-eight months. He had been one of the first local lads to join the colours on the outbreak of war and since that time had seen much service. So far luck had been with him as he had managed to come through it all without a scratch.

The final item of 6th July referred to the last item of 30th June concerning a very seriously wounded man in a French hospital, only this time the news was the worst that could have come to the White family about their son...

242248 Private Edward Keightly White, 1/5th Battalion, Lincolnshire Regiment.

Edward Keightly 'Kit' White was one of three sons of Thomas and Hannah White of King's Road, Barnetby. He was born at Ravendale (1) 1888 and in 1911 was living with his parents in Melton Ross, working as a quarry man at the Chalk Pits. He enlisted into the army at Brigg. Edward died of wounds on the 27th June 1917, aged 29. His two brothers, Christopher and Hubert, were still serving with the colours at the time of his death.

Pte E. K. White.

During the third week in March 1917 the 46th Division, with orders to transfer to I Corps, First Army, withdrew from the Gommecourt sector on the Somme and marched to the Amiens area. The 138th Brigade left Saleux, near Amiens, on 27th March bound for Lillers, west of Bethune, from where the 1/5th Lincolns moved to billets in Bourecq for training.

On completion of training the 1/5th Lincolns returned to the front line on 19th April occupying the former German front line and support trenches to the east of Cité St. Pierre, a northwest suburb of Lens. The front line, a series of advance posts mainly in houses, was accessed via trenches from cellars where the off-duty part of the battalion stayed. The first tour in the line, consisting mainly of patrols, was fairly quiet apart from occasionally being subjected to shell-fire. On 23rd April the 1/4th Lincolns relieved the Battalion.

During May, interchanging duty and relief turns with the 1/4th Lincolns, un-relaxing trench warfare activity increased, with persistent bombing, mortaring, sniping and machine-gun fire. Both sides carried out raids and patrols had frequent encounters in No Man's Land. Day or night British guns gave significant replies to the recurrent enemy shelling and barrages.

On 7th and 8th June the 1/4th Lincolns and 1/5th Leicesters assaulted the enemy in the Cité de Riaumont sector. The 1/5th Lincolns assisted the assault with support tasks and relieved them there on 9th June. On 15th June, whilst digging trenches between Crocodile and Absolom Trenches, they were subjected to trench mortar fire and in the process suffered 12 casualties.

On 18th June the 1/5th Lincolns relieved the 1/5th Leicesters at Cité de Riaumont and began to prepare for an attack the next day spending most of the night bringing up stores needed for their assault on the enemy's trenches. A and B Companies were detailed for the assault on trenches from Ball through to Brick (on the line a- b, see map) with C (in billets about a mile to the rear) as the wiring company, once their objectives were taken, and D the carrying company.

At 2.30 p.m. the attack went in behind a barrage and minutes later the enemy replied with its counter-barrage but this did not hold up the proceedings. On the Lincolns right the trench was entered without too much trouble and taken after a fierce fight, those of the enemy not being killed or taken prisoner being driven towards the Canadians assisting on their right. Meanwhile men from 'D' Coy brought bombs up to the forward dump below the slag heap. On the left heavy rifle and machine-gun fire coming from the junction of Bath, Alice, Ball and Africa Trenches checked their advance. This resistance was countered with rifle-grenades and rifle-fire with the result that the enemy was driven from those trenches.

With the objectives taken work began to consolidate the gains against counter-attack. The first, at 4.45 p.m. from Ahead Trench, and subsequent attacks at 7 p.m. and 10 p.m. were broken up by artillery, Lewis-gun and rifle-fire that exacted heavy casualties on the enemy. The enemy was also seen massing east of Admiral Trench but nothing came of that. At night two Lewis-gun posts and a listening post were put out. On 20th June the 1/5th Leicesters relieved A and B Coys who moved to Angres where, on 21st June, C and D Coys joined them after relief by the 8th Sherwood Foresters. In that attack the casualties of the 1/5th Lincolns were: twelve other ranks killed, two officers and fifty-five other ranks wounded, four other ranks died of wounds and one missing. On being relieved at Angres on 22nd June by the 5th N. Staffs the 1/5th Lincolns went into billets for rest at Petit Sains.

During the night of 25th June the 1/5th Lincolns relieved the 6th N. Staffs in the line (b-c) and proceeded to quietly capture Ahead and Admiral Trenches and the support line on the crest of Hill 65. (A Coy held Ahead, B – Admiral, C – outposts on Hill 65 with B in reserve.)

E. K. White headstone.

Next day enemy artillery was active and a mine (a booby trap in a dugout) exploded in Ahead Trench. Casualties that day were 6 killed and 32 wounded. After relief on 27th June the 1/5th Lincolns went into reserve at Liévin. 3 other ranks died of wounds that day.

That leaves the question, 'When was Pte Edward White wounded?' The 6th July *Grimsby News* reported, 'Died from Wounds': 'Private *Stit* White of the Lincolns, who was reported as very seriously wounded at the end of last week, has since succumbed to his injuries. Much sympathy is extended to his parents.' A *Hull Times* item of 21st July with a photograph of 'Kit' White stated that he was killed in action on 24th June! Edward's service records seem not to have survived so one can only guess!

Edward Keightly White is buried in Nœux-les-Mines Communal Cemetery, plot II, row C, grave 16. Field Ambulances and Units buried in the Communal Cemetery from June 1915 to April 1917; the 7th CCS used it from April 1917 to August 1917, when the Communal Cemetery Extension began.

Some local cemeteries are unkempt but this is well kept, perhaps influenced by the CWGC treatment of graves, which, together with those in the Extension, number 1,285.

On my first visit to Nœux-les-Mines to find the cemetery I asked an elderly man for directions to the British Military Cemetery. That was my mistake – I should have asked for the Communal Cemetery. Being unsure he asked the residents of some adjacent houses for help. In true French fashion, after a lot of arm waving with British Military Cemetery (in French) repeated over and

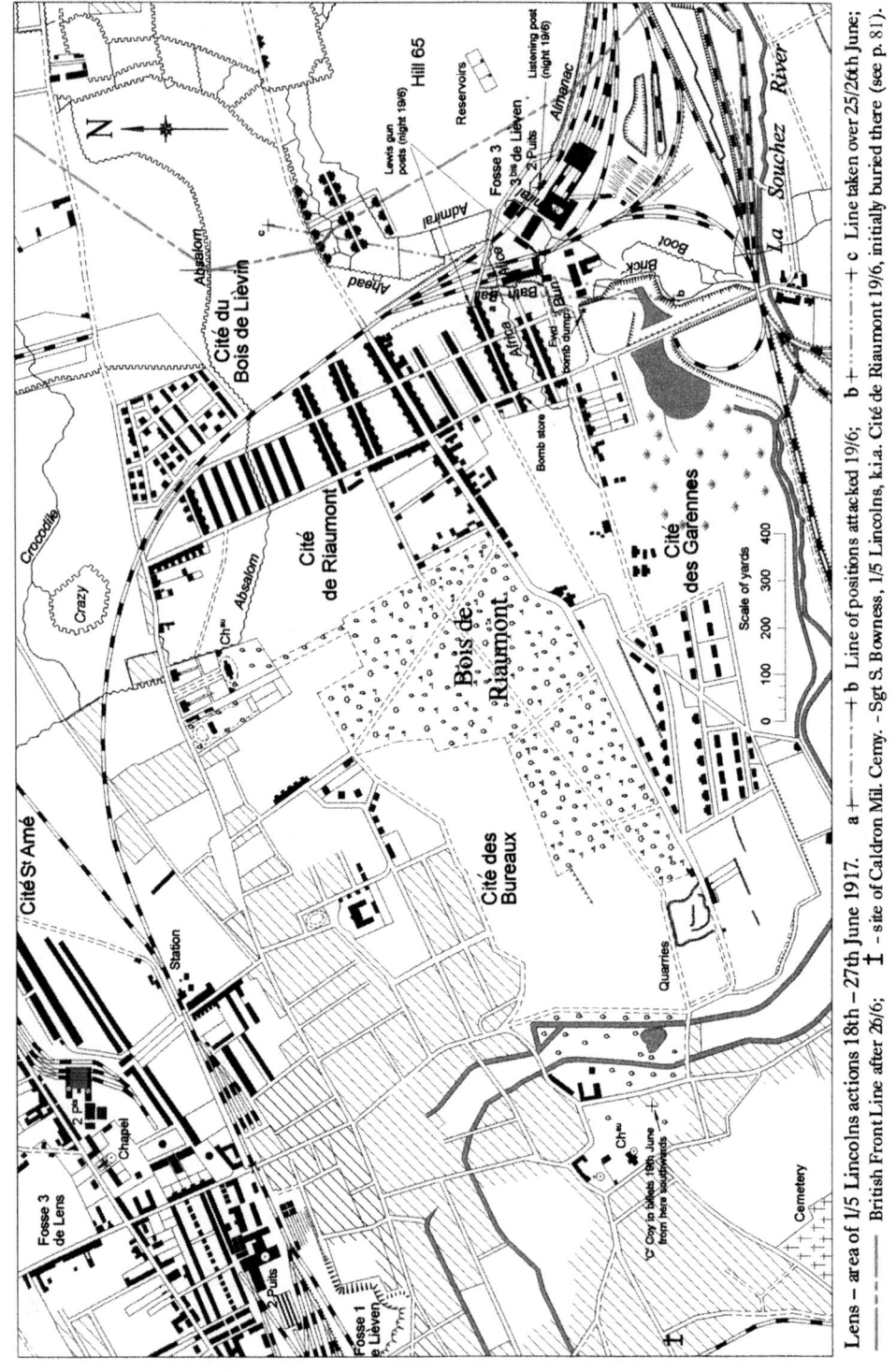

Map 19. *Lens area*

over accompanied with much head shaking and 'Non, non', etc., they eventually came to some sort of agreement.

I was directed to go to a yellow house, turn left, follow the road to the next junction, turn left again and keep to that road. I had particularly noted a high wall always on my left. I soon saw the green CWGC sign indicating the cemetery entrance through gates in that same high wall. On entering the cemetery I saw the elderly man of my earlier questioning coming through a door in the opposite wall and beyond the wall were the houses where I had stopped to ask directions! Had I asked how to get to the Communal Cemetery I too might have gone through that same door! To this day I cannot understand the logic of sending me to the other side when I had been parked near a cemetery entrance in the first place! C'est la vie!

Back in Barnetby more soldiers had been at home on leave on the first weekend in July. I have already mentioned two, namely Pte W. Smith, who had been suffering from shell shock, and L/Cpl Thomas Rowe of the wounded forearm. Pte Reg. Smith, the other soldier, was at the time in training though the report did not specify if this was basic or some sort of specialist training.

By the third week in July Gunner Henry Stephenson had arrived home for ten days leave, having earlier been admitted to a hospital to receive treatment for trench foot. That same week Mrs Peart received the news that her husband, Pte Ernest Peart of the Motor Transport Section, was also in a hospital having been seriously wounded in France.

At the end of the month Pte William Stainton, of the Lincolns, was also to be seen about the village on leave. So too was Driver Harry Cook of the RFA who was mentioned in the report as looking remarkably well. Harry, who had enlisted not long after the outbreak of war, was said to be having a well-earned leave having been in France for nearly two years.

During the evening of Tuesday 24th July the Roll of Honour erected on the Co-Operative building in Victoria Road by the Women's Adult School was invested by a Mr J. Baker of Grimsby, who gave a touching address to the large company present. The Roll of Honour, enclosed in a frame and case of wood, was the work of a Mr Shelton from Brigg. Two flower vases completed the arrangement.

This was the first permanent token to have been erected in the village to the local lads and all credit was due to Mrs Lowish and the members of the Adult School. They had also agreed that each member should be responsible, on a fortnightly basis, for placing fresh flowers in the vases throughout the summer months and using artificial flowers, or evergreens, during wintertime. Up to then 127 names were on the Roll of Honour, including 10 men from

New Barnetby. The number of 'Barnetby Boys' that had made the Supreme Sacrifice totalled 18.

To round up the news for July the Journal provided more information even though it was probably more than a month old. One more Barnetby railwayman, Harold Wilkinson, had joined the colours. Before enlistment he had been employed as a chainman in the Engineer's Dept here at Barnetby. As one man joined to serve with the colours, another left; J Tutty, a former relayer at Barnetby who joined up in the very early months of the war, had been returned to duty but at the time of the report had not resumed his duty. The final item concerned 201782 Pte Stanley Witty, 4th Battalion East Yorkshire Regiment, another former chainman from the Barnetby Engineer's Dept., reported as having been wounded and currently receiving treatment for his wounds in a hospital in Birmingham. He had enlisted around November 1915.

Moving on into August Jack Kendall, one of three sailor sons of Mr and Mrs John Kendall, sent word home that his ship had been torpedoed but he was all right. (No, I was not tempted to write the obvious and there is no prize for guessing what that was!) Only a month earlier be had been at home on leave. The following week there was a photograph of Jack in the *Hull Times* along with his two sailor brothers, Harry and Sidney. By that time Jack was safe at home with his family on survivor's leave, relating about his thrilling escape after his ship had been torpedoed and how lucky he had been when so many lives had been lost.

The Kendall Brothers.
On the left – Jack.
In the centre – Harry.
On the right – Sidney.

Several more local lads had been at home on leave from France during early August, amongst them Pte Ernest Denton of the Lincolns, who had been in France since September 1915. To signify he had been wounded twice he wore two short gold stripes *(wound stripes)* on the left cuff. Another man at home on leave who had been out in France since September 1915 and seen much fighting, was Sgt Jack Marrows, of the Lincolns who had lately been transferred to the loco. department. (Had he been permanently transferred to the Royal Engineers I wonder, which at that time was seemingly desperate for experienced railwaymen? With the enemy having pulled back to his new defensive system, the Hindenburg Line, the British were hard at work extending their lines of communication towards it.)

The last named lad reported to have been on leave during the first ten days of August was Pte W. Chambers. He had been in training and was expecting to leave England fairly soon. (One newspaper stated the name as Chamberlain; neither name is mentioned on the Roll of Honour.)

The final report for that period gave the sad news that Pte W. H. Hinchsliff, missing since last October, had at last been officially listed as 'killed in action', and much sympathy was felt for the bereaved family (the main information about Pte Hinchsliff appeared in the chapter headed 1916, pp. 106-110).

A very brief item of that same period, but not given under Barnetby news, showed a photograph of Gunner Ernest Vessey, RGA, from Owmby, Grasby, who had been killed in action on 3rd May 1917 (I referred to him earlier on in this chapter – see pp. 165-169).

By the 18th August four more boys had been on leave. The newspapers did not go into any detail, just gave out the names of the following four soldiers: – L/Cpl Walter Scott, Pte Harold Wright, Pte Rhodes and Sapper William Percival.

The following week two more local lads were at home enjoying a spell of leave. One was L/Cpl Stephen Loveday, who had gone out to France in September 1915, having joined up shortly after the outbreak of war and had seen considerable service. The other man was Pte William Frow who had recently joined the loco. battalion. (The September 1917 Journal lists chargeman G. W. Frow, from the Chief Mechanical Engineer's Dept (locomotive) here at Barnetby, as having joined the colours. Presumably this is the same man.)

The Journal went on to list a further five men from the Engineer's Dept at Barnetby who had recently enlisted namely platelayers G. Drayton, W. Rhoades, G. Rhoades, and H. Thompson and labourer C.W. Borrell. (Of those five only G. Drayton is not mentioned on the Roll of Honour and C.W. Borrell is possibly correctly listed as William *Borrill*.)

During the last week in August S/Sgt Thomas Parratt came home from Belgium for a spell of leave. He had been on the reserve list at the outbreak of hostilities in 1914 and since then had been out in France. Before the war he had been a saddler working at the Barnetby branch of Messers Lyne and Son, of Brigg.

Four more local men were at home on leave during the first week in September. One man was 122739 Pte Edgar Blake of the Royal Army Medical Corps (RAMC), who had only recently joined the colours and was expecting to be drafted abroad almost immediately. Edgar, born 2nd March 1884, eventually went on to become a Regimental Sergeant Major in that Corps. When he attained his century serving RAMC members attended his 100th birthday celebrations. Edgar, at one time a postman in the village, will also be remembered for having taken an active role in the Church here in Barnetby; he had also been a member of Barnetby Band.

Two of the remaining three men said to have been at home on leave at that time were soldiers Pte William Elwick and Pte Fred Vessey. Pte Elwick, who had been in training for a year and looking remarkably fit, was due to take a further training course in the Machine-Gun Corps. Private Fred Vessey, of the Lincolns, on leave from France, had joined up when war had broken out and seen much active service, having been sent to France in August 1914. The fourth man, said to be enjoying a holiday, was sailor George Dennis.

By the third week in September four more men had arrived home. Lt J. Waddington was home from France. (Lt J. Waddingham is not mentioned on the Roll of Honour but presumably he was sufficiently known in the village for the local reporter to include him in his news item.) Pte William Foster of the Royal Flying Corps (RFC) was still in training and the other two men were Pte A. Robinson, (? *Albert, Albert or Arthur*) of the S. Staffs and Pte Davies (*or Davis? - the Roll of Honour names an Alfred Davis*).

The final week in September had seen another trio of men arriving home for leave, namely: Pte W. Smith, Lincolns; Pte Harry Rhodes, Lincolns; and Pte William Needham. (No doubt the villagers at the time would know which W. Smith had been on leave while I can only contemplate if it was Walter or William.)

September ended with good news regarding Barnetby soldier Pte P. C. Poole, of the 10th Lincolns. Percy, the eldest son of Mr and Mrs R. Poole, had on the recommendation of his Commanding Officer duly received recognition for his services, 'for dispatch running and showing a keen devotion to duty', on the 26th August 1916 and been awarded the Military Medal. He had received a 'Card of Honour' in April for services rendered in carrying messages and for showing a keen devotion to duty whilst in action near Arras.

Pte P. C. Poole, MM.

On Sunday 30th September the Barnetby Band had given a concert during the afternoon in a field off Victoria Road kindly lent for the occasion by Mr W. Lowish (where St Mary's Avenue now is). With perfect weather for the occasion a large crowd had been attracted as the Band played musical selections appropriate for the day. Everyone agreed the Band had shown a marked improvement in its playing. Credit for this was due to the Bandmaster, Mr Rowbree, who had performed the arduous work of tutoring the many new and younger Band members that had stepped into the breach left with so many of the older Band members having joined the colours.

A collection had been made in the field during the afternoon in aid of funds the Band badly needed in order to have repairs carried out to the instruments.

Moving on into October and that month began with another group of men on leave. Two were serving in the Royal Navy, they being Jack Kendall and Cyril Catterall, who was shortly expecting to join the Grand Fleet. (*No rating was given but presumably they were both Able Seamen*). Another two were in the Royal Engineers, namely Pte Ernest Fish, who was home again after serving 15 months in France and looking remarkably well, and Pte Charles Hartley, who was doing his training. (*Privates in the RE's. does not ring true, but perhaps the local correspondent was unaware of this.*) The final two were Pte Arnold Briggs, RFC, who too was in training, and L/Cpl 'Bert' Denton, Lincolns, who was home from France.

In July it had been reported that L/Cpl Fred Maxted, RFA, at home on leave having served twenty-eight months and seen much active service, had so far come through without a scratch. His luck finally ran out and his parents, Mr and Mrs F. Maxted, received word at the beginning of October that he had been wounded in the arm and was currently receiving treatment in a hospital in Bristol.

News of a more serious nature came to Mrs Catterall with the latest situation report concerning her very sick husband, Quartermaster-Sergeant (QMS) John Catterall. John, who for some time had been lying seriously ill in a hospital in England, was not responding to treatment and had further deteriorated such that his condition was now regarded with anxiety.

The saddest piece of news came towards the end of October but its place belongs in this first week, when, on 4th October, another local lad paid the Supreme Sacrifice, he being…

1391 Private Hubert Cox, 1st Battalion, Lincolnshire Regiment.

Hubert 'Bert' Cox was born at Bigby (calculated date of birth: 9th May 1892) and baptised there on 4th June 1892. The son of John and Maria Cox of West Street, Barnetby, Hubert, a joiner, was working at home in 1911 where his father was a joiner and wheelwright. He had enlisted at Grimsby on 10th March 1915 and given his age at attestation as 21 years 305 days.

As his service documents (WO 363/C1602) are in the damaged 'Burnt Records' at the Kew National Archives, it is not known when he joined the 10th Lincolns. The local newspapers reported that on the 1st July 1916 on the Somme Hubert Cox was very badly wounded in the head with shrapnel and three gun-shot wounds in the back. Two casualty entries on his records, dated 1st and 3rd July 1916, refer to GSW head and shoulder. An entry dated 5th July 1916 simply states: sent to England. At what date Hubert returned to duty after being wounded or exactly when he was transferred to the 1st Battalion, Lincolnshire Regiment, is unclear (probably in June 1917, when that battalion was in training at Bailleulval).

The 21st Division (that the 1st Lincolns formed part of), on being transferred to Second Army, left the Arras sector on 16th September 1917 and moved north. By the 17th the 1st Lincolns had reached Cassel and from there marched to Borre. On the 20th September the battalion went by transport to a camp near Ridge Wood, southeast of Dikkebus Lake, where the men were set to work digging a cable trench from Clonmel Copse to the front line, being shelled whilst doing it.

Pte H. Cox.

On 23rd September the 1st Lincolns dug another trench, again under shellfire, from Clapham Junction to Fitzclarence Farm before moving out to the le Roukloshille area on 26th September to rejoin the rest of 62nd Brigade – 3/4th Queen's (Royal West Surreys), 12th/13th Northumberland Fusiliers and 10th Yorks (Green Howards). The 1st Lincolns returned to the front on the afternoon of 2nd October, marching via Dikkebus to a camp near Scottish Wood, and spent the night in Brigade reserve. By nightfall the following day, while plans were being made for the next battle – set for 4th October, the fine weather broke. In a change for the worse a south-westerly gale was accompanied by very heavy rain.

The 21st Division's attack was timed for 6 a.m., 4th October, using two Brigades; the 64th Brigade on the right with 9th KOYLI attacking and 10th KOYLI in support; the 62nd on the left with 3/4th Queen's (holding the line) to take the first objective (the road J11c60.55 to J11c 85.30), the 12th/13th Northumberland Fusiliers (on the right) and 10th Yorks (on the left) to take the second objective (the line J11d65.75 to J11b95.15. to J12a1.5) – see Map 20, p. 184. As Brigade reserve the 1st Lincolns allotted task was to act according to circumstances. The 7th Division was on the 21st Division's left and the 5th Division on the right.

At 9.30 p.m. on the evening of 3rd October the 1st Lincolns set off along the duck-board track north of Sanctuary Wood to their position north of the Menin Road near the eastern edge of Polygon Wood, via Clapham Junction, Fitzclarence Farm and Black Watch Corner, arriving there about midnight. In the words of the Commanding Officer, Lt. Colonel L. P. Evans, D.S.O. (Black

Watch), 'It was unlikely to be a pleasant spot'. At 5 a.m. the C.O., on having surveyed the assembly area, ordered the battalion forward to take over from the 10th Yorkshire, who had come under two heavy barrages in Glencorse Wood and at Black Watch Corner, as the left battalion for the second objective. The battalion assembled on time at about J10c2.8. (Map 28NE3), without being subjected to enemy shell-fire.

At 6 a.m. the 1st Lincolns advanced en masse, encountering much thick mud and wire, and suffered a few casualties from its own barrage 'shorts' (an 18-pounder firing short) and machine-gun fire from a 'pill-box' at J10d.5.5. This latter was silenced and the occupants surrendered to a party of Lincolns led by the C.O., assisted by a Machine-Gun Corps officer. The prisoners were escorted back but only by the wounded. By 6.40 a.m. C and D Companies, ordered ahead, assisted the 3/4th Queen's in capturing the first objective then moved up to the rear edge of the barrage and halted a hundred yards beyond their objective and reorganised. At 7.45 a.m. the Queens sent a message by pigeon reporting the first objective captured. The two companies following reorganised in Judge Trench. About this time the 1st Lincolns C.O. was badly wounded in the shoulder. Before recommencing the attack an hour and forty minutes later, A Company was brought up between C and D, leaving B in reserve.

On resuming the attack the Lincolns received further casualties, including the C.O., from a machine-gun and snipers operating near Judge Copse but continued on to the final objective (reported taken at 11.30 a.m.) that was duly consolidated, but only by a very thin line, when snipers were again troublesome. The C.O said that his men were disinclined to take prisoners during the attack and preferred the rifle to the bayonet. Not long after consolidation the C.O., by now weak from loss of blood, handed over command and went off unassisted to a Dressing Station. For his actions during the day the C.O. was awarded the Victoria Cross. For the rest of the day the Battalion was subjected to heavy shell-fire but was not counter-attacked. The following day was relatively quiet up to 10 p.m. when the right hand posts and the support company were shelled sporadically but the casualties were light. At 2 a.m. on the 6th October the 1st Lincolns moved back to Zillebeke on being relieved by two companies of the 6th Leicesters (110th Brigade, 21st Division).

In this action, known as The Battle of Broodseinde, 4th October 1917, the 1st Lincolns lost 5 officers killed, 11 wounded, 2 missing, and 1 wounded and missing (d.o.w. 4/10). Among the other ranks 24 were killed, 167 wounded and 36 missing.

Among those killed was Bert Cox. His parents received unofficial news from a 'pal' saying he was killed on 4th October by a shell whilst on duty in a wood (his

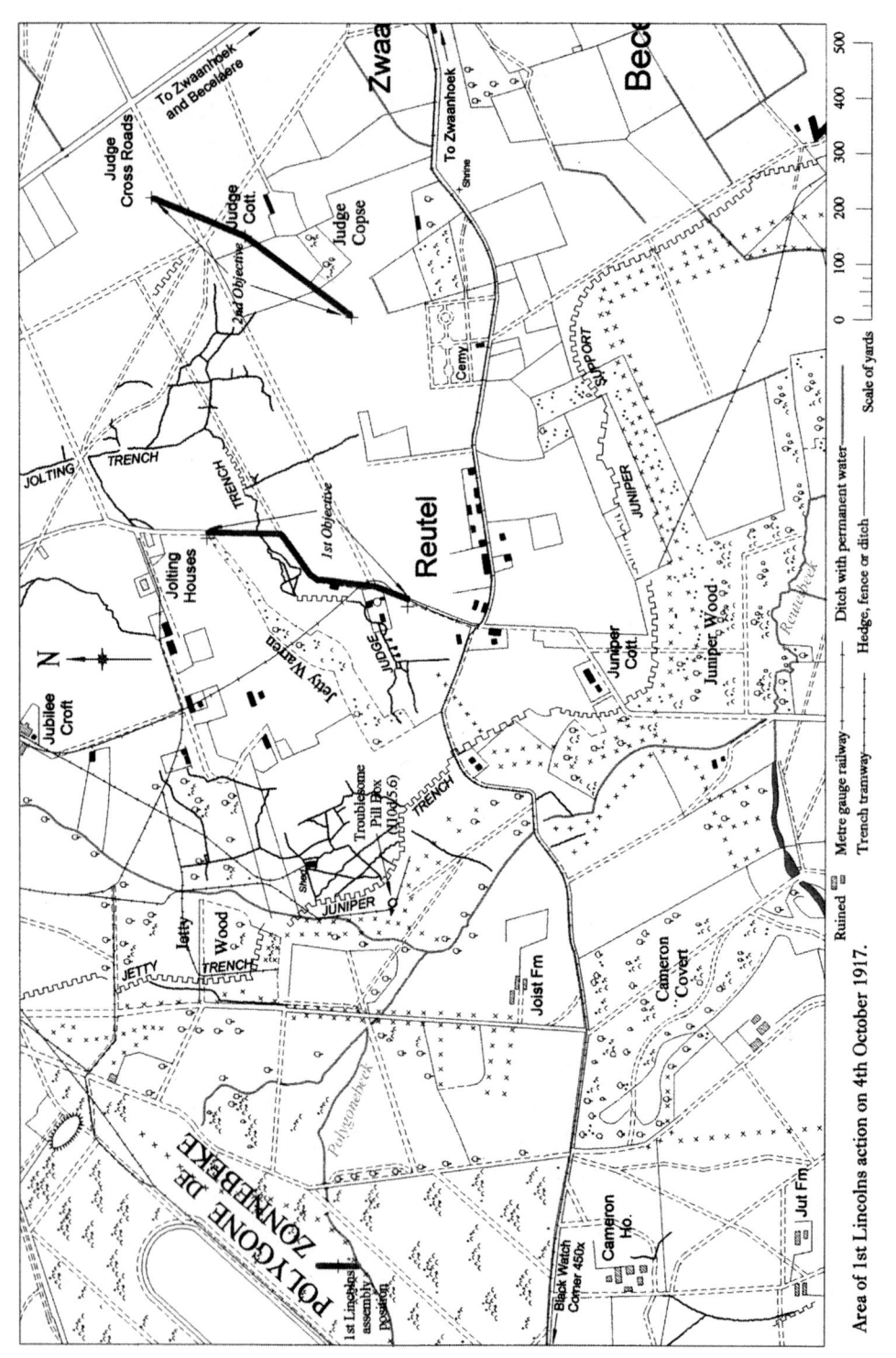

Map 20. *area of 1st Lincolns action.*

sister Ena insisted that he had been killed whilst up a tree – but trees were almost non-existent there at that time). Official news later confirmed Hubert killed in action on 4th October. (Not long after his elder brother enlisted and early in the following year joined the Royal Engineers as 169074 Sapper Harry Cox).

Private F. Plumtree wrote to Hubert's parents saying,

> *'I very deeply regret to say that your son, Bert, was killed in action on October 4th, during the attack made by our battalion in front of —. He and I were chums together, and I sincerely mourn his loss. I will ever remember him as a true and worthy comrade. I know you will feel his loss most deeply, and beg to offer you my heartfelt sympathy. He fought a good fight, laying down his life for 'Honour and Home'. I feel sure you will be pleased to learn that being killed instantly he suffered no pain'.*

Private Herbert Denton also wrote, expressing sympathy and went on to say,

> *'There is one consolation, that he gave his life for his country and humanity's sake'.*

There are ten unidentified Lincolnshire Regiment soldier's graves in Buttes New British Cemetery in Polygon Wood near to where the action took place. Bert, who is named on the Memorial to the Missing at 'Tyne Cot' Cemetery, Passchendaele, (panel 36) also has no known grave – could he be one of those ten?

Members of Bert's family named in his service records are: father, John; mother, Maria; brother, Harry 30 – Sapper RE; sisters: Mrs Edith Marshall 32, Margery 20 and Ena Mary 13. At some later date the family received his Scroll and Memorial Plaque.

Bert's youngest sister, Mrs Ena Underwood, often said she wished she knew where her brother had been killed and seen his memorial. In the autumn of 1999 son Michael, daughters Norma and Pat and their families, suggested a trip to Ypres. Ena, of Horsefair Paddock, Brigg, despite being 93 years of age and not keeping too well, didn't need too much persuasion and on 11th November 1999 visited the 'Tyne Cot' Memorial to the Missing at Passchendaele. Although deeply saddened at seeing her brother's name on Tyne Cot Memorial, Ena felt very relieved and at peace with herself knowing that at last she had visited Bert's memorial. The family also took Ena to where it is believed Bert had been killed and attended the Armistice Day Ceremony at the Menin Gate, Ypres. She enjoyed that as it made her trip to Bert's memory all the more special and memorable. Sadly, it was Ena's only visit for she died the following year on 5th July 2000.

The author, Mr Roger Frankish, of Barnetby, has a family 'connection'. Bert's brother Harry married Ethel Frankish (Roger's aunt and his father's eldest sister) on 9th May, 1923.

The Tyne Cot Memorial to the Missing forms the rear wall of Tyne Cot Cemetery, with the central apse in that wall forming the New Zealand Memorial. It carries the names of 34,950 or so United Kingdom dead (including those of 1,179 New Zealanders) who have no known grave and who fell between 15th August 1917 and the Armistice.

Men of the Northumberland Fusiliers aptly named the Passchendaele Military Cemetery 'Tyne Cot' because enemy pill-boxes in the area had a resemblance to 'Tyne Cottages' back home. In British hands these pill-boxes provided good shelter for dressing stations and stretcher bearer bases but the entrances were facing 'the wrong way' – a fact not lost on the enemy. The Cemetery originated in October 1917 from the burials by an Advanced Dressing Station using one of five pill-boxes captured by the Australians. It is the largest Commonwealth War Cemetery in the world and contains just over 11,900 burials of which almost 8,400 are of unnamed soldiers.

Three pill-boxes remain and the largest, bearing a plaque relating to its capture by the 3rd Australian Division on 4th October 1917 – the same day Bert was killed, now forms the base for the Cross of Sacrifice (suggested by H M King George V, in May 1922). In rear of the Cross of Sacrifice are the original 350 or so graves made during the war and purposefully left in the haphazard fashion that one now finds them.

Polygon Wood is a wood once more. At the time the above action took place it was a wood in name only. Photographs taken round about that time show only a few tree stumps where the wood had been. (Mr Johan Vandewalle-Temperman – owner of the café-tavern de Dreve, about half a mile from Polygon Wood, has a very comprehensive album of wartime photographs of the immediate area. He has located and is currently exploring a number of wartime underground workings, dugouts and the like, in the vicinity. This is a somewhat dirty and hazardous pastime as can be seen from photographs displayed in the tavern de Dreve bar. A Channel 4 television documentary of this work was broadcast about Armistice time 1998.)

It is quite possible that a squat square structure in a field at roughly the same map reference, give or take a few yards, that was stated in the Battalion war diary is the 'pill-box' (concrete machine-gun emplacement) that gave the 1st Lincolns so much trouble.

During the second week of October fresh faces were to be seen on leave in and around the village. Another sailor appeared on the scene, this time it

Mrs Ena Underwood, Hubert Cox's sister, age 93 years, of Brigg, at the Menin Gate Memorial, Ypres, for the first time on 11th November, 1999. Sadly, Ena died the following July.

At Tyne Cot Memorial, Passchendaele, 11th November, 1999. A sad Ena alongside the Lincolnshire Regiment panel that bears her brother's name.

Pte Hubert Cox.

Pte Hubert Cox (right) and Pals.

Driver Fred Maxted, son of Mr and Mrs Maxted, licensees of the Station Hotel, Barnetby, married Marjory 'Madge' Cox, Hubert's sister.

Pte C. R. Frankish. His sister Ethel married Hubert's brother Harry.

was Harry Kendall. The other men were in the Lincolnshire Regiment; one, Pte Percy Moss, had been in hospital for some considerable time; the other, 'Bomber' Harry Partridge, was home from France, having been out there since July 1915.

On the evening of Wednesday 10th October the Women's Adult School held their Harvest Festival thanksgiving service in the Co-Operative rooms. There the well-attended congregation heard an address delivered by Mr Horton of Grimsby and a solo rendered by Mr Horksworth. The organist for the service was Miss Edith Pashley. For the occasion the rooms had been tastefully decorated with the many gifts of fruit and vegetables received. Thanks for this was due to Mrs Lowish, Mrs Stephenson, Mrs Girdham, Mrs Parrott and Mrs Ward and the Misses Holt and Wilson. After the service the fruit and vegetables were sold off and the proceeds of the sale, amounting to £3 including the collection, donated to the Barnetby War Fund.

The following Tuesday several village ladies participated in an 'Our Day' effort selling flags in aid of the Red Cross Society. The organiser, Mrs Lowish, was assisted in the flag-sell by Mrs Girdham, Mrs Oughtred, Mrs Parrott, Mrs J. Quickfall, Misses M. and W. Broughton, Misses E. and J. Robinson, Miss Proudley, Miss M. Robinson, Miss Waite and Miss S. Denton. Purposely held so as to coincide with market day they were hoping the event would help boost their funds and make the day a big success. On opening their collecting boxes 1,083 copper coins and 203 silver coins were counted, amounting to £10. That amount was considerably in excess of the previous year's event.

News was received during the third week that Pte Bretts, of New Barnetby, had been wounded in the shoulder and was in a London hospital. Word of two Barnetby casualties had also come in. Mr and Mrs Leeson had news that their son Pte Harry Leeson, of the Lincolns, had been wounded but had not been given any details as to the nature or the seriousness of his wounding. The other family, Mr and Mrs Smith, of the Ferneries, had been notified that their son, Pte Reg. Smith, was in hospital suffering from shell shock and trench fever.

Another soldier at home on ten days leave from France, where he had been serving for nineteen months, was Mr Staniland who had been employed at Grimsby GPO before enlisting into the army postal staff. (The name of Harry Staniland is on the Roll of Honour.)

That same week, as previously mentioned, Mr and Mrs John Cox, of West Street, had also received the unofficial news, from a 'pal' of their son Hubert, informing them that their son had been killed in action on the 4th October.

Four soldiers were at home on leave during the last week in October. Pte William Smith, Lincolns, was on 48 hours leave. Pte Percy Poole, M.M. (his second distinction), 10th Lincolns, was home on leave from France, when no doubt a keen interest would have been shown in the medal he had recently received.

The two other men enjoying leave were Pte William Stainton and Pte Harry Rhodes. A Melton Ross soldier, Captain H. H. Webb, who had last been home on sick leave at the end of July was also at home for a brief 48-hour spell. He had been on the sick list for some time and during his convalescence had been recuperating at Harrogate.

The October Journal had information relating to the following Barnetby men. C. Agar, a spare fireman at Immingham had joined the colours. 240335 L/Cpl W. H. Scott, 1/5th Lincolns, was reported as having been wounded, with a remark saying he was at home at Barnetby having been gassed. There had been a report in the newspapers of mid August to say he was at home on leave. Knowing that the Journal reports were usually at least a month in arrears, I wonder if this is expanding on the August newspaper report? Before enlisting he had been a goods porter at New Holland. The final entry related to a man killed in action, with a remark saying the March Journal showed him as missing. That man was W. H. Hinchcliff (their spelling) who had been employed at Immingham. (He is not listed as missing in the March Journal but was reported as having been killed in action in the January issue as mentioned at the beginning of this chapter.)

The first week in November it was reported that Pte George Briggs, of the RFC, was at home on leave. News of a slightly different aspect of the war concerned another member of the Denton family, regarded as being one of the most patriotic families in the village. This time it was Miss Sarah Denton, the third daughter of P.C. and Mrs Denton, going off 'to do her bit.' She had left Barnetby that week for France to take up hospital duties, but the report did not say whether she had gone as a nurse or a VAD (Voluntary Aid Detachment) worker, the latter being non-medically trained. Two of Sarah's brothers were serving in France and one brother and a brother-in-law were in Egypt. The other brother was at home having been medically discharged from the Army as a result of being severely gassed.

The members of the Women's Adult School had held a whist drive on the evening of Tuesday 6th November to provide funds for sending Christmas parcels to the Barnetby lads who were prisoners of war. A good company had turned out and Mr A. Frow had officiated as Master of Ceremonies to players hoping to win the prizes donated by the Mrs Lowish, Parrott and Girdham. The proceeds from the sale of tickets and refreshments, kindly given by the members and their friends, had amounted to £3 1s 6d.

1917

On Wednesday 7th November a wedding, solemnised by the Reverend C. F. Brotherton, took place in St. Mary's Church between Corporal Percy Crabb, of the Suffolk Regiment, and Miss Adelaide L. Thorpe, the eldest daughter of Mr W. Thorpe of Silver Street. It was said to have been a pretty wedding that had aroused substantial local interest. The bridegroom had seen considerable active service with the BEF in France being among the first to go out in August 1914 and had taken part in the memorable retreat from Mons. He was now stationed in Suffolk being unfit for any further active service. His best man was Mr Jackson, the bride's uncle. The bride's sister, Miss E. Thorpe, and the bride's friend, Miss A. Slater from the Isle of Wight, had attended on Miss Thorpe.

The 17th November *Hull Times* printed a brief report with photograph, that Mr and Mrs John Cox, joiner and general draper, had received official intimation that their son Hubert had been killed in action on 4th October last. (The *Grimsby News* reported this the following week.)

Official recognition of service was not just for the military or those of a non-military capacity who were employed in a war zone. Miss Lizzie Fish had received a war worker's bronze badge 'for her long and continuous work for the soldiers.' Mrs Lowish had recommended the award for Miss Fish who had put in much hard work as an egg collector in the village for two years, having collected 1,400 eggs and a good sum of money during that time, apart from knitting a considerable number of useful wearing articles. It was believed that she was the only lady from the village at that time to possess one.

On Saturday 17th November the Teachers' Association conducted its quarterly meeting in the Station Hotel where Mr Priest, of Tealby, had presided over a good turn out. Association elections had duly taken place with Mr Pearson, of Liverpool, nominated for the vice-presidency of the Union, Mr F. C. Blackburn, of London, for the treasurership, Mr T. Cheshire, of Ashton-under-Lyne, as a member of the executive and Mr J. J. Baldwin, of Bedford, as an examiner of accounts. One of the Association members on leave at that time, Pte T. Hancock, RAMC, had been well received, as was Mr Piggram, a representative of the Union from London. The meeting discussed the allowances made to those teachers serving in the Army, feeling that they should share in the extra payments made to teachers not in uniform at the same rate.

Also on the agenda was the matter of school attendance that was being looked into by the Education Committee. It was heard how in some districts magistrates were frustrating the school attendance officers and the local education authority in their attempts to secure regular attendance. Where that had happened the remedy had been to appeal to the Board of Education and the Home Office. In other districts a marked improvement in the attitude of the magistrates had been shown. The Secretary told the meeting that local teachers had raised £32 towards the Teachers' War Aid Fund, but it was a disappointment that many members had not as yet assisted. It had been estimated in 1914 that 400 teachers might be killed, but already that total had reached 1,300, making the need for assistance to the Fund one of urgency. The council opinion was that the War Aid Deed Poll could not be altered to include the relatives of women teachers, but only covered those actually teaching before the war. At the conclusion of the meeting tea was served by 'mine hosts' of the Station Hotel, Mr and Mrs Maxted.

Sometime in the third week of November, Mr and Mrs Waite received information from the chaplain that their son Pte John Waite, of the Lincolns, who was last back home at the end of May, had been seriously wounded in the head. A card received from a nurse stated that he had undergone an operation in the 7th General Hospital at St Omer, France (known as Malassises hospital). It was hoped that he would soon be able to come home to England.

In the last week of November Mr and Mrs J. Percival received news informing them that their son, Sapper William Percival, RE, was a casualty in a hospital at Brighton, suffering from trench fever and shell shock, where his progress was satisfactory.

Soldiers continued to come home on leave. L/Cpl Harold Freeston arrived from France where he had spent nearly a year. He had earlier been wounded in the head which had impaired his sight and that had not as then been wholly restored. The other military visitor of that last November week was Pte William Borrill of the Lincolns.

Members and friends of the Christian Endeavour, in association with the Primitive Methodist Chapel had held an entertainment (no date given) in aid of local soldiers and sailors chaired by Mr W. H. Warren of New Holland. A very large audience had been well entertained to solos, duets, quartets, dialogues and recitations. Afterwards the assembled audience had sat down to a hot rabbit pie supper.

The Journal for November had just one entry relating to Barnetby. This informed that a former platelayer at Barnetby, H. Thompson, had been returned to railway duties.

More fund raising had been carried out on the evening of Wednesday 7th December when the members of the Conservative Club held a domino drive in aid of local soldiers.

The following evening in the neighbouring village of Melton Ross the residents there had held a whist drive in the village school that had resulted in £10 10s being raised in aid of their own local soldiers' Christmas parcels.

1917

During the first week of December only one soldier was reported as being on leave and that was L/Cpl Walter Scott, of the Lincolns, who had already been wounded twice.

Four men had been on leave the following week, two of them belonging to the Royal Engineers. Sapper Cyril Agar was one and the other was L/Cpl Fred Lansley, home for fourteen days from France, where he had been for the last three years with the platelayers (Fred Lansley had joined the RE Railway Troops 111th Company late in 1914). The other two men were home on sick leave, these being Pte William Holt, of the Lincolns, who had been seriously wounded in the legs a year earlier and had been in hospital ever since, and sailor Cyril Catterall who was convalescing following an operation.

The following week, two more lads arrived home on sick leave. L/Cpl Fred Maxted, RFA, had been wounded in the knee some time previously, while Pte Reg. Smith, of the S. Staffs, had been suffering from trench fever.

Following on from the Melton Ross fund-raising whist drive ten Christmas parcels had been sent to their local soldiers serving abroad. Each parcel had contained a 1lb. tin of mixed biscuits, one camp pie (or a tin of sausages), potted meat (or lobster), OXO, cocoa, sugar and milk, chocolate, military mints, some cigarettes (or pipe tobacco) and a Christmas card. A shirt and a pair of socks, courtesy of Mrs Webb, had also been enclosed in each parcel. Those men who were serving in England had their Christmas parcels attended to on the following week.

With Christmas drawing near the Barnetby Band, thinking of its members serving in the forces, had raised funds towards their aid by also holding a whist drive on the evening of Friday 14th December in the Co-Operative Rooms (the site of the present Post Office). The prizes for this occasion were donated Mr Bletcher (Worlaby), Mr Fisk (Bigby), Mr J. Havercroft (Barnetby) and Mr H. M. Webb (Melton Ross). The refreshments were courtesy of Mrs W. Needham.

Seven local men were reported to have been home on leave over the Christmas period, namely:- Transport Driver W. Chambers; Pte Charles Frankish (believed at that time to be serving with the 3rd Lincolns in Ireland); Pte Percy Moss, Lincolns; L/Cpl Fred. Maxted, RFA; and Pte Reg. Smith, S. Staffs.

When people talk about the Great War probably the most familiar name that crops up is the 'Somme'; especially the extremely high casualties of the first day, 1st July, of that 1916 battle. The 'Barnetby Boys' had got off relatively lightly throughout 1916 in terms of fatal casualties especially on the Somme. There had been just five fatalities over the four and a half month period of that battle, compared with almost twice as many fatalities for the year just ended, with five having fallen in less than a month during the Battles of Arras. Now that the fourth Christmas of the war had passed with still no sign of a let up, it must have been with some trepidation that families with sons at the front wondered what the New Year would have in store for their boys.

6
1918

THE beginning of the year on the Western Front saw both sides, as was usual during the winter months, making preparations and plans for the renewal of operations once the better weather came with the onset of Spring. Supplies were being stockpiled and new weapons brought in to augment those lost or worn out. All those commodities were relatively easy to produce providing that the raw materials were available. What both sides lacked was manpower – that was becoming much harder to come by.

At the beginning of January the British had begun taking over more territory from the hard pressed French, extending the line south from four miles north of St Quentin to five miles south of the River Oise, terminating at the village of Barisis. This extra territory now left the British Army desperately short of troops to defend it in any sort of strength, especially down in the southern part.

Apart from having to take over more of the front from the French five divisions had also been transferred to the Italian Front. Furthermore, following the heavy losses incurred in 1917 especially at Passchendaele – that was regarded as being wasteful, the British War Cabinet was reluctant to release more of the trained troops that were available. Despite this lack of manpower at the front battalion strengths had somehow to be restored. The British Army achieved this during the early part of the year by undergoing a major change in its organisation.

The result of this reorganisation was that all the United Kingdom divisions were reduced in size from 13 battalions down to 10 (including 1 pioneer battalion). To accomplish this the number of infantry battalions in each of the three brigades had been cut from 4 to 3. Some battalions were disbanded, some amalgamated into new ones and some formed into pioneer units, all the troops thus released being absorbed as replacements in one form or another.

The Allies, with America having entered the war in April 1917, also had the prospect of eventually having their numbers swelled with American troops that were slowly beginning to arrive in France. But those troops were totally inexperienced and were in need of indoctrination in the kind of warfare that they would eventually be subjected to; they were also short of essential materials, such as artillery, mortars and machine-guns. Furthermore they would only fight as American units under American command. That did not help matters.

As for the enemy, having defeated the Russians at the end of 1917, it no longer had to provide troops for that front and these were subsequently transferred to the Western Front. This situation gave the enemy a temporary advantage in numbers. But apart from that it had no other sources of manpower to fall back on.

Here at home the New Year in all probability got off to a very good start for the Briggs family. Luckily they had George at home for Christmas and his two brothers, Arnold and William joined them for the New Year. Arnold was a 2nd class Air Mechanic; George was a private serving in the Royal Flying Corps (RFC); and William was a private in the Royal Engineers (RE).

Pte Jack Wilson, Yorkshire Regiment, or to give it its full title – Alexandra, Princess of Wales's Own (Yorkshire Regiment), also had leave over the Christmas/New Year period along with those soldiers already on leave at Christmas as mentioned at the end of the last chapter.

With the New Year having just begun the village War Fund Committee promulgated its second annual statement of accounts and judging from those accounts it had had a fairly successful year. The receipts for the year from the various fund raising efforts that had been organised had amounted to £156 8s 3d, while the expenditure of providing comfort items and despatching parcels to the 'Boys' had been £124 4s 10½d, leaving the fund with a credit balance of £32 3s 4½d.

Following on from this the War Fund Committee announced that throughout the year it had sent out a total of 494 parcels at regular intervals to all the local servicemen serving at home and abroad and many other (unspecified) articles had also been distributed. Finally, to bring the report up to date, the War Fund Committee had also mentioned that during the festive season it had been busy seeing that the local lads were not forgotten at that time. There had duly been made up and despatched out to them a total of one hundred and fourteen Christmas parcels.

The Barnetby Band too had remembered its members in the forces in a similar manner during the Christmas period and had received several letters of thanks in return, extracts from which are given below.

1918

Sapper Harold Wilkinson, wrote from France saying,

> 'I thank you and all the members of the Band for the kind gift of writing pad, cigarettes and pencil, which I received from you. A writing pad is a very useful thing for us out here, when we have the time to use them, but I have been moving about just lately, or I would have written you before. I am very pleased to see that the Band is still progressing, and I hope it will keep on doing so, although I know it is no easy task as things are now.'

Sapper William H. Percival, writing to the Band from a hospital in Brighton said,

> 'Thank you very much for the parcel you sent me. You will see I am in good old Blighty again, and hope to be home shortly. I was blown up by one of Fritz's pills at ¾ on November 10th, and have been in hospital since I landed at Dover on the 23rd ¾. I often think about the Band, and wish I was back in it, but, of course, it's no good wishing. It's very kind of you all to think about us like this, and I thank the members of the Band sincerely for their kindness.'

(Shortly after writing his letter thanking the Barnetby Band for the Christmas parcel he had received Sapper William Percival, [RE attached to the E. Yorks.], had arrived home after having been in hospital for the previous two months suffering from wounds and shell shock. He was reported as looking decidedly better). Pte Jack Wilson, Yorkshire Regiment, had written,

> 'I have received parcel and beg to thank all the members of Band very kindly for the smokes, pad and pencil, which I was very pleased to receive. We have just moved, but the band has always played "Chieftain" on Church parade, and it went fine. I told my pals it was one of our old marches. We have a fine band here, consisting of six or seven cornets, three tenor, two baritones, two euphoniums, four E flat bass, three trombones, five side drums and a bass drum and a double B. Will close, wishing the band every success, and the members "A Merry Christmas and Happy New Year".'

Lastly, Pte William Baker wrote to the Band from Bungay to say,

> 'Many thanks for your very nice present and kind wishes. I send all the band my best wishes, and hope to be back among them soon.'

During the middle of January three more soldiers were to be seen about the village on leave. Pte Bob Allison, RGA, had been home on ten days sick leave while Lt J. Waddingham was over from France for fourteen days. (The latter officer's name is not listed on the Barnetby Roll of Honour.) The remaining soldier reported to have been on leave was Pte Amos Footitt, also at home from France for fourteen days.

One village youngster that had been determined to do his bit towards helping the soldiers was Master A. Lusby. Although only seven years old this boy had saved up his pennies until he had collected the princely sum of 5s. By this self-denial he was able to have some cigarettes purchased and these were subsequently sent to a soldier in hospital at Lincoln. That soldier generously handed them over to the ward Sister for further distribution amongst the other wounded soldiers. Master Lusby later received a card from the hospital thanking him for the 'smokes' that had been very much appreciated by the Tommies on the ward.

Still with the smoking theme the Women's Adult School members had held a whist-drive on the evening of Tuesday 15th January in the Co-Operative Rooms to raise monies for the War Fund to purchase smokes for the local soldiers and sailors. By all accounts the event had been another success for the hard working Women's Adult School members. During the previous six months those ladies had raised the sum of £12 6s 6d that had duly been distributed as follows:- £3 was given to the Local War Fund; £3 1s 6d was spent in providing prisoners' Christmas parcels; Waifs and Strays received £3 10s; and the proceeds of the whist-drive, for the purchase of smokes for the local lads, amounted to £3 5s. So far during the war the Women's Adult School had managed to raise in excess of £60 for the benefit of various organisations. This was quite a considerable achievement considering others were doing likewise.

Whist, apart from being a popular form of entertainment was also a useful medium for fund raising. On the evening of Wednesday 25th January it was the turn of the residents of Melton Ross to hold a whist drive in aid of their local War Fund resulting from which the fund was boosted by the sum of £9 7s 1½d. It is interesting to note that the Melton Ross whist-drive had raised almost three times the amount of money that the latest Barnetby effort had.

At a meeting of the Band Committee held on Sunday 27th January, it was reported that seven parcels had been sent to Band members serving at the Front. The report went on to state that the Band, though being badly depleted through many of its members being in the armed forces, was still endeavouring to carry on. It was to be hoped that they would have their old boys back in the fold ere long.

Another Barnetby man enlists. The Journal for January 1918 recorded that Barnetby railwayman J. W. Coupland, an engine cleaner from Barnetby locomotive depot, had joined the colours – possibly during the previous month.

The beginning of February saw five more local lads returned to the village for a spell of home leave. S/Sgt Robert Parrott was here from Belgium for fourteen days. The other four lads enjoying a brief respite from duty were L/Cpl Charles Hartley and Sapper William Frow, both serving with the Royal Engineers, and Privates Alfred Frow and Cyril Agar.

On the evening of Wednesday 6th February the Hull based Wilberforce Concert Party put on a concert in the Schoolroom, organised by Mrs R. Smith of the Temperance Hotel, in aid of the War Fund. The Concert Party had given a really talented performance that the crowded audience had thoroughly enjoyed. The sum raised for the local War Fund amounted to £10 5s.

The Station Hotel had again been the venue for a meeting when the members of the Market Rasen Teachers' Association had held their annual general meeting there. At that meeting the sum of £32 had been contributed to the Teachers' War Fund. The total amount of money held in that fund was over £120,000. The assembly had been told that up to that date a total of 1,308 teachers had been killed, or had died of wounds, during the war.

An interesting wedding with a military flavour had taken place in St Mary's Church by special licence on Saturday 9th February. The marriage was between Miss Kate Rowe, the eldest daughter of Mr and Mrs E. Rowe, and Cadet C. Bradley, of Frieston, near Boston, Lincolnshire. The bride, who was given away by her father, had looked charming as she entered the church carrying a beautiful bouquet. She had been attired in a gown of white silk crepe de Chine with a corsage of white silk brocade that displayed a gold brooch, a gift from the bridegroom, and a veil with a wreath of orange blossom.

The bridegroom, wearing uniform, had as his best man Mr W. Pearson, from Frieston. Attending the bride, as bridesmaids, were her two sisters, Margaret and Hilda. Both these ladies wore gold brooches on dresses of grey silk poplin embroidered with cerise and carried prayer books bound in grey suede, gifts of the bridegroom. The reception after the wedding ceremony was held in the schoolroom. Later the newlyweds left the proceedings to spend their honeymoon in Matlock. The bridegroom, having just completed his training for a commission, was expecting to join his regiment (not stated) in the immediate future.

Among the many presents received was a silver cake basket and lace table centre given to the bride by the staff and students of the Pupil Teachers' Centre at Cleethorpes where she had been a teacher for a number of years. The pupils of Barnetby Council Schools, where the bride's father and mother – Mr Edwin

Rowe and Mrs Ann Rowe – had respectively been headmaster and headmistress of the Council Schools at Barnetby for thirty years, presented the bride with half a dozen silver teaspoons. The School staff had presented her with a combined cream and sugar container in a silver holder.

A series of missionary lectures had been given over the previous two weeks to a well-attended congregation in the Wesleyan Chapel by the preacher Mr William Harrison of Rochdale. On Friday 8th February his lecture had been 'Nurse Cavell; heroine and saint'. (Edith Cavell, a British nurse, had been matron of a Red Cross hospital in Brussels. She was court-martialled and condemned to death by the Germans for her part in helping Allied soldiers escape to the Dutch frontier. She was executed by a firing squad on 12th October 1915.) Mr Harrison had concluded his lecture series on Wednesday 13th February when his topic had been 'Two years in a parsonage on wheels'.

Three weeks after the last concert another had been given in the school on Wednesday evening, 27th February, when the entertainers were the Sphinx Concert Party from Cleethorpes. The concert party, organised by Mrs Lowish in aid of the local War Fund, had been in the capable hands of its general manager Sgt Drummer C. V. Smith. The other members of the concert party were Drummer Coleman (accompanist), Sgt Griffiths, Cpl Eckersley, Drummer Taylor, Drummer Rothwell, Miss Lee, Drummer Nat. Gould (comedian), Sgt Drummer Smith, Drummer Rich Taylor (ventriloquist), Miss Ivy Holman and Mr Sandon.

The entertainment had been very much appreciated by the packed audience to judge by the numerous encores and had realised about £18 for the War Fund. Alas the schoolroom had been much too small to hold all those who had wished to attend. In response to a vote of thanks, proposed by Mr J. W. Naylor and seconded by Mr J. Peet, Sgt Drummer C. V. Smith said that the concert party was hoping to pay a return visit to Barnetby. Afterwards the concert party had been put up for the night by a number of the villagers.

The local newspapers of 8th/9th March carried the sad news that Mrs Catterall had been hoping would not materialise concerning her husband...

9074 Company-Quartermaster-Sergeant John Catterall, 8th Battalion, Lincolnshire Regiment

On 12th February 1918 *John Catterall,* aged 39, succumbed to the illness that had afflicted him for the past six months. In August 1917 John became very ill and was invalided from France to a hospital in England where his situation steadily worsened. By October, now very seriously ill, his situation was regarded with anxiety. His illness, consumption – today known as tuberculosis, had finally taken its toll.

John was born at Hebden Bridge, West Yorkshire, (4) 1878, the son of Thomas and Eliza Catterall. In 1891 the family was living in Wrawby; John's employment: railway clerk. In 1901 the family was living at 102 Heneage St, Clee, and John still a railway clerk. In 1911 John was living with his parents and family at 68 Silver St, Barnetby; his employment: railway labourer. His first mention in the Journal is January 1912 when appointed as a platelayer in the Engineer's Dept at Barnetby; by November 1913 he'd been transferred to the Traffic Dept as a groundpointsman. He volunteered for the army soon after war broke out and within twelve months had been promoted from private to CQMS, this rank being confirmed whilst on active service in France. Being very well known amongst many of the district GCR staff, especially drivers and guards, the sad news of John's death had been received with much regret.

CQMS J. Catterall.
Photo: GCR Journal

John's funeral took place on Friday 15th February 1918 at the Scartho Road Cemetery, Grimsby, where he was buried with full military honours in the Roman Catholic section in grave plot 76 N 11 (the Cemetery register at the Weelsby Road Crematorium gives his address as 39 Cooper Road, Grimsby). Oddly, John's name is not in the Lincolnshire Regiment Roll of Honour, neither is it mentioned in 'Soldiers Died in the War' (Lincolnshire Regiment). One suggested reason is that John was discharged from the army whilst ill and died as a civilian. If that was the case why has he a CWGC headstone? When I first visited his grave the headstone was missing; this was reported to the War Graves Commission who replaced it. John is also named on the Memorial Plaque in St Barnabas Church, Barnetby, the Barnetby War Memorial, the Barnetby Roll of Honour and the GCR Memorial at Sheffield.

J. Catterall headstone.

At the St Mary's football club sports held on August 3rd 1914 John was clerk of the sports course. Family-wise Mrs. Catterall's name kept cropping up in the news relating to various organisations and activities here in Barnetby. Cyril Catterall, a younger brother, has been mentioned from time to time as serving in the Royal Navy.

Village news relating to its soldiers or activities concerning the war appears to have been sparse throughout March. There would have been few, if any, on leave, except for those on sick leave, as all fit men would have been needed at the front for the 21st March when the enemy commenced his spring offensive – Operation Michael. The only information gleaned related to a whist drive held in the Co-Operative Rooms on the evening of Tuesday 26th March. Organised by the Women's Adult School for the purpose of providing 'smokes' for the local soldiers this had raised £3 2s 7d towards purchasing the necessary smoking requisites. Mrs Lowish, the Misses Baldwin, Frow and Worrall and Mr Oliver had donated the prizes for the occasion.

The Women's Adult School was again in the news in mid April having sent 115 parcels out to local soldiers during the previous three months. Those same ladies also presented a silver plated breakfast cruet set to Miss Baldwin on the occasion of her marriage to Driver T. Wright, of Winterton, who had been home on leave from the Italian front.

The news from the Front relating to casualties arising from the enemy spring offensive was of the worst for one village family. It reported the sad intimation that had been received by Mr and Mrs Enoch Wright that amongst those killed in action on 21st March was their son...

12736 Private Harry Wright, 1st Battalion, Lincolnshire Regiment

Harry Wright, the second son of Enoch and Maria Wright of 40 Victoria Road, Barnetby, (now 15 Victoria Road) was born at Kirmington (2)1889 (the 1911 census refers to him as Harold). Prior to joining the army Harry had been in the employ of the GCR as a goods guard based at Immingham. His name is first mentioned in the December 1911 issue of the Journal when he took up a new appointment at Barnetby Depot as a shunter. By October 1912 he had been promoted to brakesman and a year later he became a goods guard. When he transferred to Immingham is unclear yet the report of his wounding, in the November 1915 issue of the Journal, lists Harry as being Immingham based.

Harry, enlisting at Grimsby – believed to be in the early days of the war, had been in France three years up to the time he was killed. (The October 1914 Journal lists an Immingham goods guard *J. H. Wright* as having enlisted. I believe *J* is an error. No other Wright is named until November 1915, when 12736 Pte H. Wright is listed as wounded.) A 19th April newspaper report of his death, in extending much sympathy to the bereaved family, referred to Harry as 'Gunner Wright.' From that I opine he had been a battalion (Lewis) machine-gunner.

On 21st March 1918, Germany launched 'Operation Michael', the offensive that sent the British Armies reeling across the old 1916 'Somme' battlefield almost as far as Amiens. Officially referred to by the British as 'The First Battles of the Somme, 1918, 21st March – 5th April', this offensive opened with 'The Battle of St. Quentin, 21st – 23rd March' and British Forces in that area soon found themselves on the receiving end of an all-out enemy onslaught.

The enemy originally intended that this offensive be directed against the weaker southern sector where the British and French Armies joined. But, as mentioned earlier, the British had taken over part of that territory previously held by the French. This meant that the British were subsequently holding all of that part of the front targeted for the attack and would be subjected to the full force of the attack when it materialised.

At the outset, opposing a German army of sixty-four divisions on a fifty-four mile front were the British Third and Fifth Armies, with nineteen divisions in the line and ten infantry and three cavalry divisions in reserve. About a third of the enemy's northern attack was directed against part of Third Army's 28-mile front held by 14 Divisions. The remainder of the enemy attack fell on almost the whole of the weaker Fifth Army holding a 42-mile front to the south with 12 Infantry and 3 Cavalry Divisions.

As a result of re-organisation brought about by lack of manpower (as mentioned at the beginning of this chapter) divisions were re-structured on a three battalions per brigade basis. From the 3rd February 1918, the composition of the 62nd Brigade, 21st Division, was as follows: 1st Lincolns, 2nd Lincolns (from 8th Division) and the 12th/13th Northumberland Fusiliers (an amalgamation of 12th and 13th Battalions, Northumberland Fusiliers). (Regular Army battalions and 1st Line Territorial units were not disbanded. Interestingly the Lincolnshire Regiment's two regular battalions, 1st and 2nd, were now in the same brigade of a 'New Army' division.)

For the opening offensive against the British forces the 1st Lincolns (21st Division) were in VII Corps, Fifth Army, at Heudecourt – almost at the northern end of Fifth Army's front. (Unfortunately the enemy captured the Battalion diary records for the period 15th–21st March and the war diary report was subsequently written-up by the Company Sergeant-Majors.)

From 12th–16th March the 1st Lincolns, in Brigade support near Heudecourt, were in the railway embankment at W23b from where much hard work was done in putting new trenches and wiring around Vaucellette Farm about a mile distant. Each morning whilst at Heudecourt they stood–to in the Yellow Line about 1000 yards behind Vaucellette Farm. From 17th–20th March the 1st Lincolns manned the front line trenches adjacent to the Vaucellette Farm position.

On the 17th/18th March the 1st Lincolns relieved the 2nd Lincolns in the front line near Epehy, where the 62nd Brigade was holding the left sector of the 21st Divisional front. In that sector the 1st Lincolns were in trenches from Birchwood Copse on the right to Chapel Street on the left and responsible for the defence of Chapel Hill in the rear. The right of the Brigade sector, including Vaucellette Farm, was held by the 12th/13th Northumberland Fusiliers. 'C' Coy of the 2nd Lincolns was in support and two tanks were allotted for counter-attack duties.

View of the battlefield as seen from Gouzeaucourt New Cemetery approximately 2 km to the north of Chapel Hill. Indicated by arrow left to right are:- Birchwood Copse, Chapel Crossing (approx.), Vaucellette Farm (in front of trees) and Chapel Hill.

From 17th March hostile enemy shelling was practically nil until 4 a.m. on the 21st March when the enemy opened an intense four hour bombardment of gas and high explosive shells of all calibres, including trench mortars, on the entire front. Thick fog shrouded the line when the enemy advanced at about 9.45 a.m. However a vigilant Battalion Headquarters look-out spotted enemy approaching in time for Headquarters personnel, by now receiving enfilade machine-gun fire, to make a necessary forced retirement to Chapel Hill, joining 'B' Coy (in reserve) and the support company ('C' Coy, 2nd Lincolns). Shortly after 10 a.m. a 'D' Coy runner brought in a message saying that Birchwood Copse had been taken. By noon Vaucellette Farm had also fallen.

Throughout the day 'D' Coy, on the right, held Skittle Alley and Tennis Trenches to protect the right flank against the threat from Vaucellette Farm. 'C' Coy, on the left and under severe attack, was holding Chapel Street while 'A' Coy, in Cavalry and Cavalry support trenches formed a left defensive flank from its support line to Chapel Hill. 'C' Coy was forced to withdraw through 'A' to Chapel Hill where, with the other occupants, it formed a defensive line on Chapel Hill on 'A' Coy's left against any threat from the North.

Eventually 'A' Coy became outflanked, some escaping to Chapel Hill. Battalion Headquarters was later moved to Lowland Trench.

By and large the 1st Lincolns held onto their positions throughout the morning until they were reinforced at mid-day by the 4th South Africans (South African Scottish) of 9th (Scottish) Division. Small groups of the enemy were also

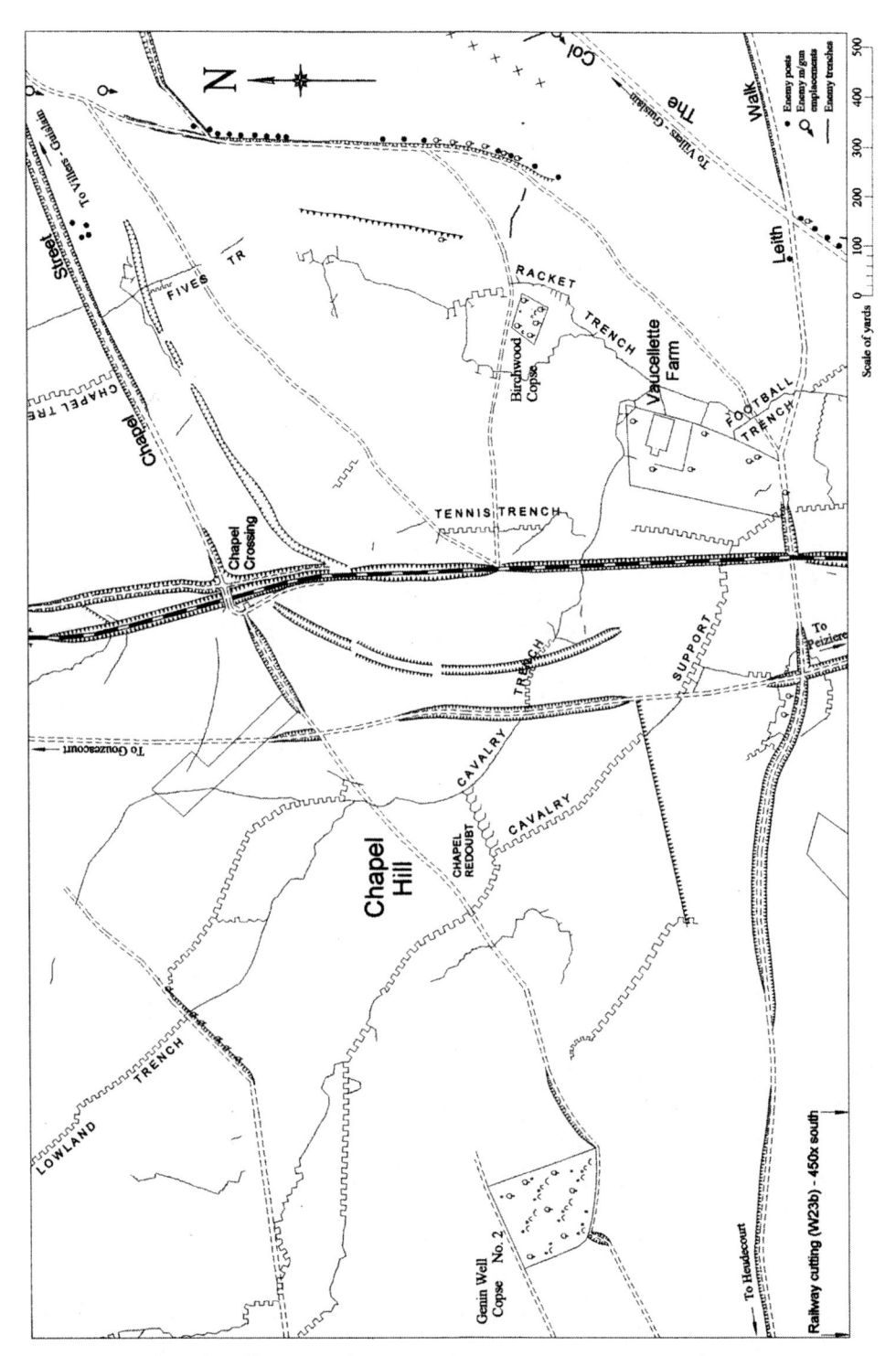

Map 21. *Chapel Hill – area of 1st Lincolns actions on 21st March 1918.*

seen around mid-day moving southward along the Gouzeaucourt–Heudecourt road in rear and were dealt with by the 2nd Lincolns. At 3 a.m. on the 22nd the 1st Lincolns moved back to Heudecourt after relief by the 4th South Africans.

The 1st Lincolns war diary simply records that there were 'Casualties' but no figures are mentioned. In the Regimental History the casualties are given for the period 21st-25th March, including the Battle of Bapaume (24th-25th March). During that period 4 officers and 66 other ranks were killed and 8 officers and 311 other ranks wounded, including many that were missing. (Two of the officers that were killed were first reported as 'wounded and missing'.)

The Battlefield as seen from the south. Chapel Hill is the dark shaded area centre to left on the skyline. Cavalry Trench ran from the right of Chapel Hill behind the clump of trees right of centre and Cavalry Support Trench ran from the centre of Chapel Hill to pass in front of the clump of trees. The railway line and Vaucellette Farm are off the photograph to the right.

Looking towards Chapel Hill from south of Vaucellette Farm, seen amongst the trees on the right. Chapel Hill is the dark shaded area in the left quarter of the photograph on the skyline. The railway line runs the other side of the clumps of bushes running left to right across the photograph. Tennis Trench was on the near side of those same bushes. Cavalry and Cavalry Support Trenches ran roughly parallel from Chapel Hill to pass either side of the clump of trees seen halfway up the extreme left hand edge of the photograph beyond the railway line.

Pte Harry Wright is listed as being killed in action on the 21st March 1918, aged 30 years. Having no known grave he is commemorated by name on the Pozières Memorial to the Missing, Ovillers-la-Boiselle (panel 24) – see photo below. Harry's name is also on the family headstone in St Mary's Churchyard, Barnetby (where his age is given as 28 years) and the GCR Memorial.

Pozières Memorial.

The Pozières Memorial forms the side and rear walls of Pozières British Cemetery and records the names of 14,644 officers and men of the 5th Army who have no known grave who fell during the Somme Battles from 21st March 1918 - 7th August 1918. (The 3rd Army, which was in action over much of the same old Somme battlefield during the same period, has its Memorial to the Missing at the Faubourg-d'Amiens Cemetery, Arras.)

The *Hull Times* of 27th April reported the sad news that had recently been received by the Slight family of Somerby concerning their son...

107608 Driver William Slight, 'B' Battery, 177th Brigade, Royal Field Artillery

William Slight, born at Brigg (2) 1891, was the eldest son of Mr John Slight. In 1911 he was working as a bricklayer at Waddingham and living with his father and two younger brothers at 12 Dunstall St, Scunthorpe. Before enlisting at Scunthorpe he had been employed as a horseman with the late Mr R. D. Coulthurst of Normanby Grange. William was killed in action on 28th March 1918, aged 27 years. He had been serving in France for over two years.

The 177th Brigade, RFA, was part of the Divisional Artillery of the 16th (Irish) Division that formed part of VII Corps, 5th Army. VII Corps was the left (northernmost) Corps of the 5th Army front that ran from just north of Gouzeaucourt in the north (about 14 km SSW of Cambrai) to Barisis in the south (30 km S of St Quentin). On 1st March 1918 the Brigade was at Ste

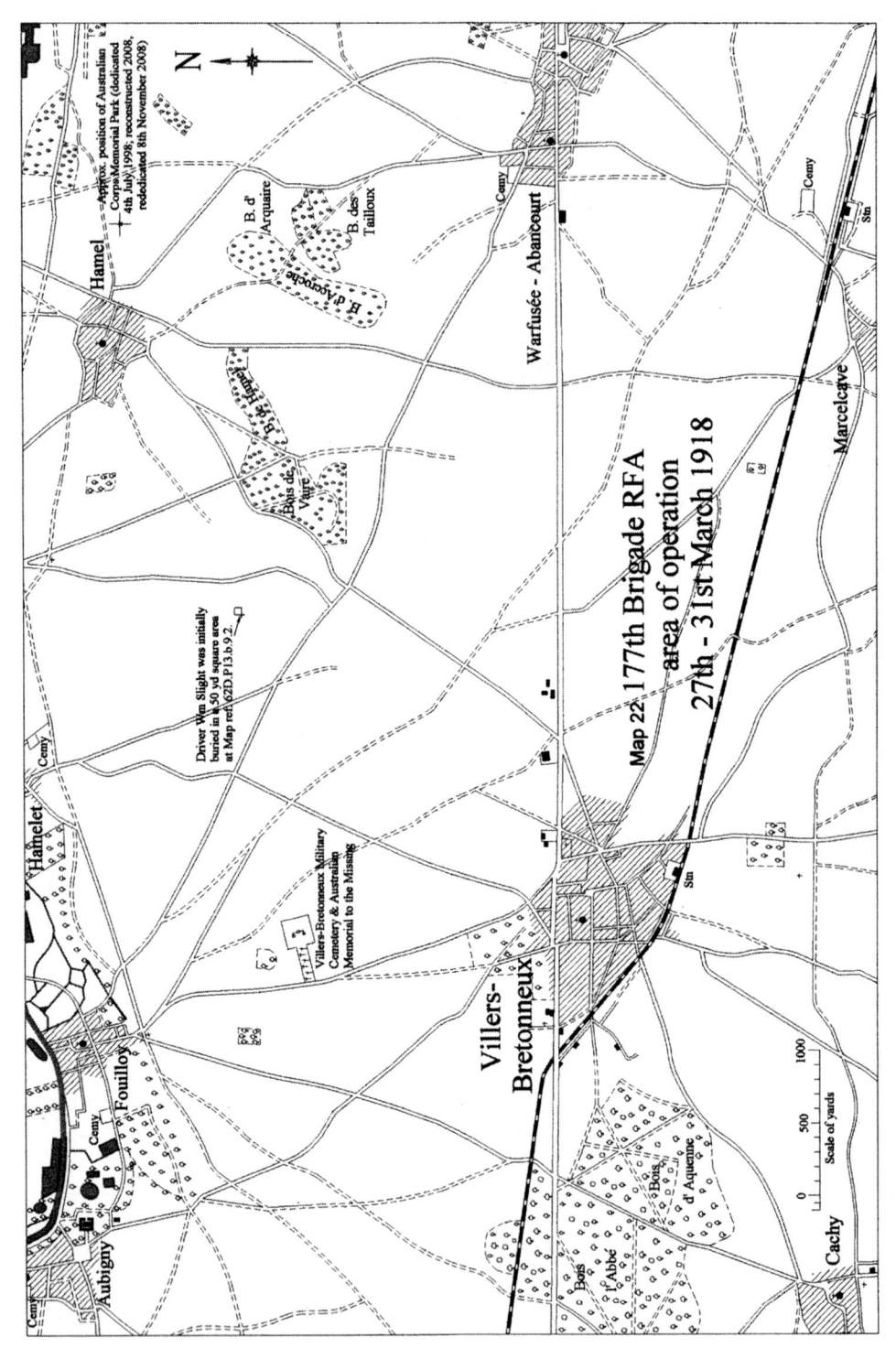

Map 22. *177th Bde RFA area of operation (Villers-Bretonneaux).*

Emilie, some 3½ km NE of Roisel (near the southern boundary of VII Corps sector), from where the batteries carried out harassing fire on selected enemy targets. The following day the Brigade became a sub group under 189th Brigade RFA. For the next two weeks each battery in turn sent out a roving section each evening to carry out harassing fire. By the 15th March it was becoming obvious that something was going to happen soon and forward wagon lines were set up near the battery positions. During the hours of darkness the horse teams and limbers were stood to at those lines. From 17th March those teams and limbers remained at the forward wagon lines. During that night a false SOS was put up (when the infantry needed urgent artillery support SOS Vary light or rocket signals would be sent up – the artillery then immediately fired on pre-arranged SOS positions).

On 21st March the German offensive Operation Michael began and during the attack 177th Brigade RFA had all its guns captured by the enemy. As a result the Brigade HQ and the wagon lines retired to Tincourt about 4 km WSW of Roisel. The following day the ammunition was dumped on gun and wagon lines then the Brigade withdrew to Biaches some 3 km SW of Peronne. The Brigade withdrawal continued the following day on roads that were becoming increasingly congested with traffic and it ended up at Dompierre about 45 km (28 miles) SW of Peronne.

The following day, 24th March, the Brigade went to the Army Gun Park at la Flaque and was re-equipped with guns. On receiving replacement guns 'B' battery and one section of 'D' (2 howitzers) was sent to the 21st Divisional Artillery at Bray. The other batteries returned to Dompierre where they went into action the next day. The Brigade withdrew to Morcourt, 8 km W of Bray, on 26th March where it was rejoined by 'B' battery and the section of 'D'. That day 'B' battery suffered heavy casualties to both men and horses.

On 27th March the Brigade withdrew to Cachy, 3½ km SW of Villers Bretonneux. The 177th Brigade RFA War Diary (WO 95/1962) records on 28th March that the Brigade went into action near Hamel, about 5 km NE of Villers Bretonneux, and repulsed a German attack during the afternoon. There is no mention of any casualties although that is the date Driver William Slight is recorded as killed in action. The following day the Brigade moved to new positions near Hamel and Bois de Vaire. The next day the enemy again attacked in strength and was repulsed. On 31st March the Brigade retired to new positions to the south of Hamelet – some 2 km NW of Hamel.

William is buried in Villers-Bretonneux Military Cemetery, Plot IV, Row A, Grave 4. He was initially buried at map reference 62D.P.13.b.9.2. about 800 yards NW of Bois de Vaire (almost in line with the Australian Memorial Park at le Hamel and approximately 2/5 of the distance from the cemetery).

The cemetery was made after the Armistice and consists of graves concentrated from other burial grounds and the surrounding battlefields.

By 1920, Plots I – XX had been completed and they contained mainly Australian graves from the period March – August 1918. Plots IIIA, VIA, XIIIA, and XVIA, together with other Plots lettered AA, contain the larger proportion of unidentified graves and from a wider area, were completed by 1925. The total 1914-18 burials number just over 2,140 of which slightly more than 600 are unidentified. There are also a number of special memorials. The cemetery also has a few burials from the 1939-45 War. That conflict left its mark on the cemetery by way of battle scars – some purposely left visible. The Australian National Memorial to the missing, a prominent landmark, stands at the rear of the cemetery. The memorial tower, complete with an orientation table, affords good views over the surrounding countryside.

W. Slight headstone.

To round off events for March the Journal listed one Barnetby railwayman as having enlisted into the colours. That was Harry Cox, who had been a relayer in the Engineer's Dept at Barnetby Locomotive Depot.

Between 9th and 29th April the Battles of the Lys took place in which three Barnetby men were killed. I have not found any newspaper reports or obituaries relating to the first casualty, named on the Roll of Honour but not on the War Memorial, namely...

48725 L/Cpl George Hurd, 13th Battalion, The King's Liverpool Regiment

George Hurd, born at Goxhill (4)1896, the son of Weldon and Eva Betsy Hurd, had lived in South Street, Barnetby (1901 census). In 1911, George was living with his parents and younger brother Charles at Habrough. 'Soldiers Died in the War' states he enlisted at Caistor and had the service number 49972, Sherwood Foresters (Notts and Derby Regiment). George was killed in action on 10th April 1918, during the Battle of Estaires, 9th - 11th April.

George has no known grave and is commemorated on the Loos Memorial to the Missing, panel 28. (Loos Memorial is about 12½ km south of where the action took place; some 2½ km northeast, the le Touret Memorial serves the same geographical area covering an earlier period.) When I first saw George's name on the Loos Memorial his Christian name initial was shown as C. The CWGC were notified and affirmed it should be G. Their French office verified it was wrongly engraved and would be altered to G. This has now been done, having seen it for myself and had confirmation from the CWGC. George is also named on the Kirmington War Memorial.

The 13th Battalion, The King's (Liverpool Regiment), was originally part of 76th Brigade, 25th Division. In October 1915 the 76th Brigade was exchanged with 7th Brigade, 3rd Division, and in April 1916 the 13th King's became part of 9th Brigade, 3rd Division. The 3rd Division at that time was part of XI Corps. In April 1918 the actions in Flanders came under the general heading of The Battles of the Lys, 9th–29th April, consisting of eight separate battles. First Army using XI Corps and XV Corps undertook the first battle, The Battle of Estaires, 9th–11th April.

On 1st April the 13th King's, out of the line at Ivergny 9 km north of Doullens, left by bus for billets in Houdain, where 431 OR's joined on 3rd April, and commenced training on the 4th. On 6th April they marched to Coupigny camp from where, on 7th and 8th, the companies were alternately employed in training and digging a new Army line near Houchin. When the Battle of Estaires began on 9th April the 13th King's received orders to 'Stand to' and at noon marched off to a point between (Hersin-) Coupingy and Béthune from where, at 9 p.m. they were taken by bus to Béthune, whence they marched about 4 km east to Gorre Château. Upon arrival they came under the orders of 165th Brigade, 55th Division and were placed in Brigade reserve.

The fighting had gone reasonably well for the 55th Division on 9th April considering that on their left the Portuguese 2nd Division, overdue for relief, overstretched (its 1st Division, less 3rd Brigade, having been withdrawn) and holding some 6 miles of line, had broken completely. The 55th Division of necessity had to form a new northeast facing defensive line on its left flank. The enemy had also considered the 55th Division to be a pushover, but the rested Division had been fairly resilient and had rebounded back after each enemy push.

Early in the morning of 10th April the enemy attacked the village of Loisne, but despite taking heavy casualties the defenders had repulsed the attack. Further attacks later that morning at Cailloux and Festubert were driven off. 13th King's were subsequently deployed as follows. Early that morning 'D' Coy was sent to replace a company of 165th Brigade in a position lining a stream northwest of Gorre Wood. In the evening 'C' Coy, ordered to report to the OC 5th King's at Festubert Keep, had two platoons in the Keep and two deployed as a defensive

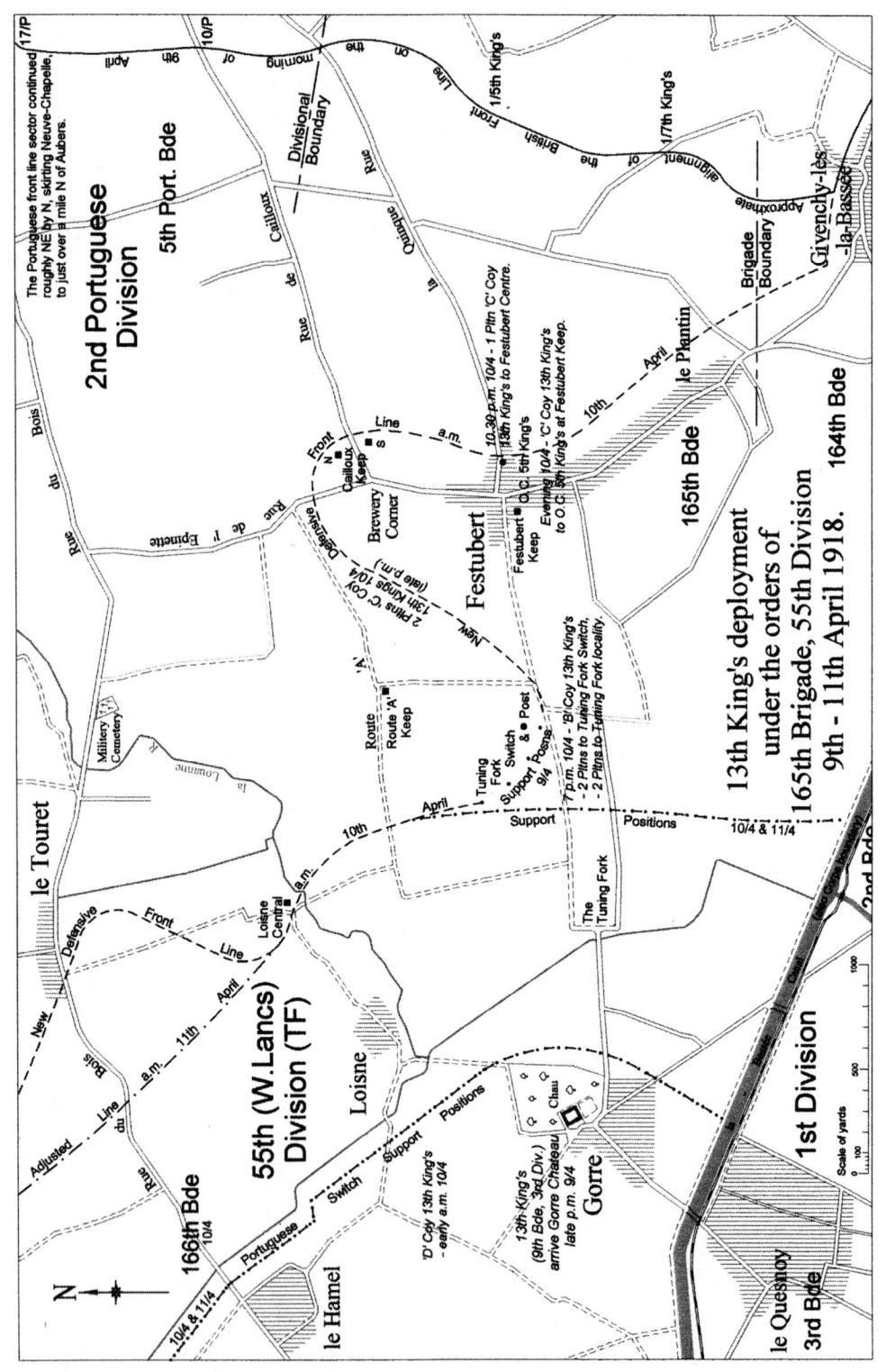

Map 23. *Gorre, 13th King's deployment.*

flank in nearby shell holes. At 10.30 p.m. one platoon from the Keep was sent to strengthen the garrison at Festubert Central. At 7 p.m. 'B' Coy sent two platoons to Tuning Fork Switch and two platoons to the Tuning Fork locality. The following day was similar, with 165th Brigade being subjected to heavy attacks. Where the enemy made inroads into the line successful counter-attacks pushed him back again. Unfortunately there is no mention of any casualties in the 13th King's war diary.

The following item appeared in the *Hull Times* of 1st June and relates to an event that occurred in April. Again it was the sad news that another Barnetby Boy had been killed in action this time on 17th April, namely...

21585 Private Thomas Wilfred Bramley, 10th Battalion, Lincolnshire Regiment.

Thomas Wilfred Bramley, the son of Hannah Bramley of Worlaby, was born at Little Coates, Lincolnshire (3)1879 and up to at least 1901 lived with his grandparents at Worlaby. He married Emma Sanderson (b. Ketsby, Lincs. (1)1883) at Louth in (4)1906 and in 1911, as a groom/gardener, was living at Kirmington Vale with wife and son Stanley Sanderson Bramley, aged 2.

He had worked as a groom for Mr Lowish at Worlaby and Barnetby before enlisting at Brigg. After he was killed in action on 17th April 1918, his Company Commander said of Thomas,

Pte T. W. Bramley.

> 'He was manning a trench and helping to keep back the continuous effort of the enemy to force us back. His presence amongst the boys in action always inspired them with renewed confidence and effort.'

That 17th April action, entitled the 'First Battle of Kemmel, 17th–19th April', was part of the 'Battles of the Lys, 9th–29th April 1918' offensive involving the British First and Second Armies. The 34th Division (and 10th Lincolns), used initially as part of XV Corps, First Army, was later involved as part of Second Army as a result of having been transferred to its IX Corps.

During the early part of 1918 the United Kingdom Divisions had undergone major restructuring. As a result of this on 3rd February the 10th Lincolns were transferred from 101st to 103rd Brigade, 34th Division. The 103rd Brigade now comprised the 9th Northumberland Fusiliers, the 10th Lincolns and the 1st East Lancashires.

At the time of this army re-organisation the 10th Lincolns were near Croisilles, southeast of Arras. They were still in the area at the start of the big enemy offensive on the 21st March taking part in 'The First Battles of the Somme, 1918', and remained there until the 23rd March when the division was relieved. After a period of rest and refitting the 34th Division left the Somme area. The 1st April saw the 10th Lincolns in trenches to the southeast of Armentières, near Bois Grenier where the line defences were found to be in a very poor state. That area had been where the 10th Lincolns had undergone their first spell of front line trench duty, after the initial trench warfare training, soon after arriving in France in January 1916. This area was soon to become the focus of another major enemy offensive, 'Operation Georgette'.

By the end of March 'Operation Michael', the enemy offensive begun on 21st March, had lost its impetus just short of Amiens in having advanced too far, too fast, out-run its supplies with over-extended supply lines running across difficult terrain (the 1916 Somme battlefield).

By implementing 'Operation Georgette' the enemy now switched his attention to the north in a planned push aimed roughly north-west from his positions to the west of Lille.

Late on 7th April the enemy subjected most of the Lens – Armentières sector of the front to a heavy bombardment of gas shell. The 2nd Portuguese Division, due for relief on the night of 9th April, was holding a Corps sector from which the 1st Portuguese Division – except for its 3rd Brigade – had been withdrawn on 5th April. Just after 4 a.m. on 9th April the bombardment was repeated. At 8.45 a.m. the barrage on the 2nd Portuguese front lifted, followed by an attack on its lines, five miles south-west of the 34th Division position. The enemy broke through the weak Portuguese lines, thereby causing problems for the British Divisions on either flank especially the 40th Division on the left. Until then those flanking Divisions had not been attacked.

The enemy now pushed out north-west and north in strength against the 40th Division, aiming for the River Lys, with the result that the 40th Division was struggling to hold the enemy. The 34th Division, on the left of 40th Division, sent the 101st Brigade to assist and to destroy the bridge at Bac St Maur. But the men arrived to find the enemy already on the far side of the river and in control of the bridge. During the afternoon, and still on the wrong side of the river, the 101st and 103rd Brigades of 34th Division and the 12th Suffolks from 40th Division formed a defensive line facing an enemy now advancing eastward on either side of the river.

On the following day, 10th April, the 34th Division was faced with further problems on the left resulting from the 25th Division's failure to hold the enemy. The 34th Division, already falling back, was now in danger of being encircled. By mid afternoon a withdrawal was ordered but this too was not without problems

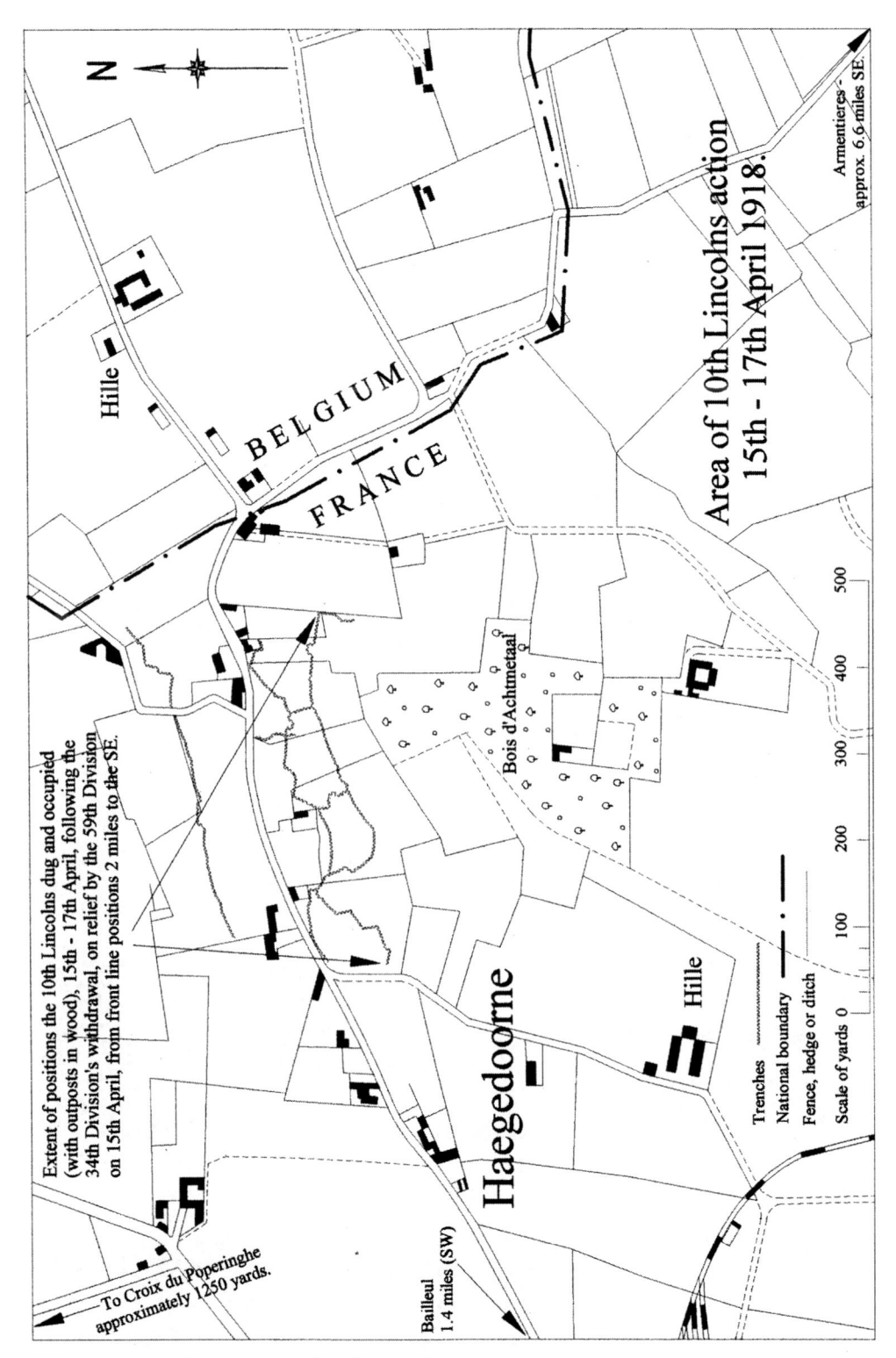

Map 24. *Haegdoorne, area of 10th Lincolns action.*

for there yet remained the river to cross and, hopefully, three bridges by which to do so. A fighting withdrawal took place during the evening through the western suburb of Armentières. The first bridge (railway) was found to be in enemy hands. The second bridge, a wooden one, was partially destroyed but proved passable only to find the enemy too close for comfort once across it. The last, a road bridge at Pont de Nieppe, was intact with the Royal Engineers waiting to destroy it once all the men were across, the 10th Lincolns CO and his headquarters company being the last to cross. The 34th Division then formed a defensive line parallel to the river roughly a quarter of a mile beyond it and remained there for the night.

The day after, 11th April, the 34th Division held off repeated attacks until the evening when it was ordered to withdraw in the direction of Bailleul. (Also on the move in the same direction were the civilian inhabitants of the area). Next day the Division established a new line, with the 103rd Brigade in reserve. The enemy shelled the 10th Lincolns line but apart from that left it alone. Later during the day the 34th Division transferred to IX Corps.

Following further enemy attacks this hold-off and withdraw action was repeated on the next two days centred on Bailleul. During the night of the 14th/15th April the 34th Division was relieved by the 59th Division; the 10th Lincolns, relieved by 4th Lincolns (177th Brigade), moved to Haegedoorne about 1½ mile NE of Bailleul. There the battalion commenced to dig-in on the forward slopes of the hill, assisted by the 209th Field Coy. Royal Engineers digging outposts around an adjacent wood, which the 10th Lincolns subsequently manned and improved.

The forward slopes of the hill on which the 10th Lincolns dug in. The trenches ran roughly central left to right. The dark shadow is cast by the wood, Bois d'Achtmetaal, in rear.

Although the day was relatively quiet by late afternoon the 34th Division found itself again in the front line when the 59th Division, having been driven out of its positions, had withdrawn through the 34th Division's front. The following day, 16th April, had started off reasonably quiet although the enemy had kept the 10th Lincolns front posts under constant machine-gun fire throughout the night. But during mid afternoon the enemy opened up a heavy bombardment of artillery and machine-gun fire on the Divisional lines followed by an assault. The enemy took the 10th Lincolns left outposts by the wood after direct shell hits there had caused the survivors to retire. They were regained at heavy cost to the enemy by a determined counter-attack a couple of hours or so later.

From 8 a.m. to noon on 17th April the enemy heavily bombarded the 34th Division's front and rear lines with guns of all calibre. Under its cover the enemy carried out local attacks against the 10th Lincolns, occupying the house south of the wood, and succeeding again in driving in the left outposts, three of which had been obliterated by shell-fire. Yet the line held and the enemy was driven off receiving heavy losses from machine-gun and rifle fire. But the bombardment had taken its toll of the 103rd Brigade. It was ordered to be relieved that night by the 88th Brigade. On relief a depleted 103rd Brigade and an equally depleted 101st Brigade were formed into a composite brigade and moved back to near Croix du Poperingue to the Army second line. The next morning the 10th Lincolns dug a new line in rear of Croix du Poperinghe, about 2 km to the northwest, where they remained until 21st April.

The fighting of the 34th Division was duly acknowledged in a special Order of the Day issued by the Army and Corps Commanders on 22nd April. The 10th Lincolns casualties over the whole period were 335, including 67 killed. Thomas Wilfred Bramley was killed in action on 17th April the last fighting in which the 10th Lincolns took part. On 11th May the 10th Lincolns were reduced to Training Cadres on a voluntary basis for the newly arrived American troops. Those men who were not part of the cadres were sent to join other units.

Thomas has no known grave and is commemorated by name on the Memorial to the Missing at Tyne Cot Cemetery, Passchendaele (panel 36).

At home *The Grimsby News* of 3rd May reported on the wedding on Tuesday 23rd April, conducted by the Rev. C. F. Brotherton, between Miss Jane Hayward and Mr Victor Alexander Williams. The bride, the niece of Mr and Mrs H. Sims, of Barnetby, had been given away by her uncle, Mr Sims. Miss Hayward, looking charming in a gown of navy blue taffeta trimmed with gold and a hat of white satin with blue ninon, carried a sheaf of lilies and wore a gold brooch – the latter being gifts of the bridegroom. Miss Cole of Middlesborough and Miss Muriel White of Barnetby had attended her. The groom Mr Victor Williams, from London, was the eldest son of the late Mr Joseph Williams, a retired naval officer, and Mrs Williams. He was an Engine Room Artificer (ERA) in the Royal Navy. Both the groom and Mr Weaver his best man, also an ERA, wore naval uniform. The newlyweds spent their honeymoon in London.

The newspaper also reported that towards the end of the month Mr and Mrs Robinson received a field card from their second son, Arthur, bearing the information that he was a prisoner of war. He was the second of their sons to have been taken prisoner the youngest having been taken prisoner in September 1915. They had just received information that he had been sent to Holland along with some other prisoners.

That same Grimsby newspaper concluded with a report on the bad tidings that were sent to Mr and Mrs Scott relating to official information received on Saturday 27th April that their son Walter had been killed in action during the recent spate of heavy fighting. Walter, who had been with the colours for a considerable time, had previously been wounded and after spending an appreciable amount of time in England had been drafted abroad. Of their three other sons serving their country, the eldest had been a prisoner of war since September 1915, one was serving in the Navy and the youngest, a soldier, had been in the Army only a short while. (The Journal of June 1918 listed an A. Scott (Arthur?), a greaser in the Carriage and Wagon Dept at Barnetby as having joined the colours. The Journals from November 1911 to March 1914 also list an A. F. Scott working at Barnetby as a shunter, brakesman, and goods guard before being transferred as a goods guard to Immingham depot. But there is no mention of him ever having enlisted.)

The final item that week gave news of a Barnetby man being a recipient of an award from the Sir Edward Watkin Special Award Fund for the year 1917. Mr R. Todd, a Barnetby goods guard in the Superintendent's Dept, had received a card of merit and 10 shillings 'for services rendered at Barnby Dun when he had found a railway wagon on fire some months ago'. (The full list of awards was in the June issue of the Journal.)

The April 1918 Journal provided information about two Barnetby men. In the list of men joining the colours it names W. Johnson, a relayer in the Engineer's Dept at Barnetby. (Only Arthur Johnson is named on the Roll of Honour.) The other reference to a Barnetby man was a brief obituary (with photograph) to the late John Catterall. (His name was in the list of those killed in action/died of other causes in the May issue of the Journal.) That same May Journal listed labourer B. Gee as having joined the colours from the Engineers Dept at Barnetby.

The Grimsby News of 17th May reported that Pte Jesse Dawson had been severely gassed and had been blind for several days and fortunately had since regained his sight and was said to be progressing favourably. The newspaper concluded with a report that two local lads were on leave: Sapper William Percival, RE, who had now recovered from wounds received last November and Pte Jack Braithwaite who had served in German East Africa for one and a half years and suffered severely from fever during that time.

The Grimsby News of 24th May reported that the Wesleyan Chapel members had held a very successful gift service on Wednesday 15th May and had raised the sum of £4 13s 6d to augment the local War fund. Numerous gifts of OXO, cocoa, cigarettes, condensed milk, soap and one hundred and twenty-seven eggs were also received and handed over to the War Fund.

News of another wounded soldier from the village came when Mrs Wilson received word that her youngest son, Pte Jack Wilson, having recently been wounded, was currently in a hospital receiving treatment for shattered arm muscles and was said to be progressing favourably.

The *Grimsby News* of 31st May carried distressing village news when it reported on the information received by ex-P.C. and Mrs Denton on 24th May. This was official notification that during the fighting of 26th April among the fatal casualties of that day was their third son...

21230 Sergeant Herbert Hanks Denton, 1st Battalion, Lincolnshire Regiment

Herbert 'Bert' Denton, born at Goxhill (2)1891, was the third son of Frederick and Mary Ann Denton, of New Brumby, Scunthorpe, and one of four sons to see service with the Army. I believe the family home in Barnetby at one time had been the police house at No 87 Victoria Road. In 1911 the parents, their six children and Frederick's mother, were living at 5 Hawthorn Villas with Bert employed with the GCR as an engine cleaner. Shortly before the out-break of war Bert had followed in his father's police footsteps by joining the Lincolnshire Constabulary and had been stationed for a brief period at Metheringham.

On 8th October 1915 a report stated that the family had received news that their son Ernest, a Private in the Lincolns, had been wounded and gassed and was in Broadstairs hospital. The following month, on 26th November, his brother Walter H. was reported as being wounded and on 10th March 1916, while serving with the 8th Lincolns, he was reported as having received a second wound, this one being to the knee. In January 1917 the family had received a more favourable report that stated that their son Bert had given blood to save the life of an officer.

A report of 10th August 1917 said that Ernest had been at home on leave after having been in France since September 1915. Two months later on the 12th October Bert, as then still a Private, was also reported as having been at home enjoying a spell of leave. *(That was possibly in late September for he is next mentioned in the newspapers on 23rd November 1917, as having written a letter of condolence to Mr. & Mrs. John Cox following the death of their son Hubert on October 4th 1917.)*

The 1st Lincolns were last mentioned as having taken part in the Battle of St.Quentin, 21st–23rd March 1918. The Battalion had remained on the Somme sector until the end of March having been involved in the fighting withdrawal across the old 1916 Somme battlefield in the face of the enemy drive for Amiens. The 1st Lincolns had finally formed parts of composite battalions in defensive positions at Baizieux (some 18 kilometres northeast of Amiens) and Bonnay (about 6 kilometres south of Baiziuex). By the 31st March the 1st Lincolns had ended up at Bourdon (about 18 kilometres northwest of Amiens) where the battalion effective number totalled three hundred and thirty-four having suffered a total of three hundred and eighty-nine casualties.

On 1st April the 62nd Brigade (including 1st Lincolns) moved north to the Kemmel area to take part in the Battles of the Lys. The 4th-7th April saw the 1st Lincolns in the line near Wytschaete having relieved Australians units. When the Brigade was relieved on 7th/8th April the 1st Lincolns moved back to Ramilles Camp. The Brigade then moved to the Divisional reserve area southeast of Ypres on 10th April where the 1st Lincolns went into Otago Camp, 550 yards SE of the Lille Gate, Ypres. There the 1st Lincolns came under 64th Brigade orders while the remaining battalions of 62nd Brigade went to assist the 26th Brigade in the Wytschaete area.

On the night of 15th/16th April the 1st Lincolns relieved the 2nd Lincolns holding the line Bogaert Farm–Stanyzer Cabaret cross-roads near Wytschaete. At 4.30 a.m. on 16th April the enemy opened up a heavy bombardment (which lasted for seventy minutes on the 1st Lincolns front) followed by an assault concentrating on the 1st Lincolns flanks in dense fog. This action forced the 1st Lincolns into a fighting withdrawal to Wytschaete and by their efforts allowed the reserve battalion into the fray to stop any enemy breakthrough. On the 17th the 1st Lincolns moved to the northwest of Kemmel where the depleted battalion number totalled five officers and just over a hundred other ranks.

On 19th April the 1st Lincolns were encamped at Ottawa Camp, about 1000 yards north of Ouderdom, and they remained there until 25th April, their numbers having been boosted by newly arrived drafts mostly of young men about twenty years of age.

During the Second Battle of Kemmel, 25th-26th April, although the 1st Lincolns took no part in any attacks they did suffer a number of casualties from enemy shell-fire in that period. The 25th April was barely two hours and a quarter old when the enemy opened up an intense bombardment on the 1st Lincolns front and support areas. Shortly after 4 a.m. the 1st Lincolns stood to and at 9

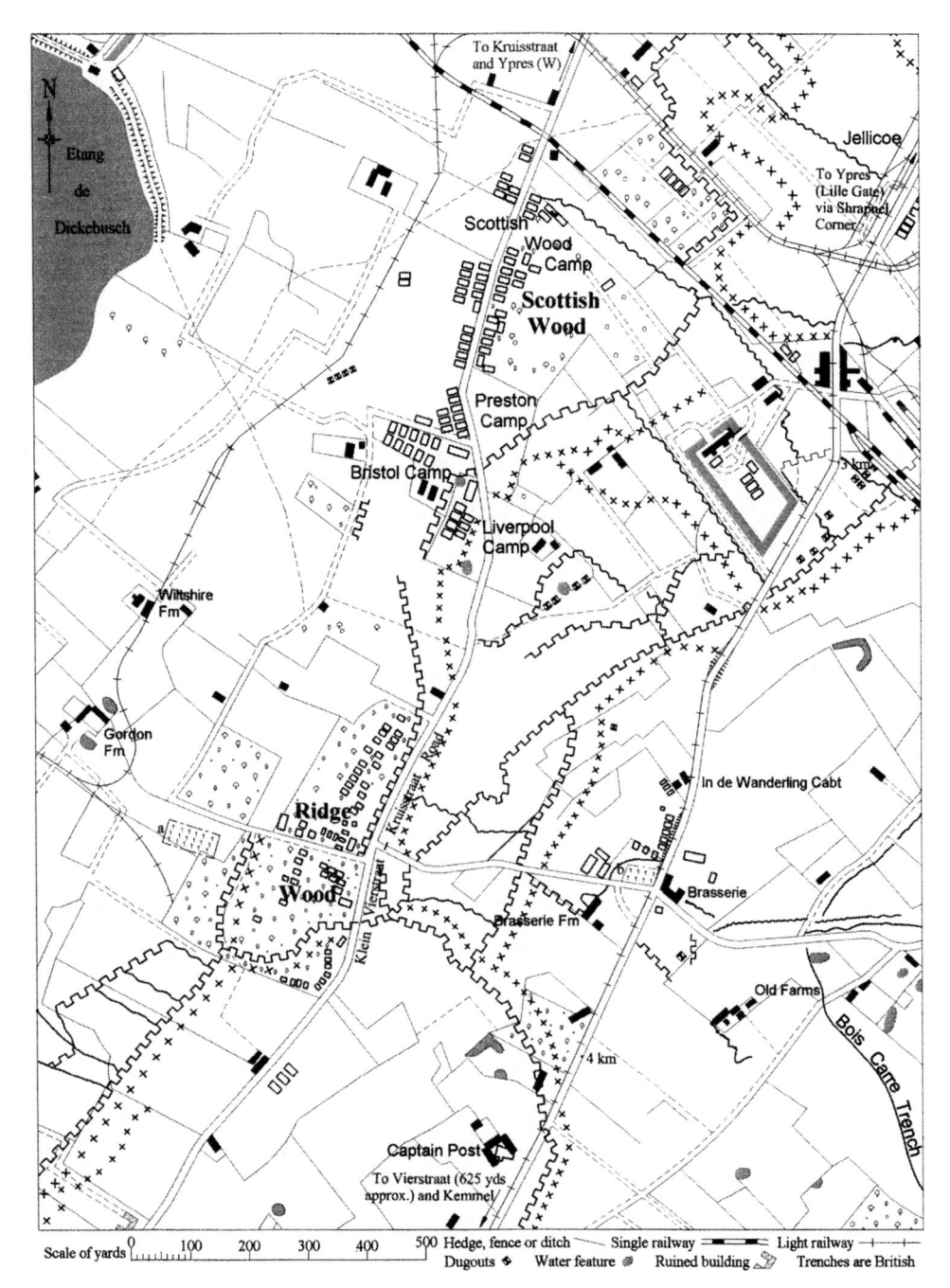

Map 25. *Ridge Wood, area where 1st Lincolns were in the line, 26th April 1918.*

a.m. moved to assembly positions southeast of the Ouderdom–Vlamertinghe road, 1000 yards northwest of Dickebusch, in readiness to reinforce the front line. At 6.30 p.m. the 1st Lincolns received orders to move into the General Headquarters Second Line along the Klein Vierstraat–Kruisstraat road (which gave little shelter) from north of Scottish Wood to the south-west end of Ridge Wood, under orders of 39th Composite Brigade (39th Division's role).

Desultory shell-fire had been received from the enemy but about 3 a.m. on the 26th April this developed into an intense bombardment in and around the Ridge Wood position that lasted for the remainder of the day causing the 1st Lincolns seventy-four casualties. The casualties of the 1st Lincolns for the period 25th-27th April was one officer and thirteen other ranks killed and fifty-four other ranks wounded.

The eastern edge of Ridge Wood taken from near the mid point of the wood's edge looking north. The trench ran along this eastern edge. Scottish Wood is in the background on the right.

One of the casualties killed in action during that bombardment of 26th April 1918, was Sergeant Herbert Denton, aged 27 years.

Oddly, for whatever reason, Bert's name has been omitted from the Roll of Honour of the Lincolnshire Regiment. The CWGC, who record Bert as holding the rank of sergeant, gave the information that after the war the Army Graves Service had been unable to locate his grave. He is therefore commemorated by name on the Memorial to the Missing at the Tyne Cot Cemetery, Passchendaele (panel 35).

Bert is also mentioned on the headstone at his mother's grave in St. Mary's Churchyard, Barnetby. (His mother, Mary Ann Denton, died ten months later on 28th February 1919, aged 59 years. Her youngest son, Wilfred, died on 17th April 1921, aged 16 years. Her third and youngest daughter, Sarah, who went to France in November 1917 to take up hospital duties, died on 27th November, 1925, aged 30 years.)

The same newspaper that reported the death of Bert Denton carried another report of a Barnetby soldier who had been wounded, Sapper W. Wilkinson.

Sapper W. Wilkinson, who had been out in France for some time, had been injured in a railway accident there and, after having had his injuries treated in a

1918

Tyne Cot Cemetery and Memorial to the Missing, Passchendaele. The cemetery rear wall forms the Memorial to the Missing (34,950 names). Shown here is the left-hand third. The Lincolnshire Regiment names begin on panel 35, the last panel before the rotunda (right) and continue in the rotunda. Sgt H. H. Denton is named on panel 35 and Ptes T. W. Bramley and H. Cox are named on panel 36.

hospital in France, had then been transferred to a hospital in Glasgow. While he had been receiving medical treatment for his injury in France he had been in a hospital that, along with some other hospitals, had been so atrociously bombed by the enemy. He was reported as saying that he had escaped injury from the bombing by getting under his bed. After the raid he had found pieces of bomb splinters on his bed. (It will be recalled that a nursing Sister from Wrawby had been killed in one such air raid on a hospital at Lillers.)

The June 1918 issue of the GCR Journal, Volume No. XIII – seemingly the last one to be published, named three Barnetby men in its various lists appertaining to those GCR employees doing military service. Amongst those who were named as having enlisted into the Colours were A. Scott (previously mentioned) and C. S. Thompson – the latter having been a cleaner in the Chief Mechanical Engineer's Locomotive Dept. The list naming those that had been 'Killed in Action' mentioned Pte H. Wright (also previously mentioned). (With the cessation of publication of the Journal a good source of information had been lost.)

The 7th June *Grimsby News* had reported both good and bad news regarding the fate of two Barnetby soldiers.

First the good news:

The Scott family had received astounding new information concerning their son Walter. He had not been killed, as had been released earlier from official sources, for that week they had received a card from Walter saying that he had been wounded and was a POW in Germany. I can imagine the great relief that must have been felt by that family on receiving such wonderful news from their son.

Prior to the previous item giving out the good news about Walter Scott, mention had also been made of bad news. A report had been made concerning the funeral of another Barnetby soldier, the son of Mr and Mrs J. Rhoades...

WR/201924 Sapper George Rhoades, Royal Engineers.

George Rhoades, the son of Joseph and Mary Ann Rhoades was born at Barnetby (1)1896, where he had lived with his parents in South Street (1901 census). In 1911 the Rhoades family was still living in South Street and George was in employment as a farm labourer. Having enlisted at Brigg George had originally joined the Lincolnshire Regiment, Service number 38804 (the Journal for September 1917 lists G. Rhoades, a platelayer in the Engineer's Dept at Barnetby, as having joined the colours.)

At some later stage George had transferred to the Rail Transportation Directorate (RTD) here in England. Being subsequently wounded, he had died of his wounds at Aldershot on Saturday 1st June 1918, aged 22 years. How, where and when George was wounded is not known. (The curator of the Royal Engineers Museum at Chatham has suggested that he might possibly have been put into a lower medical category following an earlier wounding and been transferred to the RTD in England. By being with the RTD he could continue to carry on doing useful work, especially if he had had any sort of railway background.

I believe he was the Barnetby GCR employee mentioned above as having enlisted and just the sort of man the Royal Engineers would have been looking for.) George's name is also on the Great Central Railway Memorial at Sheffield adding further weight to that belief. Unfortunately, later Journal volumes do not mention a G. Rhoades as having been wounded and the last published volume appears to be number XIII with July 1918 the last monthly entry so his death is not recorded.

George Rhoades remains, having been returned to Barnetby, were interred in St Mary's Churchyard in the family plot on Wednesday 5th June 1918, where the Rev. C. F. Brotherton conducted the funeral service (N.B. In the photo above the headstone has not been 'shortened' by the camera – it is a standard size CWGC stone but because it is set into a 'kerbed' plot filled with stones it has, of necessity, been set lower than normal).

G. Rhoades headstone.

Those Barnetby men serving in a Royal Engineers Transportation Unit who died during or not long after the war have proved a bit of a stumbling block when it came to finding out information as to their precise whereabouts during the war.

Three of those Royal Engineers have service numbers with the prefix 'WR' indicating that at some stage they were transferred for whatever reason from the infantry to a RE Transportation Unit. One reason a man may have been transferred to a Transportation Unit was because he had been downgraded medically. Alternatively towards the end of the war infantry units were scoured for men having railway trade or specialist backgrounds. Where a soldier had been attached to a Transportation Unit it helps to know what his specific unit was otherwise the task of finding out more information is almost impossible.

The fifth Barnetby man who died having served with the Royal Engineers, Sapper Frank Burdass, had no letter prefix to his Army service number so presumably he had belonged to an Engineer Field Company. Unfortunately, because he died of 'Spanish flu.' after the war he is not named in 'Soldiers Died in the War' where a specific Field Company may have been mentioned. (Each Infantry Division had three Engineer Field Companies attached (one per Brigade). The other RE was Cpl C. P. Blanchard whose details are known.

As a result of the Service Records of men who served during the First World War having become available for inspection at the National Archives at Kew, there is a possibility of gathering more information. However, as roughly 60% of the Service Records for men who served in the Great War were destroyed or badly damaged by fire and subsequently by water as a result of enemy air raids during the Second World War, the problem is not necessarily going to be solved. Unfortunately, George Rhoades' documents appear to have been amongst those that were destroyed.

In some ways the next item would also have come as a relief if only as a relief from uncertainty. It has already been mentioned in the chapter dealing with 1917 but it was not reported at the time by the newspapers, as the information was not available. The newspapers of 21st/22nd June reported the sad news concerning the fate of Pte W. F. Starkey, 2/4th Battalion, York and Lancaster Regiment. After having had to suffer the awful anxiety and suspense for a year as to the fate of her only son, Mrs Starkey had just received official intimation that he had been killed in action on or about 3rd May 1917.

Returning to more cheerful matters on Wednesday 12th June a large audience had been entertained to a service of song in the school, entitled 'Little Abe', given by the members of the Adult School. During the performance there had been a silver collection that had amounted to £3 2s 6d being raised in aid of the local War Fund

The War Fund Committee had once again been busy preparing and despatching parcels to the lads and it was reported at the end of June that on that occasion they had sent off a total of 130 parcels. That Committee would no doubt have been very pleased to receive the proceeds of any fund raising efforts that were carried out in the village to keep the War Fund topped up while they whittled away at it providing comforts for the Boys.

The Barnetby Band had likewise been active around that time for during the evening of Saturday 29th June it had paraded through the village and assisted by helpers, who carried out a house-to-house collection, had raised £6 for the Prisoners of War and War Fund.

News had also come in about that time of an award having been made to a Barnetby man. 58650 CSM Sidney G. Tilbrook had been awarded the Meritorious Service Medal (MSM) 'for constant zeal and devotion to duty.' He had been with the colours since the outbreak of war and at the time of his award had been serving with the 98th Company Labour Corps out in Salonica.

The following week news of another MSM award made the newspapers, this time the recipient being 32268 QMS Thomas W. Allcard, of the 48th Field Ambulance, RAMC. (The 48th Field Ambulance was one of three ambulance units attached to the 37th Division, the other two being the 49th and 50th Field Ambulance.) Thomas, an old soldier who had previously served in the Boer War, had joined the RAMC on the 1st September 1914 and had since seen much active service on the Western Front. At the time of his award Thomas, having been in an accident, was receiving treatment in a hospital in Reading but the newspapers did not specify the nature of his accident (the 'gazetting' or notification of the above awards appeared in the London Gazette of 3rd June 1918).

The Meritorious Service Medal (MSM), awarded to NCO's and men of the British armed Services, was for good, efficient or meritorious service, though not necessarily in the field. The medal ribbon was the same for all three Services but the medal itself differed slightly for each Service on the obverse (head) side. Precedence-wise medals are always arranged right to left, the highest award, the Victoria Cross – taking precedence over every other decoration awarded, being on the right. The MSM is worn after the Military Medal (MM) or the equivalent medal for the Royal Navy and the Royal Air Force where that medal has been awarded.

On the evening of Wednesday 10th July the half-yearly meeting of the Independent Order of Rechabites had been held in the Railway Street Temperance Hotel here in Barnetby. At that meeting the members were informed of the very impressive memorial service that had taken place at the April Council meeting held at Lincoln. The Rev. Mr Symonds had conducted the service held in memory of the 20 members of the Order who had paid the Supreme Sacrifice during 1917.

Towards the latter end of summer garden fetes had been utilised as a convenient means of fund raising. One such garden fete had been held on Saturday 20th July, in the grounds of Barnetby Manor, by kind permission of Mrs Lowish and had realised £31 6s 3d in aid of the War Fund. On that occasion the Barnetby Band had marched through the village to draw the local populace to the Manor. During the proceedings the Band had entertained those attending to a programme of popular selections. Apart from the usual items at the fete there had been had also been a jumble sale and a sale of local garden produce. A programme of sporting activities had also been organised by Mrs Lowish and friends. One unusual sports feature had been a ladies cricket match. The Women's Adult School members had raised a side for this event and played the match against an outside team. Unfortunately the newspaper did not disclose the name of the opposing team. Neither did it inform on which side had won if indeed there was a result.

During mid August the War Fund Committee, seeing as how the Fund was quite healthy with a reasonably good sum of cash in hand, had taken the decision to send 5 shillings (5s.) to each of the 130 soldiers and sailors serving with the colours. In present day terms that perhaps does not seem an awful lot of money (25p), but in those days it was the equivalent of five days' basic pay for an Army private.

The August newspapers that had related the news about the cash gifts to the troops also carried the story of another village man who had recently been wounded. This soldier was the third Worrall boy, Joseph. He was being treated for his injuries at Hoylake hospital, in Cheshire, after having been wounded in both legs. At that time his two elder brothers were Prisoners of War in Germany.

More fund raising had taken place during the third week in August in aid of the POW fund. The occasion was a Garden Fete and Sports held in the grounds of Ash Field House, by kind permission of Mr and Mrs W. Lowish. The Barnetby Band had again been in attendance and had kindly given of its services. This had been a very successful venture with £70 17s. having been realised of which £19 had come from the sale of refreshments.

The local newspapers reported the following item on 4th/5th October in the news relating to Nettleton, near Caistor. The item briefly stated that Nettleton and district had received the news with sincere regret of the death of another brave soldier. Mr and Mrs R. Witty had received official information that only intimated that the deceased was killed in action on 24th August, he being their youngest son...

201782 Pte Walter Stanley Witty, 7th Battalion, E.Yorkshire Regiment

Walter Stanley Witty, born (2)1896 at Anlaby, Hull, was the youngest son of Richard Martin Witty and Rachel Witty of Nettleton, near Caistor, Lincs. In 1911 Walter was living with his family at Nettleton and in employment as a farm labourer. Prior to enlistment he had been employed by the GCR where he worked as a chainman on the Resident Engineer's Staff at Barnetby. An exceedingly loyal lad who possessed a sunny disposition he had volunteered to join up late in 1915 (Walter's enlistment is recorded in the December 1915 issue of the Journal.) After taking part in several engagements he was severely wounded

Pte W. S. Witty.

in the chest in April 1917 as a result of which he had spent some time being treated in a Birmingham hospital. This was then followed by a long period of convalescence until he was finally pronounced fit to return to active duty in time to take his share in the big advance. Some six weeks later, on 24th August 1918, Walter was killed in action, aged 22 years.

The 7th E. Yorks, (50th Brigade, 17th [Northern] Division), being part of V Corps (Third Army), took part in 'The Second Battles of the Somme 1918', carried out by Third and Fourth Armies. The first of these battles, 'The Battle of Albert', officially classified as being from 21st-23rd August saw units still fighting on 24th August!

The British forces, having halted the rapid enemy advance just short of Amiens in April, went on to a period of active defence and at the same time reorganising the whole front line preparatory to taking offensive action later on. In Picardy the offensive started with the 'Battle of Amiens' on 8th August using its Fourth Army operating south of the Somme River with the First French Army on its right. This resulted in the enemy being pushed back about 8-10 kilometres on the first day. When this operation came to a standstill on 13th August the offensive switched to the north. So began the 'Second Battles of the Somme' 1918.'

At 4.55 a.m., 21st August, IV Corps (Third Army) began a limited attack north of the Ancre River to take the general line of the Albert – Arras railway from Miraumont northerly through to Moyenneville. The 21st Division, (V Corps), detailed to cover the right flank of IV Corps, attacked and took Beaucourt. On 22nd August, following on from this successful attack, fresh troops and guns were brought up. In the meantime the left of Fourth Army was moved forward between the Somme and the Ancre rivers in preparation for the main attack on the 23rd August, using the remainder of Fourth Army to cover the right flank south of the Somme.

During the afternoon of 22nd August V Corps HQ warned 17th Division to have a brigade detailed to relieve the 110th Brigade (21st Division) at the Ancre crossing that night and prepare to assist in an attack on the Thiepval Ridge during the night of 23rd/24th. 50th Brigade duly received the orders. Late on the night of 22nd August the 50th Brigade (17th Division) relieved the 110th Brigade in its positions along the Ancre River north of Hamel. From there at midnight the 6th Dorsets of 50th Brigade began crossing the Ancre river but by daylight of 23rd August they had not fully got into position and the 10th W. Yorks and the 7th E. Yorks had still to cross.

The 10th W. Yorks, unable to start crossing before late afternoon and with only two narrow crossing points usable, made very slow progress being further

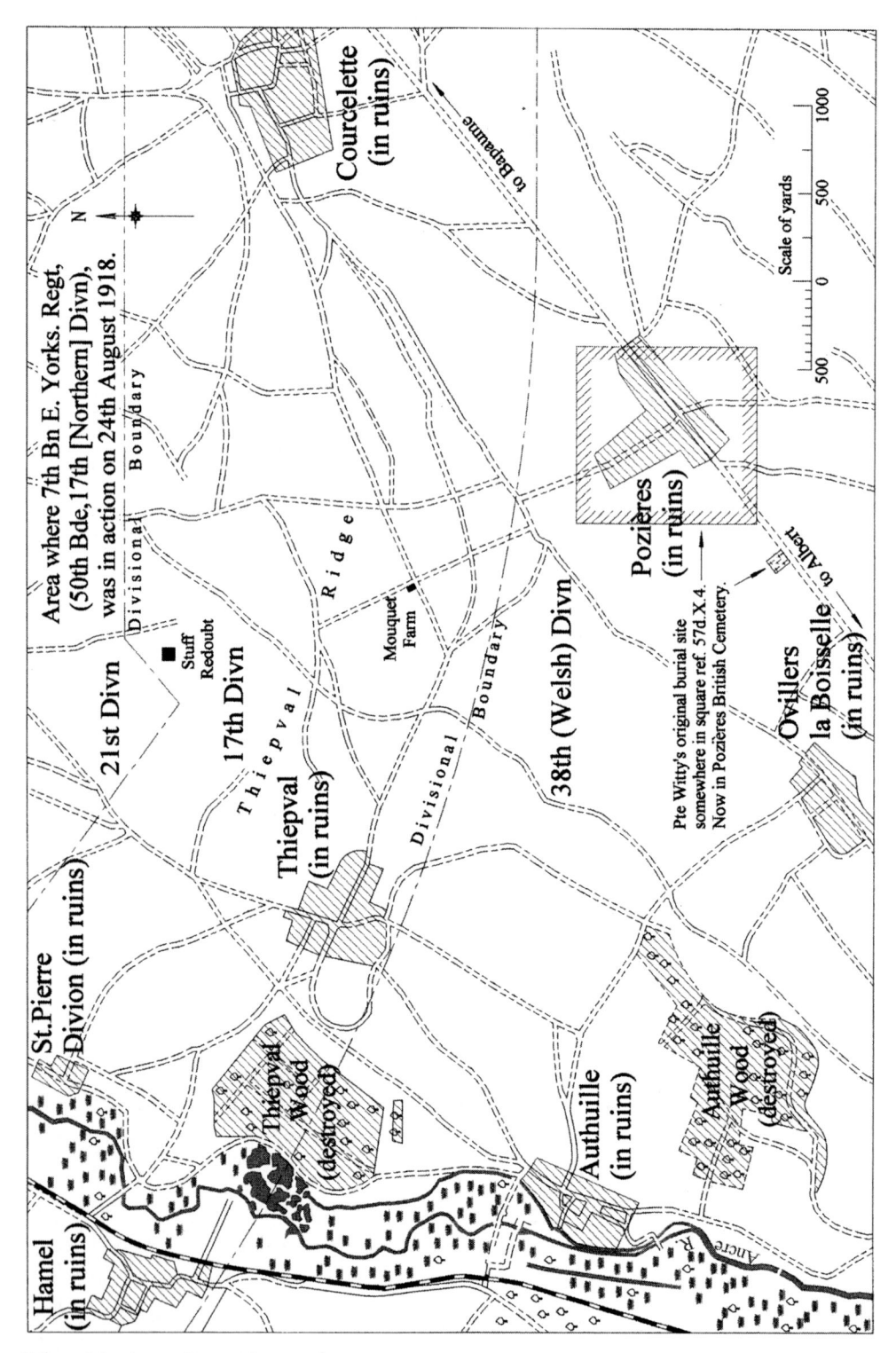

Map 26. *Area where 7th E. Yorks were in action.*

hampered by the enemy's continual shelling of the Ancre Valley, saturating it with gas, particularly near St Pierre Divion. The 7th E. Yorks eventually followed on and by midnight both battalions had crossed the river and were in position. The 6th Dorsets and 10th W. Yorks were in the first line with 7th E. Yorks in reserve and covering the gap in the left flank between the 6th Dorsets and the 21st Division.

At 1.20 a.m., 24th August, the attack went in behind the barrage, the initial objective being the Thiepval Ridge crest. The 10th W. Yorks reached their objective but heavy fire from Stuff Redoubt held up the 6th Dorsets. At first light the 7th E. Yorks, coming up in rear clearing up captured positions, found themselves forward of the Dorsets who had lost direction and were still being held up. At 4 a.m. the 7th E. Yorks received orders to press ahead with the 10th W. Yorks towards Courcelette (around this time Sgt Harold Jackson, VC, from Boston, Lincolnshire, accompanying the OC 7th E. Yorks on a forward reconnaissance, was killed by a machine-gun bullet. He is buried in A. I. F. Burial Ground, Flers).

The 7th E. Yorks advanced during the early forenoon and by 11 a.m. had captured Mouquet Farm. The Battalion paused there to ensure it was in touch with its neighbours before pressing on against heavy frontal machine-gun fire and by 2.30 p.m. it had taken Pozières. The 7th E. Yorks continued about three hundred yards further east and took up positions on either side of the Albert – Bapaume road, again ensuring that both flanks were protected, which necessitated a rearwards adjustment on the left flank. Further advance was not possible as the Battalion had by then run into their Divisional artillery fire.

The enemy made two counter-attacks during the latter part of the afternoon. The first of these was repulsed. The second, accompanied by heavy shelling, was directed against the front and right flank – the latter subjected to enfilade machine-gun fire. This caused the

W. S. Witty headstone.

7th E. Yorks to pull back to the higher ridge two hundred yards west of Pozières and make themselves secure for the night. From there, on 25th August, it was in reserve supporting the 52nd Brigade during its advance. Unfortunately the Regimental History and the Battalion War Diary do not give any casualty details for the 7th E. Yorks during that period.

Walter was originally buried near where he fell at map reference 57d.X4, an area 1000 yards square with Pozières situated almost in the middle. (By then

Pozières had quite literally been flattened during two years of fighting and no longer existed as a village.) Walter is now buried in Pozières British Cemetery, plot I, row J, grave 20. The cemetery contains 2,731 burials. Of these 1,800 are United Kingdom soldiers, 714 Australians, 209 Canadians, 7 with units unknown and 1 German soldier. 1,353 are unnamed. The original burials, made by fighting units and Field Ambulances in 1916, 1917 and 1918, are in Plot II. The remaining plots, consisting mainly of men from the autumn 1916 fighting and a few from August 1918, were concentrated into the Cemetery from the local battlefields after the Armistice.

At a memorial service held in Nettleton parish church, the Rev. J. E. Bamford paid very touching tributes to Walter. Mr and Mrs Witty also had another son, Sgt J. Witty, Royal Engineers, serving with the forces out in France.

Nettleton War Memorial (W. S. Witty). Opened 1st December 1922 by Lord Yarborough.

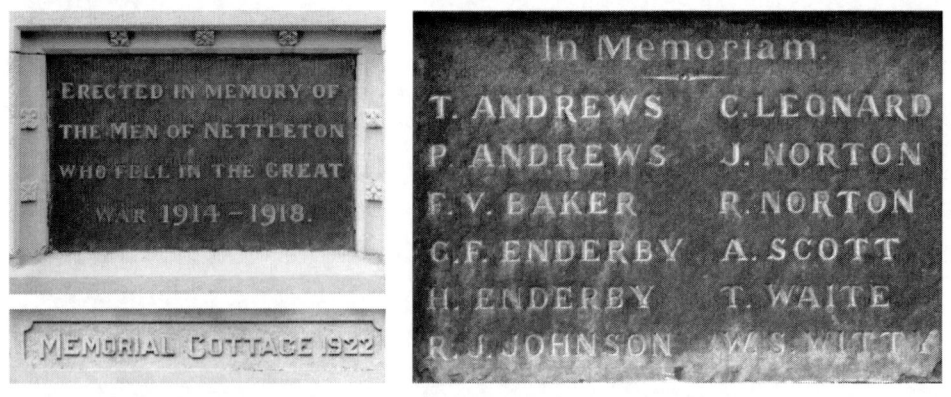

At the opening ceremony Lady Yarborough unveiled the left hand plaque and Lord Yarborough unveiled the right hand plaque.

Walter's name appears as Stanley Witty on the Roll of Honour for Barnetby but his name is not on the War Memorial although that does record the name Whitley with an indistinct initial, that is possibly S.

I believe the name Whitley on the War Memorial is an error and it should read Witty. The Regiment, E. Yorks, is correct, even if the battalion number, 4th, is wrong (fours' can often look like sevens'). The CWGC have informed me that they list no serviceman with the name Whitley and initial S in the Lincolnshire or Overall First World War Indices. I have checked various volumes of 'Soldiers Died in the War' and cannot find a Whitley S. (In Alan Tailby's book 'A Parish Camera' about Nettleton there is a photograph of a grocer's bill with the name Whitty printed on it). As Walter had GCR connections at Barnetby Locomotive Depot he fits the bill. So it is highly probable that with living in Nettleton he could have lodged here in the village, hence the inclusion of his name on the Roll of Honour and on the War Memorial in a misspelt form. Perhaps he even preferred being called Stanley! The Memorial Cottage (see photo. p. 232) and the Roll of Honour in Nettleton Church bear Walter's name. His name is also on the GCR Memorial at Sheffield.

The next item is about the man that led to my locating the Somerby Memorial plaque in Somerby church. I first noticed his name on a headstone in a family plot in Somerby churchyard mentioning a son who had died in France, namely...

104086 Gunner George William Rimmington, 287th Siege Battery, Royal Garrison Artillery.

George William 'Billy' Rimmington, born at Crosby, Lincolnshire, on 2nd May 1897, was the eldest son of John William and Mary Ann Rimmington, of Somerby, Lincolnshire. In 1911 the family was living at 1 Somerby and George was employed as a farm boy.

Prior to his enlistment George had been employed by Mr F. Chatterton of Somerby Hall and had been highly respected by all that knew him. On 10th July 1916 he joined the army at Lincoln. On 13th July he arrived at Great Yarmouth for kitting out and vaccination and from there, on 25th July, was sent to the Dundee area of Scotland for training. Whilst there George volunteered for training to be a signaller and in due course he became a signaller with the 287th Siege Battery, RGA.

When the 287th Siege Battery was first formed it was made up of four 6" (26 cwt) howitzers. On 28th February 1917 the Battery went to the Western Front

Gnr G. W. Rimmington.

forming part of the 69th HAG. In 1918 the number of howitzers was increased to six.

From then on the Battery was subsequently transferred to various HAGs. On 5th August 1917 a draft of personnel joined from the 389th Siege Battery. The Battery became part of 22nd HAG on 22nd December 1917 and at the time of the action in which George was wounded it was part of the 22nd Brigade RGA (or 22nd HAG).

During 'Operation Michael', the enemy 1918 spring offensive that had opened with effect on 21st March, the bulk of the assault had mainly been directed against the British 5th Army in the southern sector centred on St Quentin where units in the south had been driven back. By the end of the month the impetus had slackened and it finally ran out of steam during the first week of April but not before the southern elements of 5th Army had been pushed back almost as far as Amiens. Taking into consideration what had taken place in the south the British retreat in the northern sector around Arras had been relatively small. But the enemy had been held, then turned and was now in retreat. In the Arras sector by the third week in August the British were almost back to that line of 21st March.

The 22nd HAG, as part of Third Army, took part in 'The Second Battles of Arras, 1918, 26th August – 3rd September'. The first operation, 'The Battle of the Scarpe, 1918, 26th–30th August', was directed against the Hindenburg Line in the Arras sector in an attempt yet again to achieve a breakthrough of that formidable defensive system that the enemy had now been forced back to. (In 1917 between April and June the British had made several unsuccessful attempts on the Hindenburg Line in the same area that the 287th Siege Battery was about to operate in.)

26th August saw the 287th Siege Battery at map reference 51B.T7d.9.6., a road junction about 450 yards south-east of Boiry Becquerelle. During the night the Battery moved one section into action at map reference T9a.0.9., about 1,250 yards north-east from the previous position. The following day the Battery moved four guns to map reference T3d.2.6., a further 750 yards north-east. This move was completed by 2 a.m. on 28th August when the Batteries of 22nd HAG bombarded Bullecourt from 12.30 p.m. to 1.40 p.m. in support of an attack by the 167th Infantry Brigade of 56th Division.

Next day, between 11 a. m. and 1 p.m., the 287th Battery bombarded Bullecourt again and put down a creeping barrage in a south-easterly direction from about mid way between Bullecourt and Reincourt-lez-Cagnicourt. Later that day the 287th Siege Battery moved five of its guns to position T24b.5.8. about 750 yards east of Croisilles.

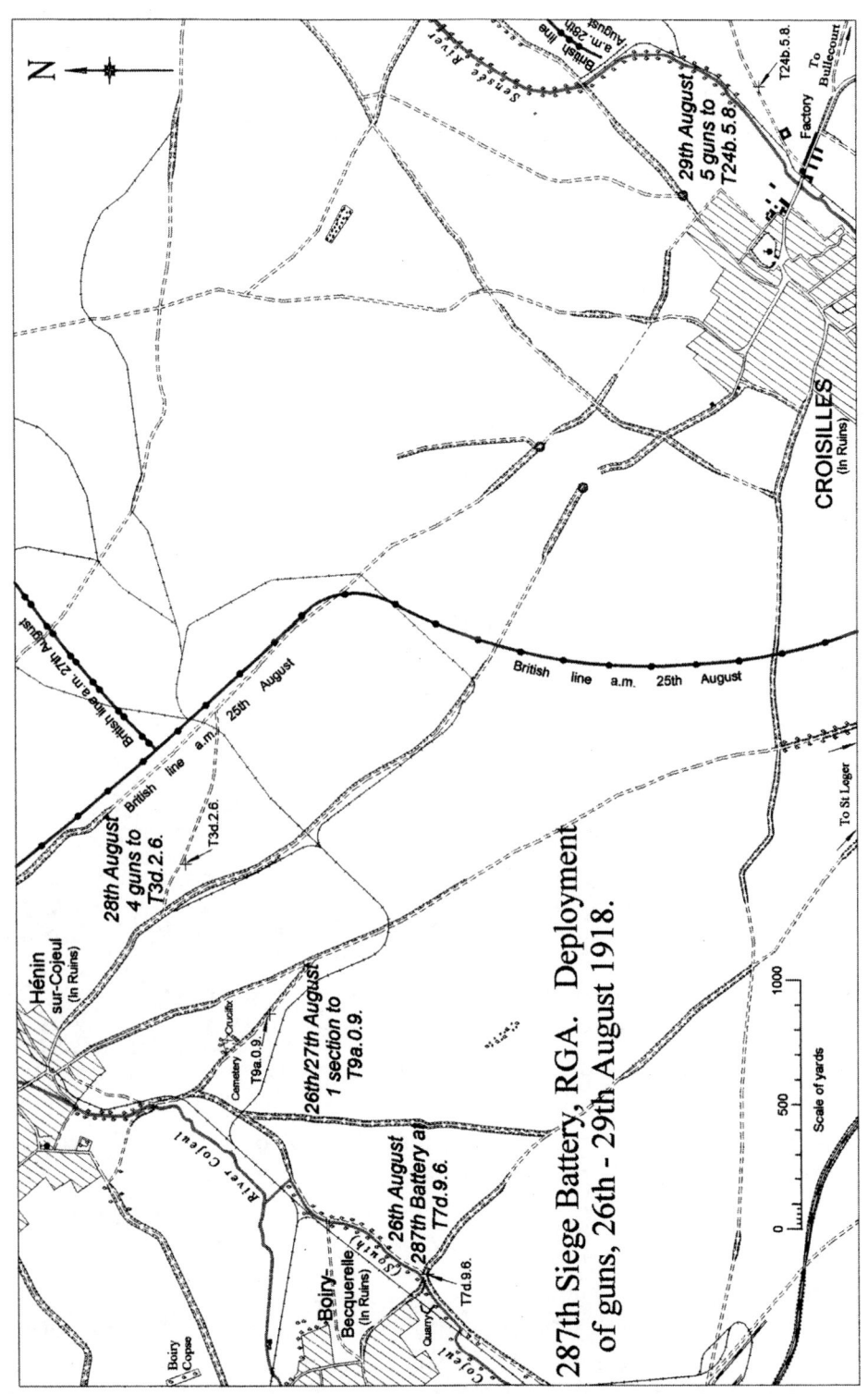

Map 27. *Gun deployment of 287th Siege Battery, RGA, in support of attacks on positions around Bullecourt during 'The Battle of the Scarpe, 26th-30th August 1918'.*

What was George's part in all this? An artillery signaller could be involved in various tasks at various places. He could be at the gun position manning field telephones or with the Forward Observation Officer (FOO) near to, or in, the front line to send messages to the battery position. Signallers accompanying a FOO usually had field telephones and carried drums of telephone wire – miles of it, laying it as they went when going to a new observation post. Other equipment included daylight signalling lamps, flags and even pigeons (wireless communication at that time being in its infancy). A signaller could be anywhere between those positions repairing breaks in the telephone wire. Each task had its share of dangers, some more than others. Thus George could have been anywhere doing any one of the tasks named.

104086 Gunner George William Rimmington, wounded in action on 29th August 1918, died of his wounds in a Casualty Clearing Station on 1st September 1918, aged 21 years. He is buried in le Bac du Sud British Cemetery at Bailleulval, Pas-de-Calais, in Plot I, Row F, Grave 1. A personal inscription on his headstone reads, *'Upright and true, one of the best. May God grant him Eternal rest. R. I. P.'*

The cemetery, situated on the northern side the N25 Arras - Doullens road, contains 743 burials – 640 from the United Kingdom, 48 from Canada and 55 German prisoners of war.

The Casualty Clearing Stations in the area at that time were Nos. 45 and 46; both used le Bac du Sud for burials. No. 45, at Bailleuval from 31st August 1918, had moved there from Auchy-les-Hesdin, about 60 km away. No. 46, at le Bac du Sud and in use there from 26th June to 1st September 1918, was moved to Bailleuval, roughly 1½ km south-east of le Bac du Sud, on 2nd September 1918. (It is most likely that George was treated for his wounds at No. 46 CCS.)

G. W. Rimmington headstone.

In Somerby churchyard, in the Rimmington plot, the headstone of brother Walter Rimmington's grave has an inscription that reads *'also George W. Rimmington, born May 2nd, 1897, died in France Sep 1st, 1918.'* George's name is also on a small brass memorial plaque on the front of the lectern in Somerby Church.

The 14th September *Hull Times* had an obituary to George complete with a small photograph. It also gave notice that a Memorial Service to George was to be held in St Margaret's Church, Somerby, on Sunday 15th September at 11.30 a.m. conducted by the Rector of Somerby, the Reverend John Smith Swann.

Sad news came to the village on Sunday 29th September during the Harvest Festival service in the West Street Wesleyan Methodist Chapel. A gloom was to be cast over that usually cheerful festive event when it was announced that Mrs Nicholls had just received news from the Chaplain about the death of her eldest son and staunch Wesleyan...

43769 Pte George Nicholls, 1/5th Battalion Lincolnshire Regiment.

George Nicholls, the eldest son of Frederick and Sabina Nicholls, was born (4)1892 at Great Coates, Lincolnshire. In 1911 he was living with his family and working on their farm at Barnetby. He had married Edith May Morwood (2)1917 and at the time of his death their address was the 'The Firs', Howsham, Lincolnshire. He had farmed with his father and brothers prior to enlistment at Scunthorpe.

It is not clear what regiment George joined on enlisting but the medal index shows service in the Leicestershire Regiment, service number 45703! (his service documents were seemingly among those destroyed in the Second World War so verification is almost impossible).

On his wedding photograph George is in uniform but the cap badge (similar to the one in the photograph, right) does not look like that of the Lincolnshire or the Leicestershire Regiment! George had been in the army about two years before he was killed in action on 23rd September 1918, aged 26 years.

Pte G. Nicholls.

In mid September the 46th Division, relieved from a long duty spell in the Bethune area, was sent south to join IX Corps, Fourth Army. On 21st September

View from a motorway bridge on 'Watling Street' approx. 300 m SW of the northern limit of 1/5th Lincolns front line sector. The white line is the approximate alignment of the Lincolns trench. Clearly seen are the embankments either side of the track, right, that runs past what's left of 'Eleven Trees' (see Map 28, p. 238).

Map 28. *Bellenlise.*

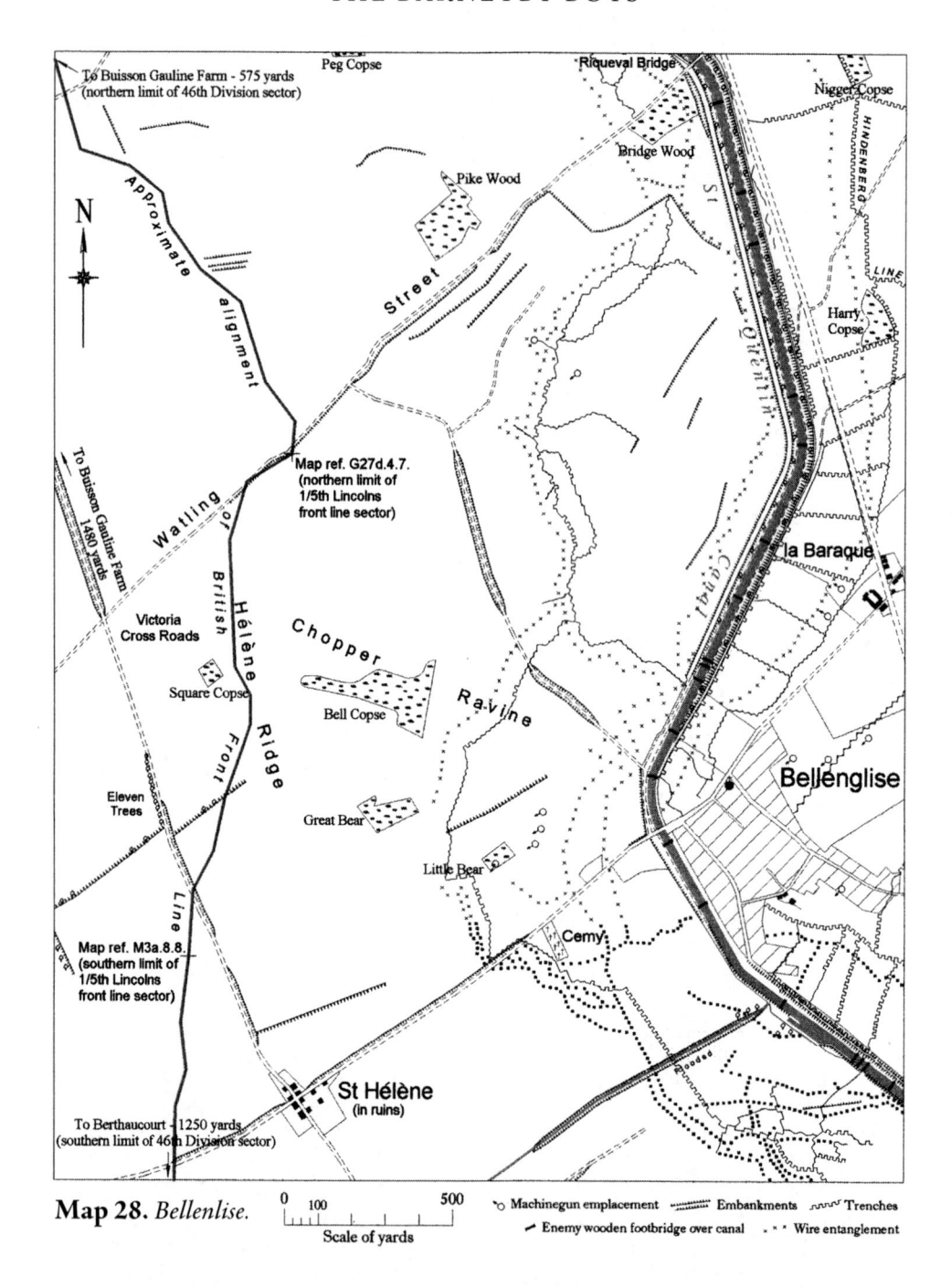

the 46th Division relieved part of the Australian 1st and 4th Divisions in positions facing Bellenglise from Buisson Gaulaine Farm, in the north, to Berthaucourt, in the south. The 30th (US) Division was on the 46th Division's left and the British 1st Division on its right. The 1/5th Lincolns relieved the Australian 46th and 48th Infantry Battalions in the front line right sub-sector holding positions

1918

Map 29.

Left – map of Bernes drawn from a trench map dated February 1918; all buildings are shown in ruins.
The road to Roisel (top right) suggests Roisel is northeast from Bernes; it is roughly due north, 4km (2.5 miles) away.

Sugar Factory
Crucifix
To Roisel (approx. N. of Bernes)
Bernes

Church: map ref. 62c.Q10b.83.85.

Map ref. 62c.Q10b.5.9., covering an area 50 yards square.

Photograph of church taken from here.

George Nicholls original burial site, also that of the rebuilt church.

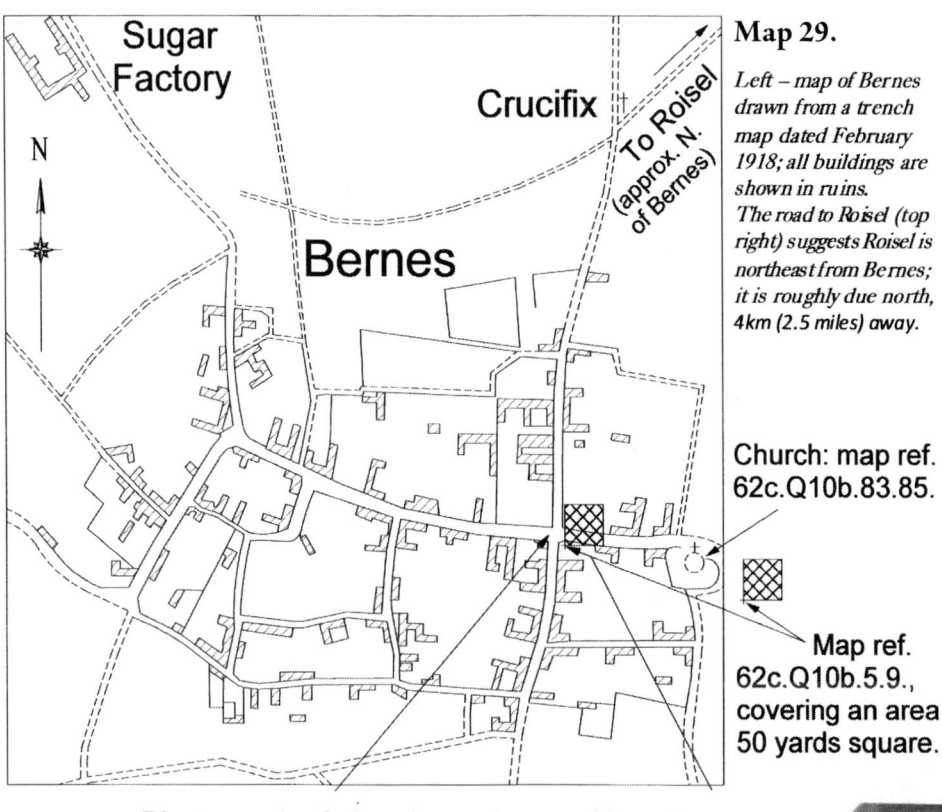

Photograph taken from the cross roads in Bernes looking east. On the map above, the church is shown at the end of the street (at map ref 62c.Q10b.83.85.) in an area that is now the village cemetery – seen on the photo as the walled area in front of the tall central tree. On the photo the rebuilt church is seen on the right, built on the site of George Nicholls' original burial (map ref. 62c.Q10b.5.9. – an area 50 yards square that extends left over the road and towards the cemetery). The area is also where the other 48 men had been buried.

from M3a.8.8. to the road at G27d.4.7. which overlooked the St. Quentin Canal and the enemy positions beyond.

The 1/5th Lincolns war diary (WO 95/2690) for 22nd September states that the enemy shelled the whole Battalion area with H.E. and gas shell and repeated the shelling on the 23rd, which resulted in two other-ranks being killed. Although no names are mentioned it is likely that Pte George Nicholls was one of those two killed.

In September 1918 the RFA and the 46th (North Midland) Division buried 49 men in Bernes churchyard. After the Armistice those burials were concentrated into Roisel Communal Cemetery Extension where George is buried in plot I, row J, grave 1, (his original burial site, map reference 62c.Q10b.5.9., is the same as the other 48 men originally buried in Bernes churchyard.) A photograph of Bernes cemetery believed taken soon after the war, showed a number of graves, later removed, marked with wooden crosses that a Bernes resident thought were German. With the cemetery next to the original church was this the churchyard referred to, were those graves British and was a map reference error made?

Roisel originally had two Military Cemeteries, the Communal and the Communal Cemetery Extension, but all the graves in the Communal Cemetery, except one, were removed into the Extension. The Germans began the Extension and the 41st, 48th, 53rd and 58th Casualty Clearing Stations developed it in the autumn of 1918.

George Nicholls' headstone.

After the Armistice 557 British and 278 Germans graves were concentrated into it from the area around Roisel. It now holds the graves of 862 British and Commonwealth troops, 120 being unnamed, and about 500 Germans.

George's daughter, the late Mrs Hastings, who with her daughter ran the Wool Shop in Brigg Market Place, told how the area around Roisel reminded her of the Nicholls' family home at Wold Farm, Barnetby.

At the time George was killed the 1/5th Lincolns, 138th Brigade, had not been carrying out any operations but settling into its new positions in preparation for the 46th Division assault on the St Quentin Canal. Beyond the canal were the formidable defences of the Hindenburg Line, so particularly strong that the enemy thought them practically impregnable.

The Canal on its own was obstacle enough. In parts it ran between cliffs 30-50 feet high at the northern end of 46th Division's sector by Riqueval Bridge, the water depth being 6-8 ft where two battalions of the assaulting unit, 137th (Staffordshire) Brigade, would make a crossing utilising various flotation devices. The 137th Brigade left boundary was at the Riqueval Bridge, the right at Bellenglise village. The rest of the Division would follow later, 138th Brigade on the left and 139th on the right, with both Brigades passing through the 137th on to their own objectives. Although the Battle of St Quentin Canal, 29th September–2nd October, does not concern the story in relation to George, it is worthy of mention because the 46th Division not only crossed the canal but also succeeded in breaching the Hindenburg Line and taking all its allotted objectives beyond, partly aided in the crossing as a result of the enemy's failure to destroy footbridges over the canal. At last the long sought after breakthrough had been made.

The next fatality is named only on the Roll of Honour though there is a strong Barnetby connection; to date I have not come across any obituary relating to…

245209 Pte Charles Braithwaite, 13th Battalion Durham Light Infantry

The name Braithwaite will be familiar to many Barnetby people through that family having been 'Mine Host' for 109 years at the Railway Inn where Kenneth Braithwaite was the last licensee of that family there. William Braithwaite, Ken's grandfather, had a brother living in the Doncaster area and *Charles*, his son, was born (3)1890 at Auckley, Yorkshire, a small village roughly four miles south-east of Doncaster. In 1911 he was in lodgings at Green Mile, Retford and working as a domestic groom. Charles had regularly visited Barnetby and eventually married local girl Elizabeth 'Liza' Mitchell of Melton High Wood, (3)1915. She was later to marry Fred Robinson of Barnetby. That marriage also ended tragically for Fred died quite young having been involved in a gassing accident at Scunthorpe Steelworks along with other workers.

Charles enlisted into the Lincolnshire Regiment at Lincoln, number 26117 and at some later stage was transferred to the Durham Light Infantry (DLI) and given the service number 245209. When Charles was transferred from the Lincolns to the DLI is not known. It could have been while the 13th Battalion was still part of 68th Brigade, 23rd Division, when that Division was sent to Italy in November 1917. In 1918, when the divisions were restructured from four battalions per brigade to three, each of the three brigades of 23rd Division lost one battalion to form the 74th Brigade, 25th Division. After restructure the 74th Brigade comprised of 13th DLI (ex 68th Brigade), 9th Yorks (ex 69th Brigade) and 11th Sherwood Foresters (ex 70th Brigade).

The 25th Division had returned to England for reforming, having suffered heavily on the Aisne at the end of May 1918. Was this the time Charles joined the 13th DLI had he been in the 10th Lincolns (during May 1918 those 10th Lincolns not used on training cadres were transferred to other units)? In mid September 1918 the 25th Division returned to France as part of XIII Corps, Fourth Army its ranks now swelled by nine battalions sent from the 7th, 23rd and 48th Divisions in Italy.

This reconstituted 25th Division, made up of the 7th, 74th and 75th Brigades had, by 3rd October, moved up to the front near le Catalet where it relieved Australian troops in the line.

C. Braithwaite headstone.

There the 74th Brigade prepared for the next days' battle in support of 7th Brigade's attack on enemy defences on the high ground to the north of and protecting Beaurevoir village, the object eventually being to take Beaurevoir, but the attack failed and orders were received to continue in the morning using 74th Brigade. 74th Brigade moved off to its assembly positions at 1 a.m. on 5th October, with the 13th DLI going to its assembly trench east of Prospect Hill. The attack went in at 6 a.m.; the 13th DLI between the 9th Yorks on the right and 11th Sherwood Foresters on the left, the Brigade objectives being Guisancourt Farm, the high ground north of Beaurevoir (A & B as far as B1- see map), la Sablonnière (a farm) and a track junction some 600 yards east of the latter farm. Tanks were detailed to take part in the operation but not all arrived.

The preparatory artillery barrage targeting hostile strong points and posts was not entirely successful in knocking out the enemy machine-guns, especially in Beaurevoir, which soon caused heavy casualties to the 9th Yorks and 13th DLI, but the 13th DLI pressed on and managed to reach a sunken road that ran roughly south-east from near Guisancourt Farm to Beaurevoir. Moving on from there the 13th DLI came upon a mass of trenches (see map) whose occupants caused problems before they were captured. The battalion then moved forward and crossed the Villers-Outréaux road. The 13th DLI was now in front of its flanking battalions and came under heavy shrapnel and machine-gun fire, especially from the high ground to the north of Beaurevoir which forced a withdrawal to the sunken road. A further retirement had to be made due to heavy machine-gun fire that found them back to within about 400 yards of their start line where they proceeded to dig in. During the operation the 13th DLI

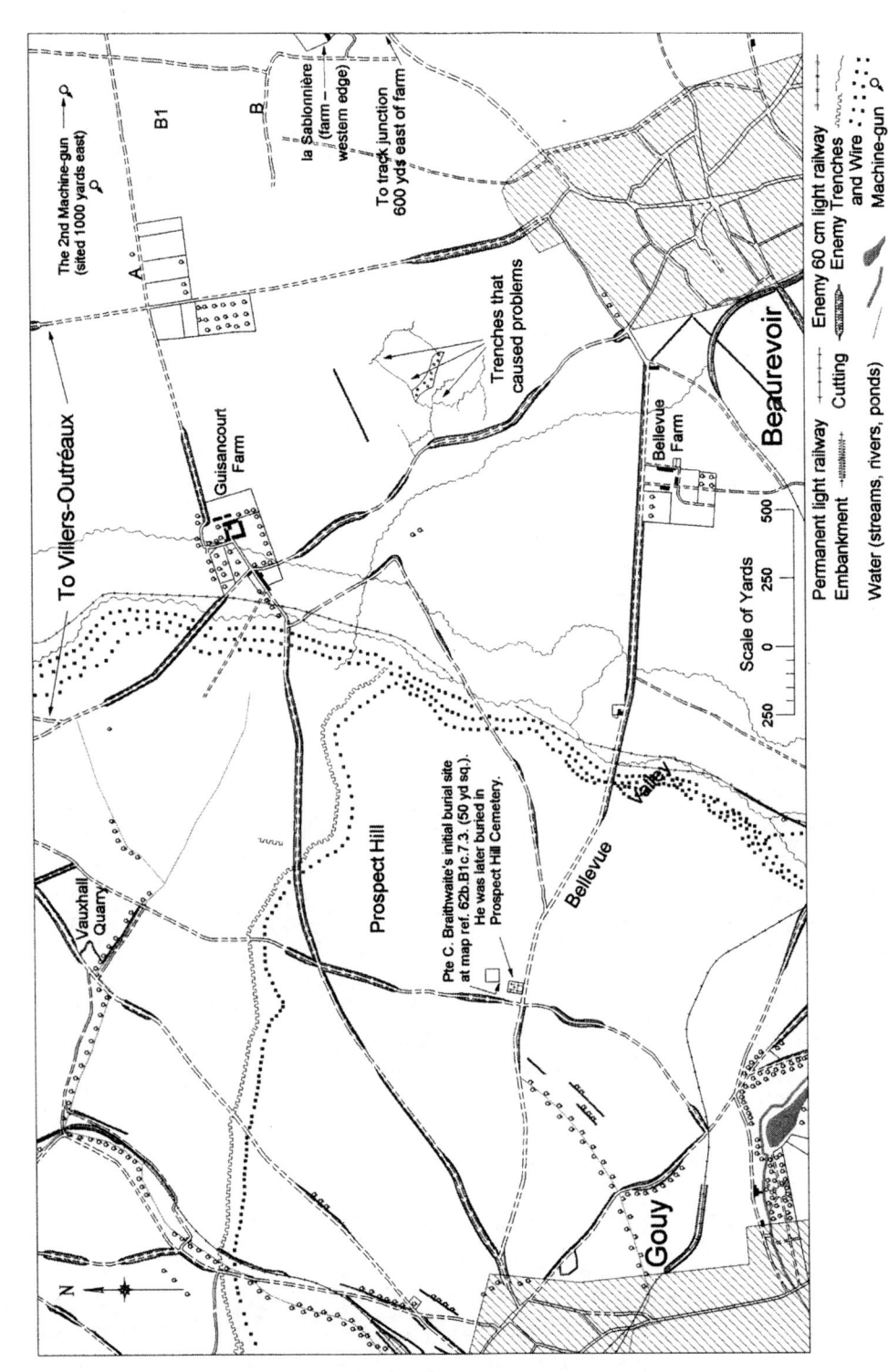

Map 30. *Area where the 13th Bn, Durham Light Infantry (74th Bde, 25th Divn), attacked eastwards from Prospect Hill on 5th October 1918.*

suffered heavy casualties but, except for naming Officer casualties, no other-rank figures are given.

Early the following morning, after a preliminary heavy artillery bombardment, the attack was resumed, resulting in the 25th Division this time reaching its objectives.

Pte Charles Braithwaite, killed in that action on 5th October 1918, was initially buried on the battlefield at map reference 62b.B1c.7.3. near to where he is now buried in plot I, row C, grave 10, of Prospect Hill Cemetery, Gouy, France. The CWGC record Charles as the husband of E. Robinson (formerly Braithwaite), of Barnetby, Lincs.

After 1st KOYLI had captured Prospect Hill on 3rd October the 50th Division and 18th Field Ambulance made the original cemetery, Plot I, by burying 78 officers and men mostly from the units involved in taking the hill. Prospect Hill Cemetery was increased after the Armistice by concentrating 459 graves of men who fell in October 1918, mainly from the battlefields to the north of Gouy. There are 119 graves in the cemetery of soldiers that are unidentified.

Prospect Hill Cemetery, Gouy. The original burial site of Charles Braithwaite was in the field in rear of the cemetery approximately where the dark patch is immediately to the left of the cross.

The newspapers at the beginning of October carried news of L/Cpl Maurice Allison (or Pte Allison depending on which paper was read) whose parents had been informed that, after having recently been at home on leave from Italy, he had been taken dangerously ill on his return journey and was in a hospital in France (or Italy, depending on which paper was read). Another casualty was Pte Harry Partridge who had been in France for more than three years. His parents had been informed that he had been gassed and was in a base hospital in

France. A third wounded casualty, also in a base hospital, was Pte Reg. Smith. His parents, of 'The Ferneries', had likewise been notified of his wounding but had received no further details.

The 18th October *Grimsby News* gave news of another Barnetby soldier having been wounded. Mr and Mrs Gee, of Silver Street, had recently received information about their son Cpl Alfred Gee. He had been wounded in the head and was receiving treatment for his wound in a hospital in England.

On Wednesday 23rd October a whist drive had been held in the Conservative Club room organised by the Women's Unionist Association, the proceeds being in aid of funds to help purchase a machine-gun for the Lincolnshire Regiment.

At the beginning of November a brief item the newspapers stated that the school had been closed due to the influenza epidemic. I wonder if that is what had laid Pte M. Allison low when he was returning to duty from home leave? News of another casualty followed. Mr and Mrs J. White had received information that their son, Pte Hubert White, had been wounded and was receiving treatment in a hospital in France. No details of his injuries had been received.

Pte Harry Partridge, who a few weeks earlier had been gassed, was at home around the beginning of November for three weeks leave. While he was in hospital he had given an infusion of blood for the benefit of a brother soldier. Harry by that time had seen much active service having been in France since July 1915.

On 9th November another Barnetby Boy died and that was…

WR/207055 Pioneer Charles Meysey Green, Royal Engineers

Charles Meysey Green, born at Barnetby (1)1886, the son of Edward and Esther Green, was the husband of Ethel Drayton (formerly Green) of Shirebrook, Mansfield, Notts.

In 1911, Charles was working as a clerk at Ulceby, lodging there in the house of Fred Woodward. He married Holton-le-Moor girl Ethel Shacklock (1)1915 (who later married George H. Drayton (4)1925).

As the name C. M. Green is on the GCR Memorial at Sheffield, it suggests that Charles had been employed by the GCR prior to enlisting into the colours at Grimsby. A name with the same initials entered in the Journals

C. M. Green headstone.

supports this. The Journal of June 1909 records that a C. M. Green, a Wombwell booking clerk, transferred to Cleethorpes Pier to take up duties of a clerk and the March 1913 Journal records that a C. M. Green, an Ulceby clerk, transferred to Grimsby D.S.O. for duties as a relief clerk. It is possible that both these records, in referring to a clerk, relate to the same man. Other information states that Charles was living at Market Rasen at the time of enlistment.

During his service with the Army Charles was in the Railway Operating Division, Royal Engineers. He died on Saturday 9th November 1918, aged 32 years, and is buried in St Mary's Churchyard, Barnetby, where the inscription on his headstone reads, 'Thy will be done'. It is likely that Charles was a victim of the influenza epidemic that claimed more victims than were killed on all sides during the Great War. It has been estimated that the figure world-wide could be as high as 27,000,000.

Just two days later, shortly after 5 a.m. on 11th November at Rethondes in the Forest of Compiègne, a German delegation signed a document accepting the terms of the Allied Armistice in a railway carriage of Maréchal Foch's special train. On completion of the signing Maréchal Foch issued orders that messages were to be sent out immediately to all Allied Commanders informing them that hostilities would cease at 11 a.m. that day, 11th November 1918.

Accordingly at the 11th hour of that 11th day of November the guns fell silent; a truce had been declared and hostilities with Germany ceased. However a state of war would still exist until a peace treaty document had been drawn up, agreed upon and finally signed. On 18th January 1919 the Allied delegates assembled in Paris to set the Peace Conference in motion. After months of wrangling and negotiation over the terms of the peace settlement, a document was finally drawn up and, on 28th June 1919 in the Palace of Versailles near Paris, the peace document, the Treaty of Versailles, was signed by the representatives of Germany and the Allied Powers.

Peace treaties for the other Central Powers that had signed armistice documents earlier, namely Bulgaria (30th September), Turkey (30th October) and Austria-Hungary (3rd November) were accordingly drawn up at other locations at different times and duly signed.

Meanwhile, now that hostilities had ceased, what of the British troops on the Western front, many of whom were 'Short Service' men who had signed up for 'the duration of the war'? It was natural that all British troops would want to return home as soon as possible seeing that Germany's forces, in accordance with the Armistice terms, had to evacuate immediately all the countries that they had occupied, namely Belgium, France, Luxembourg and Alsace-Lorraine. However once German forces were back on their own territory the Allied armies had to provide an Army of Occupation on the west bank of the Rhine in Germany. Moreover the Army still had commitments overseas, particularly with its garrisons in India. British troops were also deployed in North Russia sent as part of a multi-national force to prevent the large quantities of Allied war materials, stockpiled primarily at Murmansk and Archangel, from falling into the hands of the Russian Bolsheviks that had taken over power in Russia as a result of the Russian Revolution of October 1917.

The Army also had to have sufficient trained troops available in case hostilities flared up again and for this reason many of the 'Short Service' men were demobilised as Class Z Reserve under an Army Order of 3rd December 1918 to cater for such an eventuality. My father fell into that category and he was processed towards the end of March 1919. Men with special industrial skills had priority and for the rest demobilisation was virtually on a 'first in, first out' basis, with those conscripted being the last to leave. To process the men took time but by the end of 1919, most of the 'short service' men had been returned to civilian life. I suspect that not many men from Barnetby had been Regular soldiers and that most of the men who fought in the war had enlisted under the 'Short Service' category.

How was the news of the signing of the Armistice document and subsequent cessation of hostilities taken in Barnetby? There was nothing reported in the local newspapers under village news giving reaction to the event or that any special services had been held in thanksgiving.

Meanwhile, with men still away from home on active service duties and with Christmas approaching, one village organisation set about to provide its serving members with comforts. Around the middle of the month the Band held a whist drive in aid of raising funds to provide the serving soldiers of Barnetby Band with Christmas parcels.

During the last week of November two local soldiers had been repatriated home from prisoner of war camps. One, Cpl Fred Robinson, had been held a prisoner since September 1917. The other, L/Cpl Walter Scott, had been a prisoner for only a few months. (At the end of April his parents had received official notification that he had been killed in action!)

At the beginning of December the War Fund announced that a postal order for 10s. had been sent along with a Christmas parcel to all those Barnetby Boys who were Prisoners of War. A gift would be sent to all the other local soldiers and sailors in time for Christmas.

The following week the War Fund Committee announced that the War Fund would be disbanded, now that the War had ended, when all the soldiers and sailors had returned home.

THE BARNETBY BOYS

During the last week of the month two more local soldiers who had been prisoners of war arrived home in time for Christmas. They were Pte George Scott, who had been in Germany since September 1915 and Pte Arthur Worrall. The newspaper then went on to say that so far five local lads had returned (I find the fifth somewhat elusive!) That still left three others to come home and nothing had been heard of them since the Armistice. It was hoped that ere long they would be welcomed back home. Thus ended 1918.

7
1919
And the Immediate Post War Years

ALTHOUGH the war was over many soldiers who had volunteered for the duration of the war had yet to be demobilised. Furthermore not all Prisoners of War had been returned home. Late in the New Year two such men, Private W. Pretty and Private J. Worrall, arrived home in Barnetby newly returned from their three years and three months in captivity. Both men had been GCR employees prior to enlisting in 1914. William Pretty had been a spare driver based at Immingham and Joseph Worrall an assistant connector in the signal department at Barnetby. Still to be repatriated was Pte Ernest Grant, taken prisoner at the same time as the others.

In May 1988 my wife and I and two friends, who had traced men named on war memorials in the area covered by the Laceby branch of the Royal British Legion, had a holiday in Alsace and Lorraine. We planned to visit as many of their Memorials as possible in Cemeteries en-route to Alsace (via Verdun) and on the return from Lorraine towards Mons (via Luxembourg). One visit on the itinerary was to the French National Cemetery at Plaine in the Bas-Rhin (formerly Alsace) department (off the N420, 60 km south-west of Strasbourg, altitude 500 m).

At Plaine we visited the grave of 100086 Pte Alfred Reed, 1st Battalion Notts and Derby Regiment, who died on 16th June 1918, aged 19 years. The son of Charles and Susannah Reed of Keelby, Lincolnshire, he is buried in a small British plot that now contains the graves of over 40 1914-1918 war casualties including 12 unidentified and 9 Special Memorials. The French plot has 221 identified burials and 546 unidentified.

I was curious why British soldiers were buried there. The CWGC gave no specific reason for using Plaine for British burials but confirmed that the majority of those in Plaine and the surrounding cemeteries had been prisoners-of-war. The CWGC also informed me that the British burials in Plaine had been transferred from the (la Broque) Albet Communal Cemetery German Extension near Schirmeck, the Lièpvre Military Cemetery and the Ste Marie-aux-Mines German Cemetery. Information received at a later date stated that Pte Reed had been reburied in the French National Cemetery, Plaine, on 23rd April 1924.

Much later while looking through local newspapers of the Great War period two items of interest caught my eye. The *Grimsby News* of 3rd January 1919 told of the distressing news received in a letter on Christmas morning by a Mr and Mrs Reed of Keelby; a dramatic heading in the *Hull Times* of 18th January 1919 related to that letter.

The letter received by Mr and Mrs C. Reed on Christmas morning was from a Liverpool soldier recently repatriated from a POW camp. He told them that he was from the same camp as their son Alfred and that he had died there in June. (Mr and Mrs Reed had not heard of their son since about that time.) Further particulars received said it appeared Alfred had been placed in a cattle truck and had two days journey without food and drink. Dysentery and death followed.

The dramatic heading in the 18th January *Hull Times* that had caught my attention read: DIED FROM STARVATION. – N. LINCS. SOLDIER'S FATE IN GERMANY.

The story came from an article in the *Liverpool Courier* as related by a Pte A. H. Burbage, East Lancashire Regiment, on being repatriated home from Germany. His experiences told of how a Pte Reed had died of starvation whilst in transit to a Prisoner of War camp in Germany, but did not say where the POW camp was or where he had been buried. The report went on: –

> 'At noon we were put into trucks for our journey to Germany. We had our breakfast at 6 a.m. and nothing further in the way of food was given us. We were cooped up 42 in each truck and for 47 hours never allowed either food or drink. We arrived at Saarburg at 11 p.m. Monday, and on being allowed out the condition of most of the prisoners was pitiable, the lads fainting from pure starvation... The first death occurred through exhaustion and starvation, and it was just a matter of waiting to see who would be next. We had not long to wait, and I buried and read the service over the first two on June 19th. The men supposed to be buried were named Reed and Scudamore.'

As it turned out Scudamore was not the second man. But Pte Burbage was certain of Reed's identity having received a photograph of him from Reed's parents in Keelby, Lincolnshire.

Pte Burbage informed Mr Reed that the interpreter had given him the deceased's name and home address. He added that he was buried in a lovely cemetery and that he had made a cross and wreath for his grave. The other prisoners had attended the funeral as a token of respect.

Pte. A. Reed.

The inference on first reading the report is that Pte Reed had been buried at Saarburg (roughly 20 km south of Trier, in Germany) yet the CWGC archival records show that Pte Reed was initially buried at la Broque French Military Cemetery. Given that the train had arrived on a Monday in Saarburg, as reported, was this possibly 10th June? Seeing that Pte Reed had died shortly after on Sunday 16th June and was buried on Wednesday 19th June 1918 had the train subsequently left Saarburg and reached its final destination by 19th June and was that destination a POW camp in the Schirmeck (la Broque) area of what was then German territory in Alsace? (Schirmeck is 11 km north of Plaine on the N420.) Thinking that Pte Reed had possibly died of wounds in captivity those reports now have me wondering just how Pte Reed had died and are they to be believed?

The newspaper that ran the starvation report also had a brief item (with photograph) that had a Barnetby connection. It was a plea for information from any repatriated soldiers who could give information about Lieut B. Hutchinson, 9th East Yorks, reported wounded and missing on 3rd May 1917. At that time he was gazetted Captain in the 'University Magazine'. His mother, Mrs Hutchinson, 72 Cannon Hall Road, Pitsmoor, Sheffield, and his aunt, Mrs J. Coupland of King's Road, Barnetby, were anxiously seeking news of him.

'Soldiers Died in the War' records 2nd Lt Benjamin Hutchinson, MC, East Yorkshire Regiment, as killed in action on 3rd May 1917. The CWGC list him as 2nd Lt Hutchinson, aged 23 years, son of Betsy Hutchinson and the late Frank Hutchinson, serving with the 11th Battalion East Yorkshire Regiment. The 11th battalion seems the more likely as the 9th was a reserve unit based in England. The 11th East Yorks, raised in Hull and known as the 2nd Hull Battalion, formed part of the 92nd Brigade, 31st Division. During May 1917 the 31st Division, in XIII Corps, First Army, took part in the Third Battle of the Scarpe, 3rd – 4th May 1917, part of the Arras offensive. On 3rd May 1917, the battalion was in action at Oppy a couple of miles north of Gavrelle where Pte Hugh Dawson was killed on 28th April 1917. The 31st Division, facing an enemy strongpoint at Oppy Wood, was spotted forming up in the moonlight and subjected to a heavy artillery bombardment of its trenches causing many casualties. 2nd Lt Hutchinson has no known grave and is commemorated by name on the Arras Memorial to the Missing.

The last Barnetby Boy to be repatriated, Ernest Grant, duly arrived home during the third week in January having been held captive in Germany since September 1915. Ernest had been very appreciative of the parcels that he had received; all had been welcome and he was now able personally to thank all those who had so generously contributed to his comfort.

On Wednesday 29th January a public meeting was held in the schoolrooms to ascertain the wishes of the parishioners' regarding the erection of some form of memorial in the village to the remembrance of the servicemen of the parish who had died during the war. Mr J. W. Naylor presided over the meeting. After discussing the matter at some length Mr Ward proposed that a War Memorial Fund be should opened; seconded by Mr Charnley, this was carried unanimously.

The next proposal, by Mr Cowling, was that a public hall should be erected as the form of memorial; that was seconded by Mr Williamson and carried unanimously. Following on from this a War Memorial Committee was appointed. Representing the ladies were Mrs Blanchard, Mrs Brotherton, Mrs Cox, Mrs Ffrench, Mrs J. Manders, Mrs G. Meggitt, Mrs Moss, Mrs South, Mrs Nicholls, Mrs Stringfellow, Mrs Walker and the Misses Agar, Freestone and Lockwood. The gentlemen appointed were Dr Ffrench, The Rev. Brotherton, Mr Charnley, Mr E. Cuthbert, Mr Cowling, Mr J. Manders, Mr Naylor, Mr Williamson, Mr J. B. Vickers, Mr Fish, Mr G. Neale, Mr Ward, Mr Hartle, and Mr Foster (Stonecroft). Finally, the meeting was asked whether it was now possible to acquire a nurse for the village. After discussion it was agreed that the individual wishes of all parishioners should be sought regarding the installation of a village nurse.

By the beginning of February men were returning home after having been demobilised. Among the first was Sapper E. Fish and Ptes F. Denton, W. Denton, A. Footitt, Larder (who is not named on the Roll of Honour), H. Partridge and F. Lansley.

In February newspapers there were pleas for information about two missing local soldiers. The first concerned 21682 Pte W. H. Hinchsliff, 2nd Lincolns (No. 10 Platoon, Y Company), who had been missing since 23rd October 1916. This plea, directed to returned soldiers who might have news, asked that any information be sent to Mr C. Hinchsliff of 43 Victoria Road, Barnetby.

The next person seeking information was Mr C. Newmarsh of Mill Farm, Barnetby, who appealed for news of his son 26968 Pte Cyril Newmarsh, 6th Battalion, Somerset Light Infantry, reported missing since 23rd August 1917.

(Pte Cyril Newmarsh died on 23rd August 1917. He has no known grave and is commemorated by name on the Tyne Cot Memorial to the Missing at Paschendaele, Panel 41. 'Soldiers Died in the War' lists Cyril as formerly 22884, Lincolnshire Regiment, born at Newstead, Brigg, enlisted at Habrough and resided at Brocklesby.)

On Thursday 13th February, at the vicarage, Mr J. W. Naylor presided over a meeting of the newly formed War Memorial Fund Committee. At that meeting Mr J. W. Naylor was elected chairman, Mr G. Neale secretary and Mr H. Lowish treasurer.

The War Fund Committee announced that the fund subscription collections would be discontinued after 22nd February but it was hoped that the villagers would continue the weekly subscriptions in order to provide a nurse for the village. It was also announced that a parcel of clothing had been sent to a Miss Brown of Brigg from Philadelphia, USA. (*Intriguing!*)

The 21st/22nd February newspapers carried brief items to clear up a misunderstanding arising from the War Memorial public meeting regarding the installation of a parish nurse. Many parishioners had erroneously formed the opinion that the nurse was to be part of the memorial. The items clarified that the question of installing a nurse was an entirely separate undertaking.

On Saturday 15th February an interesting presentation ceremony had taken place in the GCR Signal Department Workshops at Barnetby Depot, when Inspector J. B. Vickers, on behalf of the men, presented a silver watch to Pte J. Worrall. Inspector Vickers had said how pleased they all were to welcome Joseph back again after his three-year sojourn in a Prisoner of War camp in Germany. In reply Joseph Worrall thanked the men for the watch, saying that he would always value it. He also took the opportunity of saying how all the parcels he had received had been most welcome. In conclusion Mr J. Overton proposed a vote of thanks to Inspector Vickers for making the presentation, which was duly seconded by Mr. Joe Waite.

Sadly March began with the reported death of another 'Barnetby Boy'...

14585 Sapper Frank Burdass, Royal Engineers

On Saturday 1st March the death occurred in Fort Pitt Hospital, Chatham, of 14585 Sapper Frank Burdass, Royal Engineers, aged 35 years. He had died from bronchial pneumonia (possibly a Spanish 'flu victim).

Frank, the son of Joseph Burdass (jun.) and the late Fanny Burdass of Barnetby was born (1)1884 at Hillsborough, Yorks. He had been in the Army for around fourteen years and had served at Singapore; in 1911 he was at the Royal Engineers Barracks, Chatham. He had been wounded twice in the war and lost an eye. During the twelve months prior to his death he was employed in the Royal Engineers Stores at Chatham. Frank was laid to rest alongside his mother's grave in St Mary's Churchyard, Barnetby (sadly she had died on 10th December 1892, aged 37 years). The funeral service was reported by the local newspapers and the *Doncaster Gazette* of 14th March 1919 had a brief obituary stating his father and stepmother were living at East View, Laughton Road, Hexthorpe, near Doncaster, Yorkshire, where his father, a cabinet maker, was a well known foreman in the Great Northern Railway Plant Works at Doncaster. Frank's name is also mentioned on his mother's headstone, where part of the brief inscription reads: *"Frank, son of the above, (Sapper of the RE) one of the British Expeditionary Force of 1914 died…".*

F. Burdass headstone.

On Saturday 8th March the wedding was solemnised in St Barnabas Church between a Miss Meggitt, the youngest daughter of Mr and Mrs G. M. Meggitt of the Maltings, Barnetby, and Lt J. Pickworth Hutchinson, of the Sherwood Foresters. Lt Hutchinson was the youngest son of the late Councillor James and Mrs Hutchinson of Belmont, near Bolton, Lancashire. The Rev. C. F. Brotherton conducted the ceremony. The bridegroom had seen much active service in West Africa and France and was entitled to wear four gold stripes (presumably these were for the time spent on active service and not wound stripes). He wore the Mons ribbon and also the ribbon of the West African campaign. Captain T. D. Wheeler, 3rd Battalion Northamptonshire Regiment, who was wearing the ribbon of the Croix de Guerre, attended Lt Hutchinson.

During April the War Fund Committee reported that the balance of the Fund, a total of £82 6s 1d, would be kept until all the men had returned home. The Committee also stated that a total of 242 pairs of socks and 137 shirts had been given to the local servicemen during the war.

Mrs Lowish and all the Committee paid thanks to all those who had collected and who had helped in any way in providing comforts for the village Sailors and Soldiers. Mrs Lowish also announced she had sent a total of 104,050 eggs from the Barnetby Depot to the National Egg Collection for the Wounded. Of that total the village had contributed 11,909 eggs and £18 2s 10d in cash. The School children sent 4,900 eggs and £0 3s 4d in money. The following children collected over 100 eggs: – Jack Agar, 163; J. and T. Dawson, 368; M., H. and F.

Cuthbert, 139; E. and H. Gibbons, 292; D. and A. Lusby, 105; R. Rowe, 344; W., M. and B. Metcalf, 113; D. and H. Nicholls, 160; A. and E. Stringfellow, 121 and the Wells children, 370.

At a War Memorial Fund committee meeting on Wednesday evening, 4th June, the ladies on the committee reported they had canvassed the village in an endeavour to obtain subscriptions for the fund. The result had not been as satisfactory as anticipated. It was believed the reason went back to the decision made at the public meeting some time earlier that the Memorial should be in the form of a public Memorial Hall. One of the main objections prevailing was that a hall would be used only for dancing and would not be kept sacred to the memory of those men who had given their lives for their Country. To dispel that idea the committee had pointed out that a hall would also be used for Council meetings, club meetings, entertainments, bazaars, lectures etc., and also for private and public functions. The committee decided to carry on in the hope that when the scheme was finally put into working order the whole of the residents would give their assistance especially those who had withheld their subscriptions for the reason stated.

July began with a newspaper report of the death of another Barnetby Boy...

Sapper WR/148130 Ernest Arthur Insley, Royal Engineers.

Ernest Arthur Insley, was born at Grimsby (1)1888, the son of William and Sarah Insley. A wagon builder by trade (one source said at Scunthorpe!) in 1911 he was working as a wagon repairer and living with his sister Florence Healey at 77 Chapman Street, Grimsby. He enlisted into the Royal Fusiliers at Hounslow on a 7 and 5 engagement (7 years with the colours, 5 in reserve) on 25th January 1915, Service Number 16954. He was posted to the 6th Battalion on 1st February 1915 and to the 3rd Battalion on 18th May 1915. In October 1915 the 3rd Battalion Royal Fusiliers, 85th Brigade, 28th Division, went out to Salonika via Alexandria as part of the Mediterranean Expeditionary Force. During July 1917, whilst in Salonika, Ernest received hospital treatment for malaria. After treatment for malaria a medical memo in his service records states that he was not to be sent anywhere where malaria was prevalent. On being discharged from hospital he was attached to the 19th Railway Operating Company R. E. for Railway Police Patrol duties. Whilst thus employed

E. A. Insley headstone.

Ernest committed a number of misdemeanours that were brought to the notice of his superiors who duly meted out just retribution.

In April 1918 the authorities received a letter from Ernest's sister, Mrs Florence Neal of Grimsby, asking for news of her brother who had not been heard from for some time. On 16th August 1918, Ernest was transferred to the Railway Troop R. E. for the purpose of being employed at his trade. A note in his service records says that he was sent to Longmoor on 28th September 1918 yet his time served with the Mediterranean Expeditionary Force is given as being from 25th October 1915 – 14th February 1919! The next period of service is 'Home' from 15th February 1919 – 1st July 1919. Ernest was demobilized on 15th March 1919 and transferred to Section B Army Reserve. He died from malaria and pneumonia on 1st July 1919, aged 31 years, whilst at home at Scunthorpe; he is buried in plot Y of Scunthorpe Cemetery.

Ernest's name is on the Memorial Plaque in St Barnabas Church, the War Memorial and the Roll of Honour where his name is in a column of those from the village who survived the war. His service documents are among the 'Burnt Records', WO 363/I70, at the PRO. On a Statement of Relatives, signed by Mrs F. Neal, the following blood relatives' names are recorded: father, W(William) Insley, Station Rd, Barnetby; brothers: H(Harry) Insley 46, Manchester; G(George) W. Insley 36, Grimsby; J. Insley 34, Scunthorpe; sisters: F(Florence) Neal 44, Grimsby; E(Edith) A. Tillbrook 41, 41 Station Rd, Barnetby; L. Kent 38, Grimsby. (Other documents show the names F. Healey and F. Headley with the same address as F. Neal. On one document Florence Healey, sister, is named as next of kin!) His father, William, had also been a railway wagon builder.

Just over a fortnight later another death from military action occurred that cast an air of sadness over the village. This was not a Great War casualty as such but that fact would not lessen the blow received by the victim's family. The Barnetby Boy in question was…

2nd Lt Ernest Dudley Ffrench, Queen Victoria's Own Corps of Guides (Frontier Force)(Lumsden's), attached 3rd/1st King George's Own Gurkha Rifles, (the Malaun Regiment).

Ernest Dudley Ffrench, born (1)1900, was the eldest son of Dr William J. L. and Helen Ffrench of Barnetby-le-Wold. On the evening of Saturday 23rd August Dr and Mrs Ffrench received word that their son, *Lt Dudley Ffrench*, had been killed in action on 16th July 1919, aged 19 years, whilst on active service in India during the 3rd Afghan War 1919. The news had cast a gloom over the village for Dr Ffrench was well known and esteemed in the district.

1919

Dudley, at Trent College, Derby, when WW1 began, went on from there to Sandhurst for training leaving there at the end of February 1918 to go to India where he entered into the service of the Indian Army on 20th December 1918. He had only been in India six months when the incident occurred. He was a keen soldier with seemingly the promise of a brilliant Army career in front of him. His tragic death at the early age of 19 years brought that promising career to an untimely end. Details of Dudley's Indian Army service can be found in the British Library.

In Afghanistan on the night of 19th/20th February 1919 the then Afghan ruler, Amir Habibulla, was murdered. There followed a brief internal power struggle that resulted in Habibulla's third son, Amanulla, being proclaimed ruler (Amir) on 28th February. At the beginning of May 1919 Amir Amanulla, the new ruler of Afghanistan, to bolster a somewhat shaky popularity declared a *jihad* (holy war) against the infidels in India (i.e. British) and called on all Mohammedans to aid Afghanistan. On 6th May, following Afghan incursions into India's North West Frontier Province, India declared war on Afghanistan. (The hilly North West Frontier Province, then in India, is now in West Pakistan.) Many Mohammedan hill tribesmen of Afghan origin living on the Indian side of the border, particularly those in Waziristan, aided the enemy when it suited them, usually for their own ends.

In the Zhob sector of the Southern Front, North West Frontier, a weekly Murgha Kibzai – Fort Sandeman provision convoy (using bullock and mule carts) left Murgha on 12th July. At Lakaband post on the night of 13th the post was attacked by some 200 enemy. The 0630 departure next day for Dewal was delayed to 1130 until the area was cleared of enemy forces.

The convoy, escorted by 191 rifles of 3/124th Baluchistan Infantry, commanded by Captain A. W. Goolden, arrived unmolested at Dewal. It left at 0600 on 15th hoping to meet the escort from Fort Sandeman 2 miles north of Babar. At Babar, acting on information that 200 tribesmen had been seen nearby, Captain Goolden left the bullock carts at the post and pressed on with the mule carts. Outside Babar a force of about 800 – 900 Wazirs attacked, causing loss to personnel and animals. A depleted convoy returned to Babar to await the Fort Sandeman escort, delayed 3 hours by doubts of the Lakaband situation. (Capt. A. W. Goolden, striving to return part of the convoy to Dewal, was killed by pursuing enemy 2½ miles north of there.) In the meantime at 1115 hrs on 14th July a telegram arrived at Fort Sandeman from 'Zhobforce':

> 'Send escort meet convoy which left Murgha on 12th. If you are fortunate enough to be attacked in Fort Sandeman should be able to deal enemy a

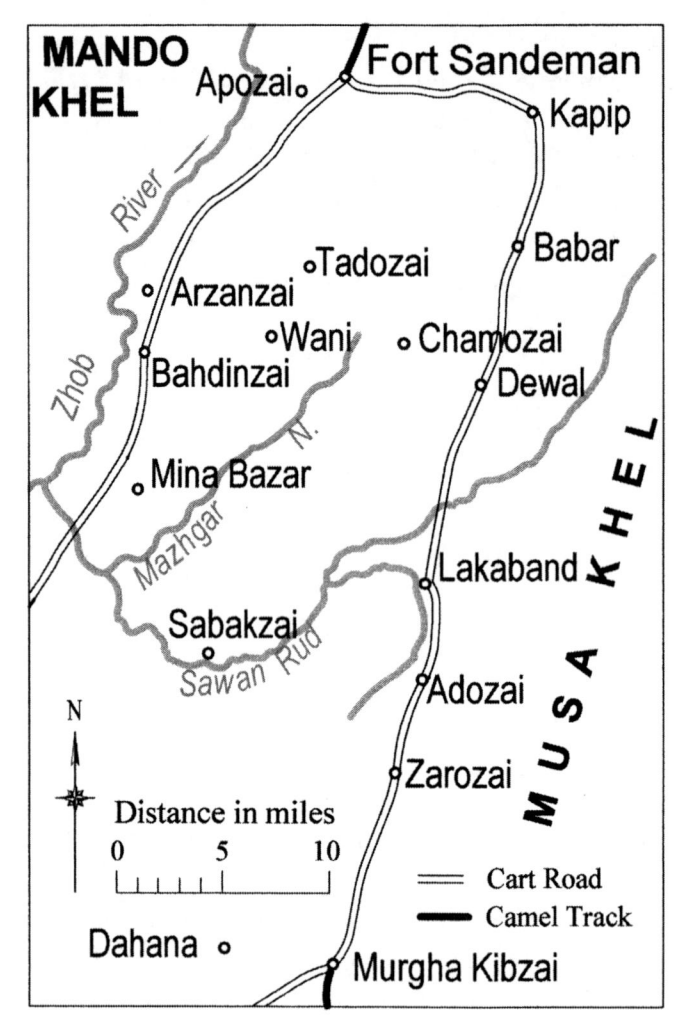

Map left:
The route of the Provision Convoy, Murgha Kibzai – Fort Sandeman, 12th- 16th July 1919, during the 3rd Afghan War 1919. Early in May 1919, Amir Amanulla, the ruler of Afghanistan, declared a jihad (holy war) against the infidels (British) in India and called on all Mohammedans to aid Afghanistan. Many aiding the enemy were hill tribesmen of Afghan origin living locally in India. Particularly hostile were the Wazirs from Waziristan, the Indian region bordering onto the northern boundary of the Zhob district. (The territory is in the hilly North West Frontier of India, now part of West Pakistan.) Fort Sandeman, now called Zhob, lies at 69° 31 'E, 32° 21 'N. From Fort Sandeman the nearest Afghan border is some 30 miles to the North West and from Murgha Kibzai the border lies some 120 miles away West North West.

Map below:
Sketched by 2nd Lt. V. J. Gilbert, Royal Artillery, and attached to his action report, it shows where the attack on the convoy took place after leaving Kapip. WO 95/5395.

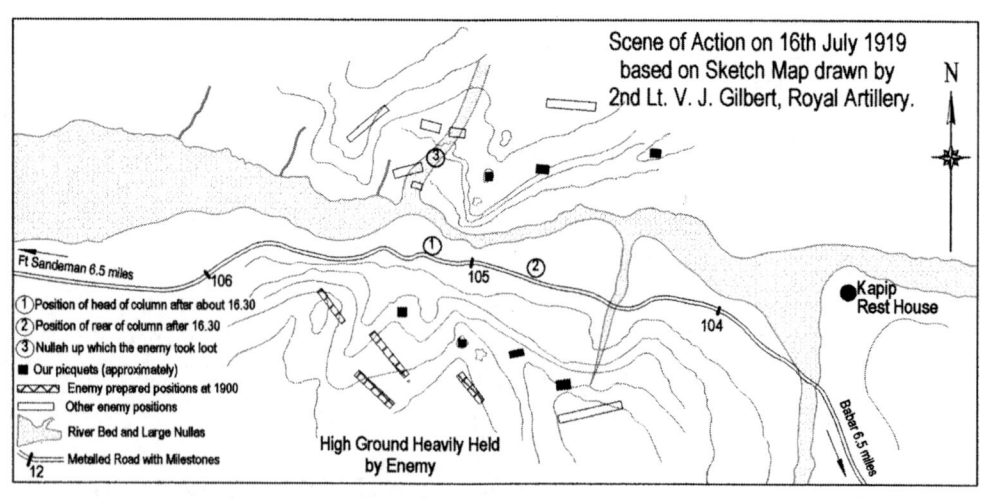

Map 31. *Murgha Kibzai – Fort Sandeman & sketch.*

hard blow. Use your discretion about attacking the 1000 Wazirs reported to be at Brunj. This force can be a considerable proposition in plains such as lie between you and Brunj considering the number of troops you have at your disposal.'

At 1235 hrs Fort Sandeman sent a reply:

'Escort despatched to meet convoy. Aeroplane here hopes to make reconnaissance this evening. At present heavy mist'.

At 1300 another telegram reached Fort Sandeman:

'Convoy due leave Lakaband detained till 15th. Arrange accordingly'.
The convoy escort, ready to depart from Fort Sandeman, was stopped.

The escort, under the command of Capt. R. W. Copland, 3/1 Gurkha Rifles, duly left at 0900 hrs on the 15th July for Babar. It was comprised of the right section of the 38th Mountain Battery, 225 rifles of 3/1 Gurkha Rifles and 75 rifles of Zhob Militia. The escort had been warned that three very big parties of Wazirs and Suleman Khels were at Oomza. It was reported that 1000 were on their way towards Lakaband and Murgha by various routes. An attempt to keep them up to date on the position would be made by aeroplane.

A message was heliographed at 1315 hrs, on 15th to Capt. Copland, OC Escort, at Kapip:

'Aviator reports 600/700 attacking convoy at Babar from Fort Sandeman side. Push on to their help. Road reported clear to Babar'.

Further messages asking for assistance were sent.
At 2315 hrs on 16th July 1919, Havildar Gammarsing of 'C' Company 3/1 Gurkha Rifles arrived at Fort Sandeman wounded through the head. Leaving 3 Gurkha other ranks some 3½ miles away he had hastened ahead to make his report that Captain Copland and another British officer had been killed and Lt Dobbin wounded in the shoulder. He said a force of about 2000 enemy had cut up the convoy, killing all the animals with the guns and capturing all the guns. Very few gunners were left.
Now follows a report on the action Babar–Kapip, Fort Sandeman Road of 15/7-16/7 by 2nd Lt V. J. Gilbert, Royal Artillery. (PRO WO 95/5395)

'Escort left Fort Sandeman to meet incoming convoy at 0900 on 15th intending to march to Babar, take over the convoy and halt for the night.

The journey was uneventful until the escort was 1½ miles from Babar when bursts of fire came from hills on the left of road (1830). Under the orders of the OC Column enemy were engaged by the Infantry and guns. Enemy fire quietened after 30 minutes and the Column moved forward under some sniping fire from flanks.

On approaching Babar Post it was seen that the convoy was parked to the E of the Post which was being subjected to heavy fire from the high ground to the E and S and from cover near the village. Troops in the Post were gallantly replying. Guns were run up, Lewis-guns brought into action and after 20/30 minutes firing the enemy ceased fire. The troops in the Post were found to be a party of 3/124th Baluchistan Infantry (Sub. Sulloh M'd, I.D.S.M), who stated that the enemy had attacked the convoy about mile 97 at 1000 hrs that morning. Convoy had retired part staying at Barbar and part moving on towards Dewal. From all the evidence the troops in the post had had an extremely heavy fight to keep the enemy out. Many enemy dead were lying round the Post about 25/30 being reported seen, the 3/124th had about 15 killed and many wounded in the post.

OC Escort took over convoy and ordered a camp for the night round the Post.

On the night of the 15/16th a few rounds were fired into the camp, nothing important.

Reports were received from people sent out from Babar (about 0900 hrs 16th inst) that Dewal was deserted, one BO (British Officer) lying dead in the camp where there were a few empty tents.

Further reports indicated that road as far as Kapip was clear. Everything pointed to the enemy having moved towards Lakaband and the OC Convoy ordered the Convoy to move to 107 Mile for the night 16/17th.

A start was made at 1100 hrs, picquets were pushed out, spies from the village were sent ahead and all was well until the 104-6 mile stone when men were sighted ahead dressed as Gurkhas. Lt Dobbin and three men went forward to investigate and find out who these men were. On nearing them the men fired on the party and wounded Lt Dobbin severely (time 1600 hrs). The Column was halted and closed up, as it was soon seen that the hills were held in force by the enemy. OC Column (Capt. Copland) now sent forward two parties, one under Lt Dobbin (who although severely wounded refused to go behind) and one under Lt Ffrench to attack and clear the hills on either side of the river and establish picquets. The guns were brought into action to assist in the task in hand and brought 'Gun Fire' to bear on the enemy on both flanks.

The attempts were partially successful a few men established themselves on the "Tangi" but all-round met with desperate resistance. Owing to enemy pressure on the rear and flank picquets the column was advanced a few hundred yards. The advanced guard could make no further progress in spite of a gun being run up level with them. The enemy in ever increasing numbers poured down fire on the column inflicting many casualties among men and animals. The OC Column now himself went forward (1800 hrs) with all the men he could collect (18/20) to try and improve the increasingly grave position that was developing. He, however found it impossible to push on, and, returning after sustaining many casualties, he again endeavoured to scrape together enough men to make a second attempt. This he found to be impossible the men being worn out after the long march, hard picquetting and the severe fighting in which they had already been engaged. Nevertheless with the few men that he could get he made a second attempt. A little later (1900 hrs) a report was received that he had been killed whilst leading the attack. During this time Lts Dobbin and Ffrench were making gallant attempts to hold the picquets already established.

On hearing that Capt. Copland had been killed I handed over the gun I had been shooting to the senior NCO and assumed command of the column. Immediately information was received that Lts Dobbin and Ffrench had been killed.

I went back along the convoy to investigate the state and found that all the cartmen had deserted.

On nearing the rear of the column I sent for Sub Gul'bad Shah of the Zhob Militia (Rear Guard Commander) and held a hurried consultation. This Indian Officer and myself made a tour of the picquets on the left flank and found them in imminent danger of being driven in. On getting level with the Advanced Guard the great strength of the enemy was realized, many of them holding strongly prepared positions from which they were pouring a heavy fire effectively preventing any advance of the column. I thought it was my duty to inform OC Sandeman of the gravity of the situation and sent him word (at 1930 hrs) by four Zhob Militia Orakzais hoping they would be able to get through the enemy position. (On arrival at Fort Sandeman I found they had succeeded in eluding the enemy arriving at Fort Sandeman at 0400 hrs 17th inst.)

Returning along the inside of the picquet position I found that the enemy were very heavy pressing the rear guard who were putting up a brave resistance. Crossing over the river to inspect the picquets on the right flank I found them in an equally serious position (2000 hrs).

Now the volume of fire increased to its greatest intensity and, shortly after this, as it grew dark, whistles were blown by the enemy who on this signal rushed the convoy in overwhelming numbers, fierce hand to hand fighting ensued and the Escort hopelessly outnumbered, was swept away. The enemy then raided the carts and proceeded to take away loot up the Nullah about 105/4 on the right bank. The rear guard who had now joined me on the hill overlooking the "Tangi" poured volleys of fire into the enemy carrying away the loot. A Lewis-gun on the other bank of the river (3/124th Baluchistan Infantry) assisted greatly in harassing the enemy carrying away loot.

After this all was chaos and our force cut off in small numbers commenced to make their ways in twos and threes in direction of Fort Sandeman.

I re-crossed the river at 0015 hrs and remained on the scene until 0115 hrs when the rear guard and myself moved off hoping to meet any force that may have been coming to assistance of the Column. After making a 'Detour' we struck Kapip–Fort Sandeman Road about 109 mile and arrived Fort Sandeman about 0900 hrs on 17th.

Casualties:
38th Mountain Battery:
(2.75" BL guns – both guns put out of action by No.1's.)
Indian other ranks: 1 killed, 11 missing believed killed, 7 wounded.
3/1st Gurkha Rifles:
British Officers: 3 killed (Capt. Copland, Lts Dobbin and Ffrench).
Indian other ranks: 34 killed, 34 wounded.
Zhob Militia:
Indian other ranks: 2 wounded.
3/124th Baluchistan Infantry:
Not possible to give figures until it is known how many men got back to their unit at Lakabad.'

The report then continued with loss and mentions of the men who displayed bravery in action including Lt F. le. F. Dobbin 6th Gurkha Rifles attached 3/1st Gurkha Rifles (Mentioned in Despatches).

2nd Lt Ernest Dudley Ffrench has no known grave and is commemorated by name on the Delhi Memorial to the Missing, India, (face number 24). A brass plaque mounted on the south wall of St Barnabas Church adjacent to the font reads:

> *To the Dear and Honoured Memory of*
> *Ernest Dudley Ffrench,*
> *2nd Lt 1st Guides, I. A. attd 3/1st Gurkha Rifles,*
> *Who fell in action near Fort Sandeman*
> *On the Afghan Frontier, July 16th 1919,*
> *aged 19 years.*
> *Elder son of William J. L. and Helen Ffrench*
> *of Barnetby-le-Wold.*
> *Malo Mori Quam Foedari*

The *Hull Times* of 26th July reported on the Peace Celebrations held in Barnetby on Saturday 19th July. They took the form of a thanksgiving service followed by an afternoon and evening of sports. (Peace celebrations were carried out throughout the county.) For the occasion the village had been bedecked with flags. The celebrations began with a procession round the village, numbering around 700 led by the Barnetby Band with Capt. Waddingham in charge. They marched to a field in Victoria Road kindly lent for the occasion by Mr Lowish.

The Delhi Memorial (India Gate) to the Missing, commemorates 13,314 Commonwealth servicemen. Among those named is Ernest Dudley Ffrench, killed in action on 16th July 1919 near Fort Sandeman on the North West Frontier during the 3rd Afghan War 1919.
(Photo CWGC)

There the marchers joined forces with people who had turned up to attend the united thanksgiving service. The Rev. C. F. Brotherton (Church of England), Rev. Howes (Brigg Wesleyans), and Mr Dunn (Brigg Primitives) addressed the congregation numbering over 1,000.

The brass plaque in memory of Ernest Dudley ffrench-mounted in the baptistery on the south wall of St Barnabas Church, Barnetby-le-Wold.

In the afternoon the children's sports took place. Other events included a cricket match, baby show, quoits match and best bouquets of wild flowers. The children had been provided with a tea in the National School at 3.45 p.m. Following the children's tea a meat tea had been provided for all soldiers and sailors, their wives and sweethearts – and any near relatives, widows, old-age pensioners and those receiving parish relief. During the tea the Rev C. F. Brotherton addressed all the soldiers and sailors. Captain Waddingham replied on behalf of the servicemen ably supported by Sergeant-Major Alcard.

In the evening the adult sports event took place. A procession formed up near the railway subway from where the marchers set off for the Victoria Road field headed by a decorated horse belonging to Mr Green and ridden by Geoffrey Walker attired in fancy dress. To complete the entertainment the Barnetby Band had been in attendance, having kindly given of its services.

1919

During the evening the prizes for the children's and adults sports event were presented as follows:

> Decorated cycle: 1st, Miss J. Smith; 2nd, Master H. Davies; 3rd, Miss Moss.
> Baby show: 1st, Mrs C. Kitchen; 2nd, Mrs Maddison.
> Wild flowers bouquet: 1st, Miss C. Coupland; 2nd, Miss E. Cuthbert; 3rd, Stanley Cuthbert; 4th, Miss N. Baxter.
> Cricket match: Lieut H. Wells' team – 35 runs, beat Mr T. Betts' team – 27 runs.
> Hidden treasure: Mr. R. Beedham. Clock golf competition: Master A. Maxted.
> Musical arms (?) – ladies: Miss A. Cook; – gentlemen: Mr F. Kendall.
> Chain measuring; 1st, Mr F. Vessey; 2nd, Sergeant Gee; 3rd, A. Adamson.
> Bowling for fowls: Mr J. Bains.   Quoits match: Mr Roe, Mr Cook and Mr Rowbree.
> High jump: Privates C. Frankish, H. Partridge and F. Denton.
> Human boat race: Messers White and Kendal; Peet and Vessey; Procter and Slowen.
> Tug-of-war: Harry Feirn's team.
> Lemon race: 1st, Mr F. Lowish; 2nd, Mr F. Wray; 3rd, Mr F. Hardy.
> 120 yards for soldiers: 1st, Pte F. Denton; 2nd, Pte C. Frankish; 3rd, Lieut H. Wells.
> Women's thread-needle race: Miss F. Peart, Miss A. Cook and Miss L. Rhodes.
> Old-age pensioner's race: Mr G. Feirn and Mr T. Stainton.
> Sack race: 1st Pte H. Partridge; 2nd Pte J. Braithwaite; 3rd Lieut H. Wells.
> Bun and whistle race: 1st, Mr R. Hall; 2nd, Pte J. Wilson; 3rd, Mr G. Johnson.
> Egg and spoon race: 1st, Miss K. Slowen; 2nd, Miss L. Rhodes; 3rd Miss G. Cook.
> 120yards for soldiers and sailors: 1, Pte C. Frankish; 2, Pte F. Denton; 3, Pte H. Partridge.
> Slow bicycle race: 1st, Mr H. Foster; 2nd, Mr. F. Slowen; 3rd, Mr P. Vessey.
> Padlock race: 1st, Mr F. Westoby; 2nd, Mr G. Johnson; 3rd, Mr Overton.

Towards the end of August Nurse Edlington was installed as the District Nurse. It was felt that a nurse was needed to attend to the welfare of the villagers. That had not been possible during the War due to the difficulty of obtaining a nurse.

Peace celebrations were conducted on Saturday 20th September for the children of the village. The Barnetby Silver Band had headed a procession that proceeded to the schools where the Vicar, the Rev. C. F. Brotherton, and Mrs Brotherton, together with other members of the committee, presented each child with a souvenir mug, a new penny and a bun.

On Sunday evening, 21st September, a Memorial service was conducted for all the Barnetby men who had paid the supreme sacrifice in the Great War. The altar had been draped with a large Union Flag while a second Union Flag, to which was attached a wreath, was carried in front of the choir as they entered the Church. At the close of the service Pte J. Braithwaite played the Last Post.

A whist drive in aid of the War Memorial Fund organised by members of the committee had been held in the school on Friday 3rd October. Miss Vickers presented the eventual winners, Miss Lockwood, Mr Orme and Mr Borrill with their prizes, donated by Mrs Blanchard, Mrs Cox, Miss Agar, and Mr Partridge. The amount raised by the event amounted to about £5.

On the evening of Monday 10th November a public meeting was held in the school to assess the wishes of the villagers with regards to the disposal of the balance of the War Fund that amounted to close on £83. Mr Foster (Stonecroft) presided. Various proposals were put forward at the meeting and it was eventually decided to erect a monument of some kind in the village in memory of the local lads who fell during the war.

On Tuesday evening, 11th November, a dance had been held in the schoolrooms in aid of the War Memorial Fund. There had been a large attendance at the function that had also been used to commemorate Armistice Day.

Towards the end of November the War Memorial Fund committee made it known that, having been authorised by the public meeting of 10th November, it would utilise the balance of the War Fund (about £75) in providing a permanent War Memorial. A decision had been made that the Memorial would take the form of a village Cross. The committee also appealed for further subscription towards this memorial. The Memorial Fund treasurer, Mr Lowish, or the secretary Mr F. Ringrose, would gratefully receive any monies up to 19th December, when the lists would be closed.

A dance was held in the school on the evening of Monday 8th December in aid of raising money for the recently appointed War Memorial Fund. Mr Hardaker, a pianist from Ulceby, had provided the dance music.

At a meeting of the War Memorial Fund committee, held on Wednesday 24th December in the Manor House, it was decided that a cross of grey granite costing £130 would be erected in the village. Granite was chosen as this was thought to be the most durable type of stone. At the time the committee only had £100 in hand and on the understanding that there were some in the village wishing to contribute towards it they would also gratefully accept any other contributions. All contributions were to be sent to the secretary, Mr F. E. Ringrose of Silver Street.

1920

In February 1920 a decision was made to purchase a large hut that would serve as a temporary War Memorial Hall until sufficient funding for a more permanent building had been raised. This would be known as the YMCA Hut and would be provided with a billiard table, a piano, some furniture and a library. Provision had already been made for a suitable location for setting the hut on. (The hut was erected on a site off Smithy Lane now occupied by the dwelling at No 95 St Barnabas Road.)

On Wednesday 10th April Dr Ffrench formally opened the YMCA Hut as a temporary War Memorial. A very full programme of attractions had been laid on commencing with a jumble sale and sale of work in conjunction with a number of guessing competitions. A tea was provided late in the afternoon and during the evening local ladies and gentlemen had put on a concert. This was followed by a dance that went on until the early hours of the morning. (The late Mrs Ena Underwood of Brigg, formerly Barnetby girl Ena Cox, recalled many pleasant memories of the numerous village dances she had attended, especially those held in the YMCA Hut, and spoke of the Kendall brothers as being 'lovely dancers'.)

The *Hull Times*, 1st May, reported that Mrs T. Gostelow had received the 1914-1915 Star and ribbon that would have been conferred upon her son Pte Cyril Gostelow had he lived. (This is not to be confused with the 1914 'Mons' Star awarded for service between 5th August 1914 and 30th November 1914, that is almost identical but for the different dates inscribed upon it.)

On Tuesday 24th August a wedding took place in St Mary's Church, Barnetby, between Mrs Elizabeth Braithwaite, widow of the late Pte Charles Braithwaite and eldest daughter of Mr Mitchell of Scunthorpe, and Mr Frederick Robinson, youngest son of Mr and Mrs H. Robinson of Barnetby. Miss Mitchell had attended her sister, Mrs Braithwaite, and Mr George Scott had been the groom's best man. The reception afterwards was held at The Railway Inn. Both the groom and his best man were returned servicemen.

On Friday 3rd September returned soldier Harry Cox, formerly 169074 Sapper H. Cox, Royal Engineers, who had come through the latter years of the war apparently unscathed, met with a serious accident while driving a pony attached to a dray. On meeting a traction engine the pony shied and Harry Cox fell from off the front of the dray close to the pony's hind hooves. The pony then proceeded to kick Harry several times before pulling the dray over his foot. Harry was taken home where Dr Ffrench found it necessary to put several stitches in the patient's head. Harry was also treated for bruising and shock. A week later the newspaper reported that Harry was progressing slowly. Harry's sister, Ena (Mrs Ena Underwood), could not recall the incident but she remembered the pony as being a bad tempered, vicious, beast that she was frightened to go near.

During the first week in December work began on erecting the Memorial Cross that had been decided would be fitting to the memory of the local lads who had fallen in the War. The site chosen was in the corner of the temporary (St Barnabas) Church grounds close to the school and the high road (St Barnabas Road). However, the funds available were insufficient to pay for having any names inscribed upon it. Not everyone was happy with that situation even though names were inscribed on other memorials in the village. (After the present St Barnabas Church was built in 1927 the temporary Church served as the Church Hall until it was demolished in 1991 to make way for the present Church Hall – opened 15th October 1991.)

On the afternoon of Sunday 5th December 1920 the newly erected Memorial Cross was unveiled in the presence of a large company. Mr W. Lowish of the Manor House carried out the unveiling ceremony. All denominations were represented and the Rev. C. F. Brotherton and others addressed the gathering. The grey granite Cross standing 10 feet high is situated on a large concrete base. Inscribed on the polished front and picked out in gold is the following:

> *'To the Glory of God and in honoured memory of the Barnetby Boys who have given their lives that we may live in freedom and peace; also as a thanksgiving for the safe return of the others who served in the great European war 1914-1919'.*

On Sunday 19th December local ex-servicemen met in the YMCA hut and unanimously decided to take steps to have the names of those who had died for their country inscribed upon the War Memorial Cross. They agreed to begin a subscription fund among the ex-servicemen of Barnetby and would gratefully accept donations from relatives and friends of those who had died.

1921

On Wednesday 5th January 1921 the committee of those responsible for the erection of the War Memorial Cross gathered to consider by what means they could clear the remaining £14 deficit. It was pointed out that the amount available towards the cost of the memorial already included the balance of £71 that had been received following the closure of the War Fund and the £52 that had been subscribed towards the Cross.

On Thursday 24th February, at The Angel Hotel, Brigg, a number of freehold Barnetby properties of the estate of the late Mr Richard Abey, of Barnetby-le-Wold (died 20th June 1876), were offered for sale by auction by Mr A. E. Dowse, auctioneer, of Scunthorpe. There were 18 lots in total, comprising of 25 cottages and gardens, 3 building plots and 1 paddock. Some tenants' names (in italics), familiar to the author Roger Frankish, crop up in the sales catalogue.

Lots 1 – 9, on the southern (railway) side of Railway Street, were from beyond the railway station towards the western end of the street. Lot 3, comprising of a cottage and garden was purchased by Mr Drury for £365; Lot 8, two cottages and gardens (tenanted by *Mr Holt* and *Mr Baldwin* at rental £7 and £7 8s 6d p.a. respectively), was purchased by Mr Wells for £122 10s. My father, C. R. Frankish, had pencilled notes in the sales catalogue that Lot 1 (tenanted yearly by *Mr Frow* and *Mr Worrall* at rental of £7 p.a. respectively), Lot 6 and Lot 7 (two cottages tenanted by Mr Gibson and *Mr Frow* at £5 18s p.a. respectively) were withdrawn from the sale.

Lots 10 – 13 were in West Street. Lot 10, a dwelling house, shop and garden, including an adjoining cottage containing about 419 square yards let on a yearly tenancy to *Mr Cox* (John) at rental of £20 2s p.a., including use of a workshop on Lot 14, was bought by Mr Green for £330. The dwelling house, built by W. Abey in 1783, is now numbered 3 West Street; the adjoining cottage has since been demolished. (My aunt Ethel, who married Harry Cox in 1923, lived there at some stage and ran the grocery shop with her husband.)

Lot 13, one cottage and garden and outbuildings, including one piggery, containing about 427 square yards and let on a yearly tenancy to Mr Frankish at a rental of £10 6s p.a., with a right to draw water from the pump and well on Lot 12, was purchased by Mr C. R. Frankish, my father, for £170. (The cottage, built by R. Abey in 1875, was eventually numbered 13 West Street and is currently owned by Mr Mick Clarke; it was my home from birth until 1960 when I purchased the property at 5 Smithy Lane, Barnetby, where I now live.)

The properties in between, Lots 11 (three cottages) and 12 (two cottages tenanted by Mr Ward and *Mr Hall* at £4 10s and £8 p.a. respectively), were withdrawn from the sale; the cottages of Lots 11 and 12 have since been demolished and replaced by a house and bungalow respectively.

The remaining Lots, 14 – 18, consisted of all the properties on the east side of Post Office Lane (now Old Post Office Lane). Lot 14, at the Queen's Road end, comprising of two cottages and gardens (tenanted by Mr Long and *Mr Stainton* at £5 6s and £5 13s p.a. respectively), including a workshop and outbuildings, was bought by J. Abey for £180; the cottages have since been demolished and a bungalow now occupies the site. Lot 15, two cottages and gardens (tenanted by *Mr Padmore* and *Mr White* at £7 7s and £7 3s p.a. respectively), was withdrawn from the sale; the cottages are still in use as one dwelling. Lot 16, a cottage and garden containing 1,577 square yards and let to Mr Waby (a photographer) on a yearly tenancy at a rental of £8 2s p.a. was purchased by Mr Fred Maxted for £230. This property contained the water well and pump for use by the owners/occupiers of Lots 14 – 18 inclusive. The cottage has since been demolished and replaced by a bungalow, 4 Old Post Office Lane, owned by Mr F. Bradley.

Lot 17, two cottages and gardens (tenanted by *Mr Grant* and *Mr Stephenson* at £7 10s p.a. respectively), was bought by Mr G. Stephenson for £180; both cottages remain but are uninhabited and two houses have since been built on the site. Of Lot 18, the cottage and garden at the northern end of the lane, my father had not made any notation in the catalogue; the cottage is still there and currently owned and occupied by Mr and Mrs Kicks.

The death occurred on 20th May, 1921, of Ernest Goodhand, aged 26 years, after a long illness. Ernest, eldest son of Mr and Mrs F. Goodhand, had served with the Royal Engineers during the war.

On Sunday 28th August an impressive service had been held in St Mary's Church in the afternoon when the vicar, the Rev. C. F. Brotherton, unveiled a beautiful marble tablet to the memory of those men who had fallen during the war. The Rev. H. T. Parry, rector of Bigby, had preached an appropriate sermon to the large congregation. The tablet was inscribed as follows:

'In Glorious Memory of these men of Barnetby-le-Wold,
who for their country gave their lives in War'

1914	Herbert Bull, R.N.	1917	E. Keightly White
1916	George H. Smith		Hubert Cox
	J. Wilfred Rapson	1918	Jno Catterall
	J. Wm Lobley		Harry Wright
	W. Hy Hinchsliff		Thos W. Bramley
	Cyril Gostelow		Herbert H. Denton
1917	Fred Thompson		Geo. H. Rhoades
	George W. Smith		Geo. Nicholls
	Walter Blair		Chas M. Green
	Reg. Robinson	1919	Frank Burdass
	Percy C. Blanchard		Ernest A. Insley
	Hugh Dawson		E. Dudley Ffrench
	Wm F. Starkey		

'Their Name Liveth for Evermore.'

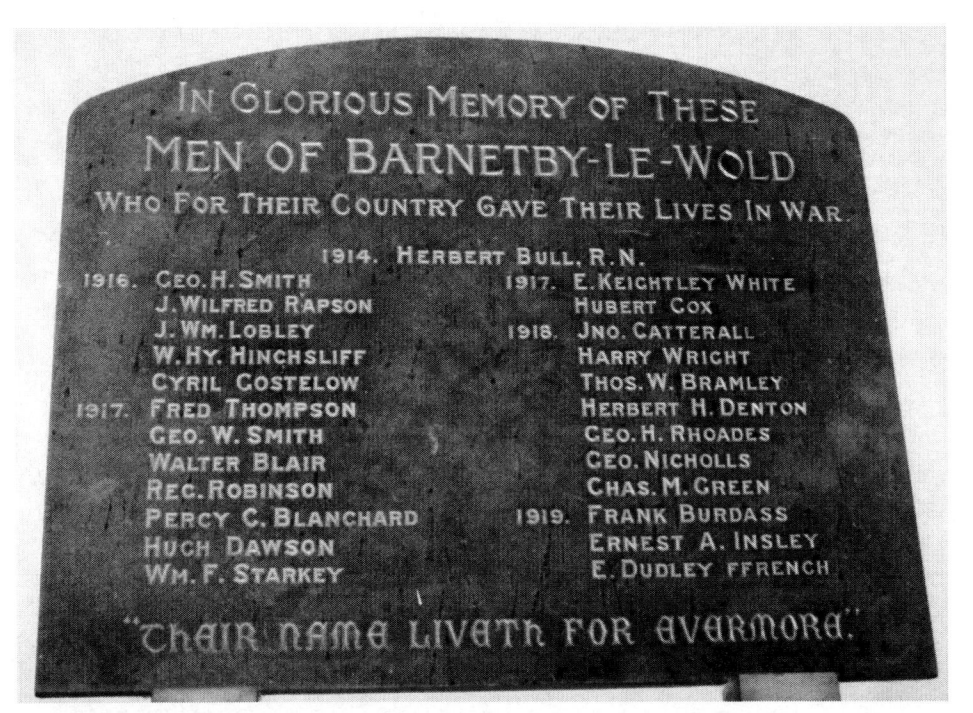

Barnetby Memorial Tablet.

The tablet is now on the north wall of the nave in St Barnabas Church. The names on the tablet are solely those of the men from the village and not those associated with the village, as is the case of the names inscribed on the War Memorial Cross situated in the Church grounds.

During the second week of November Mr and Mrs F. Gostelow had received a package containing the Memorial Plaque for their late son Cyril along with The British War Medal and Victory Medal. (Most next-of-kin of deceased soldiers received memorial plaques. This is the only newspaper reference to one having been sent to a Barnetby Boy's family that I came across.)

1922

There was no village news appertaining to the war or post war or concerning men who had served in the war reported in the local newspapers until September.

The *Hull Times* of 9th September carried a report of a fatal accident at Wrawby involving a returned serviceman from Barnetby, former Private Jesse Dawson (Regiment not known).

> Barnetby man killed by charabanc. On Thursday 7th September Jesse Dawson, platelayer of Barnetby, with a friend named Gee, was cycling towards Brigg on the Grimsby main road. When overtaking the Enterprise

and Silver Dawn charabancs near Wrawby tunnel Dawson was seen to fall from his cycle, and the hind wheel of one of the charabancs passing over him, he was killed instantly.

The funeral of Mr Jesse Dawson, who met his death under such tragic circumstances at Wrawby, took place on Monday afternoon, 11th September. Aged 26 years, he was the youngest son of Mrs Elizabeth Dawson. Jesse had joined the Army in November 1915, was wounded in France and later badly gassed.

The *Grimsby News* of 15th September carried the report of the coroner's inquest into the fatal char-a-banc accident of Barnetby cyclist Jesse Dawson that had occurred near the bridge over the railway on the road approaching Wrawby from Barnetby.

> Mr Richard Mason, the Grimsby County coroner held an inquest at Brigg on Saturday 9th September upon Jesse Dawson, single, a platelayer of Barnetby, who was killed on the road when cycling at Wrawby, through being run over by a motor char-a-banc. Victor Stratton, of Crosby, a passenger in the char-a-banc said the vehicle was returning from Cleethorpes on Thursday night and when descending the hill at Wrawby, two cyclists, one of whom was Dawson, overtook them.
>
> The cyclists, riding in single file, were passing the char-a-banc when Dawson seemed to run into the back wheel of the cyclist ahead of him. The result was that he was thrown right under the char-a-banc, the wheels of which passed over him. Bertie Gee said he was riding with Dawson from work. As they overtook the char-a-banc witness said to Dawson *'I'll go first'* and Dawson replied *'All Right, I'll follow'*. Witness rode on and passed the vehicle and was not aware anything had happened until he heard the brakes suddenly applied on the char-a-banc. Going back he found Dawson lying in the road behind the char-a-banc.
>
> Albert Parker, of Crosby, the driver of the char-a-banc, said he never saw the cyclists and did not know anything had happened until he felt a bump and heard the passengers scream. The coach would be travelling 10 –12 miles per hour. Dr F. G. Goodman said *Dawson's* injuries were of such a nature that death would be instantaneous. A verdict of *'Accidental Death'* was returned.

Nothing further was found in the newspapers relating to any village activity connected with the war or post war related matters until November, when on the morning of Saturday 11th November a special service was held in St Barnabas Church. Afterwards many beautiful floral tributes were laid on the War Memorial.

The final newspaper item for the year referred to another memorial service held on the afternoon of Sunday 10th December. For this occasion the Barnetby Band headed a parade of members of the RAOB le-Wold Lodge, together with members of their Order from Brigg and Scunthorpe, through the village to the War Memorial where they held a choral service. During the service Brother Lusby placed a laurel wreath on the Memorial in memory of the fallen. Afterwards a special service for men was held in the Church. Tea was later provided in the Station Hotel for the visitors and members of the Barnetby Band.

1923

On the afternoon of Wednesday 9th May 1923 the Rev. T. R. Menrig-Davies, the vicar of Barnetby, officiated over the wedding in St Barnabas Church between Harry Cox, eldest son of Mr and Mrs J. Cox, and Miss Alice Ethel Frankish, eldest daughter of Mr and Mrs T. Frankish. The bridesmaids were Miss Ena Cox, sister of the bridegroom, and Miss Amy Marshall, niece of the bridegroom. The best man was Charles Frankish, brother of the bride.

1924

The final item in this narrative, reported in the *Hull Times* on 16th February 1924, while not connected with the war, relates to the death at Immingham of Mr Henry Dawson, aged 44 years (no date given), a former Barnetby serviceman and railwayman.

Henry Dawson, a goods guard on the L and N E Railway, had resided at Barnetby before moving to Immingham a few months prior to his death. For many years he had been a member of the Church Choir and previous to joining the Railway had served in the Navy. Deep sympathy was felt for his widow, who was left with five children, ages between 15 years and 16 months. His mother, Elizabeth Dawson, had lost one son in the war (Hugh) and another (Jesse) under tragic circumstances a little over a year earlier. The deceased had been ill for some time.

Henry, son of Thomas and Elizabeth Dawson, was born at Barnetby in (1)1880. The 1881 census records that he had two older brothers, Thomas S. (6) and Edward (3) and at the time the family was dwelling in Commercial Road, Barnetby. Henry's name first cropped up in the GCR Journal of February 1911 on being appointed as a brakesman at Barnetby. Prior to that date he had been employed at Barnetby as a shunter; for some unknown reason that appointment was also in the February 1912 issue. However the Journal issue for December 1911 confirmed that brakesman H. Dawson has been appointed a goods guard at Barnetby. It would appear from his obituary that he had been employed in that capacity at Barnetby throughout the war.

Although this narrative of events throughout the Great War as they affected Barnetby, and particularly its menfolk, is now concluded in one respect it is still incomplete. There still remain the questions of when the names of the fallen were put on the War Memorial and why the extra names that are on the Roll of Honour were not included? It is possible the former is recorded somewhere and, judging by the number of errors, I think it was much later that the names were added when perhaps the returned soldiers no longer remembered their fallen comrades' details. The latter question will remain a mystery.

Appendix 1

Opposing Naval Forces at the Battle of Coronel

Royal Navy
Admiral Craddock's Cruiser Force

Canopus: a pre-dreadnought battleship completed in 1899 displacing 12,950 tons. Main armament: 4 x 12-inch guns, secondary armament: 12 x 6-inch guns; speed of only 18 knots.

Good Hope: armoured cruiser built in 1902/3 displacing 14,100 tons; carried 2 x 9.2-inch guns [1 forward, 1 aft], and 16 x 6-inch guns (old pattern) mounted in sponsons (or casemates).

Monmouth: armoured cruiser built in 1903 displacing 9,800 tons; carried 14 x 6-inch guns (old pattern), many mounted in sponsons.

Glasgow: light cruiser built in 1911, displacing 4,800 tons. She had 2 x 6-inch guns and 10 x 4-inch guns; all guns were of the latest type.

Otranto: a converted Orient Lines liner of 12,000 tons armed with 6 x 4.7-inch guns and not designed for a major warship encounter; maximum speed at that time, 16 knots.

The cruisers' designed speeds were in excess of 22 knots. The number of guns carried by the armoured cruisers is impressive on paper but the sponson mounted (broadside) batteries could only be fired on the side fitted; the lower sponson (main deck) batteries, being so close to the water, were vulnerable to flooding in heavy seas necessitating their doors being closed thus rendering those guns inoperable. Rangewise, the 8.2-inch guns of the enemy armoured cruisers outdistanced the British cruisers' guns, possibly even *Canopus*' 12-inch.

German Navy
Admiral Graf von Spee's Cruiser Force.

Scharnhorst and *Gneisenau*: armoured cruisers built in 1907 displacing 11,600 tons. Armament: main: 8 x 8.2-inch guns; secondary: 6 x 5.9-inch guns; designed speed of 23 knots.

Dresden: light cruiser built in 1908 displacing 3,600 tons had a speed of 24 knots; armed with 10 x 4.1-inch guns.

Nürnberg: light cruiser built in 1908 displacing 3,400 tons, speed 22/23 knots; armed with 10 x 4.1-inch guns.

Leipzig: light cruiser built in 1906 displacing 3,200 tons, speed 22/23 knots and armed with 10 x 4.1-inch guns.

Appendix 2

Captain Francis Willmer McAulay, RFA (T.F.)

Fastened to the outer Church wall adjacent to the family tomb in Aylesby Churchyard is the original wooden marker Cross from Foncquevillers Military Cemetery, France, where Captain McAulay is buried. (No name or identification plate is visible.)

Francis Willmer McAulay was born in 1891, the only son of Samuel and Maud Mary McAulay of Aylesby, a village near Grimsby. Educated at The Leys in Cambridge he went on to take his M.A. degree in agriculture and economics at St. John's College, Cambridge. During his time in residence at St. John's College he was a member of the Officers' Training Corps.

Francis McAulay returned to Aylesby where he farmed in partnership with his father. He joined the Territorial Force and was commissioned as a Second Lieutenant, Royal Field Artillery (T.F.) on 5th October 1910, serving with the 1st North Midland Brigade Ammunition Column. He was promoted to Lieutenant on 15th July 1913 and from September 1913 he was serving with the 2nd Lincolnshire Battery of the 230th Brigade RFA, part of 46th (North Midland) Division.

When war broke out he immediately volunteered for service abroad. On 21st January 1915 he was promoted to the temporary rank of Captain. February 1915 saw the 46th Division leaving for France. By May 1916 it had moved to the Foncquevillers/Gommecourt sector at the southern end of the British 3rd Army Front that joined with the northern boundary of the 4th Army Front, preparing for the forthcoming Somme offensive. The 230th Brigade RFA was situated between Bayencourt and Sailly-au-Bois and Capt. McAulay was now in charge of 'B' battery.

On 21st May at about 7.45 a.m., the enemy commenced to shell the battery heavily and accurately with 5.9" H.E. and at 8.50 a.m. increased the firing rate for about five minutes, blowing in No. 2 gun pit and the telephone dug-out. In the gun-pit the only damage was to the gun-shield, sight and fuse-indicator ring of No 2 gun. The situation in the telephone dug-out was more serious. During the bombardment Capt. McAulay was there when two shells hit it, killing him and two of the five men, telephonist 451 Corporal C. Carty and 2089 Gunner S. H. Pratt, instantaneously and wounding 1239 Sargeant G. Broadstock, 807 Gnr A. Smith and 1600 Driver A. Mumby-Croft. (Driver Mumby-Croft subsequently died of wounds next day and is buried in Doullens Communal Cemetery Extension No. 1; Corporal Carty and Gunner Pratt are buried in Sailly-au-Bois Military Cemetery.)

The men in Capt. McAulay's battery had lost an officer and a friend in whom they placed absolute confidence, with their welfare being his constant care. His Colonel spoke of him as a very popular and gallant officer. General Campbell said of him, "He was such a good officer and a specially nice one and was a great loss".

The announcement of Capt. McAulay's death gave rise to deep feelings of sympathy towards his parents. Sadly his father Samuel died on 15th June 1920, aged 64 years. That his mother grieved for a much-loved son is manifest in the memorial she had built to his memory.

In 1925 plans were drawn up to build a practical memorial, namely the McAulay Memorial Cottages. The architect, C. H. James (noted for the City Hall, Norwich), had once worked for Sir Edwin Lutyens. The builders, Hewins and Goodhand Ltd. of Grimsby, began work on the cottages in 1926, consisting of six self-contained houses and a community room all under one roof, to be built as homes for anyone in difficult circumstances (i.e. almshouses). The site at the front was lawned for bowls and croquet and planted with ornamental trees; the rear was laid out for allotments with fruit trees. The houses, some with two bedrooms and some three, each had a large lounge at the front and a scullery,

(Left) The original wooden marker cross from the grave of Captain Francis Willmer McAulay in Foncquevillers Military Cemetery is now fastened to the outer wall of St. Lawrence's church, Aylesby, adjacent to the McAulay family tomb in Aylesby Churchyard.

(Right) Captain Francis Willmer McAulay's headstone in Foncquevillers Military Cemetery.

APPENDICES

larder and a downstairs bathroom at the back. Two boilers supplied hot water to the all houses and a common laundry. The inside woodwork, British Columbian pine, was stained and polished a different colour in each house. Above the main door a memorial stone carved by a local Art School instructor reads, *"In Memory*

The McAulay Memorial Cottages at Aylesby in N. E. Lincolnshire.

The Memorial plaque above the front entrance to the McAulay Memorial Cottages. The inscription reads: In Memory of Francis Willmer McAulay, Captain R.F.A., T.F., who fell in action at Fonquevillers, France, on May 21st 1916 aged 25.

of Francis Willmer McAulay, Captain R.F.A., T.F., who fell in action at Fonquevillers, France on May 21st 1916, age 25 (note the incorrect spelling of Foncquevillers). The cottages cost: just under £11,800. The building is now a listed building.

The McAulay Memorial Cottages are now Trust managed retirement homes. Little has changed in their construction, except that the community room at the right hand end of the building, as viewed from the front, has been converted into a seventh dwelling. A three-quarter length near life size portrait of Capt. McAulay wearing RFA uniform used to hang in that room. It is at present awaiting possible re-hanging in St. Lawrence's Church, Aylesby.

Appendix 3

C. S. Lord Worsley, Lt Royal Horse Guards

(Reference to the book 'Charles Sackville Pelham, Lord Worsley' by his father and for use of facilities at the Estate Office, by kind permission of Lord Yarborough).

Two wooden Crosses hang in Brocklesby Parish Church. Both marked Lord Worsley's grave, as will be revealed in this narrative.

In St. Peter's Church, Great Limber, among the names of the fallen engraved on the Rood Screen is that of Charles Sackville Lord Worsley.

Charles Sackville Pelham, born on 14th August 1887 at 17 Arlington Street, London, was the eldest son of Charles Alfred Worsley Pelham, 4th Earl of Yarborough and Marcia Pelham, Countess of Yarborough; as heir to the family estate he held the title Lord Worsley. He grew up at Brocklesby Hall on the family estate in Lincolnshire, a few miles from Aylesby where Francis McAulay lived. At Brocklesby he soon became an accomplished horseman. Educated at Eton, but unlike Captain McAulay not a scholar, Lord Worsley always took great pride in all that he did.

In 1906 Lord Worsley entered the Royal Military College, Sandhurst, left in 1907 to join the Royal Horse Guards (the Blues) and was gazetted Second Lieutenant on 5th October, 1908.

On 31st January 1911 he married the Hon. Alexandra Mary Freesia Vivian (her older sister Dorothy had married Maj. Gen. Douglas Haig in 1905). From 1912-13 Lord Worsley was extra on the staff of General Sir Douglas Haig (GOC Aldershot). Early in 1914 Lord and Lady Worsley took up residence at Little Brocklesby in the parish of Great Limber near the Pelham family home at Brocklesby. (Brocklesby Park, courtesy of Lord Yarborough, became the field training ground of the 10th Lincolns 'Grimsby Chums'; some Labour battalions also formed there.)

When war broke out a Composite Household Battalion, comprising of one squadron from each the 1st and 2nd Life Guards and the Royal Horse Guards, was formed and sent immediately to France. That summer the remainder,

The wooden cross placed at Lord Worsley's grave by his younger brother, the Hon. Sackville George Pelham.

Original German cross found at Lord Worsley's grave; his sword and Memorial plaque are below.

Charles Sackville Pelham, Lord Worsley, Lieutenant, Royal Horse Guards.
(Courtesy Lord Yarborough)

Lord Worsley's grave in Ypres Town Cemetery Extension.

Household Brigade Memorial, Zandvoorde, the site of Lord Worsley's original burial.

APPENDICES

having been brought up to strength from cavalry of the line reservists, went into training. During this time Lord Worsley went to Hythe on a machine gun course, on completion rejoining the regiment in training at Ludgershall Camp on Salisbury Plain as officer in charge of the machine gun section (2 guns per regiment).

In October 1914 Lord Worsley embarked with the Royal Horse Guards on active service, landing in Flanders on 8th October. The next day at Bruges the regiment joined the rest of the Household Brigade, as part of the 7th Cavalry Brigade of the 3rd Cavalry Division. Mid October saw the 7th Cavalry Brigade making forays towards Roulers (Roeselare), being billeted at Passchendaele. Here Lord Worsley's gunners had the opportunity to bring a gun into action, silencing enemy rifle fire being directed towards them.

At Passchendaele they joined with the 7th Infantry Division, whose task had been to take Menin. But the enemy went on the offensive and the British began to dig in, the cavalry having to work dismounted. Early on 21st October the enemy attacked the 7th Division in Zonnebeke and the 7th Cavalry Brigade was sent in support. The Blues moved into good trenches under fire and opened up on the enemy massed on a ridge, driving them back. The Coldstream Guards later relieved them. Meanwhile the 6th Cavalry Brigade reinforced the 2nd Cavalry Division, with a gap in its line near Zandvoorde, the 7th Cavalry Brigade going into billets at Zillebeke. A thinly strung out line of Cavalry now held the line Zandvoorde – Messines. The defence of Ypres was on; the salient was in its infancy.

On 23rd October the Blues relieved the 1st (Royal) Dragoons (the Royals) in trenches at Zandvoorde, being heavily shelled whilst doing so. Relieved by the 6th Brigade on 25th October the Blues camped at Klein Zillebeke except 'C' Squadron – including Lord Worsley and his guns; they remained in their trenches in support. Little did Lord Worsley know that was where his guns

30th October 1914

A	Right-hand trenches of 7th Infantry Division.
B	Trenches held by 2nd Life Guards.
C	Trenches held by Lord Hugh Grosvenor's squadron of 1st Life Guards.
D	Trenches held by rest of 7th Cavalry Brigade.
X	Trench with Lord Worsley's machine gun.
Y	Trench with machine gun 'that got away'.
a - b	Fence
c - d	Belt of trees.

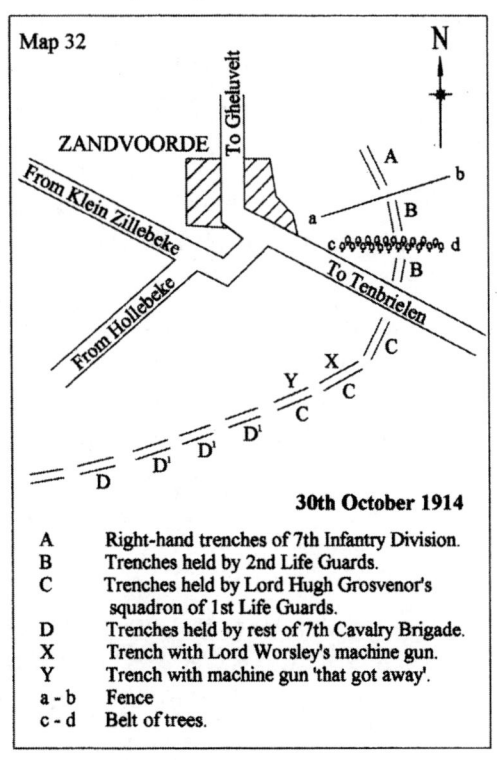

Map 32. *Zandvoorde.*

would stay, unrelieved, either reinforcing the 1st Life Guards, who had only one serviceable gun, or in support. And things were hotting up.

On 29th October, the Blues, manning widely spaced short section shallow trenches on the forward slope of the Zandvoorde ridge with no communication to flank or rear, came under fierce bombardment by heavy guns. A breach was made in the exposed cavalry line in this sector but the enemy failed to exploit the gap, which was plugged and held with the help of infantry. That evening 1st Life Guards relieved 'D' and half 'C' squadron of the Blues, Lord Hugh Grosvenor's 1st Life Guards being supplemented by Lord Worsley and his guns. With them were two troops of 2nd Life Guards. To their right were the Blues 'B' Squadron and two troops of 'C'.

Next morning at 7 a.m. a bombardment of high explosive and shrapnel lasting ninety minutes preceded an enemy attack on the weakened 7th Infantry and Cavalry Divisions on the exposed Zandvoorde ridge, destroying their trenches. The enemy, advancing in strength, attacked the right of the line first causing the 2nd Life Guards (Capt. O'Neill) at 'D' to fall back (see diagram p. 283). The Blues at 'D1', in turn also forced to fall back from the right (as were the 1st Life Guards at 'Y', with one gun and heavy losses), sent messages to Lord Hugh Grosvenor in the other 'C' trenches informing him to pull back. It is not known if they were ever received. Those trenches were by this time surrounded – their occupants fighting until annihilated. There were no wounded to tell the story and the enemy took no prisoners! The enemy subsequently took Zandvoorde in the course of the day.

> Killed in those trenches that day were:
> One squadron of 1st Life Guards:
> Capt. Lord Hugh Grosvenor, Capt. E. D. F. Kelly, Lt J. C. Close-Brooks, Lt Hon. G. E. F. Ward and 67 other ranks.
> Two troops of 2nd Life Guards:
> Capt. A. M. Vandeleur, Capt. F. J. Todd, Lt J. Anstruther and 57 other ranks. (Other ranks include cavalry of the line).
> Lt Lord Worsley's Machine Gun section, Royal Horse Guards.

For unexplained reasons the Germans were interested in Lord Worsley's death; possibly because Oberleutnent Freiherr von Prankh of the 1st Bavarian Jäger Battalion, who witnessed the fight, knew their opponents were the Royal Horse Guards. Inspecting the captured trenches he found the body of an English Lord. He ordered a Lt von Neubert to have any personal items removed and handed over, so the next of kin could be informed, and the body buried. This was subsequently carried out that same evening, 30th October.

APPENDICES

Meanwhile no one had heard any word of the men in those trenches. The first news, 'Lord Worsley missing', came from the War Office on 7th November 1914. On 15th November *The London Gazette* announced his promotion to Captain. On 5th December *The Times* reported that he and three other officers were 'missing'. The distraught wife and parents sought news from many sources. On 11th January, 1915, news arrived that Lord Worsley's name was on a German list as killed and buried at Zandvoorde, no date given. *The Times* published the official report on 20th January, and on 7th February the War Office issued a death certificate to Lord Yarborough.

Following on from the 'missing' declaration of 7th November, Lord and Lady Yarborough sought more information through diplomatic sources at The Hague. This eventually resulted in a plan of the burial site being obtained from Berlin. The plan noted that the identification tag had been removed. A second, private, source from inside Germany forwarded a similar plan to the family from Berlin.

Attempts to locate the burial site were not possible until after the war ended. Finding the site was not easy, for that part of Belgium had been blasted out of all recognition during four years of warfare. The site was located at a second attempt on 15th December 1918, by a young officer and family friend, Mr A. H. James, using the plan confided to him by Lady Yarborough, assisted by an ex-RSM of the 10th Hussars who had been in action on 30th October, 1914, near Zandvoorde. The grave, more like a filled in shell-hole, was marked with a crude broken wooden cross that bore no name. Mr. James supplemented this with a pile of stones when the site agreed with the burial plan. Before returning home arrangements were made locally for another Cross to be made inscribed with Lord Worsley's name.

On 27th January 1919 Mr James, accompanied by Lord Worsley's younger brother the Hon. Sackville George, returned to the site picking up the newly made Cross en-route. Snow made finding the grave difficult but they found it, the original German Cross in place, and proceeded to dig a hole in which to stand the new Cross, unearthing the missing broken-off piece of the original Cross a few inches down; this was also unmarked. Reporting their action to the War Graves Commission, they returned home taking with them the original German Cross. (Lady Worsley eventually purchased the burial site).

The War Graves Commission, as part of its policy to concentrate isolated graves, made arrangements for the body to be exhumed for re-burial in Ypres Town Cemetery Extension. On 8th September 1921 the Revd Swann-Mason from Immingham, representing the family, was present at the unearthing of a body about five feet down in the uniform of a Royal Horse Guards officer.

Further identification came from a maker's name in the boots and a gold tooth filling. Next day the re-burial of Lord Worsley took place with Revd Swann-Mason in attendance; the new Cross that had been made to mark the original burial site now marked the grave. It was returned to the family in 1923 when a stone marker replaced the wooden Cross.

Tucked down a narrow path dividing a row of houses on the southern edge of the village of Zandvoorde, Belgium, overlooking well tended gardens, stands the Household Brigade Memorial. In 1924 the Horse Guards had a memorial made to the Household Brigade and this was erected on the burial site previously purchased by Lady Worsley. On 24th May 1924 this memorial, inscribed *'To those of the 1st & 2nd Life Guards & Royal Horse Guards who died fighting in France & Flanders 1914. Many of them fell in defence of the ridge upon which this cross stands'*, was unveiled in the presence of Lord and Lady Yarborough, Lady Worsley and Lord Worsley's two younger brothers – the Hon. Sackville George Pelham and the Hon. Marcus Herbert Pelham. Field Marshal Earl Haig, the then President of the British Legion (and Lady Worsley's brother-in-law), carried out the unveiling.

In July 1924 the War Graves Commission located the identity tag of Lord Worsley attached to a list of names in a German Sanitary Unit, including a note that nothing else had been handed in. The disc was in good condition never having been buried. It was returned to Lady Worsley who had also received her husband's sword from officers in his regiment.

The sword is now in Brocklesby Church, as are the two wooden Crosses and Lord Worsley's Memorial disc. Beneath the sword a plaque states *'This sword was carried by Charles Sackville Lord Worsley Lt. Royal Horse Guards who died for his King and Country at Zandvoorde 30th October 1914. Buried in Ypres Cemetery. Dulcet et decorum est pro patria mori'.* By the family pew is a small monument to Lord Worsley sculptured by Mr. C. Sergeant Jagger, who had served with the 2nd Worcesters and was seriously wounded when that battalion charged and retook the village of Gheluvelt on 31st October 1914. The wording beneath the monument reads: *Vincit Amor Patræ. To the Glory of God and in memory of Charles Sackville Pelham Lord Worsley Lieutenant Royal Horse Guards who fell at Zandvoorde 30th October 1914 aged 27. This monument is erected by his sorrowing family and the tenantry of the estate. Brave courteous loving and beloved 'He died the noblest death a man may die fighting for God and Right and Liberty and such a death is immortality.'* A large memorial plaque on the south wall of the church to the fallen of the First World War from Brocklesby includes C. S. Lord Worsley.

Of the other officers and men killed in that action on 30th October 1914, nothing has ever been heard of them since that day nor anything found to identify any one of them.

APPENDICES

Mr C. Sergeant Jagger's monument to Lord Worsley by the Pelham family pew in Brocklesby Church.

The memorial plaque to the fallen of W. W. 1 from Brocklesby and Little Limber in Brocklesby Church.

Appendix 4

L/Cpl G. W. Smith Service Documents.

APPENDICES

MEDICAL HISTORY SHEET.

Surname: Smith Christian Name: George William

Examined on 23rd day of June 1915 at Vernon BC

Approved by [signature] Rank: C. appearsl. M.O

Birthplace: City or Town: Barnetby
County: Lincolnshire, Eng.

Apparent age: 32 yrs
Trade or occupation: Labourer
Height: 5 Feet 5½ Inches
Weight: ___ Lbs.
Chest measurement: Minimum 36 inches; Maximum expansion 2 inches
Physical development: ___
Small-Pox Marks: ___
Vaccination Marks: Arm Right ___ Left 3; Number 3
When Vaccinated last: 10/7/15 — Pos
(a) Marks indicating congenital peculiarities or previous disease: ___
(b) Slight defects but not sufficient to cause rejection:

Date	Result	Anti-Typhoid Inoculations, Etc.
18/7/15	Pos	
20/7/15	Pos	
4/8/15	Pos	

Enlisted on 24 day of May 1915 at Vernon BC

	Corps.	Regt'l. Number.	Habits.	Date.
Joined on enlistment	D. Coy. 54th Battn CEF	443323		24/5/15
Transferred to..				

EXAMINED OR DISCHARGED BY A MEDICAL BOARD.

Station.	Date.	Disease.	Result.

N. B.—This sheet to be disposed of in accordance with instructions in the Regulations for Army Medi[cal] Service, on the man becoming non-effective; the date and cause being stated on next page.

Medical G. W. Smith.

THE BARNETBY BOYS

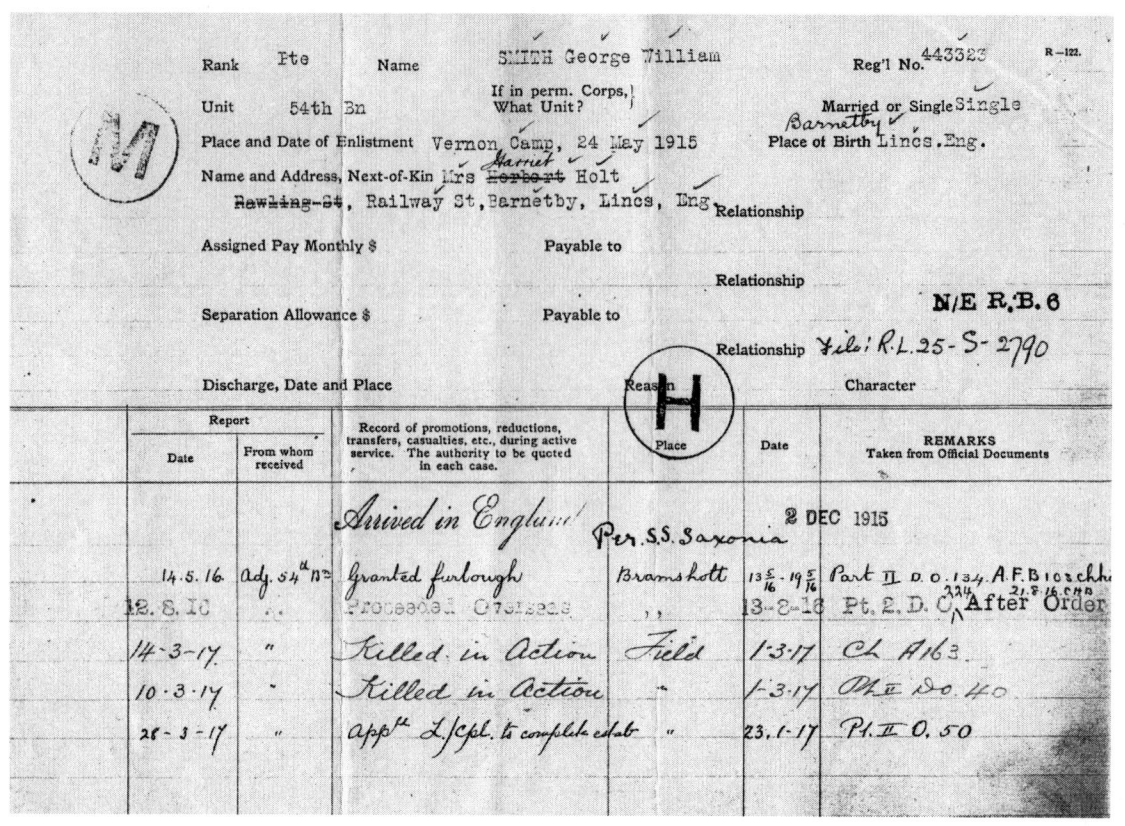

Casualty sheet G. W. Smith.

APPENDICES

M. F. B. 440.

MILITIA AND DEFENCE

In reply please quote
No. 649-S-11051

Ottawa, April 28th., 1919

From,-
    The Adjutant-General,
        Canadian Militia.

To,-
    Mrs. Harreit Holt,
        Railway Street,
           Barnetby, Lincs.
              England.

443323 Pte. George William Smith,
Canadian Expeditionary Force.

    Madam,-

        I beg to transmit herewith official certificate of death in respect of the late soldier marginally noted.

                                                          [signature]

EJW/Cas.   Enclosure 1   for Director of Records
                                              for a/Adjutant-General.

Letter G. W. Smith.

Appendix 5

Sgt G. W. Thacker Service Documents.

APPENDICES

Casualty form 1 G. W. Thacker.

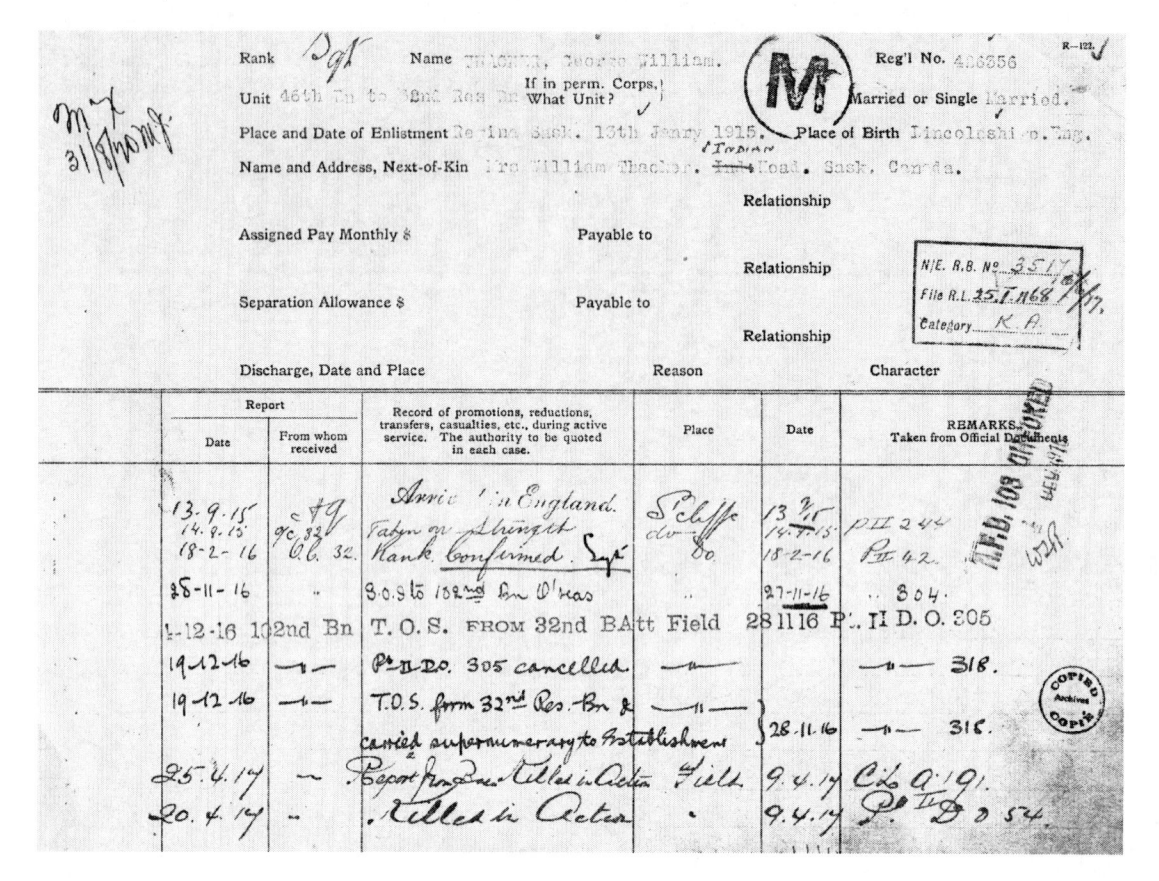

Casualty form 2 G. W. Thacker.

APPENDICES

Report Date	From whom received	Record of promotions, reductions, transfers, casualties, etc., during active service, as reported on Army Form B. 213, Army Form A. 36, or in other official documents. The authority to be quoted in each case.	Place	Date	Remarks taken from Army Form B. 213, Army Form A. 36, or other official documents.
Unit	15-4-17	KILLED IN ACTION Lieutenant. For Major D.A.A.G. Canadian Section 3rd Echelon G.H.Q.	Field	9-4-17	Pt II No.54 d/- 20-4-17 D.C.S. 131 d/- -do- Can Sec File K.I.16/2445 Letter from Unit

Casualty form 3 G. W. Thacker.

Sgt G. W. Thacker Next of Kin card.

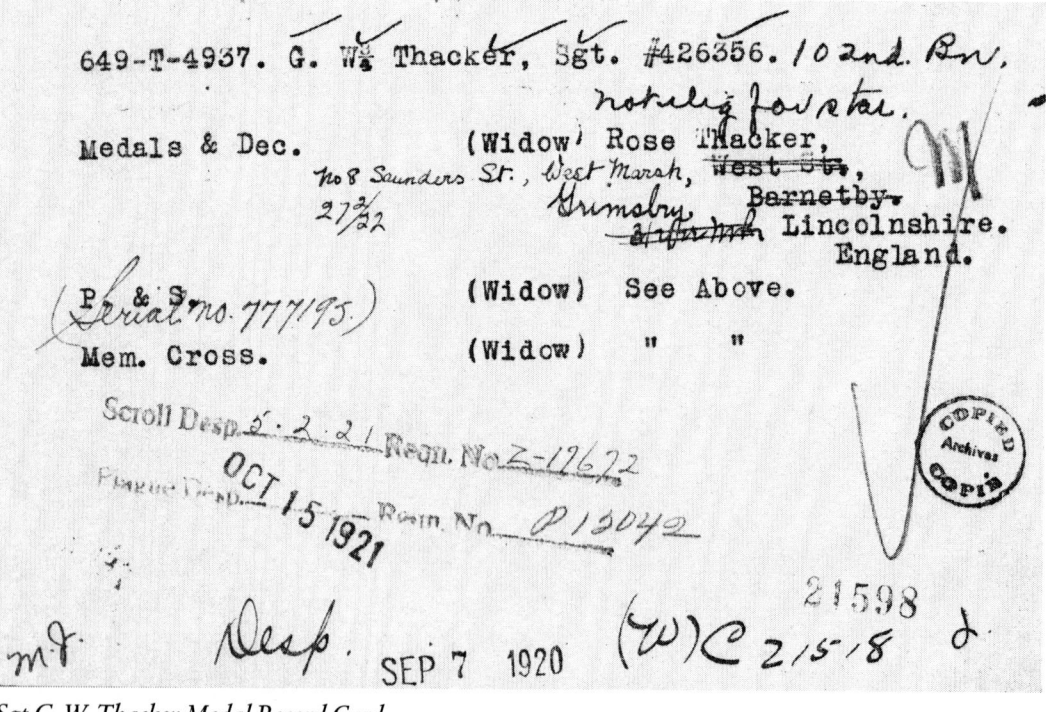

Sgt G. W. Thacker Medal Record Card.

Appendix 6

Roll of Honour

For King and Country

1914 — 1919

		Our Glorious Dead		
Agar Cyril	Fish Ernest	Andrews Charles	Lowish Henry	Scott George
Allcard Thomas	Footitt Amos	Bell Harry	Maddison Charles	Scott Harold
Allison Henry	Frankish Charles	Blair Walter	Maddison Fred	Scott Walter
Allison Maurice	Freestone Harold	Blanchard Percy	Marrows Jack	Slowen Sidney
Allison Robert	Freestone Robert	Braithwaite Chas	Maxted Fred	Smith Charles
Baines James	Frow Alfred	Bramley Thomas	Midgeley William	Smith Harry
Baker William	Frow William	Bull Herbert	Moss Charles	Smith Joseph
Baldwin Fred	Gee Alfred	Burdass Frank	Moss Frank	Smith Reginald
Barnett Fred	Gee Frank	Catterall Jack	Moss Percy	Smith Sidney
Barron Percy	Gee Herbert	Cox Hubert	Needham William	Smith Walter
Battersby Harry	Good Alfred	Dawson Hugh	Overton John	Smith William
Baxter Robert	Goodhand Ernest	Denton Herbert	Overton Fred	Spafford Percy
Bell Cyril	Gostelow William	Ffrench Dudley	Overton William	Stainton William
Blake Edgar	Grant Ernest	Gostelow Cyril	Padmore George	Staniland Harold
Borrill William	Green William	Green Charles	Parker Ernest	Stephenson Henry
Braithwaite John	Hall Alfred	Hall Thomas	Parratt Thomas	Thompson Charles
Briggs Arnold	Hall Herbert	Hinchsliffe Harry	Parrott Robert	Thompson Herbert
Briggs George	Hall Reginald	Hurd George	Partridge Harry	Thompson Thomas
Briggs William	Hall Rupert	Lobley William	Pearte Ernest	Thorpe Joseph
Broughton George	Hartley Charles	Nicholls George	Pepperdine Reuben	Tillbrooke Sidney
Catley Frank	Hollingsworth Jas	Rapson Wilfrid	Percival William	Troup George
Catterall Cyril	Holt William	Rhoades George	Ponting William	Vessey Fred
Cook Harry	Holt Wilson	Rhodes Harry	Poole Percy	Vessey Percy
Copeland Joseph	Hutchinson Edward	Robinson Reginald	Pretty William	Waite John
Cox Harry	Insley Ernest	Smith George H	Regan Joseph	Wells Horace
Davis Alfred	Insley George	Smith G. W.	Rhoades Henry	White Christopher
Dawson Jesse	Johnson Arthur	Starkey William	Rhoades William	White Hubert
Dennis George	Kendall Harry	Thacker George	Robinson Albert	Wilkinson Arthur
Denton Arthur	Kendall Jack	Thompson Fred	Robinson Albert	Wilkinson Harold
Denton Ernest	Kendall Sidney	Tweed Arthur	Robinson Arthur	Wilson Jack
Denton Fred	Kirkbride John	Vessey Ernest	Robinson Charles	Winn Thomas
Denton Walter	Lansley Fred	White E. K	Robinson Fred	Worrall Arthur
Elvidge Harry	Lee William	Witty Stanley	Rose Ralph	Worrall Joseph
Elwick William	Leeson Harry	Wright Harry	Rowe Thomas	Worrall William
Farrow John	Loveday Stephen		Scott Arthur	Wright Harold

These are the names as they appear on the Roll of Honour. The two outer columns bear the names of those men who served and returned. Ernest Insley [second column] was a war fatality – his name should be in the centre column. With no reference found of Harry Rhodes [centre column] being a war fatality I believe name should be in the fourth column. See Appendix 6a for how I believe the Roll of Honour should read.

THE BARNETBY BOYS

Roll of Honour

For King and Country

1914 — 1919

Our Glorious Dead

Agar Cyril	Fish Ernest	**Andrew Charles F.**	Maddison Charles	Scott George
Allcard Thomas	Footitt Amos	**Bell Wm Henry**	Maddison Fred	Scott Harold
Allison Henry	Frankish Charles	**Blair Walter**	Marrows Jack	Scott Walter
Allison Maurice	Freestone Harold	**Blanchard C. Percy**	Maxted Fred	Slowen Sidney
Allison Robert	Freestone Robert	**Braithwaite Charles**	Midgeley William	Smith Charles
Baines James	Frow Alfred	**Bramley Thomas W.**	Moss Charles	Smith Harry
Baker William	Frow William	**Bull Herbert**	Moss Frank	Smith Joseph
Baldwin Fred	Gee Alfred	**Burdass Frank**	Moss Percy	Smith Reginald
Barnett Fred	Gee Frank	**Catterall John**	Needham William	Smith Sidney
Barron Percy	Gee Herbert	**Cox Hubert**	Overton John	Smith Walter
Battersby Harry	Good Alfred	**Dawson Hugh**	Overton Fred	Smith William
Baxter Robert	Goodhand Ernest	**Denton Herbert H.**	Overton William	Spafford Percy
Bell Cyril	Gostelow William	**Ffrench E. Dudley**	Padmore George	Stainton William
Blake Edgar	Grant Ernest	**Gostelow Cyril**	Parker Ernest	Staniland Harold
Borrill William	Green William	**Green Charles M.**	Parratt Thomas	Stephenson Henry
Braithwaite John	Hall Alfred	**Hall Thomas**	Parrott Robert	Thompson Charles
Briggs Arnold	Hall Herbert	**Hinchsliffe Henry**	Partridge Harry	Thompson Herbert
Briggs George	Hall Reginald	**Hurd Thomas**	Pearte Ernest	Thompson Thomas
Briggs William	Hall Rupert	**Insley Ernest A.**	Pepperdine Reuben	Thorpe Joseph
Broughton George	Hartley Charles	**Lobley J. Willie**	Percival William	Tillbrooke Sidney
Catley Frank	Hollingsworth Jas	**Nicholls George**	Ponting William	Troup George
Catterall Cyril	Holt William	**Rapson J. Wilfred**	Poole Percy	Vessey Fred
Cook Harry	Holt Wilson	**Rhoades George**	Pretty William	Vessey Percy
Copeland Joseph	Hutchinson Edward	**Robinson Reg. W.**	Regan Joseph	Waite John
Cox Harry	Insley George	**Smith George H.**	Rhoades Henry	Wells Horace
Davis Alfred	Johnson Arthur	**Smith Geo. Wm**	Rhoades William	White Christopher
Dawson Jesse	Kendall Harry	**Starkey William**	Rhodes Harry	White Hubert
Dennis George	Kendall Jack	**Thacker George W.**	Robinson Albert	Wilkinson Arthur
Denton Arthur	Kendall Sidney	**Thompson Fred**	Robinson Albert	Wilkinson Harold
Denton Ernest	Kirkbride John	**Tweed Arthur**	Robinson Arthur	Wilson Jack
Denton Fred	Lansley Fred	**Vessey Ernest**	Robinson Charles	Winn Thomas
Denton Walter	Lee William	**White Edward K.**	Robinson Fred	Worrall Arthur
Elvidge Harry	Leeson Harry	**Witty W. Stanley**	Rose Ralph	Worrall Joseph
Elwick William	Loveday Stephen	**Wright Harry**	Rowe Thomas	Worrall William
Farrow John	Lowish Henry		Scott Arthur	Wright Harold

(How I believe the Roll of Honour should read. The original had a 'rope' border surrounding the fallen column with a small Cross behind the wording 'Our Glorious Dead'; I have enclosed the fallen within a large Cross.)

Appendix 7

The Barnetby Boys – Casualties, 1914-1919

1914
01 Nov   RFR/PO/B/2165 AB Herbert Bull, HMS Good Hope.

1915
26 Sept	12539	L/Sgt Thomas HALL, 8th Lincs.
	12514	L/Sgt Arthur TWEED, 8th Lincs.
	12540	Pte Charles Frederick ANDREW, 8th Lincs.

1916
15 Feb	12654	Pte William Henry BELL, 7th Lincs.
03 July	12577	L/Cpl George Herbert SMITH, 7th Lincs.
03 Aug	21575	Pte John Wilfred RAPSON, 10th Lincs.
15 Aug	1560	Cpl James Willie LOBLEY, 10th Lincs.
23 Oct	21682	Pte William Henry HINCHSLIFF, 2nd Lincs.
15 Nov	12513	Pte Cyril GOSTELOW, 8th Lincs.

1917
03 Feb	1037	L/Cpl Frederick THOMPSON, 1/5th Lincs.
01 Mar	443323	L/Cpl George William SMITH, 54th (Kootenay) Bn, (2nd Central Ontario Regt) Canadian Infantry.
09 Mar	202866	Pte Walter BLAIR, 2/4th Lincs.
09 Apl	426356	Sgt George William THACKER, 102 Bn, (2nd Central Ontario Regt) Canadian Infantry.
11 Apl	1353	Pte Reginald Walter ROBINSON, 1st Lincs.
23 Apl	194926	Cpl Charles Percy BLANCHARD, "R" Corps Signal Coy, RE.
28 Apl	27425	Pte Hugh DAWSON, 8th Lincs.
03 May	202688	Pte William Foster STARKEY, 2/4th York and Lancaster.

03 May	77473	Gunner Ernest VESSEY, 160th Siege Battery, RGA.
27 June	242248	Pte Edward Keightly WHITE, 1/5th Lincs.
04 Oct	1391	Pte Hubert COX, 1st Lincs.

1918

12 Feb	9074	CQMS John CATTERALL, 8th Lincs.
21 Mar	12736	Pte Harry WRIGHT, 1st Lincs.
10 Apl	48725	L/Cpl George HURD, 13th King's (Liverpool) Regt.
17 Apl	21585	Pte Thomas Wilfred BRAMLEY, 10th Lincs.
26 Apl	21230	Sgt Herbert H. DENTON, 1st Lincs.
01 June	WR/201924	Sapper George RHOADES, RE.
24 Aug	201782	Pte Walter Stanley WITTY, 7th East Yorks.
23 Sep	43769	Pte George NICHOLLS, 1/5th Lincs.
05 Oct	245209	Pte Charles BRAITHWAITE, 13th DLI.
09 Nov	WR/207055	Pioneer Charles Masey GREEN, RE.

1919

01 Mar	14585	Sapper Frank BURDASS, RE.
01 Jul	WR/148130	Sapper Ernest Arthur INSLEY, RE.
16 Jul		2nd Lt Ernest Dudley FFRENCH, Queen Victoria's Own Corps of Guides (Frontier Force), (Lumsden's) attd 3rd/1st King George's Own Gurkha Rifles, (the Malaun Regiment).

Appendix 8

The Barnetby Boys Memorials in France and Belgium, 1914-1918.

Ypres Memorial to the Missing, Tyne Cot Cemetery, Passchendaele, (Rear Wall):
21230 Sgt H. Denton, 1st Lincolnshire. 26/4/18. (Panel 35)
21585 Pte T. W. Bramley, 10th Lincolnshire. 17/4/18. (Panel 36).
1391 Pte H. Cox, 1st Lincolnshire. 4/10/17. (Panel 36).

Ypres Memorial to the Missing, Menin Gate, Ypres:
12654 Pte W. H. Bell, 7th Lincolnshire. 15/2/16. (Panel 21).

Nœux-les-Mines Communal Cemetery:
242248 Pte E. K. White, 1/5th Lincolnshire. 27/6/17. (Plot II, Row C, Grave 16).

Loos Memorial to the Missing, Dud Corner Cemetery, Loos-en-Gohelle:
12539 L/Sgt T. Hall, 8th Lincolnshire. 26/9/15. (Panel 32).
12514 L/Sgt A. Tweed, 8th Lincolnshire. 26/9/15. (Panel 32).
48725 L/Cpl G. Hurd, 13th King's Liverpool Regiment. 10/4/18. (Panel 28). (Not named on War Memorial).
12540 Pte C. F. Andrew, 8th Lincolnshire. 26/9/15. (Panel 32). (Not named on War Memorial).

Cabaret Rouge British Cemetery, Souchez:
443323 L/Cpl G. W. Smith, 54th Bn Canadian Infantry (2nd Central Ontario Rgt). 1/3/17. (Plot XIV, Row D, Grave 14). Initially buried at map reference 44a. S21b 10.35. on Vimy Ridge.

Givenchy Road Canadian Cemetery, Neuville-St-Vaast, (Canadian National Memorial Park, Vimy Ridge.):
426356 Sgt G. W. Thacker, 102nd Bn Canadian Infantry (2nd Central Ontario Rgt). 9/4/17. (Plot A, Grave 30).
Initially buried at map reference 44a.S21b 1.3. on Vimy Ridge.

Chili Trench Cemetery, Gavrelle:
27425 Pte H. Dawson, 8th Lincolnshire. 28/4/17. (Plot B, Grave 19). Initially buried at map reference 51b.H6c 2.4.

Arras Memorial to the Missing, Faubourg d'Amiens Cemetery, Arras:
202688 Pte W. F. Starkey, 2/4th York and Lancaster Rgt. 3/5/17. (Bay 8).

Wancourt British Cemetery:
1353 Pte R. W. Robinson, 1st Lincolnshire. 11/4/17. (Plot VII, Row B, Grave 29).
Initially buried at map reference 51b.T4b 6.5.

Haute Avesnes British Cemetery:
194926 Cpl C. P. Blanchard, "R" Corps Signals Coy., Royal Engineers. 23/4/17. (Plot C, Grave 27).

Warlincourt Halte BritishCemetery, Saulty:
1037 L/Cpl F. Thompson, 1/5th Lincolnshire. 3/2/17. (Plot IV, Row G, Grave 11).

Ancre British Cemetery, Beaumont-Hamel:
12513 Pte C. Gostelow, 8th Lincolnshire. 15/11/16. (Plot III, Row B, Grave 55).

Thiepval Memorial to the Missing:
202866 Pte W. Blair, 2/4th Lincolnshire. 9/3/17. (Pier 1, Face C).
21682 Pte W. H. Hinchsliff, 2nd Lincolnshire. 23/10/16. (Pier 1, Face C).

Pozieres Memorial to the Missing and British Cemetery:
12736 Pte H. Wright, 1st Lincolnshire. 21/3/18. (Panel 24).
201782 Pte W. S. Witty, 7th East Yorks. 24/8/18. (Plot I, Row J, Grave 20).
Initially buried at map reference 57d. X4.
(Believed incorrectly named as Pte S. Whitley, 4th E. Yorks. on War Memorial.)

APPENDICES

Albert Communal Cemetery Extension:
21575 Pte J. W. Rapson, 10th Lincolnshire. 3/8/16. (Plot I, Row M, Grave 37).

Gordon Dump Cemetery, Ovillers-la-Boiselle:
12577 L/Cpl G. H. Smith, 7th Lincolnshire. 3/7/16. (Special Memorial B23). Initially buried at map reference 57d. X15c 3.5. (This would appear to be in Gordon Dump Cemetery, where the grave is believed to be).

London Cemetery and Extension, Longueval:
1560 Cpl J. W. Lobley, 10th Lincolnshire. 15/8/16. (Plot VIII, Row D, Grave 20). Initially buried at map reference 57c. S8b 55.85.

Prospect Hill Cemetery, Gouy:
245209 Pte C. Braithwaite, 13th Bn Durham Light Infantry. 5/10/18. (Plot I, Row C, Grave 10).
Initially buried at map reference 62b.B1c 7.3. (Not named on War Memorial.)

Roisel Communal Cemetery and Extension:
43769 Pte G. Nicholls, 1/5th Lincolnshire. 23/9/18. (Plot I, Row J, Grave 1). Initially buried at map reference 62c.Q10b 5.9.

Vauxbuin French National Cemetery:
77473 Gunner E. Vessey, 160th Siege Battery, Royal Garrison Artillery. 3/5/17. (Plot III, Row B, Grave 7).
Initially buried Terny-Sorny Military Cemetery (near Soissons) map reference Soissons 33. 1/20,000. 183.65. 303.5. (Not named on War Memorial).

The Barnetby Boys Memorials Elsewhere, 1914-1919.

Barnetby-le-Wold, St Mary's Churchyard:
14585 Sapper Frank Burdass, Royal Engineers. 1/3/19.
WR/207055 Pioneer Charles Meysey Green, Royal Engineers. 9/11/18.
WR/201924 Sapper George Rhoades, Royal Engineers. 1/6/18.

Grimsby (Scartho Rd) Cemetery:
9074 CQMS John Catterall, 8th Lincolnshire. 12/2/18. (RC section, Grave 76N11).

Scunthorpe Cemetery:
WR/148130 Sapper Ernest A. Insley, Royal Engineers. 1/7/19. (Plot Y, Grave 12).

Portsmouth Naval Memorial to the Missing:
RFR/PO/B/2165 Able Seaman Herbert Bull. HMS Good Hope. 1/11/14. (Panel 2).

Delhi Memorial to the Missing, India:
2nd Lt Ernest Dudley Ffrench, Queen Victoria's Own Corps of Guides (Frontier Force), (Lumsden's) attached 3rd/1st King George's Own Gurkha Rifles, (the Makrun Regiment). 16/7/19. (Face number 24).

The Somerby Men's Memorials, 1914-1918

Bac-du-Sud British Cemetery:
104086 Gunner G. W. Rimmington, 287th Siege Battery, Royal Garrison Artillery. 1/9/18. (Plot I, Row F, Grave 11).

Villers-Bretonneux Military Cemetery:
107608 Driver William Slight, "B" Battery, 177th Brigade, Royal field Artillery. 28/3/18. (Plot IV, Row A, Grave 4).
Initially buried at map reference 62d. P13b 9.2.

Vlamertinghe Military Cemetery:
50618 L/Cpl C. F. Wilson, 16th Battalion Sherwood Foresters (Notts & Derby R.). 6/2/17. (Plot V, Row H, Grave 2).

Appendix 9

Roll of Honour

For King and Country

1939 – 1945

Adams E.	Chambers H.		Marris W. E.	Thompson E.
Allcard T. K.	Chantry H.		Mumby J. W.	Thompson E.(Miss).
Allison F.	Clixby C. R.		Mumby M.	Thompson J.
Allison W.	Clixby G.	Buckle G. C.	Naylor G.	Thompson
Altoft T.	Clixby J. S.	Chambers J. W.	Naylor G. H.	Tuxworth G.
Ashton B.	Coates R.	Freeston T. S.	Naylor T.	Vessey E.
Ashton C. N.	Cowling C.	Gravil J. H.	Overton R.	Vessey J.
Ashton D.	Cowling G.	Green G. R.	Panton G.	Vessey R.
Ashton F.	Cressey G.	Hall R.	Peart C.	Vessey Ronald
Austin A.	Curtis M.	Holdstock F. B.	Perkins G. E.	Vickers A.
Austin D.	Dale D.	Phillipson H.	Perkins R.	Walford E.
Austin H.	Davis H.	Rose F. B.	Phillips W.	Wallis
Austin W.	Dawson F.	Smith G. F.	Pilkington M. L.	Ward E.
Barnes W.	Dawson J.		Poole W. C.	Ward M.
Barnett J.	Dickinson G.		Pratt J.	Waters F.
Beacham H. R.	Dodson F.		Pretty M.	Watts S. G.
Beedham R.	Drakes D.		Proudley L.	Wells E.
Beel T. H.	Easton J. C.	Heath G. A.	Ranyard G.	Wells F.
Beeton E.	Easton R. F.	Heath W. G.	Robinson H.	Westby R.
Bell H.	Ellis L. F.	Hesketh H.	Sampson G. T.	Westoby C.
Bradley F.	Etty R.	Hill M. R.	Shephard C.	Westoby Clive.
Braithwiate K.	Fisher R.	Hirst E.	Speed B.	Westoby F.
Britcliffe D.	Frow C.	Holt J.	Speed J. W.	Westoby M.
Broughton D.	Fryer A.	Hoodlass C.	Smith E.	Whitehead J.
Brown W.	Gammidge C.	Howson G.	Smith H.	Whyld F.
Burgess G.	Girdham N.	Jenkins	Stennett R.	Williams
Carline G.	Green C. V.	Kirkby B.	Stephenson D.	Williams C.
Carnaby R	Hallam F.	Kirkby G.	Stephenson W. E.	Wilson S.
Cawkwell J.	Hartle J.	Lovock R. C.	Stringfellow J.	Wright J.
Cawkwell S.	Heath B	Markham S. MM	Stutt B.	Wray E.

Killed in Action: G. C. Buckle, J. W. Chambers, T. S. Freeston, H. Gravil, G. R. Green, R. Hall, F. B. Holdstock, F. B. Rose, G. F. Smith.

Died on Active Service: H. Phillipson.

Prisoner of War: T. Altoft, H. Austin, G. Kirkby, J. W. Speed, E. Wells.

Disabled: S. Markham MM; G. T. Sampson.

Discharged: G. Carline, D. Dale.

(N.B. Not named on the Roll of Honour: H. Green, killed in action and named on the War Memorial and Memorial plaque in St Barnabas Church; C. R. Frankish, discharged medically.)

Appendix 10

The Barnetby Boys Memorials, 1939-1945

Luton General Cemetery, Bedfordshire:
1223122 AC2 (W. Op/Air Gnr U/T) Frederick Benjamin Holdstock, RAF (VR). 25/2/41. (Grave 7648).
Son of Ernest and Martha Elizabeth Holdstock of Sparsholt, Berkshire; brother of the late Mrs Margery Neave.
Mrs Neave spoke of a premonition the family had regarding her brother: his official number adds up to 13!

The Runnymede Memorial, Egham, Surrey:
1189615 AC1 Francis Bernard Rose, RAF (VR). 5/7/41. (Panel 57).
Son of Bernard and Alice Rose; husband of Nora Emily Rose of Northolt, Middlesex.

Nicosia War Cemetery, Cyprus:
4980 Pte Horace Phillipson, 1st Bn Sherwood Foresters (Notts & Derby Regt). 2/9/41. (Plot V, Row B, Grave 6).
Son of John and Ruth Phillipson of Barnetby, Lincolnshire.

The Alamein Memorial, Egypt:
847352 Gunner George Frederick Smith, 28th Field Regiment, Royal Artillery. 6/6/42. (Column 37).
Son of Frederick and Mabel Frances Smith of Barnetby, Lincolnshire.

Tripoli War Cemetery, Libya:
T/153906 Driver John Henry Gravil, RASC. 15/1/43. (Plot VII, Row F, Grave 19)
Son of Fred and Maria Gravil; born at Thorne, Yorkshire and lived with his guardians in Barnetby, Lincolnshire.

APPENDICES

Kanchanaburi War Cemetery, Thailand:
3888127 Pte Geoffrey Charles Buckle, 6th Royal Norfolk Regiment. 20/6/43. (Plot II, Row M, Grave 49).

Syracuse War Cemetery, Italy:
2014489 Sapper Hugh Green, 725 Artisan Works Coy, Royal Engineers. 23/7/43. (Plot II, Row C, Grave 9).
Son of Thomas William and Etty Green; husband of Freda Elizabeth Green of Bonby, Lincolnshire.

Cassino War Cemetery, Italy:
T/172028 L/Cpl Thomas Smith Freeston, RASC. 24/5/44. (Plot XI, Row J, Grave 22).
Son of Mr and Mrs Walter Freeston of Broadstone, Derbyshire.

Chichester Cemetery, Sussex:
P/JX 264867 Ldg Seaman Reginald Hall, RN, HMS Aeolus. 8/9/44. (Square 159 C of E Plot, Grave 24).
Son of Percival and Alice Hall; husband of Annie Evelyn Hall of Barnetby, Lincolnshire.

Arnham Oosterbeek War Cemetery, Netherlands:
14329425 L/Bdr George Roland Green, 1 Airlanding Lt Regt, Royal Artillery. 23/9/44. (Plot XXVI, Row B, Grave 5).
Son of George Thomas Green and Ada Mary Green of Barnetby, Lincolnshire.

Berlin 1939-1945 War Cemetery, Germany:
191689 Pilot Officer (Air Gunner) John William Chambers, RAF (VR), 619 Squadron. 11/4/45.
(Plot I, Row L, Collective Grave 3 – 6).

Appendix 11

The Memorial Plaques in St Barnabas Church
Barnetby-le-Wold.

---

*'In Glorious Memory of those men of Barnetby-le-Wold,
who for their country gave their lives in War.'*

	1914	Herbert Bull, R.N.	
1916	George H. Smith	1917	E. Keightly White
	J. Wilfred Rapson		Hubert Cox
	J. Wm Lobley	1918	Jno Catterall
	W. Hy Hinchsliff		Harry Wright
	Cyril Gostelow		Thos W. Bramley
1917	Fred Thompson		Herbert H. Denton
	George W. Smith		Geo. H. Rhoades
	Walter Blair		Geo. Nicholls
	Reg. Robinson		Chas M. Green
	Percy C. Blanchard	1919	Frank Burdass
	Hugh Dawson		Ernest A. Insley
	Wm F. Starkey		E. Dudley Ffrench

'Their Names Liveth for Evermore.'

Memorial plaque of Great War.

The Great War 1914 – 1919.

APPENDICES

> ✝ *In affectionate remembrance*
> *of the men from this parish*
> *who made the*
> *the supreme sacrifice*
> *in the world war*
> *1939 – 1945*
>
> *G.C. Buckle* *H. Green* *R. Hall*
> *J. W. Chambers* *G. R. Green* *F. B. Holdstock*
> *T. S. Freestone* *J. H. Gravil* *H. Phillipson*
> *F. B. Rose* *G. F. Smith*
>
> ## Eternal Rest Grant Them O Lord.

Memorial plaque of WW2.

The World War 1939 – 1945.

Appendix 12

The names and inscription on the War Memorial at Barnetby-le-Wold (there are at least 21 errors for WW1).

Killed in Action	
Sgt H. H. Denton	1st Lincs
L/Cpl II. Wright	" "
Pte C. Gostelow	2nd Lincs
" H. Hinchsliff	" "
" E. K. White	1/5 "
L/Cpl F. Thompson	5th "
Cpl G. H. Smith	7th "
Pte H. Bell	" "
L/Cpl G. W. Smith	" "
Sgt T. Hall	8th "
Sgt A. Tweed	" "
Pte H. Dawson	" "
Q. M. Sgt J. Catterall	
A. B. H. Bull	H.M.S. Good Hope
Spr F. Burdass	R.E.

South (Left) Face.

Killed in Action	
Cpl J. Lobley	10th Lincs
Pte W. Blair	" "
" T. Bramley	" "
" H. Cox	" "
" G. Nicholls	" "
" J. Rapson	" "
" R. W. Robinson	11th "
Cpl C. P. Blanchard	R.E.
Pte G. Green	Died
Pte G. Rhoades	Died
Sgt G. Thacker	Can^{dns}
Pte S. Whitley	4th E. Y^{ks}
" W. Starkey	2/4 Y^k & Lanc^a
" E. A. Insley	N^{thrd} F^{lrs}
2nd Lt E. D. Ffrench OVO 1st Gds I. A.	

North (Right) Face.

To the Glory of God
and in honoured memory of
The Barnetby Boys
who have given their lives
that we may live in freedom and peace
also as a thanksgiving for the safe return
of the others who served
in the Great European War
1914 – 1919
'Greater Love hath no man than this'

G. C. Buckle	1939 – 1945	F. B. Holdstock
J. W. Chambers	G. R. Green	H. Phillipson
T. S. Freeston	J. H. Gravil	F. B. Rose
H. Green	R. Hall	G. F. Smith

East (Front) Face.

Appendix 13

Somerby lectern.  *A close up of the back of the lectern.*

Memorial plate, St Margaret's Church, Somerby.

"Thoughts at Lochnagar Crater on the Somme – 1st July 1996"

Eighty years on – and still we come,
Drawn by an intangible bond
To Lochnagar's deep gaping wound
That we now stand around
To remember those whose brave advance –
On that fateful July morn –
Was centred near this awesome place,
This great crater scarring the ground.
Men of Suffolk, Grimsby "Chums", Royal Scots, Tyneside
Geordies – Scottish and Irish,
Just like we who're gathered here –
Eighty years on.

We cannot know their inner thoughts
As they prepared that day,
Forever hopeful that the guns –
As they'd been led to understand –
Had well and truly cleared the way
To march – in line like on parade –
To their objectives unopposed.
But 'twas not so –
Those shells failed to destroy the foe
Sheltered deep inside the earth;
Or cut the wire;
And soon machine-guns swept their lines –
Brought into action from below
Undamaged by the weight of shell
That had rained down;

And mines were blown,
Like this one here, where we now stand –
Eighty years on.

The carnage wrought was grim indeed;
Six thousand odd soldiers fell.
Some sought refuge in this hole,
Whilst others rose no more.
Of those that did, those sorely maimed
Were Blighty bound for good.
Luckless others that survived the day –
Some with wounds just freshly healed –
Were later in the fray again
Beyond yon not too distant wood.
Many returned worse injured,
Many more did not come home;
Not far from here, where we now stand –
Eighty years on.

'Twas much the same on all the front,
From Gommecourt in the North
Right down the line to where we stand
And South to Maricourt.
As they advanced towards the foe
They never stood a chance,
For all the while those guns spat out
That murderous hail of fire,
They bravely tried to struggle on
Against that uncut wire.
Almost fifty-eight thousand were casualties –
Near a third forever gone –
That's hard for us to comprehend –
Eighty years on.

THE BARNETBY BOYS

Hundreds lie in Cemeteries near
Who paid the bitter price –
Their names inscribed upon the stones
That mark their resting place.
A Cross of Sacrifice stands guard o'er them,
Bright flowers adorn their graves –
They may rest in a foreign field
But it's made to be like home.
Memorials honour countless more –
Their whereabouts not known;
Many lie in unnamed graves,
Many more were never found;
But they are not forgotten –
They too are named on stone;
And all is tended with such care –
Eighty years on.

And so we gather here today
On this first July morn
To pay homage to their memory,
May their endeavours never fade;
We offer prayers of thanks to them
At this unusual shrine
In knowledge that their cause was just –
The fight they fought was won
That we may live in a freer world,
Their quest was not in vain.
We know their sacrifice was great;
We honour what they've done.
Pray ever let their memory live –
As eighty years on.

R. O. Frankish.
Friend of Lochnagar

Where Poppies Grew

(Sequential to and based upon the poem "In Flanders Fields",
by the late Lt Colonel John McCrae, MD, RCAMC).

In the fields of Flanders amongst the crosses poppies blew,
But now upon your graves are grown bright flowers of varied hue;
Cross engraved headstones, set in lawns, now mark where you are laid;
Rank on rank they proudly stand like soldiers on parade.
No gunfire din drowns out the larks' singing as they fly;
Clear heard below they freely soar on high up in the sky.

Alas, a score of years and one saw again the foe arise;
Although subdued he'd smouldered, angered by the Armistice.
Throughout the land the call to arms sounded out anew;
Caught in strong hands, and held on high, they took the torch you threw.
Sleep, sleep on ye Dead, they did not break their faith with thee;
And bitter were the battles fought before their victory.

Crude crosses were their markers too; of these there was no dearth,
Like the poppies that once grew in Flanders' ravaged earth.
Among your many ranks that in Flanders fields are laid
Their Memorial stones are manifest to the sacrifice they made –
Now gathered in from where they fell; and in new fields far wider spread
Lie more battalions of their Dead.

One of your ranks a poem wrote, in an off duty hour,
Inspired by the sight of the simple scarlet flower
That swayed amidst the crosses in the breeze.
It was to your Remembrance that we turned to this
For the emblem to the Fallen proudly worn at Armistice –
The poppy – whose waving blooms once set ablaze
The fields of Flanders.

R. O. Frankish.

Pte 12248 John Kirk Adlard was born on 22nd February 1891 at Grimsthorpe, Lincolnshire. He enlisted on 9th September 1914 while living at Barton-upon-Humber, Lincolnshire and joined the 6th East Yorkshire Regiment. He served in that battalion with the Expeditionary Force Mediterranean (Egypt). He was posted to the 7th Battalion East Yorkshire Regiment in February 1918 and was killed in action on 29th March 1918 on Bouzincourt Ridge. He is buried in Bouzincourt Ridge Cemetery, Somme.

On visiting my Mother's half-Brother's grave at Bouzincourt Ridge Cemetery.

R. O. Frankish

From this Cemetery's lonely viewpoint rolls a tranquil panorama,
Witness to a dreadful battle that we simply call 'The Somme'.
Below in the valley flows the Ancre, meandering past woods once familiar -
Aveluy, Thiepval and Authuille - grown anew in verdurous splendour;

This peaceful setting, almost idyllic, sorely tries the imagination
To picture scenes of devastation accompanied by the gunfire's thunder.
Now all was quiet; save for a cuckoo, its oft-repeated two-note call -
The plaintive song that heralds summer - came loudly ringing on the wind.

Thiepval's Monument breasts the skyline, intruding on this pastoral scene,
Looking o'er two tragic hillsides - one each aside the Bapaume road -
And on to Albert's gilded statue, towering agleam above the rooftops;
Each reminding of the combat that hereabouts was waged.

Inside this Cemetery lies my kinsman, slain on this soil ere I was born;
Before his grave I humbly stood, bearing thoughts and prayers from home.
Who can explain why tears should well in eyes that hath ne'er this man seen?
What justifies those deep emotions stirred by one you've never known?

His son - scarce had I known him ere he to war was gone,
To far-off Imphal's sultry plain; and he now lies in India's soil.
Among the flowers by the headstone I laid a posy of red poppies -
A silent tribute to my kinsmen - may they at peace forever rest.

Pte 5120284 Harry Adlard, born on 13th May 1913, was a native of Barton-upon-Humber, Lincolnshire. He served with the 1st Battalion Northamptonshire Regiment, and was killed in action at Imphal, India, on 15th April 1944, aged 30 years and is buried in Imphal Military Cemetery, India. The original death notice gave the regiment as the Royal Warwickshire Regiment.

Bibliography

Charles Sackville Pelham, Lord Worsley, by his father. (Privately published 1924.)

Atteridge, A. Hilliard. *A History of the 17th (Northern) Division.* Robert Maclehose & Co. Ltd, The University Press, 1929.

Banks, A. *A Military Atlas of the First World War.* Leo Cooper, 1997.

Baraston, Lt. Colonel J. H. C.B, O.B.E. and **Bax, Capt. Cyril E. O.** *The Eighth Division 1914-1918.* Naval & Military Press, 1999 (original 1926).

Bryant, P. *Grimsby Chums. 10th Lincolnshire in the Great War.* Humberside Leisure Services, 1990.

Coombs. R. E. B., M.B.E. *Before Endeavours Fade.* Battle of Britain Prints International Ltd, 1986.

Edmonds, Brig.Gen. Sir J. E., C.B., C.M.G., R.E. (Retd). *The Official History of the Great War, 1914-1918. Military Operations in France and Belgium.* The Imperial War Museum; Naval & Military Press. (DVD).

Gliddon, G. *The Battle of the Somme; A Topographical History.* Gliddon Books, 1996.

James, Capt E. A. *A Record of the Battles and Engagements of the British Armies in France and Flanders, 1914-1918.* Gale and Polden, Ltd, 1924.

James, Brig. E. A., O.B.E., T.D. *British Regiments, 1914-1918.* Naval & Military Press, 1993.

Lewis, C. *Sagittarius Rising.* Warner Books, 1994.

McCarthy, C. *The Somme, the Day-by-Day Account. The Third Ypres, Passchendaele, the Day-by-Day Account.* Arms and Armour Press, 1996 & 1995 respectively.

Middlebrook, M. *The Kaiser's Battle, 21 March 1918.* Allen Lane, 1978.

Nicholls, J. *Cheerful Sacrifice; the Battle of Arras 1917.* Leo Cooper, 1995.

Shakespear, Lt. Colonel J., C.M.G.; C.I.E.; D.S.O. *The Thirty Fourth Division, 1915-1919.* Naval & Military Press, 1998 (original 1921).

Simpson, Maj. Gen. C. R. C.B. *History of the Lincolnshire Regiment, 1914-1918.* Medici Society Ltd, MCMXXXI.

Spencer W, *Army Service Records of the First World War,* Public Record Office, 2001.

Westlake, R. *Kitchener's Army*. The Nutshell Publishing Co. Ltd, 1989.

Wintringham, J. W. *With the Lincolnshire Yeomanry in Egypt and Palestine, 1914 – 1918*.

Lincolnshire Life, Grimsby, 1979.

Yates, K. *Graf Spee's Raiders*. Leo Cooper, 1995.

Great Central Railway Journals

Ministry of Pensions. *Locations of Hospitals and Casualty Clearing Stations, British Expeditionary Force 1914-1919*.

Soldiers Died in the Great War 1914-1919. HMSO.

The General Staff Branch Army Headquarters, India. *The Third Afghan War 1919 Official Account*. Naval & Military Press (original 1926).